G. A. L

DR. G. A. LAZENBY, JR.

LECTURES ON THE HARVARD CLASSICS

HISTORY
POETRY
SCIENCE
PHILOSOPHY
BIOGRAPHY
PROSE FICTION
CRITICISM AND THE ESSAY
EDUCATION
POLITICAL SCIENCE
DRAMA
VOYAGES AND TRAVEL
RELIGION

THE HARVARD CLASSICS
EDITED BY CHARLES W ELIOT LLD

Lectures on The Harvard Classics

BY

William Allan Neilson PhD

GENERAL EDITOR

AND

George Pierce Baker, A. B.

Ernest Bernbaum, Ph. D.

Charles J. Bullock, Ph. D.

Thomas Nixon Carver, Ph. D., LL. D.

George H. Chase, Ph. D.

William Morris Davis, M. E., Ph. D., Sc. D.

Roland Burrage Dixon, A. M., Ph. D.

William Scott Ferguson, Ph. D.

J. D. M. Ford, Ph. D.

Kuno Francke, Ph. D., LL. D.

Charles Hall Grandgent, A. B.

Chester Noyes Greenough, Ph. D.

Charles Burton Gulick, Ph. D.

Lawrence Joseph Henderson, M. D.

Frank W. C. Hersey, A. M.

Henry Wyman Holmes, A. M.

William Guild Howard, A. M.

Robert Matteson Johnston, M. A. (Cantab.)

Charles Rockwell Lanman, Ph. D., LL. D.

Gustavus Howard Maynadier, Ph. D.

Clifford Herschel Moore, Ph. D.

William Bennett Munro, LL. B., Ph. D., LL. D.

A. O. Norton, A. M.

Carleton Noyes, A. M.

Charles Pomeroy Parker, B. A. (Oxon.)

George Howard Parker, S. D.

Bliss Perry, L. H. D., Litt. D., LL. D.

Ralph Barton Perry, Ph. D.

Chandler Rathfon Post, Ph. D.

Murray Anthony Potter, Ph. D.

Roscoe Pound, Ph. D., LL. M.

Fred Norris Robinson, Ph. D.

Alfred Dwight Sheffield, A. M.

O. M. W. Sprague, A. M., Ph. D.

Oliver Mitchell Wentworth Sprague, Ph. D.

William Roscoe Thayer, A. M.

Frederick Jackson Turner, Ph. D., LL. D., Litt. D.

Charles Henry Conrad Wright, M. A.

ASSOCIATE EDITORS

P F COLLIER & SON
NEW YORK

Designed, Printed, and Bound at
The Collier Press, New York

CONTENTS

CONTENTS

CONTENTS

The Lecture Series on the contents of The Harvard Classics ought to do much to open that collection of literary materials to many ambitious young men and women whose education was cut short by the necessity of contributing in early life to the family earnings, or of supporting themselves, "and who must therefore reach the standing of a cultivated man or woman through the pleasurable devotion of a few minutes a day through many years to the reading of good literature." (Introduction to The Harvard Classics.) The Series will also assist many readers to cultivate "a taste for serious reading of the highest quality outside of The Harvard Classics as well as within them." (Ibid.) *It will certainly promote the accomplishment of the educational object I had in mind when I made the collection.*

CHARLES W. ELIOT.

The Harvard Classics provided the general reader with a great storehouse of standard works in all the main departments of intellectual activity. To this storehouse the Lectures now open the door.

Through the Lectures the student is introduced to a vast range of topics, under the guidance of distinguished professors.

The Five-Foot Shelf, with its introductions, notes, guides to reading, and exhaustive indexes, may thus claim to constitute with these Lectures *a reading course unparalleled in comprehensiveness and authority.*

WILLIAM ALLAN NEILSON.

HISTORY

I. GENERAL INTRODUCTION

By Professor Robert Matteson Johnston

HISTORY alone, of all modes of thought, places the
reader above his author. While the historian more
or less diligently plods along his own narrow path,
perhaps the one millionth part of all history, every avenue
opens wide to the imagination of those who read him. To
them history may mean anything that concerns man and that
has a past; not politics only, but art, and science, and music
have had their birth and growth; not institutions only, but
legends and chronicles and all the masterpieces of literature,
reflect the clash of nations and the tragedies of great men.
And it is just because the reader is merely a reader that the
full joy of history is open to him. He wears no fetters, so
that even were he bent on mastering the constitutional documents of the United States he could turn aside with a calm
conscience to listen to the echoes of dying Roland's horn in
the gorge of Roncevaux or to stand by Cnut watching the
North Sea tide as it lapped the old Dane's feet.

In all directions, in almost every branch of literature, history may be discovered, a multiform chameleon; and yet history does not really exist. No one has yet composed a record
of humanity; and no one ever will, for it is beyond man's
powers. Macaulay's history covered forty years; that of
Thucydides embraced only the Peloponnesian war; Gibbon,
a giant among the moderns, succeeded in spanning ten centuries after a fashion, but has found no imitators. The truth
is there is no subject, save perhaps astronomy, that is quite
so vast and quite so little known. Its outline, save in the
sham history of text books, is entirely wanting. Its details,
where really known to students, are infinitely difficult to

bring into relation. For this reason it may be worth while to attempt, in the space of one short essay, to coordinate the great epochs of history, from the earliest to the most recent times.

The practical limit of history extends over a period of about three thousand years, goes back, in other words, to about 1000 B. C. Beyond that we have merely scraps of archæological evidence; names of pictures engraved on stone, to show that in periods very remote considerable monarchies flourished in Egypt, along the Euphrates, and in other directions. It was not these people who were to set their imprint on later ages, it was rather what were then merely untutored and unknown wandering tribes of Aryans, which, working their way through the great plains of the Volga, the Dnieper, and the Danube, eventually forced their way into the Balkan and the Italian peninsulas. There, with the sea barring their further progress, they took on more settled habits, and formed, at some distant epoch, cities, among which Athens and Rome were to rise to the greatest celebrity. And about the year 1000 B. C., or a little later, Greece emerges from obscurity with Homer.

Just as Greece burst from her chrysalis, a Semitic people, the Jews, were producing their counterpart to Homer. In the Book of Joshua they narrated in the somber mood of their race the conquest of Palestine by their twelve nomad tribes, and in the Pentateuch and later writings they recorded their law and their religion. From this starting point, Homer and Joshua, whose dates come near enough for our purpose, we will follow the history of the Mediterranean and of the West.

THE LEADERSHIP OF GREECE

First the great rivers, the Nile and the Euphrates, later the great inland sea that stretched westward to the Atlantic, were the avenues of commerce, of luxury, of civilization. Tyre, Phocæa, Carthage, and Marseilles were the early traders, who brought to the more military Aryans not only all the wares of east and west but language itself, the alphabet. Never was a greater gift bestowed on a greater race.

With it the Greeks developed a wonderful literature that was to leave a deep impress on all Western civilization. They wove their early legends into the chaste and elegant verse of the Homeric epics, into the gloomy and poignant drama of Æschylus, Sophocles, and Euripides. They then turned to history and philosophy. In the former they produced a masterpiece of composition with Thucydides and one of the most delightful of narratives with Herodotus. In the latter they achieved their most important results.

Greek philosophy was to prove the greatest intellectual asset of humanity. No other civilization or language before the Greek had invented the abstract ideas: time, will, space, beauty, truth, and the others. And from these wonderful, though imperfect, word ideas the vigorous and subtle Greek intellect rapidly raised a structure which found its supreme expression in Plato, Aristotle, and Zeno. But from the close of the Fourth Century before Christ, the time of Aristotle and his pupil Alexander the Great, Greek began to lose its vitality and to decay.

This decadence coincided with events of immense political importance. Alexander created a great Greek Empire, stretching from the Mediterranean to the Indus. After his death this empire was split into a number of monarchies, the Greek kingdoms of the East, of which the last to survive was that of the Ptolemies in Egypt. This perished when Augustus defeated Cleopatra and Antony at Actium in B. C. 31, exactly three hundred years after Alexander's final victory over Darius at Arbela.

THE DOMINATION OF ROME

During these three hundred years a more western branch of the Aryans, the Romans, had gradually forced their way to supremacy. It was not until about B. C. 200 that Rome broke down the power of Carthage, got control of the western Mediterranean, and then suddenly stretched out her hand over its eastern half. In less than two centuries more she had completed the conquest of the Balkans, Asia Minor, and Egypt, and the Mediterranean had become a Roman lake.

The city of Rome may go back to B. C. 1000, and the

legends and history of the Republic afford an outline of facts
since about B. C. 500, but it was only after establishing contact with the civilization and language of Greece that the
Romans really found literary expression. Their tongue had
not the elasticity and harmony of the Greek, nor had it the
wealth of vocabulary, the abstract terms; it was more fitted,
by its terseness, clearness, and gravity, to be the medium of
the legislator and administrator. Under the influence of
foreign conquest and of Greek civilization, Rome, however,
quickly evolved a literature of her own, an echo of the superior and riper one produced by the people she had conquered; it tinged with glory the last years of the Republic
and the early ones of the Empire, the age of Augustus. Virgil produced a highly polished, if not convincing, imitation of
Homer. Lucretius philosophized a crude materialistic universe in moderate hexameters. Cicero, with better success
and some native quality, modeled himself on Demosthenes;
while the historians alone equaled their Greek masters, and in
the statesmanlike instinct and poisoned irony of Tacitus revealed a worthy rival of Thucydides.

Latin and Greek were the two common languages of the
Mediterranean just as the unwieldy Republic of Rome was
turning to imperialism. The Greek universities, Athens,
Pergamon, and Alexandria, dictated the fashions of intellectualism, and gave preeminence to a decadent and subtilized
criticism and philosophy perversely derived from the Greek
masters of the golden age. But a third influence was on the
point of making itself felt in the newly organized Mediterranean political system—that of the Jews.

THE CONTRIBUTION OF THE JEWS

To understand the part the Jews were now to play, it is
necessary first of all to look back upon the general character
of the social and political struggles of those ancient centuries.
At the time of Homer's heroes, and, in a way, until that of
Alexander the Great, states were small, generally a city or a
group of cities. War was constant, and generally accompanied
by destruction and slavery. As the centuries slipped by, the
scale increased. Athens tried to create a colonial empire as

did Carthage, and the great continental states, Macedon and Rome, followed close at their heels. In the last century or so before Christ, war was nearly continuous on a vast scale, and it was attended by at least one circumstance that demands special consideration.

Social inequality was a fundamental conception of the ancient world. The Greek cities in their origin had been communities ruled by a small caste of high-bred families. The social hierarchy proceeded down from them to the slave, and war was waged on a slave basis, the victor acquiring the vanquished. The great wars of the Roman Republic against the Greek monarchies were huge treasure-seeking and slave-driving enterprises that reduced to servitude the most able and most refined part of the population of the conquered countries. Rome had created a great Mediterranean state, but at a terrible price. The civilization she had set up had no religion save an empty formalism, and no heart at all. It was the Jews who were to remedy this defect.

All through the East and in some parts of the West the Jewish merchants formed conspicuous communities in the cities of the Empire, giving an example of spiritual faith, of seriousness and rectitude, that contrasted strongly with what prevailed in the community. For materialism and epicurean-ism were the natural outcome of a period of economic pros-perity; religion was at its best formalistic, at its worst orgiastic; ethical elements were almost wholly lacking. Yet a revolt against the soullessness and iniquities of the times was proceeding and men were prepared to turn to whatever leaders could give them a system large enough to satisfy the cravings of long-outraged conscience, and large enough to fill the bounds of the Mediterranean Empire. Three Jews—Jesus, Paul, and Philo—came forward to do this work.

Jesus was the example, the man of conscience, the redeemer God. For in this last capacity he could readily be made to fit in with the Asiatic cults of the sun and of redemption which were at that time the most active and hopeful lines of religious thought. Paul was the Jew turned Roman, an im-perialist, a statesman, of wide view and missionary fervor. Philo was the Jew turned Greek, the angel of the Alexandrian schools, who had infused Hebraic elements into the moribund philosophizing of the Egyptian Greeks, and thereby given it a renewed lease of life. That lease was to run just long enough to pour the Alexandrian thought into the Christian mold and give the new religion its peculiar dogmatic apparatus.

For three centuries, until A. D. 312, Christianity was nothing in the Mediterranean world save a curious sect differing widely from the hundreds of other sects that claimed the allegiance of the motley population sheltering under the ægis of the Emperors. During those three centuries the Mediterranean was a peaceful avenue of imperial administration, of trade, of civilizing intercourse. Its great ports teemed with a medley of people in whom the blood of all races from the Sahara to the German forests, and from Gibraltar to the valley of the Euphrates, was transfused. The little clans of high-bred men who had laid the foundations of this huge international empire had practically disappeared. The machine carried itself on by its own momentum, while wars remained on distant frontiers, the work of mercenaries, insufficient to stimulate military virtues in the heart of the Empire. It was, in fact, the economic vices that prevailed, materialism, irreligion, and cowardice.

The feeble constitution of the Empire was too slight a framework to support the vast edifice. Emperor succeeded emperor, good, bad, and indifferent, with now and again a monster, and now and again a saint. But the elements of decay were always present, and made steady progress. The army had to be recruited from the barbarians; the emperor's crown became the chief reward of the universal struggle for spoils; the Empire became so unwieldy that it tended to fall apart, and many competitors sprang up to win it by force of arms.

THE CHRISTIANIZING OF ROME

In 312 such a struggle was proceeding, and Constantine, one of the competitors, casting about for some means to fortify his cause against his opponents, turned to Christianity and placed himself under the protection of the Cross. Whatever his actual religious convictions may have been, there can be no doubt that Constantine's step was politic. While the pagan cults still retained the mass of the people through habit and the sensuous appeal, Christianity had now drawn to itself, especially in the western parts of the Empire, the serious minded and better class. Administrators, merchants, men of position and influence were Christian. Constantine needed their aid, and fulfilled the one condition on which he could obtain it by adopting their faith.

Thus suddenly Christianity, after its long struggle and many persecutions, became the official religion of the Empire. But Christianity was exclusive and the Emperor was its head; so conformity was required of all citizens of the Empire, and conformity could only be obtained by paying a price. The masses were wedded to their ancient cults, their ancient gods, their ancient temples, their ancient rites. To sweep them away at one stroke and to substitute something different was not possible. So a compromise was effected. The priests, the temples, the ritual, the statues, remained, but they were relabeled with Christian labels, under cover of which Christian ideas were slipped in. A great metamorphosis took place of which the intelligent traveler and reader of to-day can still find traces:—

"The fair form, the lovely pageant that had entwined the Mediterranean with sculptured marble, and garlands of roses, and human emotion, was fading into stuff for the fantasies of dreamers. The white-robed priest and smoking altar, the riotous procession and mystic ritual would no longer chain the affections of mankind. No longer would the shepherd blow his rude tibia in honor of Cybele, no longer would a thousand delicious fables, fine wrought webs of poetic imagination, haunt the sacred groves and colonnades of the gods. Day after day, night after night, as constantly as Apollo and Diana ran their course in heaven, had all these things run their course on earth; now, under the spell of the man of Galilee, they had shivered into a rainbow vapor, a mist of times past, unreal, unthinkable, save where the historian may reconstruct a few ruins or the poet relive past lives. And yet the externals in great part remained. For it was at the heart that paganism was struck, and it was there it was weakest. It had attempted, but had failed, to acquire a conscience, while the new faith had founded itself on that strong rock. Christianity had triumphed through the revolt of the individual conscience; it was now to attempt the dangerous task of creating a collective one." [1]

THE FALL OF ROME

The establishment of Christianity at Rome came not a moment too soon to infuse a little life into the fast-decaying Empire. Constantine himself helped to break it in two, a Roman and a Greek half, by creating a new capital, Constantinople. More ominous yet was the constant pressure of the Teutons at the frontier, a pressure that could now no longer be resisted. By gradual stages they burst through the bounds, and at the time Christianity was becoming the official religion of the Mediterranean world, Germanic tribes had already extorted by force of arms a right to occupy lands within the sacred line of the Rhine and of the Danube. From that moment, for a century or more, the processes of Germanic penetration and of Roman disintegration were continuous, culminating in 375 with the great Germanic migrations and in 410 with the sack of Rome by Alaric and the Goths.

During the terrible half century that followed, the Roman world was parceled out among a number of Germanic princes, and of the old order only two things were left standing, a fragmentary empire of the East centering in Constantinople, and a bishopric of Rome of vastly increased importance that was soon to be known as the Papacy, and that already showed symptoms of attempting to regain by new means the universal dominion which the Emperors had lost.

The Germans were crude and military; the Latins were subtle and peaceful, and when the storm of conquest swept through the West they sought safety in the cloister. "There, under the protection of the Latin cross, a symbol the barbarians dare not violate, what was left of Roman intellectualism could cower while the storm blew over, presently to reissue as the army of Christ to conquer, with new-forged weapons, lands that the legions of their fathers had not even beheld." [2]

[1] Johnston, "Holy Christian Church," p. 146.
[2] Johnston, "Holy Christian Church," p. 162.

The Latin churchmen quickly learned how to play on the credulity and the superstition of the simple German, while setting before him the lofty ideals and ethics of Christianity. They not only held him through religion but they soon became the civil administrators, the legislators, the guiding spirits of the Germanic kingdoms.

Civilization had now taken on a marked change, had become a composite in which Christianity and Teutonism were large factors. Perhaps this was all clear gain; but in the economic and material sense there had been great losses. Enormous wealth had been destroyed or scattered, and imperial communication had broken down. The trader was no longer safe on the Mediterranean; the great roads of Rome were going to ruin; boundaries of military states barred old channels of intercourse. Under these conditions civilization could only be more localized, weaker than before. And in fact the Teutonic kingdoms pursued for some time an extremely checkered course.

THE RISE OF ISLAM

Then came, in the seventh century, a new and even more terrible blast of devastation. Mohammed arose, created Islam, and started the great movement of Arab conquest. Within almost a few years of his death the fanaticized hosts of Arabia and the East were knocking at the gates of Constantinople, and swept westward along the southern shores of the Mediterranean until the Atlantic barred their steps. They turned to Spain, destroyed the Visigothic kingdom, crossed the Pyrenees, and reached the center of Gaul before they were at last checked. The Franks under Charles Martel defeated them at Tours in 732, and perhaps by that victory saved Christendom. Had the Arabs succeeded in this last ordeal, who knows what the result might not have been? As Gibbon characteristically wrote: "A victorious line of march had been prolonged above a thousand miles from the rock of Gibraltar to the banks of the Loire; the repetition of an equal space would have carried the Saracens to the confines of Poland and the Highlands of Scotland; the Rhine is not more impassable than the Nile or Euphrates, and the Arabian

fleet might have sailed without a naval combat into the mouth
of the Thames. Perhaps the interpretation of the Koran
would now be taught in the schools of Oxford and her pul-
pits might demonstrate to a circumcised people the sanctity
and truth of the revelation of Mahomet."

On the wreck of the Arab hopes the descendants of
Charles Martel founded a monarchy which blazed into
ephemeral power and glory under Charlemagne. In the
year 800 the greatest of Frankish rulers revived the imperial title, and was crowned by the Pope in the basilica of
St. Peter's. But the old Empire could not be resuscitated,
nor for the matter of that could the Frankish monarchy long
maintain the preeminent position it had reached. A new
visitation was at hand, and Charlemagne before he died saw
the horizon of his northern seas flecked by the venturesome
keels of the first of the northern pirates.

THE FEUDAL SYSTEM

For about two centuries Europe passed through an epoch
of the deepest misery. Danes and Scandinavians ravaged
her from the northwest, Saracens from the south, so that
only the upper Rhine and Danube, harboring a rich Teutonic
civilization, escaped destruction. The Carlovingian Empire
broke into pieces, Frankish, Lothringian or Burgundian, and
Germanic, with the last of which went the imperial title.
And this disintegration might have continued indefinitely to
chaos had not feudalism appeared to fortify and steady de-
clining civilization.

Only force could successfully resist force, and at every
threatened point the same mode of local resistance sprang
up. Men willing and able to fight protected the community,
and exacted in return certain services. They soon began
to build castles and to transmit their powers, together with
their lands, to their heirs. Lands soon came to be viewed as
related to other lands on conditions of military and other
services. The Church followed the example, until, finally,
by the eleventh century, one general formula underlay
western European ideas: that every individual belonged to
a class, and enjoyed certain rights on the performance of

various services to a superior class, and that at the head of
this ladder of rank stood either the Emperor, or the Pope, or
both. The last step was a highly controversial one; on the
first all men were agreed.

By this time feudalism had done its best work in restoring
more settled conditions, and bringing to a conclusion the
northern and southern piracy. From Sicily to the marches
of Scotland, Europe was now one mass of small military
principalities, only here and there held together in more or
less efficient fashion by monarchies like those of France and
England, or by the Empire itself. Every trade route was
flanked by fortifications whence baronial exactions could be
levied on the traders. And when, under more peaceful conditions, great trading cities came into existence—in Italy,
Germany, the Netherlands—a fierce struggle arose for mastery between burghers and feudal potentates.

Meanwhile the Church itself had developed great ambitions and suffered the worst vicissitudes. While under
the Frankish protection, Rome had acquired the temporal
domain she was to hold until September 20, 1870, when she
was dispossessed by the newly formed Kingdom of Italy.
With this territorial standing, and impelled forward by the
mighty traditions of ancient Rome and of the Church, she
deliberately stretched out her hand under Gregory VII
(Hildebrand) in an attempt to grasp the feudalized scepter
of Europe. The Germanic Empire, the offshoot of the greater
domain of Charlemagne, resisted.   The great parties of
Guelphs and of Ghibellines, imperialists and papalists, came
into existence, and for a long period tore Germany and Italy
in vain attempts at universal supremacy.

Inextricably bound up with the feudal movement, and with
the enthusiasm for the service of the Church that Rome for
a while succeeded in creating, came an interlude, religious,
chivalrous, economic, the Crusades. Out of superabundant
supplies of feudal soldiers great armies were formed to relieve the Holy Places from the profaning presence of the
infidels. The East was deeply scarred with religious war
and its attendant butcheries, and little remained in permanent results, save on the debit side. For the Crusades had
proved a huge transportation and trading enterprise for the

thrifty republics of Genoa and Venice, and led to a great
expansion of oriental trade; while the West had once more
been to school to the East and had come back less religious,
more sceptical. And from the close of the period of the
Crusades (1270) to the outbreak of the Reformation, two
hundred and fifty years later, economic activity and the
growth of scepticism are among the most prominent facts,
while immediately alongside of them may be noted the birth
of the new languages, and, partly resulting from all these
forces, the Renaissance.

THE RENAISSANCE

For a while the Papacy, spent by its great effort of the
eleventh and twelfth centuries, went to pieces. The Latin
ideas for which it stood began to lose ground rapidly as
Dante created the Italian language (1300), and as, in the
course of the next two centuries, French, English, and German assumed definite literary shape. There was not only a
loss of faith in Latin forms, but a desire to transmute religious doctrine into the new modes of language, and especially to have a vernacular Bible. Assailed in this manner,
Rome stimulated theological studies, helped to create the
mediæval universities, and tried to revivify the philosophy
which Alexandria had given her in the creeds by going back
to the texts of the golden age of Greece with Aquinas.

It was of no avail. Europe felt a new life, a new nationalism moving within her. Voyages of discovery to India, to
America first stirred imaginations, and later poured into the
itching palms of ambitious statesmen, soldiers, artists, vast
stores of gold. The pulse of the world beat quicker. Constantinople fell, a thousand years after its foundation, into
the hands of the Turk, and its stores of manuscripts, of art,
of craftsmen, poured into Italy. Men became inventors,
innovators, artists, revolutionaries. Cesare Borgia attempted, but failed, to create an Italian empire. Martin
Luther attempted to secede from the Church, and succeeded.

He declared that a man could save his soul by the grace
of God only, and on that basis started a wrangle of ideals
and of wordy disputations that plunged Europe once more

into an inferno of warfare. It lasted until 1648, the peace of Westphalia, when it was found that on the whole the northern parts of Europe had become Protestant and the southern had remained Catholic.

FRANCE AND ENGLAND

At this very moment Louis XIV was beginning the reign that was to mark out for France the great position she held in the Europe of the last two centuries. The age of feudalism was fast passing. The last great feudatories had worn out their strength in the wars of religion. The monarchy had gained what they had lost, and now set to work in the splendor and pageantry of Versailles to reduce the once semi-independent feudal soldier into a mincing courtier. The Bourbons succeeded in large part. They remained the autocrats of France, with the privileged orders of the clergy and aristocracy at a low level beneath them, and in unchecked control of the machinery of government. That machinery they soon began to abuse. Its complete breakdown came with the French Revolution in 1789.

This dramatic event resulted from a large number of convergent and slow-acting causes. Among them we may note the fearful mismanagement of the Bourbon finances, inadequate food supply, and the unrest of a highly educated middle class deprived of all influence and opportunity in matters of government. That class got control of the States General which became a national assembly, and set to work to destroy Bourbonism in the name of liberty, equality, and fraternity. Between the inexperience of this assembly and the impotence of the Court, rose the wild force of the Parisian mob, which eventually drove France into war with outraged Europe, and brought the Bourbons, with thousands of the noblest and best as well as a few of the worst people of France, to the guillotine.

War which became successful, and the feebleness of the republican government that succeeded the Reign of Terror, inevitably made for a military dictatorship and a restoration of the monarchy. Napoleon Bonaparte, the greatest upstart in history, held France by his magnetic gaze and iron grasp

for fifteen years, while he organized her as no European
country had ever been organized, and with her might in his
control darted from torrid Egypt to arctic Russia in a
megalomaniac frenzy of conquest. He fell, leaving France
so exhausted that, for a brief spell, the Bourbons returned.

It had taken all Europe to pull down France and Napoleon, and in the end distant Russia had dealt the most
fatal wound. Yet it was England that had proved the most
constant, the most stubborn, and the most triumphant enemy.
And the quarrel between these two countries, France and
England, was that which went furthest back in history.

For a while, during the dark epoch that followed Charlemagne, the Normans had held by conquest a sort of middle
country between France and England. Under their duke,
William, they conquered England itself in 1066, and there
set up a strong insular monarchy. Their foothold in France,
however, brought the Anglo-Norman kings in conflict with
their neighbor, and wars were to rage between the two
countries with only rare intermissions until 1815. At first
their object was largely territorial possession; later economic
factors grew more apparent, until in the eighteenth century
and under Napoleon the struggle had become one for oversea colonial empire.

SPAIN AND THE HOUSE OF HAPSBURG

In the sixteenth century, with the House of Tudor on the
English throne, the perennial struggle of the English sover-
eigns against France became complicated by the appearance
of a new continental power that might under given circumstances join hands with the older enemy. This was
Spain.

Since their defeat by the Franks at Tours, in 732, the
Arabs had steadily lost ground. For several centuries, however, they had prospered in Spain, and there they had developed learning and the arts with splendid success, at a
moment when Christian Europe was still plunged in darkness. But presently the feudal principalities lodged in the
Pyrenees and Asturian mountains began to gain ground,
and finally toward the end of the fifteenth century these

states came together in a united monarchy that conquered the last Arab kingdom and founded modern Spain.

At this very moment, by one of the most remarkable coincidences in European history, marriage alliances and other circumstances almost suddenly threw the Spanish kingdom, the great inheritance of the dukes of Burgundy, and the kingdom of Hungary, into the hands of the Hapsburg dukes of Austria, who were to seat their ruling princes on the imperial throne of Germany almost uninterruptedly until the old Germanic empire closed its days in 1806.

This huge concentration of power in the hands of the Emperor, Charles V (1519-1556), gave a marked turn to the situation created by the outbreak of the Reformation. For France, which remained Catholic, and England, which became Protestant, had both to face the problem of the overtopping of the European equilibrium by the inflated dominions of the Hapsburgs. This accounted for much in the constantly shifting political adjustments of that age. It was not until the close of the reign of Louis XIV (Treaty of Utrecht, 1713) that the Hapsburg power was about balanced by the placing of a Bourbon prince on the throne of Spain. From that moment France and Spain tended to act together against England.

In England the religious upheaval lasted roughly about a century, from Henry VIII to Cromwell; on the whole, it was less violent than on the Continent. Its chief results were the establishment of the Anglican Church and of those more markedly Protestant sects from among which came the sturdy settlers of New England.

THE FOUNDING OF THE BRITISH EMPIRE

It was during the wars of religion that England came into a struggle with the new Hapsburg-Spanish power. It had its tremendously dramatic episodes in the cruise of the Great Armada, and its fascinatingly romantic ones in the voyages of discovery and semi-piratical exploits of the British seamen who burst the paper walls that Spain had attempted to raise around the southern seas. The broad ocean, the gold of the Indies, the plantations of sugar, of

tobacco, of coffee, the growing settlements and countries of a
new world, these became the subject of strife from that time
on. And as Spain declined in her vigor after the Armada,
and a century later became the client of France, so the
struggle narrowed itself to one between the latter power
and England.

In the Seven Years' War (1756-1763), England established her supremacy in this world-wide struggle, and although in the next war she lost her American colonies, yet
when she met France again in 1793, her trade and manufactures, her unrivaled geographical and economic situation, and her politic and businesslike statesmanship, had
placed her at the head of the nations of Europe. She joined
the European alliance against France in 1793, and with only
two short intervals remained in the field against her until
at Waterloo, twenty-two years later, Napoleon was finally
defeated by Wellington and Blücher.

During this gigantic struggle France faced two problems,
that of the sea and England, that of the land and the three
great military powers of northeast Europe—Austria, Russia,
Prussia. Toward the end, after Napoleon had failed in
Spain and got into a death grapple with Russia, it was the
Continental issue that obscured the other. But England
kept her eye firmly fixed on the sea, on colonies, on water-
borne trade; so that when at the Congress of Vienna (1815)
the powers parceled out the shattered empire, England was
left by common consent the only great sea and colonial
power.

MODERN EUROPE

A period of reaction followed the fall of Napoleon, but in
1848 it came to a close in a storm of revolution. Population
had grown, means of communication were multiplying fast
and promoting intellectual as well as economic activity, political privileges were unduly restricted, governments were
old-fashioned. In Italy, and in Germany where the old
empire had perished in 1806, were the seeds of a new nationalism. From Palermo to Paris, and from Paris to Vienna, a
train of revolutionary explosions was fired, and for two
years Europe was convulsed. A new Bonaparte empire

arose in France, and in Italy and Germany a national idea
was founded, though not for the moment brought to its consummation. That was to take twenty years more, and to be
vastly helped by the tortuous ambitions of Napoleon III
ably turned to use by Cavour and by Bismarck.

In 1859 France helped the House of Savoy to drive Austria
from the valley of the Po, and thereby cleared the way for
the liberation and fusion of all Italy by Cavour and Garibaldi. In 1866 Prussia expelled the House of Hapsburg
from Germany, and four years later consolidated her work
by marching to the walls of Paris at the head of a united
German host which there acclaimed William of Hohenzol-
lern chief of a new Germanic empire.

What has happened since then, and chiefly the scramble
for colonies or for establishing economic suzerainty, belongs
more to the field of present politics than of history. For
that reason it may be left out of account. And so indeed
has much else been left out of account for which the limit
of space fixed for this essay has proved altogether too narrow. If a last word may be added to help the reader to
gather in the harvest from that trampled and mutilated field
which we call history let it be this, that everything turns on
a point of view, on a mental attitude. The reader is the
spectator of the pageant; he must be cool to judge and discriminate, with no bias toward praise or blame, content
merely to observe as the constant stream unfolds itself in all
its changing colors, but with a mind ready to judge human
actions and motives, an imagination ready to seize on the
ever-living drama of fact, and a heart ready to respond to
those countless acts of heroism that have ennobled great
men and great races, and with them all humanity.

II. ANCIENT HISTORY

By Professor William Scott Ferguson

O F THE three periods of approximately fifteen hundred years each into which the history of the Western World falls, two belong to the domain of antiquity. The first of these "links in the chain of eternity" includes the rise, maturity, and decay of the Oriental civilization at its three distinct but interconnected centers, Egypt, Babylonia, and Crete-Mycenæ. The second reaches from 1200 B. C. to 300 A. D., and it too is filled with the growth, fruition, and decline of a civilization—the high material and intellectual culture of the Greeks and Romans. Overlapping this for several centuries, the third or Christian period runs down to our own time. The nineteenth century of our era may be regarded as the opening of a fourth period, one of untold possibilities for human development.

The Greeks, like the Christians, went to school for many centuries to their predecessors. Their earliest poems, the "Iliad" and "Odyssey" of Homer, are in one sense a legacy from the Cretan-Mycenæan age, in which the scene of their action is laid. None the less, like the peoples of mediæval and modern Europe, the Greeks owed the production of their most characteristic things to their own native effort.

It was in the eighth and seventh centuries B. C. that the Greeks became a new species of mankind. In this, the time of their expansion from an Ægean into a Mediterranean people, they shook off the bonds which had shackled the Oriental spirit, and, trusting to their own intellects, faced without flinching the grave problems of human life. When they then awoke to a realization of their position, they found themselves in the possession of cities which were at the same time states. Political connection between them there was none, and slender indeed were the ties of sentiment, language, and religion which bound to one another the Hellenes of Miletus, Corinth, Syracuse, Marseilles, and the hundreds of other Greek city-states then in existence. The complexity of the map may be appreciated by observing that Crete alone had twenty-three distinct states. In Greece, as elsewhere, cities in which life was at once national and municipal proved the most favorable soil for the growth of free institutions.

THE INDIVIDUALISM OF GREECE

The keynote of the formative age of Greece was the rise of individualism. Poets freed themselves from the Homeric conventions, and dealt not as of yore with the deeds of ancient heroes, but with their own emotions, ideas, and experiences. They laid aside the measure and diction of the Epos and wrote every man and woman in his native rhythm and dialect. Sculptors and painters, long since accustomed to work in the spirit of a school, and to elaborate more and more scrupulously certain types of art, now became conscious that so much of their work was of their own creation that they began laying claim to it by adding their signatures.

The problems of religion were no longer satisfactorily settled by the Homeric revelation. They forced themselves directly upon the attention of every thinking individual. One man remained orthodox, another took refuge in the emotional cults of Dionysos and Demeter, another revolted and sought to explain the world as a product of natural laws and not of divine creation. Men who had earlier been obscured by their respective families, clans, and brotherhoods, now severed themselves for all public purposes from these associations, recognizing only the authority of a state which threw open its privileges to all alike. There were revolters in politics as there were revolters in religion and in art: the tyrants are the kinsmen of the personal poets, Archilochus, Sappho, Alcæus, and of scientists like Thales of Miletus and the Ionian pyhsicists.

The Asiatic Greeks were in general the leaders at this time, and Miletus was the greatest city in the entire Greek world.

SPARTA—ATHENS—THEBES

The sixth century which followed was an age of reaction. Men shrank from the violent outbreaks of the preceding generations. It was the time of the "seven wise men," of the precept "nothing in excess," of the curbing of aristocracies with their claim to be a law unto themselves. During this epoch of repression a rich and diversified culture which had developed in Sparta was narrowed down to one single imperious interest—war and preparation for war. With the leveling down of the Spartan aristocracy went the decay of the art and letters of which it had been the bearer. The Spartan people became an armed camp living a life of soldierly comradeship and of puritanical austerity, ever solicitous lest its serfs (there were fifteen of them to every Spartan) should revolt and massacre, ever watchful lest the leadership which it had established in Greek affairs (there were 15,000 Spartans and 3,000,000 Greeks) should be imperiled. In Athens the course of development had been directly the opposite of this. There, too, the nobles were ousted from their monopoly of political rights, but on the other hand, the serfs were admitted to citizenship. The men who molded Athens in its period of democratic growth were themselves aristocrats who never doubted for a moment that the culture of their order would ennoble the life of the masses. Hence no pains or expenses were spared by them to build and maintain—at their own cost—public *palæstræ* and *gymnasia* in which poor and rich alike could obtain a suppleness and grace of body that added charm and vigor to their movements; and to institute so-called musical contests in which the people generally had to participate, and the preparation for which incited all classes to study literature and art—above all to learn the words and the music of lyric and dramatic choruses. The aristocracy died down in Athens, but the Athenians became the aristocracy of all Greece.

That they did so was largely the work of their most brilliant statesman, Themistocles, whose "Life" by Plutarch is included in The Harvard Classics.[1] Under his far-sighted guidance Athens built an invincible fleet at great financial

[1] *Harvard Classics,* xii, 5.

sacrifice, cooperated with Sparta with singular devotion and unparalleled heroism in beating off the Persians, and established her maritime empire. Aristides[2] was at first his unsuccessful rival and later his faithful collaborator, and Pericles,[3] whose interest in science, philosophy, jurisprudence, art, and literature makes him the best exponent of the culminating epoch of Greek development, profited sagaciously by their work. He both perfected the institutions of Athenian democracy and defined and organized its imperial mission. No man in high place ever took more seriously the doctrine that all citizens were equally capacitated for public service, yet no more ardent imperialist than he ever lived. The truth is that Athenian democracy with all that it implies was impossible without the Athenian maritime empire. The subject allies were as indispensable to the Athenians as the slaves, mechanics, and traders are to the citizens of Plato's ideal republic.

This empire Sparta sought to destroy, and to this end waged fruitless war on Athens for ten years (431-421 B. C.). What she failed to accomplish, Alcibiades,[4] the evil genius of Athens, effected, for at his insistence the democrats embarked on the fatal Sicilian expedition. After the dreadful disaster which they sustained before Syracuse ('413 B. C.), their dependencies revolted and ceased paying them tribute; whereupon, unable to make head against the Sicilians, Spartans, and Persians, who had joined forces against her, Athens succumbed in 405 B. C. It is doubtful whether any other city of 50,000 adult males ever undertook works of peace and war of similar magnitude. Athens led Greece when Greece led the world.

The Spartans took her place, but they held it only through the support given them by their confederates, Persia and Syracuse. When they quarreled with the Persians they at once lost it; regained it by the Kings' Peace of 387 B. C., but only to fall before Thebes sixteen years later. Thebes depended solely upon her great warrior-statesman, Epaminondas. His death in battle, in 362 B. C., meant the downfall of the Theban supremacy, and at the birth of Alexander the Great in 356 B. C. the claim could be made that what the

[2] *H. C.*, xii, 80. [3] *H. C.*, xii, 36. [4] *H. C.*, xii, 110.

Greeks had sought for two hundred years had now been accomplished: all the European Greek cities, great and small,
were again free as they had been in the seventh century. In
reality, as Plutarch's biography of Demosthenes[5] shows,
they lived rent by factional struggles, in constant fear and
envy of one another, and under the shadow of a great peril
which union, not disunion, could alone avert.

MACEDON

Philip of Macedon united Greece under his own leadership, and with the power thus secured Alexander the Great
laid the Persian Empire prostrate and open for swift and
persistent Greek colonization. As Machiavelli in his
"Prince"[6] points out, "his successors had to meet no other
difficulty than that which arose among themselves from their
own ambitions." This was sufficient, however. It led to a
thirty years' war such as had never before been seen. At
its end the Græco-Macedonian world was paralyzed by an
unstable balance of power in which Egypt, under the
Ptolemies, by using its great wealth to maintain a magnificent fleet held Macedon and Asia in check. The
unification of Italy under Rome (343-270 B. C.) and the
subsequent destruction of the Carthaginian Empire
(264-201 B. C.) brought into hostile conflict with Egypt's
enemies a military state which was far stronger than any
individual Greek kingdom. This state had a population of
5,000,000, an army list of 750,000, and it could keep 100,000
men in the field for many years at a stretch. Such a force
could be stopped only by a federation of the entire Greek
world. The Greeks again paid the just penalty for their
disunion, and after a bitter struggle they sank under the
Roman sway.

THE RISE OF ROME

The Romans who conquered the Greeks were not "gentlemen" like Cicero[7] and Cæsar[8] and their contemporaries of a
hundred and fifty years later. Their temper is only partially
revealed in Plutarch's "Coriolanus,"[9] in which a legend—

[5] H. C., xii, 197.   [6] H. C., xxxvi, 7.   [7] H. C., xii, 225.
[8] H. C., xii, 274.   [9] H. C., xii, 152.

which, however, the Romans and Greeks of Plutarch's time (46-125 A. D.) believed to be a fact—is made to illustrate the alleged uncompromising character of their political struggles and the lofty virtues of their domestic life. In fact, they had many of the qualities of Iroquois, and when they took by storm a hostile city, their soldiers—uncultured peasants, once the iron bonds of discipline were relaxed—often slew every living thing which came in their way: men, women, children, and even animals. The world was not subdued by Rome with rosewater or modern humanitarian methods.

Five generations later the Italians were in a fair way to being Hellenized, so powerful had been the reaction of the eastern provinces upon them in the interval. During this epoch of rapid denationalization, the Roman aristocracy, which had guided the state first to internal harmony, then to stable leadership in Italy, and finally to world-empire, became divided against itself. The empire had nurtured a stock of contractors, money lenders, grain and slave dealers —the so-called equestrian order—which pushed the great landed proprietors, who constituted the senate, from position to position; wrested from them control of the provinces which it then pillaged most outrageously, and helped on the paralysis of government from which the rule of the emperors was the only escape. The youth of Cicero coincided with the suicidal strife between the agrarian and the commercial wings of the aristocracy. Cicero, being a "new man," had to attach himself to great personages like Pompey, in order to make his way in politics, so that his political course and his political views were both "wobbly"; but he had at least one fixed policy, that the "harmony of the orders" must be restored at all costs.[10] This, however, was impracticable.

THE ACHIEVEMENTS OF JULIUS AND AUGUSTUS CÆSAR

The empire had also bred a standing army, and the necessity that this be used against the Teutons, Italians, Greeks, and Gauls bred leader after leader who could dictate terms to the civil government. The last of these was Julius Cæsar. He

[10] See Cicero's "Letters" in *Harvard Classics*, ix, 81.

was the last because he decided not to coerce the senate, but
to put himself in its place. His short reign (49-44 B. C.) is
a memorable episode in the development of Rome, in that it
was the first reappearance of a world monarchy since Alexander the Great's death. Cæsar is greeted in contemporary
Greek documents as "the Saviour of the entire race of men."
After his murder a quarrel arose between rival candidates
for the command of the troops—Cæsar's troops, as the
assassins found to their sorrow.   Antony,[11] his master of
horse, finally took one half of them with him to the East, to
finish Cæsar's projected campaign against the Parthians, to
live in Alexandria at the feet of Cleopatra, Cæsar's royal
mistress—who was not only an able and unscrupulous
woman, but also the heir of a bad political tradition—to bring
Egypt into the Roman Empire by annexing the Roman Empire to the Egyptian crown. The most that can be said for
him is that he was a kind of bastard Cæsar. On the other
hand, Augustus, Cæsar's adopted son, to whom the command of the rest of the troops fell, proved to be a statesman
of the highest order. He roused national and republican
feeling in Italy against Antony and his Egyptian "harlot";
but, after defeating them at Actium in 31 B. C., he had to
reckon with the demon—or was it a ghost?—which he had
conjured up. This he did by establishing a peculiar compromise between republicanism and monarchy called the
principate, which lasted, with fitful reversions to Cæsar's
model, and gradual degeneracy toward a more and more
complete despotism, until the great military revolt of the
third century A. D. occurred, when the Roman system of
government, and with it the Græco-Roman civilization, sank
in rapid decay. For two hundred and fifty years sixty millions of people had enjoyed the material blessings of peace
and orderly government. They had cut down forests, made
the desert a garden, built cities by the hundreds, and created
eternal monuments of the sense for justice and magnificence
which penetrated from Rome to the ends of the known
world. Then they became the helpless prey of a few hundred thousand native and barbarian soldiers. The decline
of the Roman Empire is the greatest tragedy in history.

[11] *H. C.,* xii, 334.

During the *principate* the prince or emperor seemed to be the source of all actions, good and bad.   Upon the will and character of a single individual hung suspended, apparently, the life and weal of every human being.   It was, therefore, natural for this age to be interested in Biography.   Hence Plutarch is at once a "document" for the time in which he lived and a charming "betrayer" of the Græco-Roman world on which he looked back.

III. THE RENAISSANCE

By Professor Murray Anthony Potter

THE Renaissance followed what is, even now, sometimes called the Dark Ages. The almost inevitable inference is that a period of darkness was succeeded by one of light. The veil of night rent asunder, the world, rejoicing in the sun's rays, with glad energy again took up its work. But much of the darkness of what are more fitly called the Middle Ages is due to the dimness of vision of those who have baptized the period with a forbidding name, and if we called the Renaissance an age of light, is it not because we are dazzled by mere glamour? After all, the Renaissance was the offspring of the Middle Ages, and a child must frequently bear the burdens of its parents.

One of the burdens of the Middle Ages was obscurantism, and obscurantism is that which "prevents enlightenment, or hinders the progress of knowledge and wisdom." Instead of dying at the close of the Middle Ages, it lived through the Renaissance, wary and alert, its eyes ever fixed on those whom it regarded as enemies, falling upon them from ambush when because of age or weakness their courage flagged, and it triumphed in the sixteenth century. It can never die as long as there are men. Neither can superstition die, nor fear, nor inveterate evil passions, which, if they smolder for a time, will unfailingly burst forth and rage with greater fury. If such be your pleasure, you can, with some plausibility, represent the Renaissance as darker than the Middle Ages. Machiavelli,[1] the Medicis, and the Borgias have long been regarded as sin incarnate in odious forms. Making all due allowances for exaggeration and perversion of truth, the Renaissance was not a golden age, and the dramas of

[1] For Machiavelli's political ideals, see his "Prince" in *Harvard Classics*, xxxvi, 5, and Macaulay's essay "On Machiavelli" in *Harvard Classics*, xxvii, 381.

horror[2] are something more than the nightmares of a madman. And yet it is a luminous age. The sun has its spots,
and the light of the Renaissance is all the more intense because of the blackness of the intermingling shadows.

THE INDIVIDUALISM OF THE RENAISSANCE

No age can be adequately defined by a short phrase, but it
was a happy thought which prompted the statement that the
Renaissance was the age of the discovery of man. Add the
importance, not only of man in general, but of the individual. It is true that men of marked individuality abounded
in the Middle Ages. You have only to think of Gregory the
Great, Gregory of Tours, Charlemagne, Liutprand, Abelard,
and Saint Bernard of Clairvaux. What is new is a general
awakening to the fact that the perfection of individuality
is so important, and the desire to force your contemporaries and posterity to regard you as different from
other men.

It might be said, with a certain amount of exaggeration
of course, that the mediæval man was Plato's dweller in the
cave, who succeeded at last in making his escape into the
light of day, and so doing became the Renaissance man en-
raptured by what lay within his field of vision, and allured
by the infinite promise of what lay beyond. And as if the
actual world cramped him, he must discover ideal realms
and live in the past and the future as well as the present.

THE REVIVAL OF CLASSICAL ANTIQUITY

His interest in antiquity is well known. With the ardor
of treasure hunters, scholars sought for classical manuscripts and antiquities, in France, Switzerland, Germany,
Italy, and the East, and the enthusiasm excited by their success could not have been greater had they discovered El
Dorado. They were generous with their treasures, door
after door opening upon antiquity was thrown back, and
men swarmed through them eager to become better acquainted with their idols and obtain from them information

---

[2] See, for example, Webster's "Duchess of Malfi" in *Harvard Classics,*
xlvii, 719.

which their teachers of the Middle Ages were powerless to furnish. Some were so dazzled and docile that, instead of freeing themselves from bondage, they merely chose new masters, but, after all, more gracious ones.

Petrarch, anticipating Andrew Lang, writes letters to dead authors. Of Cicero he says: "Ignoring the space of time which separates us, I addressed him with a familiarity springing from my sympathy with his genius." And in his letter to Livy: "I should wish (if it were permitted from on high), either that I had been born in thine age, or thou in ours; in the latter case, our age itself, and in the former, I personally should have been the better for it." Montaigne says that he had been brought up from infancy with the dead, and that he had knowledge of the affairs of Rome "long before he had any of those of his own house; he knew the capitol and its plan before he knew the Louvre, and the Tiber before he knew the Seine.[3]

THE RENAISSANCE CURIOSITY

This infatuation for antiquity may seem bizarre, but it did not exclude intense interest on the part of the Renaissance man for the world about him, his town, his country, and remote as well as neighboring nations. Petrarch likes to speak of the marvels of India and Ceylon. There were drops of gypsy blood in his veins, but he was afraid of stealing time from his beloved books, and remains an excellent example of the "far-gone" fireside traveler, who in his study roamed through distant parts, spared the inclemency of the weather and the incommodities and dangers of the road.

Montaigne, who loved "rain and mud like a duck," was of stronger fiber. "Nature," he says, "has placed us in the world free and unbound; we imprison ourselves in certain straits." "Travel is, in my opinion, a very profitable exercise; the soul is then continually employed in observing new and unknown things, and I do not know, as I have often remarked, a better school wherein to model life than by incessantly exposing to it the diversity of so many other lives,

[3] Cf. Montaigne's "Institution and Education of Children" in *Harvard Classics*, xxxii, 29-73; and especially on his own education, pp. 67-71. See also Sainte-Beuve's essay "On Montaigne" in *Harvard Classics*, xxxii, 109.

fancies and usances, and by making it relish so perpetual a
variety of forms of human nature."

From one source or another, then, the Renaissance men
acquired an immense number of facts, and were able to retain them; for much is said about their inexhaustible memory. The important thing to know is what they did with
them. Was their passion for facts that of a miser for his
gold, of a savage for shiny, many-colored beads?

A fact is a delightful, wholesome thing. To the everlasting credit of the Renaissance men they appreciated its value,
and worked hard to acquire it, thus grappling with reality.
No longer would they merely scan the surface of things;
they would pierce, as Dante said, to the very marrow with the
eyes of the mind. Two or more centuries later than Dante,
Machiavelli complained that his contemporaries loved antiquity, but failed to profit by the lessons which are implicit
in its history. But Machiavelli was not entirely just. The
Renaissance men were tender gardeners, and in their loving
care every fact, every theory, every suggestion burgeoned,
flowered, and bore fruit.

Some of them, it is true, recognized limitations to the
versatility characteristic of the spirit of the age. Pier Paolo
Vergerio, after reviewing the principal branches of study,
states that a liberal education does not presuppose acquaintance with them all; "for a thorough mastery of even one of
them might fairly be the achievement of a lifetime. Most
of us, too, must learn to be content with modest capacity as
with modest fortune. Perhaps we do wisely to pursue that
study which we find most suited to our intelligence and our
tastes, though it is true we cannot rightly understand one
subject unless we can perceive its relation to the rest."
These words might well have been written to-day. Very
probably they were equally apposite in the Renaissance; yet
they seem cautious, almost overtimorous, in a period when
so many men were not only accomplished scholars, authors
of repute, capable public servants or statesmen, connoisseurs
of the fine arts, painters, sculptors, and architects themselves. There seems to have been nothing that they could
not do if they wished.

THE AGE OF DISCOVERY

Every interest was turned to account. In their pursuit of perfection they required an ampler environment. The age of the Renaissance is the age of the great discoveries, of Diaz, Columbus, Vasco da Gama, Vespucci, the Cabots, Magellan, Francis Drake,[4] and others, whose journeys were undertaken with a far different purpose than the mere satisfying of restless curiosity.

Equally practical was the study of the heavens. The stars had long been regarded as flaming beacons in the sky, prophets and guides for man to his ultimate goal. Their influence, benign or malignant, determined the fates of individuals and nations. It behooved the prudent man to consult them, and he studied the hidden workings of nature not only to comprehend them, but to make them serve his purpose. There were many failures, but if the Renaissance is the age of Faust, it is also that of Copernicus.

In the study of the world about him, of the firmament, of the past and the future, the Renaissance man felt his subject was something created. In his turn he took up the rôle of creator. To escape from an importunate world he called into existence the Arcadia of the pastorals, the fairyland of the adult man. It has almost vanished from our sight, but its music and fragrance still hover in the air. Another manifestation of dissatisfaction with the actual world, more practical, is the creation of ideal commonwealths, Cities of the Sun, or Utopias.[5]

THE WORSHIP OF BEAUTY

The lover of beauty nowadays shrinks from the Utopias of the Renaissance, but the practical men of that age cherished beauty with an affection we can hardly conceive. It was bone of their bone and flesh of their flesh. It was the one guest ever sure of welcome. Dante, in the *tornata* of his first ode, says: "Ode! I believe that they shall be but

---

[4] For the narratives of these explorers see *H. C.*, xliii, 22ff., xxxiii, 133ff.
[5] See, for example, Sir Thomas More's "Utopia" in *H. C.*, xxxvi, 142.

rare who shall rightly understand thy meaning, so intricate
and knotty is thy utterance of it. Wherefore, if perchance
it come about that thou take thy way into the presence of
folk who seem not rightly to perceive it; then I pray thee
to take heart again, and say to them, O my beloved lastling:
'Give heed, at least, how beautiful I am.'" They would give
heed, and to such extremes did many Renaissance men go in
their worship of beauty that they prostituted her and debased themselves. The majority remained sound of heart,
and though tortured with doubts, and stumbling again and
again, they succeeded in making themselves worthy of communion with God.

Last of all, the question might be asked: is the Renaissance
more than a period of storm and stress, a link between the
Middle Ages and Modern Times? Like every age, it is one
of transition, but it is also one of glorious achievement. If
any one doubts this, let him remember only a few names
of the imposing roll call—Petrarch, Boccaccio, Ariosto, Machiavelli, Rabelais, Montaigne, Calderon,[6] Lope de Vega,
Cervantes,[7] Shakespeare,[8] and in their ranks Dante[9] takes
his place with the same serene and august confidence with
which he joined the company of Virgil and Homer.

[6] *H. C.,* xxvi, 3ff.   [7] *H. C.,* xiv.
[8] For works by Shakespeare and his contemporaries in the Elizabethan
drama, see *H. C.,* xlvi and xlvii.
[9] *H. C.,* xx.

IV. THE FRENCH REVOLUTION

By Professor Robert Matteson Johnston

THE French Revolution concentrates within the narrow space of five years, from the 5th of May, 1789, to the 9th of Thermidor, 1794, all that man can conceive as most dramatic, repulsive, uplifting, terrifying, glorious, and disheartening. There is never a happy medium about it, nothing balanced or discriminating; everything is extreme, human emotion rising to the most intense collective utterance at the pangs of starvation, of murder, of oppression, of tyranny, at the joy of decisive action and of climbing the heights whence liberty and betterment can be seen streaking the horizon with hope. That is why the Revolution fascinates the ordinary reader more than perhaps any other period of history. It sets before him the bounds of the sublime and of the ignoble, of all that lies undeveloped in himself never, in all probability, to find expression.

THE CONTRASTS OF THE REVOLUTION

How extraordinarily difficult to interpret such a movement! Even Carlyle, with all his his passionate humanity, fails to catch the figure of that unfortunate woman who tramped through the empty streets of Paris at dawn one gray autumn day, starvation and despair in her eyes, mechanically tapping her drum and lugubriously chanting: "Du pain! Du pain!" ("Bread! Bread!") That distressing figure, poignant in all its naked emotions, was to uproot the Bourbons from Versailles, to make of Paris once more the capital of France, and by that deed to divert the whole current of French history from a channel of two centuries. And that is the contrast, the difficulty, at every point. Mirabeau is a venal and corrupt individual whose turpitude insistently pursues us, and yet at moments he is the statesman of grand vision whose eye unerringly pierces through the veil of time. Charlotte Corday is but a simple and quite unimportant young woman from the country; she drives a knife into Marat's heart, and with that heroic gesture flashes light to the very depths of a terrific crisis.

HISTORIES OF THE REVOLUTION

A curious fact about the French Revolution, but not so strange as it would seem when one thinks the matter over, is that there should be no good history of it. The three outstanding books are those of Michelet, Carlyle, and Taine; and all three are destined to live long as masterpieces, intellectual and artistic; yet not one of them is wholly satisfacory to the present age, whether for its statement of facts, for its literary method, or for its mentality; while there is no sign at the present day that we are likely soon to get another great history of the Revolution. On the contrary, the tendency is for historians to concentrate their attention on the endless details or varied aspects of the movement, finding in each of these a sufficient object for the exercise of their industry and talents. Following that example, we may here perhaps best touch on the reaction between France and England in terms of the Revolution, and particularly in regard to those two famous books, Voltaire's "Letters on the English," [1] and Burke's "Reflections on the French Revolution." [2]

THE REVOLUTION OF IDEAS

The early part of the eighteenth century witnessed a great change in the current of ideas in France. The death of Louis XIV, and the coming to power of Philippe Duc d'Orléans as regent, dispelled all the old prestige of glittering Versailles, and gave France a wit and debauchee for ruler who cared nothing for pomp or etiquette. He enjoyed life after his own unedifying fashion; he gambled and encouraged stock exchange speculation; he relaxed the muzzle and let slip the courtier's leash with which Louis had

[1] *Harvard Classics,* xxxiv, 65. [2] *H. C.,* xxiv, 151.

curbed the great men of letters of his epoch. And immediately French writers dashed away into the boundless field of political satire and criticism. Montesquieu led off with his "Lettres Persanes," in 1721, and Voltaire followed hard at his heels with his "Letters on the English," in 1734. The hounds of spring were at winter's traces.

VOLTAIRE'S DARING

Montesquieu's violent arraignment of the old order passed only because he seasoned it more than generously with a *sauce piquante* that titillated the depraved taste of the Regent to a nicety. Voltaire's book was in even worse case; it was immediately condemned, and an order was issued to arrest the author and imprison him in the Bastille. Voltaire had to fly for safety. And yet, to a modern reader, the "Letters on the English" doubtless seems a perfectly mild affair.

It is only by bearing in mind the conditions of political despotism that then existed in France that one can realize the boldness of the book. In it Voltaire gives his impressions of England in his supremely lucid style, but after the fashion of the man who throws a ball at some object from which he tries to catch it on the rebound. He is writing of England, but he is thinking of France; and in the customs and institutions of the former he seeks the examples from which he can measure those of his own country.

Voltaire is, on the whole, inclined to think well of the strange people whom he visited across the Channel, though he cannot avoid the conclusion that their philosophy, liberty, and climate lead straight to melancholia. England appears to him the land of contentment, prosperity, order, and good government. Monarchy is restrained by a well-balanced parliamentary system, and above all there is toleration in matters of faith and in matters of opinion. He frankly admires, and calls on his countrymen to copy, what seems to him the most admirable of models. It may be noted, however, that he is clearly nervous of strictly political questions, and he always prefers getting around to his plea for tolerance by the circuitous road of religion.

AN ENGLISH VIEW OF THE REVOLUTION

With Burke, more than half a century later, we get the strongest possible contrast. He admires nothing; he reprobates everything; he foresees the worst. For one thing, the Revolution had now actually broken out. Already its best aspects were becoming obscured, as disorder fast grew, and as the National Assembly deliberately adopted a policy of destruction to defeat Bourbon apathy and insouciance. France appeared to be threatened with anarchy, and that seemed to Burke more intolerable than the long-continued conditions of tyranny and misgovernment that were responsible for it. He was an old man, and more conservative than in his younger days. To him the glorious revolution of William of Orange and the Whigs seemed the perfect model, and the parliamentary institutions of Britain the ideal form of government. The disorders of Paris and the methods of the National Assembly shocked and wounded him, so he turned on them and rent them. He admitted, indeed, that he was not in a position to pronounce judgment: "I do not pretend to know France as correctly as some others," and so he confined himself to the rôle of the advocate. His pleading against the Revolution echoed through the Courts of Europe, carried conviction in almost every quarter where doubt existed, and to this day remains the most effective indictment against the men who made modern France. The success of Burke's book was in part due to the fact that its publication was followed by the Reign of Terror, which seemed to prove the author's argument, but above all to its brilliant and noble, if somewhat too ample, style. Of this one example only will be given:

BURKE ON MARIE ANTOINETTE

"It is now sixteen or seventeen years since I saw the Queen of France, then the Dauphiness, at Versailles; and surely never lighted on this orb, which she hardly seemed to touch, a more delightful vision. I saw her just above the horizon, decorating and cheering the elevated sphere she just began to move in—glittering like the morning star, full

of life, and splendor, and joy. Oh! what a Revolution!
And what a heart must I have to contemplate without emotion that elevation and that fall! Little did I dream when
she added titles of veneration to those of enthusiastic, distant, respectful love, that she should ever be obliged to carry
the sharp antidote against disgrace concealed in that bosom;
little did I dream that I should have lived to see such dis-
asters fallen upon her in a nation of gallant men, in a nation of men of honor, and of cavaliers. I thought ten
thousand swords must have leaped from their scabbards to
avenge even a look that threatened her with insult. But
the age of chivalry is gone. That of sophisters, economists,
and calculators has succeeded; and the glory of Europe is
extinguished for ever." [3]

Thus Burke proudly looked down on the miseries of
France, while Voltaire had admiringly looked up to the
prosperities of England. And we who come more than a
century later, while recognizing their preeminence as men
of letters, may perceive that as thinkers they were perhaps
a little too near their objects. Burke's arguments are always
admirable but unconvincing; while Voltaire's often justified
praise of the English reposes on an obvious failure to understand them.

[3] *H. C.,* xxiv, 223-224.

V. THE TERRITORIAL DEVELOPMENT OF THE UNITED STATES

By Professor Frederick Jackson Turner

EXPANSION has been the very law of American life. In the treaties which record the successive annexations of the territory of the United States we may read the story of the nation's acquisition of its physical basis, a basis comparable in area and resources not to any single European country but to Europe as a whole. If a map of the United States is laid down upon a map of Europe drawn to the same scale, with San Francisco resting on the coast of Spain, Florida will occupy the land of Palestine, Lake Superior will be adjacent to the southern shore of the Baltic, New Orleans below the coast of Asia Minor, and the shores of North Carolina will nearly coincide with the eastern end of the Black Sea. All of Western Europe will lie beyond the Mississippi, the western limits of the United States in 1783. These treaties[1] mark the stages by which the Union acquired an area equal to all nations west of the Black Sea.

THE BOUNDARIES OF THE NEW NATION

Freed from the fear of French attack after the peace of 1763, the thirteen colonies declared their independence. Against the wishes of Spain, and even against the pressure of her French ally in the Revolutionary War, the United States secured from England by the treaty of 1783[2] boundaries which extended along the Great Lakes, west to the Mississippi, and south to Florida, as well as the free navigation of the Mississippi. Spain recovered from Britain

---

[1] The references in this lecture are to the volume of American Historical Documents, and especially to the collection of treaties, *Harvard Classics*, xliii.

[2] *H. C.*, xliii, 185.

Florida, which she had conquered in the course of the war.

But these boundaries were only paper rights, for England failed to give up her posts on the Great Lakes, alleging the neglect of the United States to carry out the provisions of the treaty in regard to loyalists and debts, and Canadian officials encouraged the Indians across the Ohio to resist the advance of the Americans. In similar fashion on the southwest Spain denied the right of England to convey to the Union the territory between the Alleghenies and the Mississippi, and withheld the navigation of the river by means of her possession of New Orleans. She also, in the period of the weak confederation, intrigued with leaders of the Kentucky and Tennessee settlements to withdraw them from the Union; and, like England, she used her influence over the Indians to restrain the American advance.

While Indian wars were in progress north of the Ohio during Washington's administration, the French Revolution broke out, and England feared not only that the American expeditions against the Indians were in reality directed against the posts which she retained on the Great Lakes, but also that the United States would aid France in a general attack on her. Breaking her historic alliance with Spain, the French Republic, in 1783, tried to involve, first the Government of the United States and then the western frontiersmen in attacks upon Florida and Louisiana.

These were the critical conditions which in 1794 resulted in Jay's mission and treaty by which England agreed to give up the western posts.

THE STRUGGLE FOR THE MISSISSIPPI

Alarmed at the prospect of a union of England and the United States, Spain not only made peace with France at Bâsle in 1795, but also, by Pinckney's treaty in that year, conceded to the United States the Mississippi boundary and the navigation of the river. The latter concession was vital to the prosperity of the Mississippi Valley, for only by way of this river could the settlers get their surplus crops to a market.

It had become clear by 1795 that, with rival European nations threatening the flanks of the American advance, interfering in domestic politics, and tampering with the western frontiersmen, the United States was in danger of becoming a mere dependency of the European state system.[3] Partly to ensure such a dependence of the United States upon herself, and partly to procure a granary for her West Indian Islands, France now urged Spain to give her Louisiana and Florida, promising protection against the American advance.

The Alleghenies seemed to the leaders of French policy the proper boundaries for the Union. At last, in 1800, Napoleon so far mastered Spain as to force her to yield Louisiana to him; and the Spanish Intendant at New Orleans, pending the arrival of French troops, closed the Mississippi to American commerce. The West was in a flame. It had now acquired a population of over three hundred and eighty thousand, and it threatened the forcible seizure of New Orleans. Even the peaceful and French-loving President Jefferson hinted that he would seek an English alliance, and demanded the possession of the mouth of the Mississippi from France, arguing that whoever held that spot was our natural enemy. Convinced that it was inexpedient to attempt to occupy New Orleans in view of the prospect of facing the sea power of England and an attack by the American settlers, Napoleon capriciously tossed the whole of the Province of Louisiana to Jefferson by the Louisiana Purchase Treaty[4] of 1803, and thereby replenished his exchequer with fifteen million dollars, made friends with the United States, and gave it the possibility of a noble national career by doubling its territory and by yielding it the control of the great central artery of the continent.

EXTENSION OF THE ROCKY MOUNTAINS

The expansive spirit of the West grew by what it fed on. The Ohio valley coveted Canada, and the South wished Florida, where England exercised an influence upon the

[3] Compare "Washington's Farewell Address," in *H. C.,* xliii, 255, 256; 261-264.
[4] *H. C.,* xliii, 267.

Spanish administration. It was the West that took the lead
—bringing on the war of 1812. In the peace negotiations in
1814 Great Britain tried to establish a neutral zone of Indian country between Canada and the Ohio Valley settlements, but by the treaty[5] the United States retained its
former possessions. By the convention of 1818 they extended the boundary between Canada and the United States
from the Lake of the Woods to the Rocky Mountains along
the forty-ninth parallel, leaving the disputed Oregon country open to each nation for a term of years without preju
dice to the rights of either.

ACQUISITION OF FLORIDA AND TEXAS

In the same years the United States was pressing Spain
to relinquish Florida. Claiming West Florida and Texas
as a part of the Louisiana Purchase, the Government annexed the former piecemeal in 1810 and 1812. Taught by
General Jackson's successful although unauthorized invasion of Florida in 1818 that she held that position on the
Gulf only at the pleasure of the United States, and hopeful
perhap., to avert the threatened recognition of the revolting
Spanish-American colonies, Spain ceded Florida in 1819,
drawing an irregular line between her possessions and those
of the United States which left Texas as well as the other
southwestern territory in Spain's hands. Recognition of
the revolted republics followed in 1823 and thereafter the
Union had to deal with Mexico in place of Spain in acquiring mainland possessions. Russia withdrew her claims to
territory south of 54° 40' in 1824, and as a result of the
negotiations which preceded this action, as well as by the
prospect of European intervention in Spanish America,
President Monroe in 1823 announced the famous Doctrine[7]
which declared the American continents no longer subject
to European colonization or intervention to oppress them or
control their destiny.

Early in the thirties American missionaries entered the
Oregon country where the Hudson's Bay Company held
sway under the English flag. American settlers, chiefly

[5] *H. C.*, xliii, 273.   [6] *H. C.*, xliii, 286.   [7] *H. C.*, xliii, 296.

descendants of the hardy frontiersmen of the Mississippi Valley, also made settlements in Mexico's province of Texas. In 1836 the Texans revolted, declared their independence, and appealed to the United States for annexation. The northeastern boundary was settled by the Webster-Ashburton treaty[8] in 1842, leaving the fate of Oregon still undetermined. In that very year an emigration of American farmers began across the plains and mountains to that distant land, and relations between the Union and England became strained. In Texas also European interests were involved, for in the long interval between the formation of the Texan Republic and its annexation by the United States, England and France used their influence to keep it independent. California, moreover, furnished reason for apprehension, for England had shown an interest in its fate, as Mexico, torn by internal dissensions, gave evidence that her outlying provinces were likely to drop from her nerveless hands.

The slavery contest now interrupted the old American expansive tendencies, for while the South raised its voice of warning against the possibility of a free Texas under British protectorate and demanded its annexation, the Whigs and anti-slavery men of the North, alarmed at the spread of slavery and the prospect of new slave States, showed opposition to further territorial acquisition in the Southwest. But in the election of 1844, which was fought on the issues of the "reoccupation of Oregon and the reannexation of Texas," Polk, a Tennessee Scotch-Irishman, representing the historic expansive spirit, won the Presidency. Texas was annexed as a State under a joint resolution of Congress in 1845, before Polk was inaugurated, and immediately thereafter he determined that if Mexico made this annexation an occasion for war, she should be compelled to cede us California and her other Southwestern lands as the price of peace.

TO THE PACIFIC

He compromised the Oregon question with England by the Treaty of 1846, accepting the forty-ninth parallel as the

[8] *H. C.,* xliii, 299.

boundary, in spite of the campaign cry of "fifty-four forty or fight." The same year the Mexican war began, in which American troops overran California and the intervening land.

With the American flag floating over the capital of Mexico, a strong movement began to hold Mexico itself, or at least additional territory. But by the Treaty of Guadalupe-Hidalgo[9] in 1848 the line was drawn along the Gila River and from its mouth to the Pacific. Agitation for a southern route to the Pacific led to the further acquisition of a zone south of the Gila by the Gadsden Purchase of 1853.

By these annexations between 1846 and 1853 the United States gained over 1,200,000 square miles of territory. Gold was discovered in California in 1848, and unimagined riches in precious metals, timber, and agricultural resources were later revealed in this vast new empire. But most important of all was the fact that the nation had at last made its lodgment on the shores of the Pacific, where it was to be involved in the destiny of that ocean and its Asiatic shores.

The South, deprived of the benefits of these great acquisitions by the compromise of 1850, tried in vain to find new outlets by Cuban annexation. But the Civil War resulting from the rivalries of the expanding sections engrossed the energies of the nation. At the close of that war, Russia, which had given moral support to the North when England and France were doubtful, offered the United States her Alaskan territory and, not without opposition, Secretary Seward secured the ratification of a treaty[10] in 1867 by which nearly six hundred thousand square miles were added to our domains.

For nearly a third of a century after the Civil War the energies of the Union were poured out in the economic conquest of the vast annexations in its continguous territory. In 1892 the Superintendent of the Census announced that the maps of population could no longer depict a frontier line bounding the outer edge of advancing settlement. The era of colonization was terminating. The free lands were being

[9] *H. C.*, xliii, 309.   [10] *H. C.*, xliii, 459.

rapidly engrossed and the Union was reaching the condition of other settled states.

THE ISLAND POSSESSIONS AND THE PANAMA CANAL

In this era the old expansive movement became manifest in a new form by the Spanish-American War and the acquisition of land oversea. It was the recognition of the independence of Cuba[11] by the United States in 1898 and the intervention to expel Spain which brought about the Spanish-American War; but once involved in that war, the naval exigencies led to the conquest of the Philippines, and Porto Rico as well as Cuba. Considerations of strategy also facilitated the annexation of Hawaii[12] in 1898.

By the treaty of peace[13] in 1898 Spain ceded the Philippines and Porto Rico and withdrew from Cuba, which obtained its autonomy by the recall of the American troops in 1902.

The events of the war, and especially the dramatic voyage of the *Oregon* around Cape Horn from the Pacific coast to share in the fight off Santiago, gave an impetus to the long debated project of constructing the Isthmian Canal by the United States. With her vastly increased power in the Pacific, her new possessions in the Caribbean Sea, and the astonishing growth on the Pacific coast, the canal seemed a necessity, and almost a part of our coast line. By the Hay-Pauncefote treaty of 1901, England withdrew the obstacles arising from the Clayton-Bulwer treaty of 1850, and the United States acquired the rights of the French Company, which had failed in its undertaking to pierce the isthmus. When in 1903 Colombia rejected a treaty providing for the canal, a revolution broke out in Panama. President Roosevelt with extraordinary promptness recognized the Republic of Panama and secured a treaty[14] from this republic which was ratified in 1904, granting the canal zone and various rights to the United States.

Thus at the beginning of the twentieth century the long process of attrition of the United States upon the Spanish

[11] *H. C.*, xliii, 467.   [12] *H. C.*, xliii, 464.   [13] *H. C.*, xliii, 469.
[14] *H. C.*, xliii, 478.

Empire was brought to this striking climax. The feeble Atlantic colonies had won a land extending across the continent, they had acquired dependencies in the Caribbean, in the Pacific, and off the coast of Asia, and they had provided for connecting the two oceans by the Panama Canal.

POETRY

I. GENERAL INTRODUCTION

By Carleton Noyes, A. M.

THE human heart has ever dreamed of a fairer world than the one it knows. No man, however dark his spirit, however cramped his senses, is quite without the yearning after wider horizons and a purer air. In a happy moment earth seems to hold for all the promise of larger things. The moment passes; and the world closes in again, actual, bare, unyielding, as before. Yet among men there are some endowed with vision, an insight more penetrating and more sustained. To their liberated spirit the world unfolds a farther prospect. Earth clothes itself for them in radiant vesture, mute forms are speaking presences, the riddle of life resolves itself into a meaning. To them it is granted to arrest the moment of illumination, otherwise so fleeting; and, gifted further with a shaping power, they are able to re-create the moment in enduring forms. The men of vision are the seers and prophets; the shapers of the revelation, re-creating it, are the artists and the poets.

What each of us is seeking the poet has already found. Poetry is the step beyond, which we were about to take, but were not certain of the way. In our experience from year to year, we are not without glimpses of beauty in the world, a sense of meaning somewhere within the shows of things. Of this beauty and this meaning poetry is a fuller revelation. The poet gives us back the world we already know, though it is a world transfigured; he draws his material from stores to which we all have access, but with a difference. His vision, clearer and more penetrating, transfigures the facts and discloses the beauty only waiting to be thus revealed. His fresh sight of this beauty quickens in him an

51

emotion of wonder and of joy which impels him to expression. Seeing the world in new combinations, he selects from the common store of experience certain images colored by his mood. Of these images he weaves a pattern of words, which re-create the beauty he has seen and are charged with that deeper significance he has divined within the outward manifestation. It is just because he sees farther and feels more intensely that he is a poet; and then because he is able to phrase his experience in words which have the power to create the vision and the meaning in us. So the poet fashions that fairer world of which the heart has dreamed; and by the mediation of his art it becomes ours for an enduring possession. If this be indeed the office and destiny of poetry, we may well ask whence it draws its inspiration and by what means it accomplishes its high ends.

THE ORIGIN AND COURSE OF NARRATIVE POETRY

The older poetry of a people takes shape around a story. Childhood dearly loves a tale; for its simple heart finds the way out of a reality it does not understand by contriving a world of make-believe. The young imagination, not yet beset by too urgent actualities, admits no bounds to its wide exercise. In the childhood of the race, objects are spirits, moved by their own inner life. Natural forces are gods, acting capriciously upon the fortunes of men. A man more cunning or more powerful than his fellows becomes a hero or a demigod in memory and tradition. So a child too animates the common things of his little world with a life of their own that suits the purposes of his active fancy. He endows them with a part in his play, and they act out the story that he weaves around them. The imagination of childhood demands action, deeds done and stories told,— high adventures of gods and heroes, or the tangled fortunes of princes and damsels, of knights and captive ladies, of fairies and sprites. So a fable builds itself out of free imaginings.

The love of a story never passes. All through its long history, in every land and among every people, poetry has not ceased to interest itself in all conceivable happenings of life. But the stream of poetry is fed by many sources, and it takes color and volume according to the channels through which it flows. From the "Iliad" to "Enoch Arden," to cite typical instances which by no means set the farther or the nearer bounds of narrative poetry, both the subject and the form have undergone varied and profound changes. This movement, as each nation develops its own art and culture, has been in the direction from the general to the particular, from the interests of the entire nation to the affairs of private persons. Out of the stirrings and strivings of a whole people toward expression is gradually evolved the separate individual artist or poet.

CHARACTERISTICS OF PRIMITIVE POETRY

In elder days men worked and played *together*. The single member of the clan or the individual citizen was completely merged in the unity of the tribe or the state. His welfare depended upon the welfare of the group, his interests were bound up inextricably with the life of the community as a whole. This fact explains the range and character of the earlier poetry of any people. All nations have their own distinctive beginnings, and these are widely distributed in time: the term "earlier," therefore, is relative to each nation. Examples of such earlier poetry are the "Iliad" and the "Odyssey," on the one hand—though these represent the culmination rather than the beginning of an age, which, however, is relatively early—and on the other hand, the English traditional ballads.[1] In point of time these two instances are separated from each other by about two thousand years, but as earlier poetry they have this trait in common, that they are not the work of any one man. Such poetry as this is not made; it grows. It springs as a kind of spontaneous expression of the life of the group. An incident of common concern to the whole people, a situation involving the fortunes of all, furnishes the occasion and the motive of the tale. Necessarily some one, any one, —unknown by name,—starts it on its course. The story is told and retold: passing from lip to lip, it receives changes

[1] See *Harvard Classics*, xl, 51-130.

and additions. Again, finally, some one, unknown by name, gives it the form in which it is written down and so pre- served. But it is the poetry of a people rather than of a man.

This poetry has certain traits which serve to mark it as popular or national. In the case of poems of greater scope, like the "Iliad" or "Beowulf," it deals with action in the large. The heroes whose deeds it celebrates are the posses- sion of the kindred or the race; they are kings and men of might or valor, known to all in the national traditions. Even the gods are not absent; they play a dominant part in the action. Similarly in the popular ballads, the persons of the story, though drawn from humbler life, acquire a legendary interest which makes them typical figures and invests them with general importance. Such poetry, then, mirrors the ideals of the group or the nation. It is shaped and colored by the religious beliefs of the people or by vague question- ings and vaguer answers as to the nature and meaning of things. By the kind of persons it sets in action, by the deeds they do and the passions they feel, this poetry becomes the projection and expression of life at its best as the whole people conceives it to be. It is the nation's interpretation of itself.

One characteristic these tales have which, apart from their form as verse, makes them poetry. The world which they give back is idealized. They come into being in re- sponse to men's love of a story. But the action which they embody is not the petty and commonplace round of daily af- fairs; the action is heightened and intensified. What we call the "glamour of romance" is over it. The free imag- ination is at work to fashion a more engaging and significant world. The stories told are of a time long past, in a hap- pier and golden prime. This, they say, is the world as it was; would that it were so now, or might be again! Across the obscure yearnings of the present need, seen at a dis- tance in the fresh light of mornings gone, the men of an elder age are figured of heroic mould. Their virtues, their passions, and their faults are nobler than the common breed. The world in which they move and do is an ampler scene, bathed in a freer air. This transfiguring of things, making them bright, intense, and full of a farther meaning, is the spirit of poetry.

THE GROWTH OF INDIVIDUALISM

As civilization progresses, the individual begins to define himself more sharply against the background of his group. The common effort of the group has wrought out for itself the arts of life; the store of culture is gradually enriched by collective striving. Then a time comes when the various functions of life tend to be distributed more and more among the separate members of the community; and to them it becomes possible to develop their own special gifts and aptitudes as potter, weaver, smith. One day a man arises who has the gift of song. Conscious of himself now as an individual, he takes the stories which the fathers have told, threads of legend and tradition, and weaves them into a new pattern. As the earlier poetry was the expression of the collective ideals of the group, so now the poem conceived and shaped by a single maker is animated by his own special purpose; colored by his personal emotion, it reflects the world as he himself sees it: and it becomes in this wise the expression of his individual interpretation of life.[3]

Thus a new spirit comes into narrative poetry. Less and less it is spontaneous, impersonal, objective; more and more it is the product of a deliberate, self-conscious art; the choice of subject and the manner of presenting it are determined by the poet's own feeling. The world from which he draws his material is nearer home. His characters are more immediate to everyday experience; what they lose in glamour they gain in directness of appeal. Interest in the action for its own sake does not flag, but the persons who move in it are more closely and definitely expressive of what the poet thinks and feels. He chooses his characters because they embody concretely and so exemplify the conception he has formed of a significant situation. The story of the mythical

[3] As illustrating the contrast in point of view of the work of the individual poet and of national poetry, it is interesting to compare the acute self-consciousness of Tennyson's "Ulysses" (*H. C.*, xlii, 1007) with the downrightness of Homer's hero.

hero Beowulf and his fight with the weird sea-monster
Grendel is succeeded by Chaucer's "Canterbury Tales." [3]
Here the poet assembles a motley company, of high and low
degree, of clerical and lay, sketched from the life with exquisitely humorous fidelity. The stories they tell to pass
the stages of their pilgrimage are as varied as themselves
—none, however, more characteristic of the new temper of
poetry than the Nun's Priest's tale. Now

> A povre widwe somdel stope in age,
> Was whylom dwelling in a narwe cotage,
> Bisyde a grove, stondyng in a dale. [4]

And the hero of the tale is "Chauntecleer"! The cock
discourses learnedly of dreams, and for authorities he in-
vokes the great names of antiquity. But he succumbs to
inexorable fate, figured by "Russel the fox," while the
denizens of the barnyard act the chorus to his tragedy. The
poem in its mock heroics is a sly satire of the grand manner
of the romantic epic. But beyond the entertainment it furnishes by the way, in it is reflected Chaucer's own genial
though shrewd criticism of life; and we enjoy this contact
with the poet's own personality. So in all narrative poetry
of conscious art, whether the "Faerie Queene" or "Paradise Lost," Keats's "Endymion" or "Enoch Arden," whether
it portrays the figures of romance and fable, or whether it
treats the high argument of God's ways with man or a
tragedy of humble souls, we discern the image of a heightened and intenser world, which serves finally to express the
poet's own way of conceiving life, his interpretation of experience.

THE RISE OF THE LYRIC

The same trend toward greater personality in expression
which changes the import of narrative poetry gives rise to
poetry of a different kind and purpose. As the individual
emerges out of the mass into consciousness of himself, he
is made aware that life comes to him, in contrast to other
men, with a difference. The world is *his* world, passions
are his passions, events take their significance as they re-

[3] *H. C.*, xl, 11.   [4] *H. C.*, xl, 35.

late themselves somehow to his own experience. The great
sky arches overhead, brightly blue or piled with tossing
clouds. Outward in every direction reaches the broad earth,
a crowded pageantry of color and form and sound and stir.
Just at the center, the meeting point of all these energies,
stands a man, thinking, feeling, willing. Upon him as a
focus converge all rays of influence from the inclosing
world. Responding to their impact, he perceives a sudden
harmony within the tumult of sensation and flashing idea, a
harmony which is beauty, and his whole being is flooded
with emotion. His joy, wonder, worship, surge to expression. Out of the chaos he compels a new order, the image
of his perception; and this he bodies forth in material form
through the medium of words, shaping it after the pattern
of his perception, and moulding it to his mood. The mighty
pulse of nature bids him to sing, to voice his insight and his
feeling in accordant rhythm. So out of the fullness of his
spirit, quickened by the beauty of the world and its inner
meaning, wells a song. The lyric is born.

> It lies not on the sunlit hill
> Nor in the sunlit gleam
> Nor ever in any falling wave
> Nor ever in running stream—
>
> But sometimes in the soul of man
> Slow moving through his pain
> The moonlight of a perfect peace
> Floods heart and brain.[5]

So the external world weaves endlessly its subtle patterns
of beauty and meaning, at times well hidden indeed, but
yielding finally their secret to the ardent searchings of the
human heart. Often the lyric springs, as it seems spontaneously, out of a sheer joy of things.

> Sumer is icumen in,
> Lhude[6] sing cuccu!
> Groweth sed, and bloweth med,
> And springth the wude[7] nu—[8]
> Sing cuccu!

[5] William Sharp. [6] Loud. The final e's are pronounced as syllables.
[7] Wood. [8] Now.

Awe[9] bleteth after lomb,
Lhouth[10] after calve cu;
Bulluc sterteth,[11] bucke verteth,[12]
Murie sing cuccu!

Cuccu, cuccu, well singes thu, cuccu:
Ne swike[13] thu naver nu;
Sing cuccu, nu, sing cuccu,
Sing cuccu, sing cuccu, nu!

The bird's note gives the key. The poet responds, his joy overflows into images, his melody voices the music of *Spring!* As this is one of the earliest lyrics in our language, so it is also, in spirit, form, and content, a veritable spring song of the lyric mood.

For the lyric poem is born in emotion. Its moving spirit is song.

Piping down the valleys wild,
Piping songs of pleasant glee,
On a cloud I saw a child,
And he laughing said to me:

"Pipe a song about a lamb!"
So I piped with merry cheer.
"Piper, pipe that song again;"
So I piped: he wept to hear.

"Drop thy pipe, thy happy pipe;
Sing thy songs of happy cheer!"
So I sung the same again,
While he wept with joy to hear.

"Piper, sit thee down and write
In a book that all may read."
So he vanish'd from my sight;
And I pluck'd a hollow reed,

And I made a rural pen,
And I stain'd the water clear,
And I wrote my happy songs
Every child may joy to hear.[14]

The impulse to music is the lyric's source. But the fragile, delicately wrought vessel of lyrical form is capable of inex-

[9] Ewe.   [10] Loweth.   [11] Leaps.   [12] Runs to the greenwood.
[13] Cease. The music to which this lyric was sung in the first half of the thirteenth century still exists.
[14] William Blake. *H. C.*, xli, 599.

haustible variety and wealth of content.   It may hold as an
aroma the evanescent mood of a moment; or into it may be
poured the accumulated treasures of a ripe experience.   The
only limitation of a lyric is that it shall sing; otherwise it
is free to range earth and sky and the inmost chambers of
the heart.

THE SCOPE OF THE LYRIC

The lyric, therefore, is a poet's fullest outpouring of himself.   More than any other form of poetry it is toned to his
mood, and breathes the intensity of his emotion.   But it is
capable also of a burden of thought, provided only that the
thought take wing and rise from the shell of abstraction
into the full-embodied life of warm and colored image.   In
its simplest import the lyric is a cry.   A sudden fresh vision
of beauty releases the deep sources of joy, and the emotion,
gathering about the image that has quickened it, wells forth
in rhythmic pulse, into surgent, glowing words.

> Hail to thee, blithe Spirit!
> Bird thou never wert,
> That from heaven, or near it,
> Pourest thy full heart
> In profuse strains of unpremeditated art.
>
> Higher still and higher
> From the earth thou springest
> Like a cloud of fire;
> The blue deep thou wingest,
> And singing still dost soar, and soaring ever singest.
>
> In the golden lightning
> Of the sunken sun
> O'er which clouds are brightening,
> Thou dost float and run,
> Like an unbodied joy whose race is just begun.[15]

The song of a skylark, playing across the strings of the
poet's interpreting and transfiguring temperament, is ethe-
realized into a rarer music.   It floats us back the bird's
song; but it *is* the very spirit of poetry.

Another poet thus describes this instant experience of
beauty in its full immediacy:

[15] Shelley. *H. C.*, xli, 851.

> The sounding cataract
> Haunted me like a passion : the tall rock,
> The mountain, and the deep and gloomy wood,
> Their colours and their forms, were then to me
> An appetite; a feeling and a love,
> That had no need of a remoter charm,
> By thought supplied, nor any interest
> Unborrowed from the eye.[16]

But fresh, immediate vision may be attended by insight; the poet sees deeper, feels more, and into the precious vessel of his verse he pours a richer meaning:

> I have learned
> To look on nature, not as in the hour
> Of thoughtless youth; but hearing oftentimes
> The still, sad music of humanity,
> Nor harsh nor grating, though of ample power
> To chasten and subdue. And I have felt
> A presence that disturbs me with the joy
> Of elevated thoughts: a sense sublime
> Of something far more deeply interfused,
> Whose dwelling is the light of setting suns,
> And the round ocean and the living air,
> And the blue sky, and in the mind of man:
> A motion and a spirit, that impels
> All thinking things, all objects of all thought,
> And rolls through all things.[17]

As poetry, these verses in themselves have not quite the lyric impetus. They move to a stately music suited to the calm elevation of mind, in which "the spontaneous overflow of powerful feelings" is now "recollected in tranquillity." They describe, however, rather than illustrate, the lyric temper. They are still charged with emotion which heightens and intensifies the actual material stuff out of which they are woven, and so they are true poetry. But the burden of thought tends to impede that upward spring of feeling which is the essence of the lyric mood.

The range of lyric poetry is limited only by the capacities of the human spirit; it is coextensive with the height and depth of man's mind and heart. A lyric is some one poet's interpretation of the beauty, the wonder, the profound mystery, of life as he perceives and feels it, by the magic of

[16] Wordsworth. *H. C.,* xli, 650ff. [17] Wordsworth. *H. C.,* xli, 650ff.

word-image made visible to the inward eye, by the weaving of tone and measured beat made vocal in the soul. In swift, vivid phrase it may picture a butterfly or a world; in richly-freighted word it may seem, for an illumined moment, to unlock the vast secret of life, discovering truth. The lyric may be an iridescent jet of song, piercing the silence; it may be a mighty hymn, resolving discords and voicing the praise of things. No mood is denied it; joy and sorrow, hope and regret, tears and laughter, lie within its compass. Its characteristic note is intense personality. But the true poet transfigures the beauty he has seen in his little corner of the earth into cosmic vistas, opening to infinity, and trans-mutes his private joys and griefs into the great passionate fountains of universal happiness and suffering accessible to all men.

THE ELEMENTS OF POETIC FORM

Any subject may be turned to the uses of poetry accord-ing as the poet conceives it in a certain way. At once more sensitive and more creative than other men, the poet sees life more intensely and more beautifully. He is stirred by the splendor or tenderness of nature's pageantry of shifting colors and impressive forms; he is quickened to penetrating thought by his insight into the living principle which shapes the world, and by his sense of the varying significance of men's purposes and destiny. His emotion impels him to ex-press his perception, carrying lightly also its burden of thought, in an ordered pattern of word-symbols, which re-produce images from the external world, but which invest them with associations and implicate further meanings. To this transcript of the immediate and actual world he adds:

> The gleam,
> The light that never was, on sea or land,
> The consecration, and the poet's dream.

Thus to transfigure the world and life, under the stimulus of feeling and by the power of insight, is the magic and the mystery of the poet. So, too, poetry may range through the vast, complex whole of experience, to draw thence its inspiration and its material. But life may be thus conceived poetically, and yet the idea may be expressed in prose. To give it poetical expression, there must pulse through the subject matter, whatever guise it wear, that deep upwelling of emotion which prompts the poet to phrase his thought in the word-pattern which is a poem.

The poetic impulse, rising out of vision and emotion, utters itself in speech, but speech flowing in measured pulse and cast in a determinate mould. As the stuff out of which the web of poetry is woven is both intellectual and emotional, though the two elements may combine in varying proportions, so these elements together go to the shaping of the final total form. This form, comprising both the measured flow of words and their ultimate arrangement in a pattern,[18] is a poem. And this form is not accidental or arbitrary, but is conditioned by the nature itself of the human mind and spirit.

THE NATURE AND SOURCE OF RHYTHM

Within the texture of every poem beats a pulse like the throb of coursing blood in a living body; and this pulse or *rhythm* is the life of poetic form. Indeed rhythm is the very heart of the universe itself. No manifestation of the active principle in the great frame of things is so intimate or so pervasive. Day and night, flow and ebb, the perfect return of the seasons, the breath of our nostrils and the stars in their courses echo alike its mighty music. In the little practical affairs of life, no less than in earth's orbic sweep through stellar spaces, rhythm is a law of movement, to which all sustained action instinctively conforms. It makes movement easier, as in labor—whether the quick tap of a smith's hammer on his anvil or the long-drawn tug of a gang at a rope. Soldiers, marching to an ordered step lighten the fatigue of weary miles. Rhythm also makes movement pleasurable, as in the dance. And, conversely, the perception of rhythm in things external to oneself is both easy and pleasurable. Alike in its subjective and its objective aspects, therefore, rhythm is in essential harmony with the spirit of man.

[18] For this suggestion of poetry as a "pattern" I am indebted to Professor J. W. Mackail's Oxford Lectures on Poetry.

As the order of the universe is shot through with a living pulse, so emotion, too, if sustained, tends to express itself in rhythm. The emotional stimulus of the perception of beauty, or the excitement attending insight into the deeper truth of life, quickens the heart-throb; this heightened activity overflows to expression in words which reproduce the measured beat of the impetus out of which they spring. And so a poem comes to birth. In its most primitive forms, some scholars tell us, poetry is but the voice accompaniment to the rhythms of bodily movement in work and play.[19] A woman grinding corn back and forth between two stones, keeps time by the crooning of unreasoned words in endless repetition. A fragment of an old spinning song echoes in Ophelia's ravings: "You must sing *Down-a-down, An you call him a-down-a*. O, how the wheel becomes it!" Lithe-bodied men shout in unison their war chant, as they tread the circle of the dance. Youths and maidens in common festival recite in turn the verses of a ballad, caught and flung back in the refrain. The principle holds true through-out the age-long evolution of poetry. From the earliest to the latest manifestations of the poetic impulse, in the in-stinctive voicing of physical movement and in the highly wrought creations of mature art, the great deep pulse at the heart of things finds utterance.

> Lo, with the ancient
> Roots of man's nature,
> Twines the eternal
> Passion of song.
>
> Deep in the world-heart
> Stand its foundations,
> Tangled with all things,
> Twin-made with all.
>
> Nay, what is Nature's
> Self, but an endless
> Strife toward music,
> Euphony, rhyme?
>
> . . . . . .
>
> God on His throne is
> Eldest of poets:
> Unto His measures
> Moveth the Whole.[20]

[19] See F. B. Gummere, "The Beginnings of Poetry." [20] William Watson.

This is the origin and reason-why of rhythm in poetry.
Whatever the poet's mood, whether it be an outburst of
sheer joy or the chastened calm of meditation, his verse is
the counterpart, made audible, of his emotion, and moves
to an accordant rhythm. The swift but sustained flow of
Homer's dactylic hexameters, reciting the deeds of heroes;
the stately procession of Milton's iambic pentameter, unfolding a drama of Heaven and Hell; the soaring flight of
Shelley's skylark; the pounding hoof-beats of Browning's
mad ride,

> I sprang to the stirrup, and Joris, and he,
> I galloped, Dirck galloped, we galloped all three;[21]

whether forward thrust or steady march or winged flight,—
the lilt of the verse expresses the emotional stress and impetus within it.

THE EFFECT OF RHYTHM

And more. For the rhythm of verse not only expresses
the emotion out of which it springs; this it also communi-
cates. It imparts to the hearer its own energy and kindles
him to a like emotion. Poetry has much in common with
other kinds of literature. Prose may render a heightened
image of the world, as in the novel; it may rouse to action,
as in oratory. In essence, imaginative literature may have
a constant element within its various manifestations. What
primarily distinguishes poetry from prose is this element of
definite rhythm. By virtue of it, poetry is more immediate
and more intense in its appeal. The "imitative movements,"
psychologists would say, set going in our own organism,
rouse in us a corresponding emotion. Rhythm, too, makes
for ease of perception, and is in itself a source of pleasure.
When rightly managed, it serves also to emphasize the intellectual content of the verse. The rhythm of poetic form
is not a mechanical contrivance, but is the inevitable thrust of
the passion within. At its best, it is never monotonous. It
should not be a regularly recurring series of alternate beats,
or "sing-song"; by subtle variations of stress, corresponding
both to the emotional impetus and to the meaning of the

[21] *H. C.,* xlii, 1107.

words, it may unfold itself in undulations; the surge of the
inner tide may break in dancing wave crests, an infinite
variety of light and shade, playing over the surface of the
great central unity. The meter may change step at need,
obedient to an inner law.

> Come lovely and soothing death,
> Undulate round the world, serenely arriving, arriving
> In the day, in the night, to all, to each,
> Sooner or later delicate death.[22]

And so on through a surpassingly beautiful poem. The
meter, or measured foot, is not evident here, but inevitably
we feel a deep-drawn throb that lays hold on us, and carries
us to its own mood. To such lines as these we gratefully
accord the honorable name of poetry.

Rhythm alone, however, is not enough to constitute a
poem. A mere drone of words in meaningless repetition,
though it may illustrate one of the origins of poetry, is not
poetry itself. There must be progress in the recurrence,
and the repeat must build itself up into a pattern. Any bit
of experience, to be truly understood or vitally assimilated,
must be apprehended as a whole. In the tumult of the world
external to him the mind of man insistently demands order
and significance. Nature has compelled the poet to her own
rhythm; that is his inspiration. The poet must now compel
nature to his purposes of expression; that is his art. His
temperament has vibrated to the sweep of cosmic influences;
now his mind enters as a controlling and organizing force
to shape his perception and his meaning into a single total
unity. Out of rhythm in repetition and combination he
frames a harmony. And so his poem presents a wholeness
of impression. His pattern is built of the repeat of single
elements: metrical bars or feet compose the line or verse;
lines combine into stanzas; and stanzas fashioned after a
common design succeed one another in progress to the end.
Here again, the structure is not mechanical or arbitrary:
each *verse* is measured to the *turn* of the thought; and the
formal unity of the whole poem corresponds to the unity of
mood or idea that the poem is framed to express.

[22] Walt Whitman, *H. C.*, xlii, 1503.

THE WORD-ELEMENT IN POETRY

The poet's medium, or means of expression, is words. The painter works with color, the sculptor with form, the musician with tone. Color and form and tone are pleasurable in themselves, as sensations; they become beautiful and significant by force of what they may be made to express. So words in themselves also have a sensuous value. When used as instruments of beauty, they may add to the rhythmic structure of a poem the element of *melody*. This tonal quality is secured most easily and obviously by *rhyme,* which is perfect concord of vowel sounds together with the consonants following to complete the syllable, as in *sight, night.* Besides adding musical value to the phrase, rhyme, when adroitly managed, serves to define the pattern of the poem and to emphasize the meaning of the words in which it falls. Lesser components of the melodic element are *assonance, alliteration,* and *tone-color.* Assonance is the repetition of the same vowel sound within syllables, but with different consonants, as sh*a*pe, m*a*te. Alliteration is the agreement in sound of initial syllables, as in "The *l*isp of *l*eaves and the *r*ipple of *r*ain." Alliteration, combined with stress, is the essential verse-principle of Anglo-Saxon poetry; it is used to-day at the risk of obscuring the sense by overloading the ornament. The melodic quality of tone-color is more subtle; it is the suggestion of the meaning of the words by the tonal quality and value of their syllables, as in "Sweet dimness of her loosened hair's downfall," where the slow change in vowel quality, ē, ĭ, ō, ā, seems to invest the image with a kind of "penumbra" of sound. These are the notes of the poet's gamut; the master craftsman employs them with a just reticence to enhance the sensuous appeal of his art.

But poetry is not only emotional and sensuous in its appeal. By virtue of its medium of words, it is adapted—to an extent that the arts of painting, sculpture, and music are not—to the expression of intellectual ideas. It gains in potency, however, in the measure that it phrases these ideas not in abstract terms but concretely. Words are not color or form, but they can suggest it by means of images. Emotion always has an object, which calls it out and represents it. The image in the word becomes the expression of the poet's own feeling; and it is also the symbol and occasion to others of a like emotion. How much Wordsworth's apostrophe to Duty gains in persuasion by the beauty of suggested images! So the idea embodies itself and becomes warm and vivid, rousing the hearer's imagination to vision and kindling him to emotion. This evocative power of words is the secret of the poet, and is hardly to be analyzed. It attaches to the tonal beauty of their syllables, in themselves and in rhythmic combination; it derives from their vividness of image, and from the associations, both intellectual and emotional, which cling around them like an aroma and an exhalation.

> Bright Star! would I were steadfast as thou art:—
> Not in lone splendour hung aloft the night,
> And watching, with eternal lids apart,
> Like Nature's patient sleepless Eremite,
> The moving waters at their priestlike task
> Of pure ablution round earth's human shores.[23]

Who can say wherein lies the witchery of this word-music! It can only be felt. In addition to the common meaning of its terms, therefore, language seems to have a further expressiveness. This new significance is the creation of the poet, wrought out of the familiar words by his cunning manipulation of them. The wonder of the poet's craft is like the musician's,—

That out of three sounds he frames, not a fourth sound, but a star.[24]

THE ONENESS OF CONTENT AND FORM

Poetic form rouses the whole being to sympathetic action by its rhythm; it delights the ear by its melodious tone; the logic of its coherent harmonic structure satisfies the mind; its word-images stimulate the imagination by their power of evocation. So poetry adds to fact its intellectual worth and all the emotional value inhering in it. Finally form and meaning become *one*. And most intimately so in lyric

[23] Keats, *H. C.,* xli, 922.
[24] Browning's "Abt Vogler," *H. C.,* xlii, 1144-1148.

poetry. Here we feel that just this idea could not be expressed, just that emotion could not be communicated, in any other way. The essence and mystery of the song are in the singing.

A poem is a fragment of life rounded into momentary completeness. It compels the chaos of immediate sense impressions into forms of beauty, and so it builds a fairer world. It catches the rhythms that pulse at the mighty heart of things and weaves them into subtle and satisfying patterns; its verbal melodies waken in the soul dim echoes of the desired music of the spheres. It floods life with unaccustomed light. But it is illusion only in that it sees beyond the changing shows of nature and discerns the loveliness which the human spirit would fain believe is the vesture of the Eternal. Poetry is not illusion, but rather the express image of a higher reality. The poet would compass life and utterly possess it. Not as a patient observer of nature's processes, not a passive spectator of the moving play of human fate, he *loves* what he beholds. To him, as to a lover, the world yields something of its secret. By force of imaginative, creative vision, he sees life in its wholeness, though but for an illumined moment. Emotion and insight fuse into an image of perfection. To the poet truth reveals itself as beauty. But the revelation is never finished. Therefore all great and true poetry is the utterance of an inspiration. It is the dream of a world ever realized and yet ever to be won. In the words of one of its prophets: "Poetry is the first and last of all knowledge—it is as immortal as the heart of man."

II. HOMER AND THE EPIC

By Professor Charles Burton Gulick

EPIC poetry might be described as that in which fewest poets have achieved distinction. Homer, Virgil, Milton are the names which occur to the mind when we try to define the type, but beyond these three it is hard to find any who have successfully treated a large theme with the dignity, grandeur, and beauty which the heroic poem demands.

This is because the standard was set at the beginning; and when we analyze the method and the purpose of these great poets, Homer emerges as the one supreme and incomparable master of them all. For, in "Paradise Lost,"[1] Milton was too often diverted from the true office of the poet by theological controversy; Virgil's "Æneid"[2] is the highly studied product of a self-conscious age, and was deliberately written to exalt the greatness of imperial Rome.

THE PREDECESSORS OF HOMER

And yet, although the art of Homer is more naïve and unconscious than Virgil's, it is a mistake to think, as the eighteenth century thought, that Homer represents the childhood of the race. Fresh, vigorous, spontaneous, swift, he none the less stands at the end of many generations of singers. From them he inherited traditions of versification, diction, and phrase that reach back to the very earliest emergence of the Greeks from barbarism.

The material of the first epic songs was quite simple. In the beginning the tribal gods would be the theme of a hymn of praise or thanksgiving; and since the heroic ancestors of the chieftains were thought to be the sons of gods, it was easy to pass from god to man, and contemporary exploits in

---

[1] *Harvard Classics*, iv, 89-362.   [2] *H. C.*, xiii.

some famous raid were not forgotten. Sacred hymn became heroic lay. Popular poetry it was, in the sense that it appealed strongly to popular interest and local pride. But it remained the possession of heaven-gifted singers whose profession was hereditary.

THE DEVELOPMENT OF THE EPIC

During the twelfth century before Christ there came a mighty upheaval, involving the fall of Mycenæ and the final ruin of her splendid civilization. New adjustments of territory took place, and wholesale migrations of Greek-speaking peoples, calling themselves Achæans, Æolians, Ionians, or Bœotians, to the littoral of Asia Minor. The stir and adventure of moving tribes, the prowess of their champions, the mingling of men of the same race, though of different clans, on the edge of a country where barbarians filled the hinterland, developed a new pride in national achievement, and furnished, in fact, just the conditions most favorable for the development of the epic. Legends brought from home, where the fathers had lived a simpler life, began to expand to larger proportions. Achilles and Hector, who had possibly been rival chiefs on the border between southern Thessaly and Bœotia, now became, in the conception of the bards, magnificent princes, fighting, not for cattle, but for national existence. The scene of their exploits is shifted from the old homeland to the new, and as the imagination of the emigrants grew with their larger life in the new country, so their legends came to embody more incident, to take on more brilliant coloring, and to voice higher national pretensions.

Thus Agamemnon, whose power on the Greek mainland had by no means been limited to the one small citadel of Mycenæ, snugly built among the hills of Argos, had room to expand to something like imperial dimensions through the patriotic impulse of these later epic singers. Growing more skillful in characterization, they helped to rear the great antithesis between Achæan and Trojan, between Greek and barbarian, the West and the East; they founded Hellenism.

THE TROY OF HISTORY

That the story of the Trojan War, embellished as it is
with mythical details, reflects historical facts—actual conflicts between the Achæan and Æolian immigrants on the
one hand, and the Dardanian inhabitants of the Troad, on
the other, is now no longer doubted. The "Iliad," which in
its present form is the work of a single genius, is the result
of complicated processes which include the borrowing,
adaptation, and enlargement of old material and the invention of new.

It is not free from inconsistencies in detail and occasional lapses in interest. "Even the good Homer nods,"
says Horace. But though he nods now and then, he never
goes to sleep,

The "Odyssey"[3] probably belongs to a somewhat later era
than that in which the "Iliad" took final shape. The wanderings of Odysseus reflect newer experiences of the same
Achæan stock which had won success in stirring conflicts in
Asia, and was now pushing out in ships over the Mediterranean to compete with the Phœnician trader. The
"Odyssey" presupposes the events described in the "Iliad";
unlike the "Iliad," it is not a story of battles and sieges,
but of adventure and intrigue which center about a bold
sailor.

It is full of the wonder of a new world; of strange escapes;
of shipwreck and the terrifying power of winds and waves; of
monsters and witches and giants; of encounters with pirates,
and exploration into wild countries, even to the borders of
the earth and to the underworld. It has furnished the model
of some of Sindbad's[4] adventurers, and is the precursor of
Gulliver and Munchausen. It has given to later poetry the
lotus-eaters[5] and the Sirens, and to the language of proverb
Scylla and Charybdis, and has enriched our nursery books
with some of their most entrancing characters. As a relief
to the stir and trial of the hero, it pictures the happiness and
beauty of rural life, and presents the noblest portrait of a
faithful wife in all literature.

[3] *H. C.,* xxii, 9.   [4] *H. C.,* xvi, 242-309.
[5] Cf. Tennyson's poem in *H. C.,* xlii, 1062.

THE STRUCTURE OF THE "ODYSSEY"

The dramatic structure of the "Odyssey" has always been admired. The entrance of the hero is postponed in order to develop the situation and introduce his lovable, if somewhat futile, son Telemachus, together with some characters made familiar by the "Iliad": Nestor, Helen, and Menelaus. We are then transported to Calypso's Isle, there to find Odysseus chafing under restraint. There ensue the departure, the anger of Poseidon, the wreck, and the rescue in the land of the Phæacians. The scene shifts to the brilliant court of their king, Alcinous, before whom Odysseus recounts the wonderful adventures which preceded his arrival at Calypso's island. In Phæacia Odysseus meets Nausicaa, the fairest and most radiant girlish figure in Greek literature. Nothing will better illustrate the difference between Homer and Virgil than a comparison of Nausicaa's words of parting with the violent outpourings of Dido's spirit when Æneas leaves her.[6] This part of the "Odyssey" is also highly interesting and important for the way in which the bard Demodocus represents the traditions and methods of the heroic lay.

The second half of the story begins when the Phæacians carry Odysseus home. Disguised as a beggar, he meets with a series of encounters which give full play to the dramatic devices of recognition and irony, so skillfully practiced later on the Greek stage. He discloses himself to Telemachus. Then his old dog Argos recognizes him, in a scene full of pathos. Finally, after a supreme trial of strength and skill, and the slaughter of the suitors, the husband makes himself known to his wife, and then to his aged father. Faults of repetition there are in plenty; but they only show with what fondness the epic poets loved to linger on the story, and how eager their audiences were to have the tale prolonged.

THE AUTHORSHIP OF THE HOMERIC POEMS

The Greeks were fond of recounting personal details about their great men, but they were able to tell about

[6] See "Æneid," in *H. C.*, xiii, 167ff.

a real Homer. The later legends concerning his life are meager, and almost wholly disregarded by the scholars of Alexandria. His blindness is a trait often remarked to-day among the popular singers in the villages of Greece and Macedonia. It is beautifully portrayed in the well-known bust in the Naples Museum. Seven cities claimed the honor of being his birthplace. They were mostly on the shores of Asia Minor or the adjacent islands—a fact which attests what we knew before from the language of the poems, that their latest composers were Ionian Greeks, and that the poems had a vogue on that coast a long time before wandering rhapsodists carried them to the mainland. It is not known when they were first committed to writing. Although the Greeks knew how to write as early as the ninth century before Christ, and possibly long before that time—indeed, writing is mentioned once by Homer—it played no important part in the earlier transmission of the poems, and it was not until the reign of the tyrant Pisistratus in Athens, in the sixth century, that they were gathered together and set down definitely in the form in which we have them. Thus virtually committed to the guardianship of the Athenians, who were the leaders of culture from the sixth to the third centuries, the poems passed to the custody of the Alexandrines, who prepared elaborate editions with notes, and divided them into the "books"—twenty-four each—in which they appear to-day.

The Romans studied them sedulously, and to Quintilian, as to Plato, Homer was the fountain of eloquence. The western world during the Middle Ages had more frequent recourse to Roman versions of the tale of Troy, but with the revival of learning Homer sprang almost immediately into his rightful position at the head of the ancients, and has ever since held firm hold of the affections of all cultivated men and women.

III. DANTE

By Professor Charles Hall Grandgent

DANTE ALIGHIERI (1265-1321) is rightly called the
supreme exponent of the Middle Ages. In no other
writer, ancient or modern, do we find the spirit of a
great period so completely reflected as the mediæval soul is
mirrored in him. It was the epoch of mighty builders and
mighty theologians, of religious exaltation, of sturdy, militant faith—the age that produced the grand cathedrals and
the "Summa Theologiæ," the age of the Crusades, of St.
Bernard and St. Dominic, the age of St. Francis. So essentially is Dante a poet of God that the epithet "Divine"
has by universal consent been attached to the work which
he called a "Comedy"; and so manifest is his architectural
genius that his poem inevitably suggests comparison with a
huge Gothic church. The troops of figures that live eter-
nally in his pages, representing all types of contemporary
man from burgher to Pope, diversify without obscuring the
symmetrical outlines of his plan—a plan sufficiently vast to
embrace nearly all that was of much importance in profane
and sacred science.

THE PLAN OF THE "DIVINE COMEDY"

The "Commedia,"[1] with its three books and its hundred
cantos, relates the whole progress of a soul from sin,
through remorse, meditation, and discipline, to the state of
purity that enables it to see God. Lost in wickedness, the
poet suddenly comes to his senses and tries to escape from
it, but in vain. Reason, moved by grace, thereupon leads
him step by step to a full understanding of evil, in all its
ugliness and folly; and he at last turns his back upon it.
His next duty is to cleanse his soul by penance, until its

[1] See *Harvard Classics*, xx, and General Index, under *Dante*, in vol. L

innocence is gradually restored. Then Revelation descends to meet him, and lifts him heavenward, higher and higher, even to the presence of his Maker. All this is set forth allegorically in the form of a journey, under the guidance of Virgil and then of Beatrice, through the underground kingdom of Hell, up the lonely mountain of Purgatory to the Garden of Eden, and thence through the revolving spheres to Paradise.

THE MEDIÆVAL VIEW OF THE WORLD

To us the universe of the Middle Ages seems small. The whole duration of earthly life, from Creation to Judgment Day, is limited to some 7,000 or 8,000 years. Our globe, a solid, motionless ball, surrounded by air and by fire, is the center of the material world. About it turn the nine successive skies, transparent, shell-like, hollow spheres, bearing the sun, the moon, the planets, and the fixed stars, which together constitute the force called Nature. Outside this round universe of matter is the Paradise of pure spirit, the limitless abode of God, the angels, and the blest. The angels, ministers of the Lord, direct the movements of the celestial bodies, thus shaping existence here below and the characters of men. Of the earth's surface much more than half is covered by water; but on one side, with Jerusalem in the middle, is the clover-shaped continent of Europe, Asia, and Africa. The Christian world is ruled by two great powers, one spiritual, one temporal, both ordained by God: Papacy and Empire, founded by Christ and by Cæsar. Unrighteous ambition has brought them into conflict with each other.

Of ancient history, and of all the wealth of classic literature and art, but little was known, and that little was translated into terms of the present; for the historical sense was quite undeveloped, and so was the idea of progress, so dear to us moderns. To the mediæval mind, Solomon, Alexander, Cæsar, Charlemagne were very much alike. The most noteworthy survivors among the authors of pagan Rome were Virgil, Ovid, Lucan, Statius, Cicero, and Livy; to these should be added the Christians, Boethius and St.

Augustine, and the scholars and theologians who followed. Greek was lost; but Aristotle, in Latin garb, began in the thirteenth century to dominate European thought, and Platonism had been potent in shaping St. Augustine's doctrine some 800 years before.

THE LEARNING AND LITERARY CHARACTERISTICS OF DANTE

Most of the learning of his age Dante possessed—the science of Albertus Magnus, the philosophy of Aristotle, the theology of St. Thomas Aquinas, the fragment of Latin literature that time had spared. We find abundant evidence of it, not only in the "Divina Commedia," but also in the unfinished "Convivio," or "Banquet," an encyclopædic work in the shape of a commentary on some of the author's poems.

He wrote Latin with fluency and vigor: besides his letters and a couple of eclogues, he composed a treatise, "De Monarchia," on the relation of state to church, and began a discussion of verse forms and the use of the Italian language in poetry, called "De Vulgari Eloquentia"; there is ascribed to him also a lecture, the "Quæstio de Aqua et Terra," debating a curious problem of physical geography. But while his facts, ideas, and interests were those of his day, certain traits differentiate him from his fellows: with Petrarch he shares intensity of feeling and strong personality; with Chaucer and Boccaccio, clearness of vision and the gift of vivid, dramatic characterization; with none, his artistic reaction to the wilder aspects of nature, his stupendous imagination, his conciseness, his power of suggestion. In language, too, he stands quite apart from his predecessors and contemporaries. Such picturesqueness, such wealth of vocabulary, had never been conceived since classic antiquity. Before him, in fact, clerical Latin had been the regular medium of serious discourse. His use of the vernacular for the elucidation of philosophy and religion was a daring innovation, which he defends in the "Convivio." Especially in his own country was the modern tongue despised, and the literary output in Italian, before the fourteenth century, was correspondingly meager.

LITERARY FASHIONS OF THE MIDDLE AGES

Northern France had long since witnessed a glorious development of narrative poetry, of warlike epic and courtly romance—songs of kings and feudal lords, adventures of knights (particularly those of the Round Table[2]) in distant lands and times. Out of liturgical service had grown the drama. Symbolism, long familiar in the interpretation of ancient poetry and of holy writ, had made its way into creative art, and had produced the "Romance of the Rose," that wonder of the thirteenth century. Satire, which in this poem is combined with the allegorical theme of the quest of love, had found separate expression in the versified episodes called "fabliaux," and in the tales of Reynard the Fox. Much of this literature had been carried to Italy, as to other countries of Europe. No less renowned than the North French epic,[3] and hardly less influential abroad, was the great school of amatory lyric poetry that had sprung up in southern France—a poetry of restricted scope but of exquisite artistry, which in the twelfth and thirteenth centuries was sung and imitated at many an Italian court. Not until the time of Frederick II, however, do we find similar verse composed in an Italian tongue. About this great emperor clustered a band of clever, artificial love poets known as the Sicilian School. In Tuscany the vernacular was used for lyric purposes by a group of uninspired but ingenious rhymesters, for the most part close followers of Provençal models. At Bologna, too, the famous university town, the new art began to be cultivated in the middle of the thirteenth century. Here lived Guido Guinizelli, whom Dante calls his master, the first poet to formulate definitely that theory of love which was to govern the "sweet new style."

DANTE'S CONCEPTION OF LOVE

According to this doctrine, love is an attribute of the "gentle" heart alone. There it slumbers until aroused to activity by a worthy object. The woman who awakens this

[2] See Dr. Maynadier's lecture on "Malory" in the course on Prose Fiction.
[3] Cf. "The Song of Roland" in *H. C.*, xlix, 97ff.

"gentle" love must be a symbol of the angelic nature, or "heavenly intelligence"; and devotion to her is worship. In the generation after Guinizelli his teaching was extended by a circle of gifted writers, who introduced the poetic fashion into Florence, a busy commercial town, already perhaps the most prosperous of the bustling, ambitious, jealous, quarrelsome little commonwealths of Italy. Members of this literary company were Dante's "first friend," Guido Cavalcanti, and Dante himself. We find, to be sure, a less novel conception of love in some of our poet's works: in his sweet verses on a certain young lady who pitied him in his bereavement, in his occasional complimentary sonnets and ballads, in his wildly passionate and beautiful songs concerning a youthful person whom he calls "Pietra." In his *canzoni* to Lady Philosophy we have excellent examples of the amatory form put to an allegorical use. For a more literal expression of the new thought we must look to the compositions inspired by his ideal lady, Beatrice—and, among them, to the maturer ones. Some years after the death of his beloved, Dante selected from his previous verse a series of poems illustrating the phases of his inner life under Beatrice's influence, and surrounded them with a dainty prose explanation. This is the "Vita Nuova," or "New Life."

IV. THE POEMS OF JOHN MILTON

By Dr. Ernest Bernbaum

THOUGH most of us acknowledge that Milton dwells on the heights of English poetry, we are likely, because of his very sublimity, to look up to him with awe, as unapproachable. The charm of the minor poems of his youth may be felt without difficulty; but the obstacles to loving intimacy with his most important works, those into which he poured "the precious lifeblood of a master spirit," seem many and forbidding. We remember that Byron sneered at his angels and archangels joining in quibbles, and we apprehend that his theology must be dull or perplexing. We open "Paradise Lost"[1] at almost any page, and meet with phrases and allusions that are unfamiliar. Habituated by our contemporary literature and journalism to receive an easy delight from the shocking, the bizarre, and the exceptional, we are not immediately attracted by an art whose characteristics are dignity and restraint. In Dr. Johnson's words, "we desert our master and seek for companions." As if to encourage our truancy, there arise those who question whether, after all, Milton is a master. The chief of a prominent American library refuses to advise the reading of "Paradise Lost," an ultra-modern critic professes to have discovered "new literary valuations" which at last destroy the poet's long-established reputation, and respectable literary journals actually find it necessary to defend a fame that had seemed imperishable.

THE SOURCES OF MILTON'S GREATNESS

The serious-minded who, despite such babblings, conclude that he to whom every great man of letters from Dryden to Meredith has granted the crowning laurel must surely be

[1] *Harvard Classics*, iv, 89-362.

one whom it is an honorable privilege to know, may be assured that the obstacles to familiarity with Milton are not at all insuperable. From three sources especially does his greatness arise—the strength of his imagination, the harmony of his verse, and the truth of his thought. Each of these will become more clearly apparent to the reader if he will accept certain practical suggestions. To grow aware of the astounding imaginative power of Milton in "Paradise Lost," "Paradise Regained," [2] "Samson Agonistes," [3] and even the "Nativity Ode," [4] one should before turning to those works read the biblical passages, in each case brief, which gave the poet the outlines of his themes. It need hardly be said that such a story as that of Adam and Eve has in the Bible a simple and poignant beauty which is perfect in its way; but when one turns from the few chapters that contain it and follows the course of the great epic, one begins to realize how sublimely Milton's imagination enlarges our conceptions of the past, the distant, and the unseen. Nor is it only realms, forces, and spirits unvisited and unknown that he reveals. Read the short account of Samson, or of the temptation of Christ; observe how few, though graphic, are the strokes of characterization; and you will thereupon in "Samson Agonistes" and "Paradise Regained" recognize with what vision Milton has penerated into the hearts of hero and Lord and devil.

The mistake which prevents a full enjoyment of the musical beauty of Milton's blank verse is to read it silently —a sure way to make it seem like prose curiously printed. Aloud the blind poet uttered the most and the best of it; and aloud it should be read. Only thus can the artistic sense that slumbers within us be aroused to feel responsively the grandest rhythm and resonance that ever proceeded from an English tongue. Like ocean breakers, in varying lengths and with tireless energy, it beats and surges upon our emotions; and presently we are ready to receive those elevated thoughts it is marvelously designed to instill, because the sound has lifted us into a mood exalted above our ordinary state. He who thus comes to feel the artistic powers of Milton has taken a decisive step toward literary culture: he

[2] H. C., iv, 363.   [3] H. C., iv, 418.   [4] H. C., iv, 7.

will thenceforth not easily be imposed upon by whatever is imaginatively weak or fantastic; and his ear, once attuned to the "grand style" of the master, will no longer delight in verse that is thin or harsh.

MILTON AS PROPHET

But Milton did not use his poetical powers for the mere pleasure of exercising them. In him, as in Isaiah, the great artist is embodied in the greater prophet. This is a commonplace, yet many approach Milton as if it were untrue. In the case of "Paradise Lost," admittedly the fullest expression of his message, the first two books are mistakenly recommended as typical. In them, to be sure, are superbly displayed his artistic powers, but certainly not his dominant thought. In fact, to confine oneself to them has proved a direct way to misunderstand him. Because they deal with the fallen angels, we have arising the persistent error that Satan is the hero of "Paradise Lost," and that the archrebel preoccupied the poet's interest. The result in our day, when belief in a personal devil is faint, is the impression that Milton devotes his genius to themes that, however picturesque, possess for us slight moral significance. And so we have the pitiable result that the mere artist is admired, but the prophet not hearkened to. Yet his message, grasped as a whole, comes home to our very hearts.

THE THEME OF "PARADISE LOST"

The theme of Milton is not primarily Satan, nor even God and angels, but humanity. Not only do the opening lines of "Paradise Lost" proclaim the subject "man's disobedience," but throughout the epic it is the fate of man that is made the issue of every event in the universal creation. Thus Milton begins his story, not when Satan is conspiring against God, but when the defeated devil turns his revengeful thought toward the future inhabitants of the earth. Of that new world man is solemnly made the lord, God himself descending to breathe into him a spiritual life. It is to warn man against his fall that the rebellion in heaven is related;

and in the central books it is the glory and the weakness of human nature that we see displayed. Finally, the future history of the world is communicated to Adam, not so much to manifest the absolute power of God or the futility of Satan's hate, as to assure the children of God of his eternal love toward them. In short, the subject is not theology but religion—not the nature of God and of Satan, but the relation of the powers of good and of evil to ourselves. Could a poet deal with a problem of more compelling and everlasting interest to us? The reader who focuses his attention upon the human beings in "Paradise Lost" will do what the poet did, and will, though accidental details may elude him, follow Milton's essential thought. The descriptions of heaven and hell, which may not correspond precisely to the reader's notions of the states of bliss and of misery, will recede into the background, where they belong; and gradually there will rise before him Milton's idea of the true meaning of human life.

MILTON'S VIEW OF HUMAN NATURE

To reduce that idea to a prose formula would be to impoverish and debase it; but a hint or two concerning its general character may suggest its importance to the individual conscience. On the one hand, no poet, not even Shakespeare, has thought more nobly of the glorious capacities of man. Man is to Milton no miserable puppet of chance, no slave of his environment (Adam and Eve sin despite ideal surroundings), but an unhampered master of his fate, God himself endowing him with freedom of the will, and all the spirits of the universe interested in the use he may make of that liberty. On the other hand, no poet has felt more profoundly the constant peril of man's exalted state. Unless he in his freedom throws off all worldly temptations, even the most seductive, punishment for his disloyalty to spiritual laws is visited not only upon himself but upon his innocent fellow men. The grave moral predicaments of the Lady in "Comus," [5] of Adam and Eve, of Christ in "Paradise Regained," and of Samson, are not ex-

H. C., iv, 46.

ceptional, but typify the real state of man in every moment
of his life. Here a sublime opportunity, there a fatal danger, the decision absolutely in his own hands! Yet there
is no panic, no wild cry for relief; the spirit is as serene as
the utterance is restrained. Uncompromising independence
in earthly concerns, patient humility before God—these are
the virtues that will redeem us at last.

Hasty as this glance at Milton's ideas must be, it reminds
us of the source of his power. In his first good poem, the
"Nativity Ode," he yearned to hear that music of the
heavenly spheres, hymning divine truth, to which most
mortal ears are ever deaf; and from then until his end, amid
the din of terrestrial turmoil, he was hearkening for the
voice of God. Thus inspired, he has ever revived those who
have learned to resort to him, sending each forth with a
braver heart, a serener mind, and a reawakened conscience.
Wordsworth, sadly observing the worshipers of earthly
idols, exclaimed:

Milton, thou shouldst be living at this hour!

and the best in succeeding generations have echoed the
sentiment. Sceptics may question parts of Milton's doctrine;
but they will not easily shake its center, for that is embedded
in the pertinacious moral convictions of the English peoples.
The noblest American tradition, which founded the New
England commonwealths, and from which to depart is a
kind of betrayal of our inmost selves, is precisely that ideal
of freedom from man's dominion and conscientious obedience to God's stern will, which is the very spirit of Milton.
To commune with him is therefore to gain patriotic enlightenment as well as religious insight and poetical culture.[6]

[6] See also Bagehot's essay on Milton in *H. C.*, xxviii, 171.

V. THE ENGLISH ANTHOLOGY

By Carleton Noyes, A.M.

T HE English Anthology, contained in Volumes XL to
XLII of The Harvard Classics, comprises a selection
of representative poems in English from Chaucer to
Walt Whitman, a period of about five hundred years. In
the range and variety of subject and forms, these volumes
bear eloquent witness to the manifold creative power of
poetry. But the very abundance of their treasures suggests
certain problems, at the same time that it offers material for
their solution. What is the subject of poetry, and what the
meaning of these varied forms? How shall the reader find
his way to the poetry that is truly for him, and how may he
win from it what it holds of present delight and of lasting
service?

It is evident that the spirit of poetry, intensely real but
elusive as a sky-born Ariel, may incarnate itself in many
forms and wear a rainbow vesture. As indicated in the
General Introduction, the shaping purpose of a poem is
either the narrative interest or the lyric mood. But these
two impulses are subject to wide modifications. The differences do not affect the character of each instance as
poetry; to note them, however, furnishes a convenient
formula of description and provides a clue to the fuller comprehension of the motive of a given poem.

THE KINDS OF POETRY

When the poet's interest lies in action, incident, and situation, his poem takes the form of narrative. When such a
poem attains a certain magnitude, when the action is on a
large scale, and the personages are of sufficient eminence
and importance, it becomes an *epic*. The epic may be rel-

atively primitive and single-hearted like the "Iliad," the "Odyssey," [1] "Beowulf," [2] or the "Nibelungenlied." It may still recite the deeds of heroes in an earlier golden prime and yet be the product of a conscious, highly elaborated literary art, like Virgil's "Æneid." [3] Or again, while celebrating a lofty theme, it may be the deeply personal expression of the poet's own interpretation of experience and the world, as with Dante and Milton. In lesser compass than the epic, a narrative poem, like the *ballads* [4] or the more conscious poetical *romances* and *tales*, [5] may range over the whole wide domain of men's adventures and fortunes, finding nothing human foreign to it.

Narrative thus stories forth the doings of others; the lyric rises out of oneself. And here again the scope is limitless. A lyric may phrase emotion in its purest essence: it is then the absolute *lyric* or song. The emotion, gathering about a simple little scene in nature, may utter itself briefly and beautifully in an *idyl;* conceived on a more extensive scale, a poem of rustic life, actual or feigned, becomes a *pastoral*. [6] The passion of grief finds voice in the *elegy*. [7] A lyric may mirror the large aspects of nature as colored by the poet's feeling, and so it passes over into descriptive poetry. Sensuous elements may be subordinated to thought or to sympathy; and the poem so inspired expresses reflection and sentiment. Exaltation of thought and mood, moving through sustained and complex metrical form, finds a fitting medium in the *ode*. [8] Even wit and satire, if feeling mingle with the intellectual element, are not outside the scope of poetical expression, as in the *epigram*. Poetry also—provided only that it still be poetry—may be didactic. Although the true function of poetry, as of all art, is not to teach, but to interpret life beautifully, to touch the heart and kindle the whole being to heightened activity, yet a poem may voice moral ideas, as in Wordsworth's "Ode to Duty":

[1] *Harvard Classics*, xxii, 9ff.   [2] *H. C.*, xlix, 5ff.
[3] *H. C.*, xiii, 75ff.   [4] *H. C.*, xl, 51ff.
[5] Cf., for example, Chaucer's "Nun's Priest's Tale," *H. C.*, xl, 35ff, or Burns's "Tam o' Shanter," vi, 411ff.
[6] For examples, see *H. C.*, xl, 252, 259, 411; xli, 569, 630, 783.
[7] For examples, see Milton's "Lycidas," *H. C.*, iv, 74; *H. C.*, xl, 459; xli, 879; xlii, 1176.
[8] For examples, see *H. C.*, xl, 305, 389, 394, 459, 463ff.; xli, 488, 551, 609, 665, 745, 856, 899ff.

Stern lawgiver! yet thou dost wear
The Godhead's most benignant grace;
Nor know we anything so fair
As is the smile upon thy face:
Flowers laugh before thee on their beds,
And fragrance in thy footing treads;
Thou dost preserve the Stars from wrong;
And the most ancient Heavens, through thee, are fresh
and strong.[9]

Out of the narrative interest, a primary instinct with men,
and out of the interest, only gradually developed, in individual character for its own sake, is evolved a special literary form, called *drama*.   Here the poet embodies his
feelings and ideas in the persons of others.   He no longer
speaks for himself; he endows the figures of his creation
or observation with an independent substantive life of their
own.   The narrative interest is still strong, for the dramatist
shows his personages in action, but he allows them to work
out their own destiny in accordance with the inner necessity
of their natures.   In the drama, then, the poet's own "criticism of life" is implied rather than directly expressed.   The
drama, as a literary form, is a domain by itself.   In so far
as it is poetical, it does not differ essentially from other
kinds of poetry, and the same principles hold true throughout all manifestations of the poetic spirit.

Distinctions of motive and form, though numerous and
varied, are not to be emphasized for their own sake.   These
categories may be recognized in the large, but in concrete,
single instances they tend to overlap and to intermingle.
The narrative poem has another interest than the lyric, but
it may be touched with the lyric passion; the drama is different from either and combines both.   For the lover of
poetry, however, it is not important to devise labels and
apply them correctly.   Classification suggests the arrangement of a museum.   But poetry is a spirit, a living energy.
We cannot imprison it in a definition.   It calls for welcome and response.

In essence and in effect poetry is an interpretation of experience.   A poem is an expression, in beautiful and significant form, of the poet's passion to understand and to

[9] *H. C.,* xli, 666.

possess his world. But, though a poem embodies what some one man has thought and felt, we must not mistake the poet's representative character nor fail to grasp the universalizing power of his work. The individual poet is but an instrument: he speaks for all men. So, in our turn, as we enter by imaginative sympathy into his mind and feeling, we re-create his experience in ourselves. The kind of poetry which finds us first is that which relates itself somehow to our immediate interests. Its appeal depends upon what we bring to it of our own knowledge and sensibility. We understand it because it phrases what we have ourselves perceived and felt, though vaguely. Thus it interprets our present lot, intensifying its quality and weaving its tangled threads into a satisfying pattern. The poetry which seems to beckon to us and is able to hold us longer is the figuring forth of experience, already ours in part, into which we may enter more abundantly; it helps us to take the step beyond. The poetry to which we finally make our way—the great things of all time—is the revelation of farther depths of insight, of unsounded depths of emotion. Such poetry as this compels us to its own temper and mood. It is not only revelation, it is creation; for out of the otherwise common things of life it builds a quite new world for our possession.

If we seek a standard by which to try the quality and value of a poem, we find it most immediately in our present need. But we must be sure that the need is real, not a passing caprice, that it is intrinsically and profoundly a part of our expanding life. That poem is truly for us, and so far good, which reveals beauty to us and some kind of significance; for it can thus sustain and nourish us and minister to our growth. But there is an objective standard as well. This is found first of all in the poet's genuineness of feeling. Does the word exactly measure the emotion it is intended to express? Without this primary and underlying sincerity of purpose, all the graces of form and phrase cannot satisfy for long. Granted this sincerity, however, we may say that that greatest poetry is that which gathers into itself and radiates the most of reality, that which discloses the deepest insight into life, and is charged with the fullest intensity of emotion, matched by the greatest fitness and power of expression.

By the witchery of its music and the radiance of image, poetry may rightly give pleasure to a leisure moment. Apprehended in its deeper import, it may be one of the serious pursuits of life. To see the world poetically is itself a kind of success. Although some quiet spirits are content with the passive reception of beauty in nature and in art, yet the poetic interpretation of life is not incompatible with high moral endeavor, and may even be a stimulus to it, kindling in us a passionate ardor to know and to do. The revelation which poetry affords carries us beyond the enjoyment of the instant; as it leads us out into a more beautiful world, it brings us deeper into the true significance of things, and so it widens our spiritual horizon. As we see farther and feel more intensely, we are enabled more amply to understand the meaning of our own life in its relation to the whole.

The reading of poetry, therefore, helps toward the organization of experience. The ideal waits in the actual. It is the privilege of the poet, gifted with vision, to discern the ideal, and by the energy of creative phrase to summon it into warm and vivid reality. He marshals the fragments of experience into a harmony with which we may link up our own broken efforts; disclosing the inner meaning of our blind purposes, he brings them into a unity of direction and achievement. So he reveals us to ourselves. As the poet interprets it for us, the big scheme of things is seen to be more beautiful and more intelligible. In effect, the real appreciation of poetry is communion with the great souls of earth: In their struggles and their conquests we read the purpose of our own efforts and the aspiration of our hearts.

Yet the beauty and significance which perhaps we had missed without his leading the poet but restores to us after all. For the poet is not final; nor is poetry, with the appreciator, an end in itself. In the result it sends us back to life, to possess the world more abundantly in ourselves. It gives us, in terms of wide-ranging subject and in varied forms, the great moments of experience; but it is to make those moments intimately and wholly our own. We must love poetry, if we are to understand it; appreciation, therefore, is a discipline and a development. But if we are to win from poetry its deepest final meaning, we must actually live it. Though it has power to console, sustain, inspire, poetry is not a substitute for life, it is not an escape or refuge. Rather, it is a challenge to fuller living; and to that end it is a guide and a support.

Poetry is a fruition and a promise. Exhaustless and immortal, the spirit of poetry is ever conquering new beauty and new truth. So equally there is no limit set to what we may compass for ourselves in appreciation. Our enjoyment at any moment is the measure of our own capacity. Like the sea's horizon, the bounds of poetry are traced only by the sweep of our vision. The ocean's verge advances always before us with our progress; there is always an infinite which still awaits.

This day before dawn I ascended a hill and look'd at the crowded heaven,
And I said to my spirit *When we become the enfolders of those orbs, and the pleasure and knowledge of everything in them, shall we be fill'd and satisfied then?*
And my spirit said *No, we but level that lift to pass and continue beyond.*[10]

[10] Walt Whitman.

NATURAL SCIENCE

I. GENERAL INTRODUCTION

By Professor Lawrence J. Henderson

NATURAL science is the latest of man's great achievements. The other important agents of civilization long ago attained their full stature, and many of the finest products of human endeavor, like literature and the fine arts, have been through many centuries the common possession of the race. Even music, the most modern of the arts, is no longer young. But only in the last half century has science reached maturity and revealed its titanic power for good and evil in the reconstruction of the surroundings of our life. Yet to-day, after a few brief decades of the scientific era, agriculture, transportation and communication, food, clothing and shelter, birth and death themselves—in truth almost all of man's experiences and activities—are different from what they were before, and the earth which he inhabits is transformed so that it is with difficulty that he can imagine the conditions of life in past centuries.

Meantime, these very changes which science has wrought have combined with the great generalizations of science to modify philosophy and to direct the current of religious thought. Here again the effects are sometimes good, sometimes evil, but they are always profound and widely influential. Most wonderful of all is the growth of natural knowledge itself, the basis of these changes. Ever more extensive and complete is the description of nature; all things are counted, measured, and figured, then analyzed and classified. Out of such orderly knowledge generalizations and laws arise, and with the help of experiment and mathematical analysis receive their confirmation, until at length positive knowledge appears to extend to almost all phenomena, and, except the origin of things, little seems quite obscure or wholly unknown, while much is very securely established.

The history of science and of its influence on civilization is in some respects the simplest of the departments of history, for it is less complicated by those incalculable forces which, springing from man's passions and personal interests, make up much of the charm and difficulty of general history. Deprived of these psychological elements, the history of science is in fact more nearly a part of the natural history of man; it is concerned with the latest stage of his struggle with the environment, with his cunning and deliberate devices to master it, and with the marvelous structure of theoretical knowledge which he has built up in the process.

ANTHROPOLOGY

Our lives are mainly occupied with the material world with production and distribution of food and clothing, and the construction of dwellings which shall adequately protect us from the cold, the wind, and the rain. All higher human activities rest upon the successful establishment of these as a foundation. Hence progress, as the word is commonly understood, is most often a step in the control of the environment to the end of better production, construction, and distribution of some commodity. Such progress is not perhaps what the heart of man most ardently desires, but it is, at all events, the one kind about which there can be no doubt.

Many of the most wonderful advances in mastery of the environment are prehistoric, the results of good fortune and gradually widening experience utilized by primitive men of native intelligence. Thus clay is used as the filling for a basket, its baking is accidentally observed, and pottery results; again a log, through a long series of gradual changes and small inventions, becomes transformed into a good boat or canoe.

Sophocles, in a famous chorus of the "Antigone," has celebrated such achievements:

STROPHE I.

Many the forms of life,
Wondrous and strange to see,
But nought than man appears
More wondrous and more strange.
He, with the wintry gales,
O'er the white foaming sea,
Mid wild waves surging round,
Windeth his way across:
Earth of all Gods, from ancient days, the first,
Unworn and undecayed,
He, with his ploughs that travel o'er and o'er,
Furrowing with horse and mule,
Wears ever year by year.

ANTISTROPHE I.

The thoughtless tribe of birds,
The beasts that roam the fields,
The brood in sea-depths born,
He takes them all in nets
Knotted in snaring mesh,
Man wonderful in skill,
And by his subtle arts
He holds in sway the beasts
That roam the fields, or tread the mountain's height;
And brings the binding yoke
Upon the neck of horse with shaggy mane,
Or bull on mountain crest,
Untameable in strength.

STROPHE II.

And speech, and thought as swift as wind,
And tempered mood for higher life of states,
These he has learnt, and how to flee
Or the clear cold of frost unkind,
Or darts of storm and shower,
Man all-providing.[1]

Many will always regard this as the final expression of
man's wonder and admiration at that which man has done
in winning his civilization. But while we admire and marvel at the feats of primitive man, we must not forget to

[1] See *Harvard Classics,* viii, 253-254, for another translation of this
chorus.

distinguish a very important difference between such and many achievements of civilized man—in fact, between pre-historic works and deeds and all the greatest scientific achievements. Very wonderful as the early progress was, —think of civilized man's failure to domesticate animals, and, incomparably important, think of the winning of fire,— it lacked a certain germ of growth, which is familiar to us in our own times. Each thing came by itself, it came by accident, and it did not directly lead to other things. Beyond living one's life and waiting for something to turn up so that one's ingenuity might be exercised, there was no method of discovery or invention; the knowledge that existed was not systematized; there was no generalization from experience; and each invention, aside from its particular utility, led to nothing else. How different have been the effects of Pasteur's discovery of the place of micro-organisms in nature![2] Almost at once the causes of many of the gravest diseases of man and other animals became known. There followed the discovery of means of avoiding disease, of curing disease, and we are now well on the way to blot out some of the oldest scourges of humanity. Such are a few of the results in medicine. When the chemical and agricultural results are added, Pasteur appears already to have influenced the life of almost every civilized man.

Clearly the early advances of practical knowledge are not to be confounded with natural science. They belong to the period of human development which is the concern of the anthropologist, and they only concern us as they help to an understanding of what science really is.

ANCIENT SCIENCE

A very little true science did, however, exist at the dawn of history, such as a description of the zodiac and astronomical knowledge, upon which more or less perfect calendars could be based, and knowledge of the properties of triangles which was useful in surveying after the Nile floods. To this slender store the earliest of the Greek philosophers contributed new discoveries, but before long the genius and

[2] *H. C.*, xxxviii, 382-402, and Lecture IV in this course.

power of the Greek mind led to overweening confidence in speculation unaided by observation and experiment, and, as a result, the great period of Athens is not scientifically of the highest importance. Aristotle, to be sure, and his pupil Theophrastus, contributed very greatly to sound knowledge of animals, plants, and rocks, but in the theoretical sciences vague ideas based upon words rather than phenomena or clear and precise concepts led them astray.

"The most conspicuous example," says Bacon, "of the first class [i. e., of the Rational School of philosophers] was Aristotle, who corrupted natural philosophy by his logic: fashioning the world out of categories; assigning to the human soul, the noblest of substances, a genus from words of the second intention; doing the business of density and rarity (which is to make bodies of greater or less dimensions—that is, occupy greater or less spaces), by the frigid distinction of act and power; asserting that single bodies have each a single and proper motion, and that if they participate in any other, then this results from an external cause; and imposing countless other arbitrary restrictions on the nature of things; being always more solicitous to provide an answer to the question and affirm something positive in words than about the inner truth of things; a failing best shown when his philosophy is compared with other systems of note among the Greeks. For the Homœomera of Anaxagoras; the Atoms of Leucippus and Democritus; the Heaven and Earth of Parmenides; the Strife and Friendship of Empedocles; Heraclitus's doctrine how bodies are resolved into the indifferent nature of fire, and remolded into solids; have all of them some taste of the natural philosopher—some savor of the nature of things, and experience, and bodies; whereas, in the physics of Aristotle you hear hardly anything but the words of logic; which in his metaphysics also, under a more imposing name, and more, forsooth, as a realist than a nominalist, he has handled over again. Nor let any weight be given to the fact that in his books on animals and his problems, and other of his treatises, there is frequent dealing with experiments. For he had come to his conclusion before; he did not consult experience, as he should have done, in order to do the framing of his decisions and axioms; but, having first determined the question according to his will, he then resorts to experience, and, bending her into conformity with his placets, leads her about like a captive in a procession; so that even on this count he is more guilty than his modern followers, the schoolmen, who have abandoned experience altogether." [3]

Later, when Alexandria became the center of the Greek world, and the limitations of metaphysics had become somewhat more evident, there was a return to positive science. For nearly a thousand years men, notably Aristarchus, Eratosthenes, Hipparchus, Euclid, Hero, and Ptolemy, labored at Alexandria, employing the true methods of science and collecting valuable stores of information in astronomy, geometry, trigonometry, optics, heat, and even anatomy. The greatest of the scientific work of antiquity was done during the Alexandrine period by Archimedes at Syracuse. It consists in the creation of the science of statics.

The Romans, practical men—according to Disraeli's definition, those who practice the errors of their forefathers—did little to advance the sciences, and, when the dark ages extinguished all intellectual endeavor, it was little enough that men had achieved in science, compared with their other deeds.

Yet it is certain that both true science and the true methods of science had been established in antiquity. It was not so much the errors of the ancient world as the errors of the Middle Ages in interpretation of the ancient world, and the undue importance that was assigned to Aristotle, which held back science during the first centuries of the Renaissance.

On the other hand, it cannot be denied that if the science of antiquity at its best, in the mechanics of Archimedes, the descriptive astronomy of Hipparchus, the geometry of Euclid, and the zoology of Aristotle, did manifest most of the characteristics of method and treatment which we know to-day, nearly all of the results of modern science, the modifications of life and civilization, are lacking in antiquity. Ancient science was in great part sterile; modern science is now the principal agent in social evolution.

[3] Bacon's "Novum Organum," Bk. I, lxiii.

RISE OF MODERN SCIENCE

It was not until the seventeenth century that modern science gained a secure footing. Just as in antiquity, the minds of men once more ranged over the whole field of the intellectual and the imaginative, and produced many works of commanding genius in many different subjects before again buckling down to the more sober tasks of science, which they were doomed to labor upon till now, and quite possibly forever.

Leonardo da Vinci, most versatile of all men, had, to be sure, successfully sought the solution of problems in mechanics, and patiently studied anatomy and, in truth, almost every department of science. But, great as was his insight into the phenomena of matter and motion, and it was perhaps not less than his insight into the fine arts, his work remained without effect, because unknown.

Before Galileo there are but two modern men of science whose importance is capital, Copernicus and Vesalius. The work of Copernicus,[4] though destined finally to tear a veil from before the eyes of men, did not amount to a proof of the heliocentric hypothesis, nor was it at once profoundly influential upon thought. As for Vesalius, he labored upon human anatomy, a subject which has never exerted a wide influence upon the large affairs of civilization. The number of men who, in the sixteenth century and even before, pursued natural science with industry was considerable. But tradition, belief in authority, and the superstitions of the pseudo-sciences of astrology and alchemy, long and successfully resisted the advance of knowledge. Time-honored ideas, nevertheless, had received a rude shock at the hands of Copernicus, and by the year 1600, when Giordano Bruno was burned at the stake, the far-spreading influence of the heliocentric hypothesis, both in its direct hearing, and as an illustration of the power of the untrammeled human intellect, was evident to most thoughtful men.

There followed in the next century such a revolution in thought as has seldom occurred in the whole course of history. To this many factors contributed; the commanding

[4] *H. C.*, xxxix, 55-60.

genius of a few great men, Newton, Galileo, Harvey,[5] Kepler, Huygens, Descartes,[6] Bacon,[7] Leibnitz; the growth of algebra, which made possible the invention of analytical geometry by Descartes, and the calculus by Newton and later independently by Leibnitz; the inventions of the telescope and compound microscope, greatly increasing the powers of the eye; finally, that indefinable modernizing of the human mind wrought by the whole Renaissance, which made sound thought once more possible, and for the first time produced in Galileo a man worthy to stand beside Archimedes.

NEWTON'S "PRINCIPIA"

In many respects the seventeenth century is the most interesting in the history of science, and certainly science is the most important human interest in the history of this century. Galileo begins it. "Modern science is the daughter of astronomy; it has come down from heaven to earth along the inclined plane of Galileo, for it is through Galileo that Newton and his successors are connected with Kepler."[8] The investigation of the falling body, and the establishment of the algebraical and geometrical laws of fall by Galileo, joined with Kepler's great discoveries of the laws of planetary motion, and informed by the hypothesis of Copernicus, led to Newton's "Principia,"[9] a work (the only other one by an Englishman) that stands out like that of Shakespeare, towering over all else.

This incomparable book contains all the essential principles of the science of mechanics. Since the year 1687, when it was published, the labor of many men of great genius has only availed to polish, to refine, and to embellish a subject which they could not really extend. In the course of the studies leading up to this work, Newton, incidentally as it were, invented the differential and integral calculus, which became the source not only of countless achievements in mathematics and science, but of perhaps the bitterest controversy in the annals of learning.

The work of Newton in establishing the science of me-

[5] *H. C.*, xxxviii, 65ff. [6] *H. C.*, xxxiv, 5ff. [7] *H. C.*, xxxix, 122ff.
[8] Bergson, "Creative Evolution," translated by Mitchell, p. 335.
[9] *H. C.*, xxxix, 157ff.

chanics was dependent upon a variety of other achievements
of the century, in addition to the idrectly contributory labors
of Kepler and Galileo. Especially important were the earlier
progress of mathematics, marked by the invention of
logarithms by Napier and independently by Bürgi, and the
above mentioned discovery of analytical geometry by Descartes. Newton's work was also dependent upon the growing power and precision of scientific instruments and
measurements.

This development of mechanics from Galileo to Newton
is perhaps the best illustration of the method of scientific
progress. Upon a vast basis of accurate descriptive knowledge, erected partly by Tycho Brahe and partly by earlier
astronomers, observations with instruments of precision and
high power, quantitative experiments, and finally mathematical calculations produced in little more than half a century a work which it taxes the highest powers of the spe-
cially trained human mind to understand, and which has
withstood all criticism for two centuries, the most critical in
history.

HARVEY AND THE CIRCULATION OF THE BLOOD

Only less important than that of mechanics was the development of biology in the seventeenth century. William
Harvey, supported by the excellent work of anatomists that
had begun with Vesalius, but held back by many vestiges of
the old superstitious belief in authority and the garbled
teachings of Hippocrates and Galen, in the early years of
the century discovered the circulation of the blood.[10] After
long and most admirable investigations and self-criticism, in
the year 1628 he gave this discovery to the world.

It is impossible to imagine a more illuminating contrast
between the false learning of the Middle Ages and the sound
positive knowledge of modern times than is presented in
Harvey's book. For at almost every point the work of Harvey himself has quite as much the modern flavor as that of
Newton. The introduction presents the old traditional
views on the physiological functions of heart and lungs, and
bewilders with its meaningless play with words. There fol-

[10] *H. C.*, xxxviii, 65ff.

low upon this the simplest descriptions of observations and experiments, and the soundest reasoning from such positive knowledge, till one feels that he has passed from a dream into reality.

The work of Harvey, like so much of the work of great Englishmen, was isolated, and the full development of biology came somewhat later, in mid-century and thereafter. In this later growth, aided by the microscope and the principles of mechanics, the studies of Swammerdam, Grew, Malpighi, Redi, Borelli, Leeuwenhoek, and others, provided many important data in the most widely different departments of biology. But natural history lacked the great foundation of accurate descriptive knowledge, arranged in order, that astronomy possessed, and, as a result, much of the great work which the biological renaissance began was interrupted for a century. Among the feats of seventeenth-century biology were microscopical studies of the anatomy of both plants and animals (Nehemiah Grew, Malpighi, Leeuwenhoek), the beginnings of embryology (Harvey, Swammerdam), mechanical physiology (Borelli) including recognition of the nature of reflex action by Descartes, experimental studies tending to overthrow belief in spontaneous generation (Redi), and even observations on the physiological action of poisons.

In this century, in spite of the admirable work of Robert Boyle, somewhat overestimated in his own day however, chemistry languished under the sway of a false theory. Similarly, heat, electricity, and magnetism were of no great importance, unless the magistral work on magnetism of William Gilbert, physician to Queen Elizabeth, published in 1600, be reckoned.

Two other departments of physical science, however, the study of atmospheric pressure and optics, were more fortunate. Torricelli and Viviani, pupils of Galileo, Otto von Guericke, Pascal, and Boyle investigated the barometer and the pressure of gases and worked up the fundamental conclusions. Optics was investigated by no less men than Newton and Huygens, and at their hands underwent a wonderful practical transformation. But this subject requires a peculiarly subtle theoretical foundation, and the times were

not yet ripe even for a Newton to enter the true path of
theoretical speculation.

THE EIGHTEENTH CENTURY

The great result of seventeenth-century science was to
show the world that simple and exact laws of nature can be
discovered.   At the time of their discovery the most important thing about Galileo's law of falling bodies and Newton's
"Principia" was their amazing novelty.   Familiarity with
such results of science has bred the modern contempt for
superstition and anti-intellectual views concerning the phenomena of nature.

It must be confessed, however, that the immediate results
of man's new-found confidence in the intellect were often
very unfortunate. For there can be little doubt that it was
the successes of the Newtonian dynamics and of mathematical analysis which gave the philosophers of the eighteenth century their assurance of the possibility of like
simple, exhaustive, accurate, positive, and wholly satisfactory treatments of the most complex of human affairs,
including economics and politics, to say nothing of the biological sciences.   Vain efforts in such directions consumed
much of the best energy of the century, and such striking
failures tended to obscure the real progress of knowledge
when more modest or at least more simple problems were
involved.

There were three principal tasks for eighteenth-century
science. The organization of scientific men which had been
begun in the preceding century with the Royal Society of
London and the Académie des Sciences of Paris had to be
widened and enlarged. The work of Newton had to be
evolved and spun out finer and finer with the aid of a more
and more flexible mathematical art. Above all, the description of nature had to be extended in every direction and
classified, as the basis of further progress. In promoting
the organization of science Leibnitz is the great figure. In
the development of mathematical physics there are to be
noted the Bernoulli family, Euler, Lagrange, and Laplace.
In natural history Linnæus stands out preeminent, though

Buffon must not be forgotten, and, as the century nears its close, biologist in the modern sense begin to appear.

One achievement of the century could not be foreseen— the creation of scientific chemistry by Lavoisier, aided by Scheele, Priestley and others, a deed hardly second to that of Newton and Galileo in its importance of science and civilization, and far the most important scientific advance of a hundred years.

THE NINETEENTH CENTURY

The last decades of the eighteenth century and the first of the nineteenth were a period of profound change politically, socially, economically, and industrially, and not less scientifically. The scientific renaissance had come in the seventeenth century and culminated in Newton. The succeeding period had sufficed to develop his immortal work and to collect a vast array of facts in the descriptive sciences. At the same time the spirit of positive knowledge had been applied to the steam engine and the arts, and in very different directions had influenced the work of Voltaire, Rousseau, Gibbon, Adam Smith, and many others. However they may have differed among themselves, all these men felt the new forces, and responded to them with novel criticism of religion, society, history, and political economy.

Lavoisier had provided the instruments and methods for a revolution in chemistry quite as great as Newton's in physics. But chemistry differs very greatly from physics in the applicability of mathematics, and a vast experimental edifice had to be raised before, toward the end of the nineteenth century, anything like the completeness of the Newtonian mechanics could be attained in the younger science. Moreover the atomic theory had to be developed, had to be interwoven with the kinetic theory of gases which sees the molecules in endless motion, had to be extended with the help of geometry, before this was possible. Still, a new tendency had formed, which now has become one of the steadiest streams of scientific progress.

Following upon the work of Franklin and Coulomb and many others, the discoveries of Galvani and Volta, of

Oersted and Ampère, and above all, of Faraday,[11] in electricity, providing batteries and currents, showing the relationship of electrical to magnetic, chemical, optical, mechanical, and thermal phenomena, constituted another tendency, and both of these have had a profound influence upon the arts. Young and Fresnel created a new science of light. Heat became yearly more important with the development of the steam engine and the growth of physiological and electrical science. The work of Sadi Carnot, Mayer, Joule, Helmholtz,[12] Lord Kelvin,[13] and others led, in the middle of the century, to the principles of thermodynamics, and to the laws of the conservation and degradation of energy.

THE BIOLOGICAL SCIENCES

Microscopical anatomy was revived and, advancing through the work of many trained observers, led to the recognition of the cell as the morphological element of living things, with this as a basis, to the systematic development of the whole of histology; and so to a new embryology and pathology. Thus the names of Schleiden, Schwann, Von Baer, and Virchow have become immortal.

Rigid ideas based upon classification, which had long tottered before the assaults of Lamarck, Goethe, Erasmus Darwin, Geoffroy Saint-Hilaire, and others, finally fell before Charles Darwin's[14] triumphant conception of natural selection by survival of the fittest, perhaps the most influential idea upon the thought of his time that has ever been put forward by any man. Out of this have grown the study of heredity and, partly through the efforts of Darwin's cousin, Francis Galton, a new doctrine of perfectibility.

In another department of biology, the study of the phenomena of digestion, fermentation, putrefaction, etc., after varying fortunes, culminated in Pasteur's[15] discovery of the rôle of micro-organisms, confirming the views of Redi and Swammerdam against spontaneous generation. The results of Pasteur's discoveries have now swelled into the greatest material benefit ever conferred by one man upon

11 *H. C.*, xxx, 5-178.   12 *H. C.*, xxx, 181-259.   13 *H. C.*, xxx, 263ff.
14 "Origin of Species," in *H. C.*, xi.   15 *H. C.*, xxxviii, 287-402.

his fellows. They have led to antitoxins, immunity, and the greater part of preventive medicine, as well as to antisepsis and asepsis (Lister),[16] and so to the principal triumphs of surgery.

THE ORGANIZATION OF RESEARCH

Experimental methods, guided by mechanics, optics, heat, electricity, and chemistry, were now systematically applied to physiology, then to psychology, and, with the help of the cellular hypothesis and the sciences of embryology, evolution, heredity, immunity, etc., they have transformed biology.

Everywhere, if other mathematical methods fail, the statistical method is being applied and in suitable cases, as, for example, life insurance, with great success; thus literally bringing order out of chaos.

Meantime the world has learned that science pays. Accordingly professorships have multiplied, societies have become more numerous, journals are endowed, institutes of research established, the Nobel prizes founded, and a livelihood is provided for large number of workers.

The number of working scientists, if not their quality, has enormously increased. An army has been organized and disciplined, and an amount of work which can scarcely be imagined has been produced. Scientific literature has now become a flood that has to be canalized with the help of special journals of various descriptions devoted solely to its review, description, and orderly classification, in order that it may be utilized at all.

The forward march of science has now become inevitable, like that of civilization itself. This vast army of workers are engaged, with no stake in the outcome, with no concern for the influence of their work upon church or state or any other human institution or interest, according to known and tried and proved rules, by description, measurement, experiment, and mathematical analysis, in multiplying our reliable, positive knowledge of the world around us. Year by year this knowledge grows, by leaps and bounds when commanded by genius, slowly and painfully at the hands of most men, but steadily and surely always.

[16] *H. C.,* xxxviii, 271.

SCIENCE AND THE STATE

One of the principal results of the extension of science is its incorporation with the state. Astronomers royal have existed for three centuries, but to-day we have Departments of Agriculture with many scientific bureaus, and we badly need Departments of Public Health. Moreover, the vast increase of knowledge of a highly technical character has made it impossible for the executive, the legislative, and the judicial departments of government even to have an intelligent opinion regarding much with which they must deal. Hence the expert is acquiring an importance which is scarcely guessed even by most thoughtful persons, and government by expert commissions and expert advisers of the legislature and the judiciary appear to be inevitable features of the future state.

THE GROWTH OF SPECIALIZATION

The main currents of nineteenth-century science have produced more and higher specialization than ever before. Descartes was philosopher, scientist, and mathematician; some of the great men of the eighteenth century were hardly less so. Even through a large part of the nineteenth century many of the greater men ranged widely over the field of science and mathematics. To-day the force of circumstances has largely changed all that. The chemist is likely to look upon the physicist, or even the physical chemist, with suspicion on account of his mathematical interests. On the other hand, the mathematician, unlike Newton, Euler, and Gauss, is commonly no longer a physicist at all. There are to-day very few men who possess even a superficial acquaintance with all the principal departments of science, and between the work of the astronomer, on the one hand, and that of the anatomist, on the other, there is perhaps no closer relationship than the fact that both employ optical instruments in their researches.

The nineteenth century will ever be known in history for at least two of its scientific achievements—the unification of our knowledge of matter, energy, and life, and the final organization of the army of scientific workers, whereby discovery ceased to be dependent solely upon the individual and became a part of the business of humanity at large, at length and for the first time systematically undertaken.

THE UNIFICATIONS OF SCIENCE

1. *Conservation of Energy*

The middle of the nineteenth century witnessed the discovery of all three of the great unifications of science. These are the unification of energy by the discovery of the principle of the conservation of energy, the unification of matter by the discovery of the periodic system, and the unification of life by the work of Charles Darwin.

Not for decades after Bolton and Watt, as the result of commercial necessity, introduced the idea of measuring energy in horsepower, was the real nature of the relationship between heat and mechanical power critically examined, save once in a quickly forgotten investigation by Sadi Carnot. But at length the speculations and calculations of Julius Robert Mayer, the admirable experimental researches of Joule, and the profound studies of Helmholtz and others established the principle of the conservation of energy[17]—in short, demonstrated the proposition that energy is one and indestructible, however it may manifest itself as heat, or light, or electricity, or otherwise.

2. *Periodicity*

Somewhat later the work of Newlands, Lother Meyer, and Mendeléeff brought to light an extraordinary series of relationships, periodically recurring properties, among the elements. It would be impossible briefly to explain this relationship, but a simple analogy may serve to show its nature.

11	12	13	14	15
21	22	23	24	25
31		33	34	35
41	42	43		45
51	52	53	54	55

[17] *H. C.*, xxx, 181ff.

Giving the numbers above arranged, there can be no doubt, first, that they have been correctly arranged, and secondly, that the numbers 32 and 44 are missing, but have a place in the table. In other words, it is possible to predict the "properties" of the two missing numbers. In like manner, the studies of Mendeléeff showed similar connections among the elements. These could be arranged, as he showed, in the order of their atomic weights, in a table very similar to the above, in which the variation in properties was regular and periodically recurrent, but with certain gaps in the classification. Judging from the elements surrounding such gaps, Mendeléeff predicted the properties of the missing elements in certain cases in which the missing elements have now been supplied by chemical research. The results have invariably confirmed the Russian chemist's predictions, as may be seen from the following data concerning the element germanium:

	PREDICTION	OBSERVATION
Atomic weight......................	72.0	72.3
Specific gravity	5.5	5.469
Atomic volume	13.	13.2
Specific gravity of oxide............	4.7	4.703
Boiling point of chloride...........	Less than 100°	86°
Specific gravity of chloride..........	1.9	1.9
Specific gravity of ethyl compound...	0.96	Lower than water

Thus it has become clear that the elements are all related to one another. It is not known how to explain this relationship—perhaps they have been evolved in an orderly manner from something else—but, at all events, matter is not only indestructible (Lavoisier), but it makes up a unitary system. To-day we feel sure that we are acquainted with nearly all the stable varieties of matter that exist in the universe, though of course there remain a great variety of arrangements of this matter which are unknown to us.

3. *Biological Evolution*

The only well-known phenomenon that cannot be completely described in terms of matter and energy is life, with its peculiar characteristics of consciousness and thought. In the year 1859 biology yielded to the unifying idea of Charles Darwin. Many had previously suspected that all living things are blood relations; the discoveries of embryologists in particular had proved that the similarities among living things are far more profound than had been formerly realized. But Darwin provided a plausible explanation of the development of more complex beings by a continuous evolutionary process, and this led to the world's final decision in favor of the hypothesis of transformation.

It is possible that some of Darwin's hypotheses may in the end be discarded, but it appears to be wholly unlikely that the world will ever give up its belief in the evolution of organic beings, in all their multitudinous forms, from earlier and simpler types, and probably originally from one or more exceedingly simple forms.

Finally the change in the relation of science to civilization, accomplished in the nineteenth century, marks a new epoch in history. For the first time humanity has systematically undertaken the task of conquering the environment. A new organ of the social body, like the financial or the military, has been created and has assumed relations with the other parts of the great organism of modern society.

System replaces chance in the greater part of human affairs, manufacturing, warfare, medicine, commerce itself, have become "scientific"; they advance steadily, ruthlessly, and carry man with them; whither he cannot guess.

II. ASTRONOMY

By Professor Lawrence J. Henderson

ASTRONOMY was destined to liberate the modern intellect from the bondage of the Middle Ages, and by teaching man that the earth is not the fixed center of the universe, but a satellite of one among many stars, to shake the confidence with which he had long regarded the universe as made for him, the earth for his abode, the heavens for his enjoyment. This is the great contribution of astronomy to thought; to civilization it has also contributed some of the most important advances, such as an accurate calendar, the standard of time, and the exact measure of time, sound methods of navigation and geography; and commencing earlier than all the other sciences, it has built up one of the most admirable structures of scientific knowledge.

Astronomy was long the leader among the sciences, and as such gave to the world trigonometry, in part logarithms, and Newton's dynamics. But though astronomical progress has by no means ceased, the accelerated growth of other sciences—first physics, then chemistry, and of late biology—has rendered it less conspicuous. The continued importance of astronomy is, however, well illustrated by the marvelous results of spectrum analysis, while to-day the study of nebulæ and of the physics of the sun possesses the highest interest.

HIPPARCHUS AND THE PTOLEMAIC SYSTEM

The principal results of ancient astronomy go by the name of Ptolemy (the Ptolemaic system), but are mainly due to the labors of Hipparchus.

Hipparchus knew the latitude and longitude of 150 fixed stars within a fraction of a degree, when, in the year 134 B. C., a new star of the first magnitude suddenly appeared.

Encouraged by this extraordinary event, he applied himself diligently to astronomical measurements, establishing the position of more than 1,000 fixed stars. It was no doubt this sound basis of accurate quantitative data, and the familiarity with his subject which such work provided, that led to his great achievements. He discovered the precession of the equinoxes, and measured it with considerable accuracy; he measured the length of the day with an error of but six minutes; but his great achievement was a mathematical device whereby the position of the sun and, with less accuracy, the positions of the moon and planets could be calculated.

The essential features of this device consisted in imagining the sun to move in a circle of which the earth was not quite the center; this is the *excentric* of ancient astronomy. Another more difficult idea was that of *epicycles*. These two mathematical ideas did very good service in the work of Hipparchus, for the practical purposes of the calendar. But later, in the hands of Ptolemy, and in the succeeding centuries, they ceased to be arbitrary assumptions, or even mere theories, and in the Middle Ages became dogmas which were held most tenaciously and blindly. As astronomical knowledge slowly increased, it became necessary to make the theory more and more complex in order to fit the facts, and, long before the work of Copernicus, astronomical theories had reached a degree of absurdity that could not have endured in any other age. Yet more than one of the astronomers of antiquity had believed that the earth moves, either rotating on its axis, or revolving round the sun, or both.

THE COPERNICAN THEORY

Copernicus was born at Thorn in Poland (1473) of a German mother. Educated first in medicine, he studied astronomy in Vienna, and he was later in Italy (1495-1505) at the height of the Renaissance. When he returned home, his uncle, the bishop of Ermeland, presented him with a clerical position at Frauenburg. Here for forty years he labored to bring astronomical calculations and observations into harmony, and finally, long after he had become convinced of the soundness of the heliocentric view published the work[1] which marks the first great step in modern science, a work which he saw for the first time on his deathbed in 1543.

Copernicus showed that all the difficulties which the movements of the planets present would become very much less if the moon were left the only satellite of the earth, and the earth itself and all the planets were assumed to move around the sun. He did not prove—in truth being wise and realizing his own limitations, he did not seek to prove—this hypothesis, but only to present the reasons why it must appear the most probable explanation of the principal astronomical phenomena.

The new doctrine made converts slowly. At first it was opposed by the professional astronomers, with whose time-honored habits it interfered, and who were, for the most part, not competent to understand it. Later the opposition of the great Tycho Brahe worked against it for many years. Still later the opposition of theologians effectually cut off many converts, most notably Descartes. But the discovery of Kepler's laws completely destroyed the Ptolemaic system, and must have convinced nearly all reasonable men of the correctness of that of Copernicus. These famous laws are as follows: The line joining the sun with a planet sweeps over equal areas in equal periods of time. Every planet moves in an ellipse with the sun at one focus. The squares of the times of the revolution of any two planets are in the same ratio as the cubes of their mean distances from the 'sun.

GALILEO AND NEWTON

The next important step in the growth of knowledge of the solar system was Galileo's study of the laws of fall and the composition of two kinds of motion, like fall and projection, as in the case of a projectile. This was followed by Newton's magnificent extension of gravity from the earth to the whole of space, with the assumption and proof that the intensity of gravitational attraction varies inversely as the square of the distance.

[1] See his Dedication of his "Revolutions of Heavenly Bodies," *Harvard Classics*, xxxix, 55-60.

These ideas, combined with Kepler's laws, led at once to the theory of planetary motion and its proof, in Newton's "Principia." [2] The motion of the planets appeared as the resultant of their tendency to go on in the direction in which they were moving (inertia), and their tendency to fall to the sun (gravitation). The problem yielded completely, so far as two bodies are concerned, to the mathematical genius of Newton.

Still the revolution of the earth about the sun was not, by many astronomers, considered to be proved, while some even denied it. For if the earth really revolved about the sun, the relative positions of the stars ought not to appear the same to us from different parts of the orbit. Yet no difference in their places at the two solstices could be detected, although the stands of the observer were separated by a hundred and eighty million miles in the two instances.

James Bradley was the first person to obtain important results from the investigation of this problem of *parallax*. He found, not, to be sure, a periodic change of the apparent position of the stars that could be explained as parallax, but a different change of position, quite unexpected. This he called *aberration*, and recognized that it was due to a composition of the motion of the earth and of the light from the star itself, which is analogous to the entry of rain falling straight down, yet into the open front of a moving carriage. Here, nevertheless, was a proof, the more valuable because unexpected, of the earth's motion. It was not till 1837 that Bessel finally measured the parallax of a fixed star, and this finally ended the problem. The whole difficulty had been due merely to the enormous distance which separates us from the nearest of the stars.

SPECTRUM ANALYSIS

A new period in the history of astronomy followed upon the discovery of spectrum analysis by Bunsen and Kirchhoff. At the outset the chemical composition of the sun revealed itself. Later that of the stars became known; still later it became possible to classify the stars on the basis of their

[2] *H. C.,* xxxix, 157, and see General Index in vol. 1, under *Newton.*

spectra, and at length it has become evident that variations in spectra are at least largely due to differences in the age of suns (the length of time during which cooling has gone on), that all stars are probably very much alike both chemically and physically, and that our sun is probably very much like all other stars. The geological doctrine of uniformity has been extended to astronomy.

This results in renewed interest in the nebular hypothesis and in novel speculations regarding the origin of the solar system. In like manner, the problem of the physicochemical nature of the sun, and of the processes which take place within it, assumes great interest; for, if the universe be homogeneous, we may extend our local discoveries to the utmost confines of space. These, however, have themselves turned out not so unapproachable as a few years ago they seemed to be. Certain peculiarities of star spectra enable astronomers to judge of the motion of stars both relative to the earth and in rotation. The behavior of variable stars can also in part be accounted for by ingenious hypotheses.

Thus the old science preserves its youth and promises to continue its contributions to the growth of human understanding.

III. PHYSICS AND CHEMISTRY

By Professor Lawrence J. Henderson

THE history of physical science in the ancient world is marked by few notable results. The monochord, earliest of scientific apparatus, led to the discovery of the elements of harmony; geometrical optics in its simplest form was developed; Hero of Alexandria and others familiarized themselves with some of the phenomena of steam and air pressure; even Aristotle, whose influence in this department was on the whole so harmful during two millenniums, possessed much curious and interesting information. But, apart from the great work of Archimedes in mechanics, there is little that bears the imprint of genius in the physics and chemistry of antiquity. Most of the knowledge of the time was no better than a collection of rules of the various trades, such as dyeing, for instance.

THE ACHIEVEMENTS OF ARCHIMEDES

Archimedes established the science of statics. He discovered the law of the lever, that unequal weights are in equilibrium when their distances (from the fulcrum) are inversely proportional to their weights; he developed the idea of center of gravity, and discovered rules concerning it; and he discovered the laws of floating and immersed bodies, including the so-called principle of Archimedes, which enabled him, as the story goes, by weighing Hiero's crown in air and then in water, to detect that the goldsmith had debased the metal. This work of Archimedes, together with his remarkable mathematical feats, marks him as one of the mightiest of human intellects, fully worthy of a place among the greatest of the Greeks.

But, in spite of Archimedes, it was in fragmentary and

disjointed form that the physical science of antiquity was transmitted without important change through the Middle Ages to the Modern World. We have already seen somewhat of the additions which the seventeenth century contributed, especially in dynamics, from Galileo to Newton. It does not appear that, apart from the chemical work of Lavoisier, the eighteenth century provided much of the very highest novelty and value in this field. Perhaps the researches of two Americans, Benjamin Franklin and Benjamin Thompson, who became Count Rumford, in electricity and in heat respectively, are among the best which the century affords, as they are at the summit of all American scientific work.

LAVOISIER AND THE RISE OF MODERN CHEMISTRY

Lavoisier's achievement consisted in his recognition of the fact that weight is neither increased nor diminished in chemical changes, and in the elevation of this discovery, which has since been many times confirmed with ever-increasing accuracy, into the guiding principle of chemical investigation, the law of the conservation of mass. This advance involved the introduction of the balance as the chief instrument of chemical research. Lavoisier's great success depended, further, upon the fact that he chose the process of oxidation and reduction (the reverse of the reaction of oxidation) for study. Not only is oxygen the most active of chemical elements, if both intensity and variety of chemical behavior be considered, and far the commonest upon the earth's surface, but also the most important chemical processes are reactions of oxygen.

The partial tearing off of oxygen from the carbon of carbonic acid and the hydrogen of water is the first step in the formation of all organic substances in the plant, and the recombination of oxygen with plant products the chief chemical activity of the animal. All this and much more Lavoisier recognized, and thereby revealed the true nature of another great phenomenon of nature. These investigations also disclosed, in the sequel, the chief source of all the energy which is available for the purposes of man.

It is only the energy stored up in the plant (originally the energy of the sunlight shining upon the green leaf of the plant and transformed by the action of chlorophyll) which is contained in all coal, wood, all kinds of oil, including petroleum, alcohol, in short every fuel. And it is exclusively by the union of the fuels with oxygen once more to form water and carbonic acid that this energy is liberated, as in the human body itself, and utilized by man.[1] The resulting water and carbonic acid can then be used over again by the plant. The nature of this cycle of matter was clearly recognized by Lavoisier. This is the basis of nearly all our industry and commerce.

THE WAVE THEORY OF LIGHT

The next great achievement of physical science is commonly regarded as the establishment of the wave theory of light[2] by Young and Fresnel. This view had been put forth in the seventeenth century in a very weighty form by Huygens, and it had even been held before him by the versatile Hooke. On the assumption that light is propagated as undulations, Huygens had given a most satisfactory account of the laws of reflection and refraction; and he had had good success even in his application of the theory to the very difficult problem of double refraction in Iceland spar. Huygens, however, did not succeed in establishing his hypothesis, and Newton's preference for the so-called emission or corpuscular theory of light weighed heavily against the theory of waves.

Newton himself never quite rejected the wave theory of light, and, in truth, at many points in his writings seems strongly to favor it. But there are propositions in his works which led his followers to the positive assertion of the emission hypothesis. The great mathematician Euler, on the other hand, adopted, in the eighteenth century, the undulatory theory. Between his purely theoretical views and the Newtonians there was great controversy.

Again at the beginning of the nineteenth century the un-

[1] See Faraday on the "Chemical History of a Candle" in *H. C.*, xxx, 89-178.
[2] See Kelvin's account of the theory in *H. C.*, xxx, 263-286.

dulatory theory was set forth, this time, however, on the basis of exact observations upon the colors of thin plates, by Thomas Young, one of the most versatile men of genius of the country. The contributions of Young were destined to prevail, but, in spite of their soundness, they were treated with contempt by his contemporaries and forgotten for twenty years, until revived by the confirmations of Fresnel. Fresnel, moreover, gradually developed the mathematical theory of this intricate subject, and at length, supported by Arago, he won over the scientific world to the belief in light waves and the luminiferous ether with its strange and paradoxical characteristics.

THE WORK OF FARADAY

Of all the results of scientific experimentation, those of Faraday probably contributed most to the recognition of the connection between the different manifestations of energy, which was a necessary preliminary to the discovery of the principle of the conservation of energy.[3] This is but one of the merits of Michael Faraday, whom many have thought the very greatest of scientific experimenters, and who was certainly one of the noblest and most inspired of men.

The work of Faraday is of a richness and variety that baffles description. He was interested in every department of physical science, and he was a great discoverer wherever his interests rested. His earliest work was chemical, following that of his teacher Davy. Here he discovered new compounds of carbon, for the first time liquefied several gases, studied the diffusion of gases, the alloys of steel, and numerous varieties of glass. Next he turned to electricity, his chief interest thenceforth. With a voltaic pile he decomposed magnesium sulphate. This led later to his fundamental electrochemical law. Choosing purely physical problems, he for the first time produced the continuous rotations of wires and magnets round each other, and in 1831 he discovered induced currents. The greatness of his work in this department has been explained by the most competent of all critics, Clerk Maxwell.

[3] See Faraday on "Forces of Matter," *H. C.*, xxx, 5-88.

"By the intense application of his mind he had brought the new idea, in less than three months from its first development, to a state of perfect maturity. The magnitude and originality of Faraday's achievement may be estimated by tracing the subsequent history of his discovery. As might be expected, it was at once made the subject of investigation by the whole scientific world, but some of the most experienced physicists were unable to avoid mistakes in stating, in what they conceived to be more scientific language than Faraday's, the phenomena before them. Up to the present time, the mathematicians who have rejected Faraday's method of stating his law as unworthy of the precision of their science have never succeeded in devising any essentially different formula which shall fully express the phenomena without introducing hypotheses about the mutual action of things which have no physical existence, such as elements of currents which flow out of nothing, then along a wire, and finally sink into nothing again.

"After nearly half a century of labor of this kind, we may say that, though the practical applications of Faraday's discovery have increased and are increasing in number and value every year, no exception to the statement of these laws as given by Faraday has been discovered, no new law has been added to them, and Faraday's original statement remains to this day the only one which asserts no more than can be verified by experiment, and the only one by which the theory of phenomena can be expressed in a manner which is exactly and numerically accurate, and at the same time within the range of elementary methods of exposition."[4]

[4] "Encyclopædia Britannica," 9th ed., ix, 30.

IV. THE BIOLOGICAL SCIENCES

By Professor Lawrence J. Henderson

AMONG the central problems of biology and scientific medicine, those which group themselves about the bacteriological and pathological investigations of Pasteur[1] have been very fully represented in The Harvard Classics. This is due partly to the fact that Pasteur, in providing an explanation of the conditions of life of microorganisms and of the effects of their activities, contributed many missing links to the science of life, and unified our knowledge of the interrelations of living things. For, in its various ratifications and connections, Pasteur's problem is one of the most extensive, as it is one of the most important, in the whole domain of science. It includes or touches the subjects of fermentation and putrefaction, with the old problem of spontaneous generation and the whole question of genesis, the cause of infectious diseases and the manner of their communication, the nature and mechanism of immunity, including vaccination and antitoxins, and a host of other equally important matters. The work of Pasteur has led to modern surgery through the work of Lister,[2] to a large part of modern hygiene, sacrificing the lives of many investigators in the process; to new methods in chemical industry and agriculture, and it has created untold wealth and saved countless lives.

THE QUESTION OF SPONTANEOUS GENERATION

Aristotle, though his knowledge of embryology in at least one instance—that of the smooth dog-fish—was very great and very exact, appears at times to have been willing to assume spontaneous generation of such large animals as the eel, for

[1] *Harvard Classics,* xxxviii, 289ff.
[2] See Lister, "On the Antiseptic Principle," in *H. C.,* xxxviii, 271ff.

instance, as a common occurrence. But there can be no doubt that even in antiquity common sense sometimes felt itself more or less in opposition to such an idea, and it was natural enough for the men of the seventeenth century, when stirred by the new spirit of scientific research, to seek to solve a problem which has always been of the highest interest, and never far from the minds of thoughtful naturalists.

In this great century the most important investigations of such problems were those of Harvey, Redi, and Swammerdam. Harvey's embryological observations are far less valuable than his study of the circulation of the blood.[3] It may, in truth, be questioned if he surpassed Aristotle in any way as an embryologist. But, at all events, his work served to draw the attention of his successors to this subject, and, however vague his ideas about spantaneous generation in certain lower forms of life, he at least took a firm stand in favor of the theory of generation from the egg in most cases.

The work of Redi is of greater interest and importance. He made elaborate studies of the putrefaction of flesh, saw flies lay their eggs therein, and on gauze when the flesh was protected with it. He saw maggots develop in the unprotected meat, while the use of gauze prevented their development. He found that meat of one kind could support maggots which formed more than one kind of fly, and that the same species of fly could come from different kinds of meat. Hence he concluded that the generation of the fly is from an egg, and that there is no spontaneous generation involved in the putrefaction of meat.

Swammerdam, one of the greatest of naturalists, and many others confirmed the observations and conclusions of Redi, and, by observing again and again normal generation from the egg in many other species of minute organisms, did much to undermine the confidence with which the unaccountable appearance of living things was ascribed to spontaneous generation.

Meanwhile the microscopical studies of Leeuwenhoek had

[3] See Harvey, "On the Motion of the Heart and Blood of Animals," in *H. C.*, xxxviii, 63ff.

revealed the presence of hosts of minute organisms in putrid fluids and, in the eighteenth century, the problem of spontaneous generation was transferred to the origin of microscopic life. This problem in turn was answered unfavorably to spontaneous generation by Spallanzani. His new method of investigation was to seal up an infusion of meat in a glass flask; next the flash was immersed in boiling water until the contents had been thoroughly heated throughout, and then the behavior of the solution on standing was observed. After thorough heating no signs of putrefaction were revealed to the eye or to the nose; no living things were ever visible in the solution under the microscope. But on admitting the air to the flasks putrefaction soon set in and thus proved that the fault was not with the effect of heat upon what is to-day called the culture medium, but that putrefaction had not previously occurred simply because all germs originally present had been killed by heat; sterilized, in short.

THE CELL THEORY AND FERMENTATION

The early nineteenth century made two highly important new contributions to the old problem: the view that all living things are made up of cells as their ultimate structural elements; and, secondly, acquaintance with various digestive ferments contained in liquids like the gastric juice, which are now known to be cell free, yet are capable of bringing about processes resembling fermentation. The latter discovery led at a later date to the distinction between organized (living) and unorganized ferments.

Out of the cell theory have grown the wonderful modern sciences of embryology, largely through the efforts of K. E. von Baer, and pathology, in which Rudolf Virchow has a similar position. The study of ferments and fermentation, and of simple chemical agents which can produce like changes, has led to many new problems and to new methods of attacking old ones.

The chemical aspects of fermentation[4] have a special historical importance because they are especially associated

[4] See Pasteur, "The Physiological Theory of Fermentation," in *H. C.*, xxxviii, 289ff.

with Pasteur's discoveries. Trained as a chemist, he applied the exact methods of physical science to the biological problem, and solved what had been thought by many insoluble. The studies of Pasteur convinced the scientific world that life as we know it never originates spontaneously, that minute living organisms—microbes, germs, bacteria—are far more active agents in this world than had been guessed. Such organisms turned out to be the essential factors in fermentation of all kinds, save only those due to digestive ferments; it is such organisms which form alcohol, sour milk, make vinegar, etc. Thus in the organic cycle the rôle of the organisms formed of a single cell at length appeared to be a great one. Everywhere present, borne by the wind, they are the true scavengers; for nothing, no matter how small, can escape them. But they are more than this. Wherever they find organic matter, dead or alive, that can support life, they seize upon it; they transform many of the most important waste products of the animal into the food of the plant; they grow within larger living things, and by their growth cause disease, or do not, according to their nature. In short, it is their activity, invisible but omnipresent, fitting in at every point where gaps would otherwise occur, which completes the organic cycle.

IMPORTANCE OF THE WORK OF PASTEUR

At length the chemical processes of life upon the earth were unified. Living things were seen to make up a single community, the great laboratory through which alone matter flows in its everlasting cycle.

The results of Pasteur's discoveries and of the methods of investigation which he introduced are probably already greater than the results of Napoleon's life. The simple great man, who almost alone among the scientists of the nineteenth century equals the genius and virtue of Faraday, shares with the latter the first position among those who have revolutionized our twentieth-century world.

Pasteur's discoveries explained at once such observations as those of Oliver Wendell Holmes.[5] They gave a clue to

[5] See Holmes, "The Contagiousness of Puerperal Fever," in *H. C.*, xxxviii, 271.

such mysterious processes as vaccination.[6] And one after another each great pest has yielded up its secret cause—a specific micro-organism—to the disciples of Pasteur.

TOXINS, ANTITOXINS, AND IMMUNITY

Yet such discoveries are but a beginning in the explanation of disease. It soon appeared that there is something vastly more important about a bacterium than its ability to grow in the body—viz., the kind of poison which it yields; else why the difference between typhoid fever and tuberculosis? Thus arises the search for such poisons or *toxins,* a fruitful and important department of medical investigation. But what of the fate of the toxin in the body—what of this effect upon the host? The result of researches upon this line has been the discovery of antitoxins and the science of immunity.

In another direction the progress of micro-biology has been quite as important. Evidently it is not with the help of toxins that yeast forms alcohol and carbonic acid from sugar; it is with the help of *enzymes* or soluble ferments. These are imprisoned within the cell, but otherwise they resemble pepsin and the other soluble ferments of digestion. But if the yeast cell performs its chemical functions with the help of soluble ferments, why not all other cells as well? Such is in truth the case. Hence the study of the chemical processes which make up the activity of unicellular organisms has explained much that takes place in every living thing. In short, our progress in the solution of the fundamental problem of physiology, the physico-chemical organization of protoplasm, depends in no small degree upon studies of those minute living things which have but a single cell within which to enclose all the activities of an individual being.

[6] See Jenner's original publications on vaccination against smallpox in *H. C.,* xxxviii, 153ff.

V. KELVIN ON "LIGHT" AND "THE TIDES"

By Professor W. M. Davis

SCIENTIFIC essays, like those by Lord Kelvin on Light[1] and The Tides,[2] should be read several times by the studious reader, and each time from a different point of view. In the first reading, the reader seeks for information offered by the author; in the second, the reader examines the scientific method by which the author has gained his information; in the third, the reader's attention should be directed to the style of presentation adopted by the author in telling his story. After an attentive study of Kelvin's essays from these different sides, many a reader will find that he has made a distinct intellectual advance.

THE ESSAYS AS STATEMENTS OF SCIENTIFIC RESULTS

The first reading of either essay will disclose some of the most marvelous results that have been reached by scientific investigation. For example, it has been discovered that light is of an undulatory nature; that the vibrations of light quiver at the rate of several hundred million of million times a second; that light is transmitted over interplanetary distances with a velocity of nearly 200,000 miles a second; and that for the transmission at such a speed through what seems to us to be empty space, as between the sun and the earth, there must be a continuous, extremely tenuous, and highly elastic medium, all pervading and universally extended, to which the name, luminiferous ether, is commonly given. It is of course not to be expected that all these and many other results, physical, geometrical, and numerical, can be easily acquired; some paragraphs must be

---

[1] *Harvard Classics,* xxx, 263ff.   [2] *H. C.,* xxx, 287ff.

gone over more slowly than others, and many of them should
be reviewed more than once; some are difficult of comprehension because they are without the vivid experiments by
which they were illustrated in the original lecture; and
others because they are compressed into terse statements
without explanation. But at the end of what is here called
the "first reading," many of the conclusions announced regarding the nature of light should be fairly familiar. Similar examples may be drawn from the lecture on the tides;
the larger share of mathematical considerations here encountered may make the second essay more difficult than the
first; if some readers do not clearly understand, for example, the statement regarding diurnal inequality (p. 305),
they may be excused, for the statement is very brief; similarly, the account of the tide machines (pp. 307-312) is too
dense to be really comprehended by a non-mathematical
reader, previously uninformed on such matters as harmonic
analysis.

THE ESSAYS AS EXAMPLES OF SCIENTIFIC METHOD

The second reading of the essays, directed to an examination of the scientific method employed by the author, should
have for its most valuable result a better appreciation of the
nature of "theorizing" than most persons possess. The immediately observable elements of such phenomena as light
and tides are called "facts"; but an intelligent inquirer is
soon persuaded that the facts of observation are really only
a small part of the total phenomena. For example, some
invisible factors must determine that the noonday sky overhead is blue, and the horizon sky near sunset or sunrise is
yellow or red. Or, some unseen factors must determine the
strength of the tides and their hour of occurrence varying
from day to day. How can light travel at its incredibly
rapid velocity? How can the moon cause changes of sea
level on the earth? The true answers to such questions
would acquaint us with phenomena that, in spite of their
invisibility, take place just as truly as the phenomena that
we observe. Such unseen phenomena might be called "facts
of inference," to distinguish them from "facts of observa-

tion." To discover the facts of inference and to demonstrate their connection with the facts of observation is the effort of all theorizing. A theory is, in brief, a statement in which the supposed facts of inference are reasonably connected with the known facts of observation. How is such a statement reached? and when it is reached, how do we know that it is right? To answer such questions fully would demand a whole treatise on scientific method, here impossible; our intention is simply to point out that an introductory understanding of scientific method, much better than none, can be gleaned by a careful second reading of Kelvin's and of the other scientific essays in this collection, with the constant effort to learn how the announced results have been attained.

Notice, first, that for an active mind, it is "impossible to avoid theorizing" (p. 294). The lesson from this is to beware of those so-called practical persons who say they do not theorize; what they really do is to theorize in an unsafe, unscientific manner; for they, like everyone else, wish to understand more than they can see. The desire to theorize should not be resisted, but theorizing should be carefully cultivated and its results should be carefully held apart from those of observation. Notice, second, that, some facts of observation having been gained, the inquisitive mind at once sets about inventing schemes that may possibly include the mental counterparts of the unseen phenomena, or facts of inference, and then proceeds to determine the correctness of the inventions by certain logical devices or tests. That particular scheme is finally adopted as true which stands all possible tests. The tests are mostly experimental in the study of light; they are largely computational in the study of the tides. Notice, third, how ingenious the scientific mind must be to conceive the extraordinary schemes by which the unseen phenomena are supposed to combine with the seen, so as to make a reasonably working total process; how far these mental processes must go beyond the mere determination of visible facts by observation; how active the imagination must be to picture the invisible processes of the invented scheme; and also how free from prepossessions, how docile the scientific mind must be, in order to follow the experimental or computational demonstrations wherever they may lead! Still more important, notice how large a share of the standard content of science, as illustrated by the essays on light and tides, is made up of what are here called "facts of inference," and not simply of facts of observation.

THE MERE OBSERVER *versus* THE THEORIZER

The problem of the tides may be illustrated by a parable. Once there was a keen, unimaginative observer living on a seacoast, where a perpetual pall of clouds covered the sky, concealing the sun and moon, but where the tides, with their periodic variations, were familiar matters; he would gain a good knowledge of the facts of observation, but he would have no knowledge of their meaning as revealed by the unseen facts of inference. At the same time a philosophical hermit was living alone under the clear skies of a desert continental interior, where he was totally ignorant of the oceans and their tides, but familiar with the motions of the sun and moon, and acquainted with the law of gravitation, in accordance with which the heavenly bodies move; he might from this beginning go on with a series of inferences, or deductions, which would in the end lead him to say: "These distant bodies must exert unequal attractions on different parts of the earth, but the earth is too rigid to yield to them; if, however, a large part of the earth's surface were covered with a sheet of water, the attractions of the sun and moon would produce periodic variations in the level of such a sheet" . . . and so on. After a time, the long-shore observer sets out upon his travels and meets the hermit in the interior desert, who asks him: "Do you happen to have seen a large sheet of water, in which periodic changes of level take place?" "I have indeed," the observer exclaims, "and I was on the point of telling you about the changes of level in the hope that you could explain them; but how did you know that the changes occurred?" "I did not even know," the hermit replies, "that there was a vast sheet of water in which they could occur; but I felt sure that, if such a water sheet existed, it must suffer periodic changes of level, because . . ." The evident point of the parable is that the keen observer and the speculative hermit are both combined in a trained scientific investigator; he performs the two tasks of observation and of explanation independently, as if he were two persons; and his philosophical half finally accepts as true that particular scheme or theory which leads to the best understanding of the facts gained by his observational half.

THE ESSAYS AS MODELS OF EXPOSITION

The third reading is devoted to the style of presentation, and this brings the reader more closely into relation with the author. The object of the third reading is thus unlike that of the second, which considered the author in relation to his problem; while both these are unlike the first, in which the reader did not think of the author but only of the subject treated. A few leading characteristics of presentation in the first essay may be pointed out; the reader may afterward make for himself a similar analysis of the second essay. Note first that the more difficult subject of light is introduced by the analogous and easier subject of sound (pp. 264-268); this is as if the author kindly took the reader by the hand and guided him along an easy path toward a lofty summit. Note again the care which the author takes to lead the reader by easy steps from small to large numbers, and the sympathetic encouragement that he gives: "You can all understand it" (p. 270). Consider the homely illustration of the teapot (p. 271) and the large concept which it aids you in reaching. Recognize the personal touch given by the reference to the famous work of the American physicist, Langley (p. 272); and a little later to the epoch-making discovery of the spectrum by Newton. See again a homely illustration in the mention of shoemaker's wax, and with it Kelvin's quaint allusion to his Scotch birth (p. 276). Passing over several other matters, consider the care which this profound investigator, himself able to grasp the most complicated mathematical formulæ, gives to illustrating the nature of ether vibrations by means of a small red ball in a bowl of jelly (p. 284).

The first reading ought to excite a desire to learn more about light; the second, to understand more fully the method of science; the third, to know more intimately some of the great men of the world. Thus the careful reading of one thing creates an appetite for reading many other things: and therein lies the greatest teaching value of any reading whatever.

PHILOSOPHY

I. GENERAL INTRODUCTION

By Professor Ralph Barton Perry

How charming is divine philosophy!
Not harsh and crabbed, as dull fools suppose,
But musical as is Apollo's lute,
And a perpetual feast of nectar'd sweets.
Where no crude surfeit reigns.

SINCE Milton wrote thus gallantly in its behalf, philosophy has fairly succeeded in living down its reputation for being "harsh and crabbed." No one who has made the acquaintance of Scholastic Philosophy, the philosophy of the Middle Ages, and still the established philosophy in Milton's day, can escape a secret sympathy with the view of these "dull fools." But in the course of the last three centuries, philosophy, especially English and French philosophy, has become more free in form, more imaginative, and more self-expressive. So that the critics and belittlers of philosophy to-day, too numerous, alas! to make it safe to call names, have taken up new ground. Philosophy is condemned, not for being unmusical, but for being unpractical. The music of Apollo's lute is itself under suspicion, being too unsubstantial and too remote to suit the temper of an age of efficiency and common sense.

PHILOSOPHY AND EFFICIENCY

I sincerely wish that I could recommend philosophy on grounds of efficiency and common sense. I should be listened to, understood, and believed. I should at once insinuate myself into the confidence of my reader. If I could but say: "Now look here! Philosophy is just a matter of plain, hard-headed common sense"; or, "If you want to succeed, try philosophy. It will help you to make and to sell, to outstrip competitors, and to be efficient in whatever you undertake"; if I could make such an appeal to you, your instincts and prejudices would secure me your ready sympathy. But I should have deceived you. What I should thus have recommended to you would not be philosophy. For philosophy is neither plain nor hard-headed; nor is it a means of success, as success is ordinarily construed. This is the case, not accidentally, but in principle. The very point of philosophy lies in the fallibility of common sense, and in the arbitrariness of vulgar standards of success. Philosophy is one of those things that must be met on its own ground. You must seek it where it is at home; if you insist upon its meeting you halfway it will turn out not to be philosophy at all, but some poor compromise—the name or husk of philosophy with the soul gone out of it. No one can understand what philosophy means unless he lets it speak for itself and in its own language. If philosophy is good, it is because it contributes to life something *different,* something peculiarly its own, and which cannot be measured by any standards save those which philosophy itself supplies.

PHILOSOPHY AND COMMON SENSE

If we cannot justify philosophy by common sense, we can at least contrast it with common sense, and so approach it from that more familiar ground. Since we must admit that philosophy is at odds with common sense, let us make the most of it. What, then, *is* common sense? First of all it is evident that this is not a common-sense question. One of the things peculiar to common sense is that it must not be questioned, but taken for granted. It is made up of a mass of convictions that by common consent are to be allowed to stand; one does not ask questions about them, but appeals to them to determine what questions shall be asked. They are the conservative opinion, the solidified and uniform belief, on which men act, and which is the unconscious premise of most human reasoning. As a man of common sense, I *use* common sense to live by or to think by; it is a practical and theoretical bias which I share with my fellows, but which I do not think about at all.

Now suppose that in some whimsical and senseless mood I *do* think about common sense. Something very startling happens. This once unchallenged authority is proved to be highly fallible. Its spell is gone. It at once appears, for example, that common sense has had a history, and that it has varied with times and places. The absurdities of yesterday are the common sense of to-day; the common sense of yesterday is now obsolete and quaint. The crank of the sixteenth century was the man who said that the earth moved; the crank of the twentieth century is the man who says that it does not. Moreover, once common sense is thus reflected upon, it is seen to be in part, at least, the result of wholly irrational forces, such as habit and imitation. What has been long believed, or repeatedly asserted, acquires a hardness and fixity from that fact; in the future it is always easier to believe, more difficult to disbelieve, than anything recent or novel. And what others about us believe, we tend unconsciously to reflect in our own belief, just as our speech catches the accent and idioms of our social circle. Furthermore, a belief once widely diffused takes on the authority of established usage. It is supported by public opinion, as anything normal or regular is supported; unbelievers are viewed with hostile suspicion as unreliable and incalculable. "You can never tell what they will do next." Or they are forcibly persecuted as a menace to the public peace. I have called habit and imitation "irrational" forces. By that I mean that they have no special regard for truth. They operate in the same way to confirm and propagate a bad way of thinking as a good way of thinking. It does not follow that common sense is necessarily mistaken; indeed reasons can be adduced to show that common sense is a very good guide indeed. But if so, then common sense is justified on other grounds; it is not itself the last court of appeal. Common sense, despite its stability and vogue, perhaps on account of its stability and vogue, is open to criticism. We cannot be sure that it is true; and it may positively stand in the way of truth through giving an unwarranted authority to the old and familiar, and through shutting our minds so that no new light can get in.

The philosopher, then, is one who at the risk of being

thought queer, challenges common sense; he sets himself against the majority in order that the majority may be brought to reflect upon what they have through inertia or blindness taken for granted. He is the reckless critic, the insuppressible asker of questions, who doesn't know where to stop. He has a way of pinching the human intelligence, when he thinks it has gone to sleep. Every time there is a fresh revival of philosophical interest, and a new philosophical movement, as there is periodically, this is what happens. Some eccentric or highly reflective individual like Socrates, or Bacon, or Descartes, or Locke, or Kant, strays from the beaten track of thought, and then discovers that although it was easier to move in the old track, one is more likely to reach the goal if one beats out a new one. Such a thinker demands a re-examination of old premises, a revision of old methods; he stations himself at a new center, and adopts new axes of reference.

Philosophy is opposed to common sense, then, in so far as common sense is habitual and imitative. But there are other characteristics of common sense with which the true genius of philosophy is out of accord. We can discover these best by considering the terms of praise or blame which are employed in behalf of common sense. When ideas are condemned as contrary to common sense, what is ordinarily said of them? I find three favorite forms of condemnation: ideas are pronounced "unpractical," "too general," or "intangible." Any man of common sense feels these to be terms of reproach. It is implied, of course, that to be agreeable to common sense, ideas must be "practical," "particular," and "tangible." And it is the office of philosophy, as corrective of common sense, to show that such judgments, actual and implied, cannot be accepted as final.

PHILOSOPHY AND THE PRACTICAL

What is meant by "practical," in the vulgar sense? Let me take an example. Suppose a man to be trapped on the roof of a burning building. His friends gather round to make suggestions. One friend suggests that a ladder be brought from next door; another friend suggests that the man climb to an adjoining roof and descend by the rain pipe. These are practical suggestions. A third friend, on the other hand, wants to know what caused the fire, or why the man is trying to escape. He is promptly silenced on the ground that his inquiries are beside the point. Or approach a man in the heat of business and offer him advice. You will soon find out whether your advice is practical or not. If you have invented something, a physical or industrial mechanism, that will facilitate the matter in hand, you show that you are a practical man, and there is a chance that you will be listened to. But if you ask the business man why he is trying so hard to make money, and express some doubt as to its being worth while—well, let the veil be drawn. He may see you "out of hours," but you will scarcely recover his confidence. "Practical," therefore, would seem to mean *relevant to the matter in hand*. It is usual with adults to have something "in hand," to be busy about something, to be pursuing some end. The practical is anything that will serve the end already being pursued; the unpractical is anything else, and especially reflection on the end itself. Now the philosopher's advice is usually of the latter type. It is felt to be gratuitous. It does not help you to do what you are already doing; on the contrary, it is calculated to arrest your action. It is out of place in the office, or in business hours. What, then, is to be said for it? The answer, of course, is this: It is important not only to be moving, but to be moving in the right direction; not only to be doing something well, but to be doing something worth while. This is evidently true, but it is easily forgotten. Hence it becomes the duty of philosophy to remind men of it; to persuade men occasionally to reflect on their ends, and reconsider their whole way of life. To have a philosophy of life is to have reasons not only for the means you have selected, but for what you propose to accomplish by them.

PHILOSOPHY AND GENERALIZATION

Common sense also condemns what is "too general." In life it is said to be a "situation" and not a theory that confronts us. The man who is trusted is the man of experience, and experience is ordinarily taken to mean acquaintance with some group of individual *facts*. In political life what one needs is not general ideas, but familiarity with concrete circumstances; one must know men and measures, not man and principles. Historians are suspicious of vague ideas of civilization and progress; the important thing is to know just what happened. In the industrial world, what is needed is not a theory of economic value, but a knowledge of present costs, wages, and prices. As a preparation for life it is more important to train the eye and the hand, which can distinguish and manipulate, than the reason and imagination, which through their love of breadth and sweep are likely to blur details, or in their groping after the ultimate are led to neglect the immediate thing which really counts. Common sense would not, of course, condemn generalization altogether. It has too much respect for knowledge, and understands that there is no knowing without generalizing. There must be rules and classifications, even laws and theories. But the generalizing propensity of mind must be held in restraint; after a certain point it becomes absurd, fantastic, out of touch with fact, "up in the clouds." The man of common sense, planted firmly on the solid ground, views such speculations with contempt, amusement, or with blank amazement.

Philosophy offends against common sense, then, not because it generalizes, for, after all, no one can think at all without generalizing; but because it does not know when to stop. And the philosopher is bound to offend, because if he is true to his calling, *he must not stop*. It is his particular business to generalize as far as he can. He may have various motives for doing this. He may be prompted by mere "idle curiosity" to see how far he can go. Or he may believe that the search for the universal and the contemplation of it constitute the most exalted human activity. Or he may be prompted by the notion that his soul's salvation depends on his getting into right relations with the first cause or the ultimate ground of things. In any case he is allotted the task of formulating the most general ideas that the nature of things will permit. He can submit to no limitations imposed by considerations of expediency. He loses his identity altogether, unless he can think more roundly, more comprehensively, or more deeply, than other men. He represents no limited constituency of facts or interests; he is the thinker at large.

PHILOSOPHY AND THE TANGIBLE

It is significant that facts are reputed to be "solid," general ideas to be of a more vaporous or ghostly substance. Thus facts possess merit judged by the third standard of common sense, that of "tangibility." If we go back to the original meaning, the tangible, of course, is that which can be touched. Doubting Thomas was a man of common sense. Now we have here to do with something very original and elemental in human nature. Touch is the most primitive of the senses. And if we consider the whole history of living organisms, it is the experience or the anticipation of *contact* that has played the largest and the most indispensable part in their consciousness. That which can have contact with an organism is a body; hence bodies or physical things are the oldest and most familiar examples of known things. The status of other alleged things is doubtful; the mind does not feel thoroughly at home and secure in dealing with them. Physical science enjoys the confidence of common sense because, though it may wander far from bodies and imagine intangible ethers and energies, it always starts with bodies, and eventually returns to them. Furthermore, even ethers and energies excite the tactual imagination; one can almost feel them. The human imagination cannot abstain from doing the same thing even when it is perfectly well understood that it is illegitimate. God and the soul are spirits, to be sure; for that there is the best authority. But when they have passed through the average mind they have a distinctly corporeal aspect, as though the mind were otherwise helpless to deal with them.

Philosophy is not governed by an animus against the physical. Indeed philosophy is bound to recognize the possibility that it may turn out to be the case that all real substances are physical. But philosophy *is* bound to point out that there is a human bias in favor of the physical;

and it is bound so far as possible to counteract or discount that bias. Philosophy must nurture and protect those theories that aim especially to do justice to the non-physical aspects of experience, and protest against their being read out of court as "inconceivable" or inherently improbable. A generation ago philosophy was usually referred to as "mental and moral" philosophy. There is a certain propriety in this, not because philosophy is to confine itself to the mental and moral, but because philosophers alone can be depended upon to recognize these in their own right, and correct the exaggerated emphasis which common sense, and science as developed on the basis of common sense, will inevitably place on the physical.

OUR UNCONSCIOUS PHILOSOPHIZING

Philosophy, then, can afford to accept the unfavorable opinion of common sense, and may even boast of it. Philosophy *is* unpractical, too general, and intangible. If the condemnation implied in these terms were decisive and final, then philosophy would be compelled to give up. But philosophy is not merely contrary to common sense, for it *emancipates* the mind from common sense and establishes the more authoritative standards by which it is itself justified.

Though I should have persuaded you that philosophy is a strange thing which you must visit abroad in its own home, nevertheless I now hope to persuade you that you once entertained it unawares. Though, if philosophy is now to enter, you must expel from your mind the ideas that make themselves most at home there, this same philosophy was once a favorite inmate. Only you were too young, and your elders had too much common sense, to know that it was philosophy. Unless you were an extraordinary child you were very curious about what you called *the world;* curious as to who or what made it, why it was made, how it was made, why it was made as it is, and what it is like in those remote and dim regions beyond the range of your senses. Then you grew up, and having grown up, you acquired common sense, or rather common sense acquired you. It descended like a curtain, shutting out the twilight, and enabling you to see more clearly, but just as certainly making your view more circumscribed.[1] Since then you have come to feel that the questions of your childhood were foolish questions, or extravagant questions that no busy man can afford to indulge in. Philosophy, then, is more naïve than common sense; it is a more spontaneous expression of the mind. And when one recovers this first untrammeled curiosity about things, common sense appears not as the illumination of mature years, but rather as a hardening of the mind, the worldliness and complacency of a life immersed in affairs. It would not be unfair to say that the philosophical interest is the more liberal, common sense having about it something of the quality of professionalism.

But there is another and a more important sense in which philosophy is entertained unawares. It underlies various mature activities and interests whose standing is regarded as unquestionable. When these activities or interests are reflected upon, as sooner or later they are sure to be, it appears that they require the support of philosophy. This is most evident in the case of religion. We all of us participate in a certain religious tradition, and with most of us the principal elements of that tradition are taken for granted. We assume that there is a certain kind of life, a life of unselfishness, honesty, fortitude and love, let us say, that is highest and best. We assume that the worth of such a life is superior to wordly success; that it betokens a state of spiritual well-being to which every man should aspire, and for which he should be willing to sacrifice everything else. We assume, furthermore, that this type of life is the most important thing in the world at large. Thus we may suppose that the world was created, and that its affairs are controlled, by a being in whom this type of life is perfectly exemplified. God would then mean to us the cosmic supremacy of unselfishness, love, and the like. Or we may suppose that God is one who guarantees that those who are unselfish and scrupulous shall inherit the earth, and experience eternal happiness.

[1] Cf. Wordsworth's "Ode on Intimations of Immortality from Recollections of Early Childhood," in *Harvard Classics,* xli, 609.

DOUBT

Now observe what happens when one is overtaken with
doubt. One may come to question the worthiness of the
ideal. Is it not perhaps a more worthy thing to *assert* one's
self, than to sacrifice one's self? Or is not the great man
after all one who is superior to scruples, who sets might
above right? Who is to decide such a question? . Surely
not public opinion, nor the authority of any institution, for
these are dogmatic. Once having doubted, dogma will no
longer suffice. What is needed is a thoughtful comparison
of ideals, a critical examination of the whole question of
values and of the meaning of life. One who undertakes
such a study, every one who has made even a beginning of
such a study in the hope of solving his own personal problem, is *ipso facto* a moral philosopher. He is following in
the steps of Plato and of Kant, of Mill and of Nietzsche,
and he will do well to walk for at least a part of the way
with them.

Or suppose that our doubter questions, not the correctness
of the traditional ideal, but the certainty of its triumph.
Suppose that, like Job, he is impressed by the misfortunes of
the righteous, and set to wondering whether the natural
course of events is not utterly indifferent to the cause of
righteousness. Is not the world after all a prodigious accident, a cruel and clumsy play of blind forces? Do ideals
count for anything, or are they idle dreams, illusions, a
mere play of fancy? Can spirit move matter, or is it a helpless witness of events wholly beyond its control? Ask these
questions and you have set philosophical problems; answer
them, and you have made philosophy.

It is possible, of course, to treat doubt by the use of
anæsthetics. But such treatment does not cure doubt. With
many, indeed, anæsthetics will not work at all. They will
require an intellectual solution of intellectual questions;
their thought once aroused will not rest until it has gone to
the bottom of things. And problems forgotten in one generation will reappear to haunt the next. But even if it were
possible that the critical and doubting faculty should be
numbed or atrophied altogether, it would be the worst ca-

lamity that could befall mankind. For the virtue of religion must lie in its being true, and if it is to be true it must be open to correction as enlightenment advances. Salvation cannot be won by a timid clinging to comfortable illusions.

What should be done for the saving of our souls depends not upon an imaginary state of things, in which the wish is father to the thought, but upon the real state of things. Salvation must be founded on fact and not on fiction. In short, the necessity of philosophy follows from *the genuineness of the problems that underlie religion*. In religion, as in other activities and interests, it will not do forever to assume that things are so; but it becomes important from time to time to inquire into them closely and with an open mind. So to inquire into the ideals of life and the basis of hope, is philosophy.

PHILOSOPHY AND ART

Let us turn to another familiar human interest, that of the fine arts. There exists a vague idea, sometimes defended by the connoisseur, but more often ignored or repudiated by him, that the greatest works of art must express the general or the universal. Thus we feel that Greek sculpture is great because it portrays man, whereas most contemporary sculpture portrays persons; and that Italian painting of the Renaissance, expressing, as it does, the Christian interpretation of life, is superior to the impressionistic landscape which seizes on some momentary play of light and color. Now I do not for a moment wish to contend that such considerations as these are decisive in determining the merit of art. It may even be that they should not affect our purely æsthetic judgments at all. But it is clear that they signify an important fact about the mind of the artist, and also about the mind of the observer. The Greek sculptor and the Italian painter evidently have ideas of a certain sort. They may, it is true, have come by them quite unconsciously. But somehow the Greek sculptor must have had an idea not of his model merely, but of human nature and of the sort of perfection that befits it. And the Italian, over and above his sense of beauty, must have shared with his times an idea of the comparative values of things, perhaps of the superiority of the inner to the bodily life, or of heaven to this mundane sphere. And the observer as well must have a capacity for such ideas, or he will have lost something which the artist has to communicate. The case of poetry is perhaps clearer. Historical or narrative poems, love poems to a mistress's eyes or lips, evidently dwell on some concrete situation or on some rare and evanescent quality that for a moment narrows the mind and shuts out the world. On the other hand, there are poems like Tennyson's "Higher Pantheism," and "Maud," Browning's "Rabbi Ben Ezra," Wordsworth's "Tintern Abbey," or Matthew Arnold's "Dover Beach,"[2] in which the poet is striving to express through his peculiar medium some generalization of life. He has had some wider vision, revealing man in his true place in the whole scheme of things. Such a vision is rarely clear, perhaps never entirely articulate; but it betokens a mind struggling for light, dissatisfied with any ready-made plan and striving to emancipate itself from vulgar standards.

And one who reads such poetry must respond to its mood, and stretch the mind to its dimensions.

It is not necessary for our purpose to argue that the merit of poetry is proportional to the breadth of its ideas; but only to see that breadth of ideas is an actual feature of most poetry that is with general consent called great. The great poets have been men whose imagination has dared to leave the ground and ascend high enough to enable them to take the world-wide view of things. Now such imagination is philosophical; it arises from the same impulse as that which generates philosophy, requires the same break with common sense, and fundamentally it makes the same contribution to life. There is this difference, that while the poetic imagination either boldly anticipates the results of future arguments, or unconsciously employs the results of arguments already made, philosophy *is* an argument. Poetry, because it is a fine art, must present a finished thing in sensuous form; philosophy, because it is theory, must present definitions of what it is talking about, and reasons for what it says. And there is need of both poets and philos-

[2] See *H. C.*, xlii, 1038, 1052, 1148, 1183; xli, 650.

ophers since for every argument there is a vision and for every vision an argument.

The term "science" is now commonly employed to designate a band of special knowledges, headed by physics, pushing rapidly into the as yet unknown, and converting it first into knowledge, then into invention, and finally into civilization. Science is patronized and subsidized by common sense; and it is a profitable investment. But science, although often like Peter it repudiates philosophy and disclaims ever having known it, is of philosophical extraction and has philosophical connections that it cannot successfully conceal. Precisely as you and I were philosophers before the exigencies of life put a constraint upon the natural movements of the mind, so human knowledge was philosophical before it was "scientific," and became divided into highly specialized branches, each with a technique and plan of its own. There are many ways in which the philosophical roots and ligaments of the sciences are betrayed. The different sciences, for example, all have to do with the same world, and their results must be made consistent. Thus physics, chemistry, physiology, and psychology all meet in human nature, and have to be reconciled. Man is somehow mechanism, life, and consciousness all in one. How is this possible? The question is evidently one that none of these sciences alone can answer. It is not a scientific problem, but a philosophical problem; and yet it is inseparably connected with the work of science and the estimate that is to be put on its results.

Again, science employs many conceptions with no thorough examination of their meaning. This is the case with most, if not all, of the *fundamental* conceptions of science. Thus mechanics does not inform us concerning the exact nature of space and time; physics does not give us more than a perfunctory and formal account of the nature of matter; the greater part of biology and physiology proceeds without attempting carefully to distinguish and define the meaning of life; while psychology studies cases of consciousness without telling us exactly what, in essence, consciousness is. All of the sciences employ the notions of law and of causality; but they give us no theory of these things In short, the special sciences have certain rough working ideas which suffice for the purposes of experimentation and description, but which do not suffice for the purposes of critical reflection. All of the conceptions which I have mentioned furnish food for thought, when once thought is directed to them. They bristle with difficulties, and no one can say that science, in the limited sense in which the specialist and expert use the term, accomplishes anything to remove these difficulties. Science is able to get along, to make astonishing progress, and to furnish the instruments of a triumphant material civilization, without raising these difficulties. But suppose a man to ask, "Where do I stand, after all is said and done? What sort of a world do I live in? What am I myself? What must I fear, and what may I hope?" and there is no answering him except by facing these difficulties. There is no one who will even attempt to answer such questions except the philosopher.

THE PROBLEM OF ETHICS

When philosophy goes about its work it proves necessary to divide the question. There are no sharply bounded sub-divisions of philosophy; as problems become more fundamental, they tend to merge into one another, and the solution of one depends on the solution of the rest. But the mind must do one thing at a time in philosophy as in other affairs. Furthermore, the need of philosophy is felt in quite different quarters, which leads to a difference of approach and of emphasis.

Perhaps that portion of philosophy that is most easily considered by itself is Ethics, or what was a generation ago usually referred to as Moral Philosophy. There is no better introduction to Ethics than Plato's famous dialogue, "The Apology," [3] in which Socrates, defending himself against his accusers, describes and justifies the office of the moralist. As moralist, Socrates says that he took it upon himself to

[3] *H. C.,* ii, 3.

question men concerning the why and wherefore of their
several occupations. He found men busy, to be sure, but
strangely unaware of what they were about; they felt sure
they were getting somewhere, but they did not know where.
He did not himself pretend to direct them, but he did feel
sure that it was necessary to raise the question, and that in
that respect, at least, he was wiser than his fellows. The
moral of Socrates's position is that life cannot be ration-
alized without some definite conception of the *good* for the
sake of which one lives. The problem of the good thus becomes the central problem of Ethics. Is it pleasure, or
knowledge, or worldly success? Is it personal or social?
Does it consist in some inward state, or in external achievement? Is it to be looked for in this world, or in the hereafter? These are but variations of the same problem, as it
is attacked in turn by Plato, Aristotle, Christian theologians,
Hobbes, Rousseau, Kant, Mill, and the whole line of moral
philosophers. Other special problems emerge, and take their
place beside this. What, for example, is the relation of
moral virtue to the secular law? In Plato's "Crito,"[4] Socrates teaches that it is the first duty of the good man to
obey the law, and submit to punishment, even though he be
innocent; because the good life is essentially an orderly
life, in which the individual conforms himself to the political community to which he belongs by birth and nature.
Hobbes reached the same conclusion on different grounds.
Morality, he says, exists only so far as there is authority
and law; to save himself from the consequences of his own
inherent selfishness and unscrupulousness, man has delivered himself up forever to the state, and save so far as
enforced by the state there are no rights or duties at all.
Either one obeys the law or one lapses into that primitive
outlawry in which every man is for himself, the hunter and
the prey. How different is the teaching of Rousseau,[5] who
prophesied for an age in which men were sore from the rub
of the harness, and longed to be turned out to pasture. The
law, Rousseau preaches, is made for man, not man for the
law. Man has been enslaved by his own artificial contrivances, and must strive to return to the natural goodness and

[4] *H. C.*, ii, 31.   [5] *H. C.*, xxxiv, 167.

happiness that are his rightful inheritance. These are the questions that still lie at the basis of our political philosophy, and divide the partisans of the day, even though they know it not.

A somewhat different and perhaps more familiar turn is given to moral philosophy by Kant.[6] With him the central idea in the moral life is *duty*. It is not consequence or inclination that counts, but the state of the will. Morality is founded on a law of its own, far deeper than man-made statutes. This law is delivered to the individual through his "Practical Reason," and it is the last word in all matters affecting the regulation of conduct. Thus Kant puts the accent where Protestant and Puritanic Christianity puts it; whereas Plato, bidding us look to the rounding and perfecting of life, is the spokesman of that perennial Paganism that flourishes as vigorously to-day as it did before the advent of Christianity.

THE PHILOSOPHY OF RELIGION

Closely connected with Moral Philosophy there stands a group of problems that forms the nucleus of what may be called Philosophy of Religion. Suppose that a provisional answer has been obtained to the questions of Ethics. The good has been defined, and the duty of man made clear. What hope, then, is there of the realization of the good? May we be sure that it lies within the power of man to perform what duty prescribes? Thus there arises, first of all, the question of the status of man. Is he a creature, merely —a link in the chain of natural causes, able at most to contemplate his own helplessness? Or is he endowed with a power corresponding to his ideals, a power to control his destinies and promote the causes which he serves? This is the old and well-known problem of *freedom*. If you want to know what can be said for the prerogatives of man, read Kant; if you want to know what is made of man when he is assigned the status of creature merely, read Hobbes.[7] And what shall be said of the chance of man's surviving the dissolution of his body, and entering upon another life in

[6] *H. C.,* xxxii, 323, 337.   [7] *H. C.,* xxxiv, 323.

which he is not affected by the play of natural forces? The *immortality* of man is most elaborately and eloquently argued in Plato's "Phædo," [8] and again in Kant's "Critique of Practical Reason." But the crucial question in this whole range of problems is the question, not of man, but of God. What, in the last analysis, controls the affairs of this world? Is it a blind, mechanical force, or is it a moral force, which guarantees the triumph of the good, and the salvation of him who performs his duty? This is the most far-reaching and momentous question that can be asked, and it takes us over to that branch of philosophy that has acquired the name of "Metaphysics."

METAPHYSICS

The term "Metaphysics" has acquired a colloquial meaning that will mislead us unless we are on our guard. It is commonly used to mean such theories as have to do with the mysterious or occult. There is a certain justification for this usage, in that metaphysics is speculative rather than strictly experimental, and in that it takes us beyond the first appearances of things. But this is a question of method, and not of doctrine. To be a metaphysician one must push one's thinking to the uttermost boundaries, and one must not rest satisfied with any first appearances, or any common-sense or conventional conclusions. But there is no unnecessary connection whatever between metaphysics and the doctrine that reality is mysterious or transcendent or supernatural or anything of the kind. It is entirely possible that metaphysics should in the end conclude that things are precisely what they seem, or that nature and nature alone is real. Metaphysics is simply an attempt to get to the bottom of things, and ascertain if possible what is the fundamental constitution of reality, and what its first and last causes. There are two leading alternatives: the theory that justifies the belief in God; the theory that discredits it, reducing it to a work of the imagination, an act of sheer faith, of an ecclesiastical fiction. The classic example of the latter type of metaphysics, ordinarily known as Materialism, is to be found in

[8] *H. C.,* ii, 45.

Hobbes. An excellent example of the former is to be found in the writings of Bishop Berkeley.[9] As Hobbes sought to show that the only substance is body, so Berkeley sought to show that the only substance is spirit. The nature of spirit, according to Berkeley, is first and directly known in that knowledge which each man has of himself. Then, in order to account for the independent and excellent order of nature, one must suppose a universal or divine spirit that causes and sustains it, a spirit that is like ourselves in kind, but infinite in power and goodness.

THE THEORY OF KNOWLEDGE

A fourth group of problems that assumes great prominence in the literature of philosophy is called the Theory of Knowledge. Although of all philosophical inquiries this may seem at first glance most artificial and academic, a little reflection will reveal its crucial importance. Suppose, for example, that it is a question of the finality of science, or the legitimacy of faith. The question can be answered only by examining the methods of science in order to discover whether there is anything arbitrary in them that limits the scope of the results. And one must inquire what constitutes genuine knowledge, or when a thing is finally explained, or whether there be things that necessarily lie beyond the reach of human faculties, or whether it be proper to allow aspirations and ideals to affect one's conclusions. Bacon[10] and Descartes,[11] the founders of modern philosophy, devoted themselves primarily to such questions, so that all thought since their time has taken these questions as the point of departure. Furthermore, philosophy has called attention to a very peculiar predicament in which the human thinker finds himself. He seems compelled to begin with himself. When Descartes sought to reduce knowledge to a primal and indubitable certainty he found that certainty to be the knowledge that each thinker has of his own existence, and of the existence of his own ideas. And if a thinker begins with this nucleus, how is he ever to add anything to it; how is he ever to be sure of the existence of

[9] *H. C.*, xxxvii, 201.　　[10] *H. C.*, xxxix, 122, 150.　　[11] *H. C.*, xxxiv, 5.

anything which is not himself or his ideas? On the other hand, while my knowledge is most certainly of and within myself, yet it can scarcely be knowledge unless it takes me beyond myself. This has become the central difficulty of philosophy. It is a genuine difficulty, and yet everybody neglects it except the philosopher. Berkeley was led by an examination of this difficulty to conclude that if reality is to be assumed to be knowable, then it can be composed of nothing but thinkers and their ideas. And in this conclusion Berkeley has been followed by the whole school of the idealists, the school which has numbered among its members the most eminent thinkers of later times, and has inspired notable movements in German and English literature. Other schools have been led by an examination of the same difficulty to quite different conclusions. But this difficulty has been the crux of modern thought, and no one can hope to debate fundamental issues at all without meeting it.

Such, then, are some of the matters that at once come under discussion when one attempts to think radically and fundamentally. Philosophy is brought to these and like problems because it expresses the profound restlessness of the mind, a dissatisfaction with ready-made, habitual, or conventional opinions, a free and unbounded curiosity, and the need of rounding up the world and judging it for the purposes of life.

II. SOCRATES, PLATO, AND THE ROMAN STOICS

By Professor Charles Pomeroy Parker

WHEN Socrates grew up in the city of Athens, in the generation just after the Persian Wars, any Athenian citizen, however poor he might be, was at liberty to arrange his own life as he wished. Socrates made up his mind that money-making was not worth while, in comparison with the liberty to spend his time in thinking about truth. There was a great deal of lively thinking in the Greek world then, and Athens, under Pericles,[1] not only was winning her empire, but was finding that great thinkers, or at any rate their thoughts, loved to come to her. Pythagorean philosophers were wide awake in those days. They were discovering truth about the art of healing, they spent much successful work on astronomy, they were making progress in music, they studied mathematics, especially geometry. Many philosophers of other schools were studying fire, air, water, and earth, claiming that they changed into each other, as we say solids melt into liquids, and liquids dissolve into gases, and as some thinkers suppose that gas atoms are made up of electric units. Others were impressed by the great expanse of the sky, and said that the only way to find truth was to think of the universe as a great unchanging sphere. Others, again, held a doctrine of atoms, tiny invisible shapes of hard matter, which by combining or separating made the changing world.

SOCRATES AND ANAXAGORAS

Socrates, eagerly studying all these theories, heard at last of a philosopher, Anaxagoras, who said that Thought makes the world; but Anaxagoras did not seem to him to show the

[1] *Harvard Classics*, xii, 36ff.

rational way in which Thought would work. Rational
Thought, as Socrates viewed it, always tries to obtain some
practical good. Merely to show how one physical thing
changes into another, or sets another in motion, does not
account rationally for the world; and Anaxagoras, though
he talked about Thought, did not seem to Socrates to get at
the heart of rational activity. But Socrates, having once
caught the suggestion of Thought as a cause, never could set
it aside. To inquire into the nature of rational activity implies a careful study of men and of human minds.

SOCRATES AND THE PYTHAGOREANS

Now in that Age of Pericles there was a great interest
in men and all that concerned human life. Socrates loved
to talk with men. This put him in especial sympathy with
the Pythagoreans, who valued human souls and said that
men are immortal. Pythagoras, the founder of that school
of thought in the previous century, had organized a brotherhood of students, bound to each other by ties of religion,
austere life, and high thinking. This brotherhood had tried
to influence and improve the political life of the cities where
they lived. In the days of Socrates they had given up
politics, but never had lost their religious and human interest. Not only did they work in healing, in astronomy,
in music, and in geometry; they wanted to find the essence
of justice, beauty, life, and health. Such essences seemed
to give all the reality to human life. The Pythagoreans
conceived of them, strangely enough, as somehow mixed up
with geometry. Indeed, we ourselves are apt to speak of
justice as the square thing; but this metaphor of ours was
perhaps a reality to their minds. Different forms or shapes,
cubes, spheres, pyramids, triangles, circles, and squares, may
have seemed to them the essences of the world, and they
took a Greek word, ἰδέα, which meant *form* in those times,
to express their notion of essence; in that sense they tried
to find the *ideas* of beauty, or of temperance, or of health.
Socrates, being interested in this line of thought, made up
his mind to find the *ideas*. But he was not satisfied with '
such a geometrical notion of things as the Pythagoreans

seem to have held. He wanted to talk with men, and study life as it was reflected in human thoughts, hoping thus to get clearer notions of reality which would be a practical help to himself and others. A thing is made beautiful by the beauty in it. What is beauty? This was an important question for a Greek thinker; and to find the ideally beautiful life might be worth our effort also. An act is made just by the justice in it. What is the essence of justice? We and Socrates alike want to know that. Socrates found such inquiries puzzling, and was reduced to a kind of despair.

THE MISSION OF SOCRATES

Perhaps it was at this time that the Oracle of Delphi, which was controlled by influences highly sensitive to all the life of the time, said one day to an inquirer that Socrates was the wisest of men. This declaration was very perplexing to Socrates himself, who felt keenly his own ignorance. Eagerly questioning all kinds of men, to see if they could not give him wisdom after all, he soon found that their notions about the real essences of things were confused and contradictory. He realized that his mission was to clear up the thoughts of men. This is the first step in rational thinking, to define clearly our thoughts and agree about the essential nature of the things which our words denote.

SOCRATES AND PLATO

The "Apology," "Crito," and "Phædo"[2] of Plato present to us dramatically, in Plato's words, the thoughts of Socrates. They all deal with the last days of his life, in which his thoughts may well have been at their ripest. Very probably Plato developed some of the thoughts of Socrates to their logical results, going beyond what the master actually said, and giving the tendencies of his thinking. But we shall hardly get nearer to the essence of the real Socrates than by reading these dialogues. For instance, he would seem to have felt that souls are the permanent things; their very essence is to live and give life; justice, temperance, piety, beauty, and such *ideas* are eternal essences which give

[2] *H. C.,* ii, 3, 31, 45ff.

reality to the human world. Possibly the greater flights of imagination in the "Phædo" belong to Plato, and the perfecting of the whole theory; many have supposed that all the philosophy of the dialogue is Plato's. To disentangle his thought from his master's is hard; the two are really one great movement of human thought, which has affected the world profoundly. One line of its influence is seen in Aristotle, who, in spite of all his differences, was strongly influenced by the doctrine of real essences. Another line of Socrates's influence is seen in Stoicism.

ZENO AND STOICISM

Zeno, the founder of the Stoic school of philosophy, was a native of Cyprus, perhaps a merchant, who was shipwrecked on a certain voyage, and as a result of this apparent misfortune turned to philosophy. Men who wanted to be philosophers were likely to come to Athens in those days, two or three generations after Socrates. Zeno, being at Athens, one day sat down, so the story goes, by a bookseller's stall, where the bookseller was reading aloud from a book of Xenophon, the "Memorabilia," which described the conversations of Socrates. Greatly interested, Zeno inquired of the bookseller where such men as Socrates lived. Just at that moment Crates, a good man, a poor man, who formed his life on the life of Socrates, was passing by. The bookseller pointed to him, saying: "Follow this man." Zeno rose up and followed Crates; and the result was that Socrates's belief in the supremacy of reason and in the human soul and in the value of human life and freedom profoundly affected the teaching of Zeno. We may not search out now the other influences felt in Stoicism. The scientific, religious, and logical doctrines of this school are very important, and their development is interesting. But certainly the Socratic thought is strongly felt in this famous school.

THE ROMAN STOICS

Four or five centuries later, Epictetus,[3] a slave (afterward a freedman), and Marcus Aurelius,[4] an emperor of Rome,

[3] *H. C.,* ii, 117ff.   [4] *H. C.,* ii, 193ff.

in their meditations or conversations on human life show
the living flame of thought which was kindled in Socrates,
and handed down from him for many generations. We are
apt to think of Stoics as men who crushed all their feelings,
and went about the world with solemn faces and sad hearts,
bearing trouble as they might. But the best Stoics of all
times cared much for human nature and human freedom.
They studied men, and found man's nature to be essentially
rational. The terrible thing to them was to see this rational
soul losing its self-control and, bewildered in a vain struggle to find happiness by submission to the outside world,
getting into a turmoil of fluttering excitement over things
which were not in its own power. But what was in their
own power they tried to handle divinely, with real energy.
For they felt that man's rational soul is akin to the good
Power which makes and moves the universe. And herein
they agreed with Socrates. The slave and the emperor were
in harmony with the free Athenian.

III. THE RISE OF MODERN PHILOSOPHY

By Professor Ralph Barton Perry

W E WERE once taught that after having slept
soundly through "the Dark Ages," Europe was
suddenly awakened in 1453 by the Fall of Constantinople. We now know that it had been light all the
while and that Europe had, to say the least, been in a very
lively state of somnambulism. We know that for many centuries before 1453 men had been living very intensely and
very nobly; and with a seriousness and elevation of thought
that have perhaps had no parallel. The age that created
Gothic art, and dreamed so splendid a dream as the Holy
Roman Empire, can scarcely be said to be lacking in imagination and enlightenment.

But that something important happened to the European
mind in and about the fifteenth century no scholar is so
iconoclastic as to deny. It was not so much an awakening
of thought as a change of direction which proved in the
sequel to be amazingly fruitful. It may perhaps best be
described as *a return to the sources*. This is characteristic
of all of its more notable manifestations, such as the retro-
spect of antiquity, the reexamination of institutions, and
the more direct observation of nature. This turn of thought
back to the originals and roots of things, this general fresh-
ening up by the admixture of new experiences, had its
effects upon every interest and work of man. So there was,
among other things, a Renaissance philosophy, which meant
chiefly a new study of some ancient philosophy. Pico of
Mirandola founded a new cult of Plato; Pomponatius defended the Greek or Alexandrist interpretation of Aristotle
against the Averroist and orthodox interpretations; while

Montaigne[1] revived the ancient scepticism. But what was more significant for the future of philosophy, came not directly through the influence of the spirit of the age upon philosophy, but through the influence of this spirit first upon science, and, indirectly through science, upon philosophy. The great men of the age, so far as the future of philosophy is concerned, were not Pico and Pomponatius, but Copernicus and Galileo.

THE COPERNICAN DISCOVERY

Copernicus[2] ventured to assert that the earth moved. He could scarcely have astonished and disturbed men more if he had actually set it moving. The belief in the earth as the firm center of creation, lighted by sun and moon, encircled by celestial spheres, and furnished for the great drama of man's fall and redemption—this belief was itself the firm center of all human belief. It seemed impossible to move it without bringing down in ruin that whole grand scheme of things to which man had been fitting himself for centuries, and where he had at length come to feel himself at home. How shall one find a place for God, and a place for man, and how shall they find one another, in a universe with neither beginning nor end, neither center nor boundaries? This was the problem to which the great martyr Bruno devoted himself, and his death in 1600 may well serve as a monument to mark the beginning of modern philosophy.

Bruno saw that the world can no longer be divided into terrestrial and celestial regions, with the empyrean beyond. There can be no God above nature, or before or after nature, because nature itself is infinite. The universe is a system of countless worlds, none more divine than the rest. God is therefore not local, but universal; he is the life and beauty of the whole. This idea, recovered by Bruno from Stoicism and Neo-Platonism, and appropriated to the needs of the age which Copernicus had robbed of its ancient land-

[1] For Montaigne, see *Harvard Classics*, xxxii, 5, 9; and on the Renaissance in general see Lecture III in the series on History and Lecture III (on Cellini) in the series on Biography.
[2] See Copernicus's Dedication of his "Revolutions of the Heavenly Bodies," *H. C.*, xxxix, 55.

marks, persisted in the latent pantheism of Descartes and his followers, and in the avowed pantheism of Spinoza, was suffered to lapse during the eighteenth century, was revived again by Lessing[3] and Herder, and became one of the central ideas of the great Romantic and Hegelian movements in Germany in the nineteenth century.

THE CONTRIBUTION OF GALILEO

Copernicus contributed to modern thought an epoch-making hypothesis. Galileo contributed something less definite, but even more germinal—a new method. It would be safer to say that he represented two methods, the method of *discovery,* and the method of *exact or mathematical description.* He was neither the only discoverer of his age nor the only mathematical physicist, but he was the preeminent embodiment of both of these moving ideas.

In 1610, a year or so after the construction of his telescope, Galileo published his "Sidereal Messenger," "announcing," to quote from the title-page, "great and very wonderful spectacles, and offering them to the consideration of every one, but especially of philosophers and astronomers; which have been observed by Galileo Galilei . . . by the assistance of a perspective glass lately invented by him; namely, in the face of the moon, in innumerable fixed stars in the milky-way, in nebulous stars, but especially in four planets which revolve round Jupiter at different intervals and periods with a wonderful celerity." This is the Galileo of the telescope, the prophet of an age of discovery. But greater than the Galileo of the telescope is the Galileo who formulated the three laws of motion, and so became the founder of the modern science of dynamics. He explained the fall of bodies to the earth, not by ascribing them to a vague force of gravity, but by formulating exact mathematical ratios of time and distance, so that it was possible to deduce, predict and prove, with quantitative exactness. In other words, he brought the clearness and certainty of mathematics into the field of physical events.

[3] See Lessing's "Education of the Human Race," *H. C.,* xxxii, 195.

MODERN EMPIRICISM

Now this twofold influence of Galileo is the most important source of what is new in modern philosophy. Bacon
and Locke were philosophical observers, trusting sense above
reason, and animated by the spirit of discovery. Descartes,
Hobbes, and Spinoza were mathematical philosophers, advocates of reason, not so much concerned at first to widen
knowledge as to make it more certain.

Bacon (1561-1626) was the founder of modern "empiricism," or the philosophy of sense-experience. He criticized
those faults of his age that he thought stood in the way of
clear *seeing,* such faults as verbalism, anthropomorphism, or
undue regard for tradition and authority. He formulated
a new "Organon" ("Novum Organum"[4]), a logic and
methodology which was to correct and supplement the
Aristotelian organon, and afford a basis for scientific procedure. But Bacon was significant not so much for what
he formulated as for what he prophesied. He was the first
to dream that magnificent dream which has been so largely
realized in the course of the last century: the dream of the
progressive control of nature through the patient and self-
denying study of it. The kingdom of man, the "New
Atlantis,"[5] is to be founded on knowledge. "Human knowledge and human power meet in one; for where the cause is
not known, the effect cannot be produced. Nature to be
commanded must be obeyed; and that which in contemplation is as the cause, is in operation as the rule." Observe
nature in order that you may use nature, thus converting
it into the habitation, instrument, and treasure of man.
Here is the supreme maxim of our modern world, and the
chief ground of its peculiar confidence and hopefulness.

MODERN RATIONALISM

Descartes and Hobbes were the founders of modern
rationalism, but each in a different way. Descartes (1596-
1650) found mathematics a *model* of procedure. In other
words, he proposed that men should philosophize after the

[4] *H. C.* xxxix, 122, 150.   [5] *H. C.,* iii, 151.

manner of mathematics. He did not believe that mathematics, with its applications to physics, was itself the highest knowledge. He sought rather to formulate a logic that should be as exact as mathematics, but more fundamental and universal; thus affording a basis for the demonstration of the higher truths concerning God and the soul. The "Discourse on Method"[6] is a record of the author's profound regard for mathematics and of his own search for a like certainty in philosophy.

But Hobbes (1588-1679) was a follower of Galileo in a different sense. He proposed not so much to imitate mathematics as to adopt and extend it. He represents that idea which La Place so eloquently proclaimed a century later, and which the work of Newton seemed so nearly to realize, the idea of a universal mechanism, in which the laws of bodily motion should apply even to the origins of nature and to man. It was hoped thus to bring it about that all things should be as demonstrably known, and as certainly predictable, as the velocities and orbits of the planets. To this end the author of "The Leviathan"[7] regards both man and society, the little man and the giant composite man, as simply delicate and complicated mechanisms, moved by an impulse of self-seeking.

These, then, are the three forms in which the science of the Renaissance as embodied in Galileo is communicated to modern philosophy. Bacon, Descartes, and Hobbes became in turn the sources of the new tendencies that make up the philosophy of the seventeenth and eighteenth centuries. The empiricism of Bacon was renewed in Locke,[8] who applied "the plain historical method" to the study of the human mind; continued by Berkeley,[9] who reduced even being to perception ("esse est, percipi") ; was brought to a sceptical crisis in Hume;[10] but persisted as the national philosophy of England. The rationalism of Descartes afforded a basis for the great metaphysical systems of Continental philosophy, for the monism of Spinoza and the pluralism of Leibnitz; was degraded to a mere formalism and dogmatism in Wolff; but nevertheless persisted in the new idealistic

---

[6] H. C., xxxiv, 5.   [7] H. C., xxxiv, 323.   [8] H. C., xxxvii, 9.
[9] H. C., xxxvii, 201.   [10] H. C., xxxvii, 305.

German philosophy which was inspired by Kant. The physical philosophy of Hobbes, mingled with similar elements drawn from the philosophies of Locke and Descartes, developed into the French materialistic movement which attended the outbreak of the Revolution, and remains the model for all philosophers who seek to make a metaphysics out of physics. The forms which these three tendencies assumed during the eighteenth century, and especially their excessive emphasis on facts and necessities, provoked the great reaction which bore fruit in the following century, but which was already anticipated in Pascal's philosophy of *faith*,[11] in Rousseau's philosophy of *feeling*,[12] and in Lessing's philosophy of *development*.[13]

[11] *H. C.*, xlviii. [12] *H. C.*, xxxiv, 167. [13] *H. C.*, xxxii, 195.

IV. INTRODUCTION TO KANT

By Professor Ralph Barton Perry

I T IS generally admitted that Kant is one of the great
epoch-making philosophers, like Socrates and Descartes.
There are two things that are universally true of intellectual epoch-makers: first, they embody in themselves
certain general tendencies of their age, which are usually
due to a reaction against the more pronounced tendencies
of the previous age; second, their thought is peculiarly germinal, and among their followers assumes a maturer form,
in which the originators would scarcely recognize it as their
own. Let us consider these two aspects of the philosophy
of Kant.

REVOLT AGAINST PURE EMPIRICISM AND PURE RATIONALISM

From among the pronounced tendencies of the seventeenth and eighteenth centuries I shall select two for special
emphasis. In the first place, it was characteristic of these
two centuries to isolate and over-emphasize either one or
the other of the two great sources of human knowledge,
sense-perception or reason. Locke and his followers attempted to convert reason into a mere echo of sense; while
for Descartes and his followers, sense was always viewed
with suspicion as confusing the intellect, or as supplying
only an inferior sort of knowledge which must yield precedence to "rational science." Extreme sensationalism or
empiricism seemed to have reached an impasse in Hume;
while rationalism degenerated into formalism and word-
making in Wolff. Thus Kant's greatest work, the "Critique
of Pure Reason" (1789), was an attempt to correct these
extreme views by making the necessary provision for both
sense-perception and reason. Perception without conception, he said, is blind; while conception without perception

159

is empty. Kant's critique was aimed first at excessive emphasis on sense-perception. He showed that the bare sequence of sense-impressions can never yield the connections, necessities, unities, laws, etc., which are required for science. The intellect must supply these itself. They constitute what Kant called "categories," the instruments which the mind must use when it works in that peculiar way which is called knowing. But it follows that they are not by themselves sufficient for knowledge. They cannot themselves be known in the ordinary way because they are *what one knows with*. And since they are instruments, it follows that they require some material to work upon; they cannot spin knowledge out of nothing. Hence the data of sense are indispensable also. In short, to know is to systematize, by the instrumentalities native to the mind, the content conveyed by the senses. This is the Kant of the first Critique, the Kant of technical philosophy who numbers many faithful devotees among the thinkers of to-day.

REASSERTION OF THE SPIRITUAL

A second and more general tendency of seventeenth and eighteenth century philosophy was its comparative neglect of what are vaguely called the "spiritual" demands. These centuries themselves may be regarded as a reaction against what was thought to be the excessive anthropomorphism of earlier times. Man had erred by reading himself into his world; now he was to view it impersonally and dispassionately. He might prefer to record the findings of perception, or the necessities of reason, but in either case he was to repress his own interests and yearnings. Of course at the time it was confidently expected that morality and religion would in this way be served best. Men believed in the possibility of a "natural religion," without mystery or dogma, a rational morality without authority, and a demonstrable theology without either revelation or faith. But gradually there developed a sense of failure. Man had left himself too much out of it, and felt homeless and unprotected. Early in the seventeenth century Pascal had announced the religious bankruptcy of the mathematical rationalism of Descartes.[1] Natural religion was readily converted into atheism by Hume. The most vigorous and stirring protest against the whole spirit of the age was made by Rousseau, who urged men to trust their feelings, make allowance for the claims of the heart, and return to the elemental and spontaneous in human nature. The same note was caught up by Jacobi and Herder. Finally Lessing, in his "Education of the Human Race" (1780),[2] turned the attention of philosophy to the history of culture, to the significance of human life in its historical unfolding. It is a strange paradox that Immanuel Kant, valetudinarian and pedant that he was, should have represented this rising revolt of sentiment and faith. But such was the fact. Let us, then, view him in this light.

THE KANTIAN REVOLUTION

One of the most famous of Kant's remarks was that he proposed to effect a Copernican Revolution in thought. As Copernicus had established a new center for the planetary system, so he proposed to establish a new center for knowledge. This new center was to be the mind itself. The errors of the earlier period had been largely due, he thought, to the attempt to make knowledge center in the object, it being expected that the mind should reflect, either by perception or reason, the nature of an outward and independently existing thing. This method leads inevitably, said Kant, either to scepticism or to what is just as bad for philosophical purposes, dogmatism. The new way is to expect that the object shall conform to the mind. Thus nature, which in the earlier view was construed as an external order by which the mind is affected, or which the mind is somehow to reproduce by its own ratiocination, is now construed as the original creation of the mind. It owes all of its arrangements and connections, even its very distribution in space and time, to the constitution of the knower. The mind imposes its conditions on the object, and thus gets out of nature what it has already put into it. The bearing of

[1] See Pascal's "Thoughts," *Harvard Classics*, xlviii, 33f.; 414f.
[2] *H. C.*, xxxii, 195.

this on man's spiritual claims is apparent. It is now nature that is creature; and man, in virtue of his intelligence, that is creator. The fatal world of fact and necessity, that seemed so alien to spirit, turns out to be but an expression of the intellectual part of spirit.

THE SPHERE OF THE WILL

But a Rousseau might still complain that this victory of spirit over matter was dearly bought, since it left the rest of spirit in harsh subjection to the intellectual part. What guarantee is there that the intellect, thus clothed with authority, will make due allowance for the claims of sentiment and conscience? Kant's answer lies in his famous doctrine of the "primacy of the practical reason."[3] Nature, he says, is indeed the work of the theoretical faculties; and the theoretical faculties can recognize only facts and laws. But the theoretical faculties are themselves but the expression of something deeper, namely, the will. Thinking is a kind of action, and action in general has its own laws, revealed in conscience, and taking precedence of the rules that govern any special department of action, such as knowing. This does not mean that conscience over-rules the understanding, or that the will can violate nature; but that conscience reveals another world, deeper and more real than nature, which is the proper sphere for the exercise of the will. This is the world of God, freedom, and immortality. It cannot be known in the strict sense, only nature can be known; but it can and must be believed in, because it is presupposed in all action. If one is to live at all, one must claim such a world to live in. So Kant, who began by justifying science, ended by justifying faith.

THE FOLLOWERS OF KANT

I have said that it was the fate of epoch-makers to have their ideas promptly converted into something that they never meant. Kant was a cautious, or as he terms it, a "critical" thinker. He concerned himself with questions

[3] *H. C.*, xxxii, 323ff, 337ff.

regarding the possibility of knowledge and the legitimacy of faith; and avoided so far as possible making positive assertions about the world. But his followers were fired with speculative zeal, and at once passed over from "criticism" to metaphysics.

There resulted the great Romantic and Idealistic movement that formed the main current of philosophical thought during the nineteenth century.

In the idealistic movement the Kantian theory of knowledge is united with a pantheistic tendency that may be traced continuously back even to Plato himself. According to this pantheistic view, nature and God are the same thing viewed differently. God, foreshortened and taken in the limited perspectives defined by man's earth-bound intelligence, is nature; nature, consummated, seen in its fullness and harmony, is God.

For all we have power to see, is a straight staff bent in a pool;

And the ear of man cannot hear, and the eye of man cannot see;
But if we could see and hear, this Vision—were it not He? [4]

Nature, on Kantian grounds, is the work of intelligence, and intelligence, in turn, obeys some deeper spiritual law. That law, when interpreted according to the Platonic-pantheistic tradition, is the perfection of the whole. There are many possible variations of the view. The perfection of the whole may be regarded as a moral perfection, the ideal of the moral will, as suggested by Kant, and more positively and constructively maintained by Fichte; or as the ideal of reason, as was maintained by Hegel and his followers; or as a general realization of all spiritual values, a perfection transcending moral and rational standards, and more nearly approached in the experience of beauty, or in flashes of mystical insight, as was proclaimed by the sentimentalists and romanticists. In the popular literary expressions of the view, these varieties have alternated, or have been indiscriminately mingled. But it is this view in some form that has inspired those English poets and essayists, such as Coleridge, Wordsworth, Carlyle, Emerson, Tennyson, and

[4] Tennyson, "The Higher Pantheism," *H. C.*, xlii, 1038.

Browning,[5] who so profoundly influenced the men of the
last generation.   There is thus a continuous current of
thought from the closest philosophy of the sage of
Königsberg to the popular incentives and consolations
of to-day.

[5] See reference in *H. C.*, 1, 39.

V. EMERSON

By Professor Chester Noyes Greenough

"**HE IS,**" said Matthew Arnold of Emerson, "the friend and aider of those who would live in the spirit." These well-known words are perhaps the best expression of the somewhat vague yet powerful and inspiring effect of Emerson's courageous but disjointed philosophy.

EMERSON AS LAY PREACHER

Descended from a long line of New England ministers, Emerson, finding himself fettered by even the most liberal ministry of his day, gently yet audaciously stepped down from the pulpit and, with little or no modification in his interests or utterances, became the greatest lay preacher of his time. From the days of his undergraduate essay upon "The Present State of Ethical Philosophy" he continued to be preoccupied with matters of conduct: whatever the object of his attention—an ancient poet, a fact in science, or an event in the morning newspaper—he contrives to extract from it a lesson which in his ringing, glistening style he drives home as an exhortation to a higher and more independent life.

EMERSON AND CALVINISM

Historically, Emerson marks one of the largest reactions against the Calvinism of his ancestors. That stern creed had taught the depravity of man, the impossibility of a natural, unaided growth toward perfection, and the necessity of constant and anxious effort to win the unmerited reward of being numbered among the elect. Emerson starts with the assumption that the individual, if he can only come into possession of his natural excellence, is the most godlike of creatures. Instead of believing with the Calvinist that as a man grows better he becomes more unlike his natural self (and therefore can become better only by an act of divine mercy), Emerson believes that as a man grows in excellence he becomes more like his natural self. It is common to hear the expression, when one is deeply stirred, as by sublime music or a moving discourse: "That fairly lifted me out of myself." Emerson would have said that such influences lift us *into* ourselves.

THE OVER-SOUL

For one of Emerson's most fundamental and frequently recurring ideas[1] is that of a "great nature in which we rest as the earth lies in the soft arms of the atmosphere," an "Over-Soul, within which every man's particular being is contained and made one with all other," which "evermore tends to pass into our thought and hand and become wisdom and virtue and power and beauty."[2] This is the incentive —the sublime incentive of approaching the perfection which is ours by nature and by divine intention—that Emerson holds out when he asks us to submit us to ourselves to all instructive influences.

These instructive influences, according to Emerson, are chiefly Nature, the Past, and Society. Let us notice how Emerson bids us use these influences to help us into our higher selves.

NATURE

Nature, which he says[3] "is loved by what is best in us," is all about us, inviting our perception of its remotest and most cosmic principles by surrounding us with its simpler manifestations. "A man does not tie his shoe without recognizing laws which bind the farthest regions of nature."[4] Thus man "carries the world in his head."[5] Whether he be a great scientist, proving by his discovery of a sweeping physical law that he has some such constructive sense as that which guides the universe, or whether he be a poet beholding trees as "imperfect men," who "seem to bemoan

[1] Perhaps most clearly put in "The Over-Soul," *Harvard Classics*, v. 137ff.
[2] *H. C.*, v, 138.   [3] *H. C.*, v, 238.   [4] *H. C.*, v, 241.   [5] *H. C.*, v, 241.

their imprisonment, rooted in the ground,"[6] he is being brought into his own by perceiving "the virtue and pungency of the influence on the mind of material objects, whether inorganic or organized."[7]

THE PAST

Ranging over time and space with astonishing rapidity and binding names and things together that no ordinary vision could connect, Emerson calls the Past also to witness the need of self-reliance and a steadfast obedience to intuition.[8] The need of such independence, he thought, was particularly great for the student, who so easily becomes overawed by the great names of the Past and reads "to believe and take for granted."[9] This should not be, nor can it be if we remember what we are. "Meek young men grow up in libraries believing it their duty to accept the views which Cicero, which Locke, which Bacon have given, forgetful that Cicero, Locke, and Bacon were only young men in libraries when they wrote these books."[10] When we sincerely find, therefore, that we cannot agree with the Past, then, says Emerson, we must break with it, no matter how great the prestige of its messengers. But often the Past does not disappoint us; often it assists us in our quest to become our highest selves. For in the Past there have been many men of genius; and, inasmuch as the man of genius has come nearer to being continually conscious of his relation to the Over-Soul, it follows that the genius is actually more ourselves than we are. So we often have to fall back upon more gifted souls to interpret for us what we mean but cannot say. Any supreme triumph of expression, therefore, should arouse in us not humility, still less discouragement, but renewed consciousness that "one nature wrote and the same reads."[11] So it is in travel or in any other form of contact with the Past: we cannot derive any profit or see any new thing except we remember that "the world is nothing, the man is all."[12]

[6] H. C., v, 240.   [7] H. C., v, 248.
[8] The uses of the past and the right spirit in which to approach it, are finely set forth in "The American Scholar" (H. C., v, 5ff).
[9] Bacon, "Of Studies" (H. C., iii, 128).
[10] H. C., v, 9.   [11] H. C., v, 11.   [12] H. C., v, 23.

SOCIETY

Similar are the uses of Society. More clearly than in Nature or in the Past, we see in certain other people such likeness to ourselves, and receive from the perception of that likeness such inspiration, that a real friend "may well be reckoned the masterpiece of nature." [13] Yet elsewhere Emerson has more than once urged us not to be "too much acquainted" [14] : all our participation in the life of our fellows, though rich with courtesy and sympathy, must be free from bending and copying. We must use the fellowship of Society to freshen, and never to obscure, "the recollection of the grandeur of our destiny." [15]

EMERSON'S UNIVERSALITY

Such, in some attempt at an organization, are a few of Emerson's favorite ideas, which occur over and over again, no matter what may be the subject of the essay. Though Emerson was to some degree identified, in his own time, with various movements which have had little or no permanent effect, yet as we read him now we find extraordinarily little that suggests the limitations of his time and locality. Often there are whole paragraphs which if we had read them in Greek would have seemed Greek. The good sense which kept him clear of Brook Farm because he thought Fourier "had skipped no fact but one, namely life," kept him clear from many similar departures into matters which the twenty-first century will probably not remember. This is as it should be in the essay, which by custom draws the subjects for its "dispersed meditations" from the permanent things of this world, such as Friendship, Truth, Superstition, and Honor. One of Emerson's sources of strength, therefore, is his universality.

HIS STYLE

Another source of Emerson's strength is his extraordinary compactness of style and his range and unexpected-

[13] *H. C.,* v, 116.   [14] *H. C.,* v, 217.   [15] *H. C.,* v, 217.

ness of illustration. His gift for epigram is, indeed, such
as to make us long for an occasional stretch of leisurely
commonplace. But Emerson always keeps us up—not less
by his memorable terseness than by his startling habit of
illustration. He loves to dart from the present to the remotest past, to join names not usually associated, to link
pagan with Christian, or human with divine, in single rapid
sentences, such as that[16] about "Scipio, and the Cid, and Sir
Philip Sidney, and Washington, and every pure and valiant
heart, who worshiped Beauty by word or by deed."

Not less notable than his universality of thought, his
compactness of style, and his swiftness and range of illustration, is Emerson's delightful benignity of tone. It would
be hard to find any one whose opposition is so high minded,
whose refusal is so gentle, whose good will—though perhaps never anxious—is so uniformly evident. The sweetness of Emerson's face, as we know it from his most famous
portrait, is to be felt throughout his work.

If, in spite of all these admirable qualities, Emerson's ideas
seem too vague and unsystematic to satisfy those who feel
that they could perhaps become Emersonians if there were
only some definite articles to sign, it must be remembered
that Emerson wishes to develop independence rather than
apostleship, and that when men revolt from a system because they believe it to be too definite and oppressive, they
are likely to go to the other extreme. That Emerson did
go so far toward this extreme identifies him with a period
notable for its enthusiastic expansion of thought. That he
did not systematize or restrict means that he was obedient
to the idea that what really matters is not that by exact
terminology, clever tactics, and all the niceties of reasoning
a system of philosophy shall be made tight and impregnable
for others to adopt, but rather that each of us may be persuaded to hitch his own particular wagon to whatever star
for him shines brightest.

[16] *H. C.*, v. 222.

BIOGRAPHY

I. GENERAL INTRODUCTION

By WILLIAM ROSCOE THAYER

BIOGRAPHY is the key to the best society the world has ever had. By the best society I do not mean those exclusive circles, based on wealth, privilege, or heredity, which have flourished at all times and in every place. I mean the men and women who, by the richness of their talents or the significance of their careers, or, it may be, by some special deed, have emerged from the throng. One of the strongest instincts planted in us is our aversion to bores. Biography, as by a short cut, admits us to the fellowship of the choice spirits of the past four thousand years, among whom we shall find entertainment in endless variety. And not entertainment only; for entertainment is not the end of life, but its sweetener and strengthener.

To develop our talents for good, to build up character, to fit ourselves, like the cutwater of a ship, to cleave whatever seas of experience Fate may steer us into, to set ourselves a high, far goal and always consciously, through storm or shine, to seek that goal that is the real concern of life. On this quest biography shows the way by example.

Most of us have intervals of tedium or depression when we try to get out of ourselves. Or it may be some stroke of ill-fortune, some sorrow, some moral lapse, some desperate blunder, locks us up within ourselves as in a dungeon. Then biography comes to our rescue, and we forget ourselves in following the career of other men and women who may have passed through similar ordeals. The loneliness of grief loses some of its poignancy, the agonizing isolation which sin creates round the sinner is broken in upon by the knowledge that others have suffered or failed. and yet found strength to endure and to return

Evidently, great fiction, whether it be in the form of drama, tragedy, or novel, serves the same purpose of taking us out of ourselves, by teaching us how imaginary persons plan and act, undergo joy or pain, conquer or fall. I do not wish to belittle any fiction which can justify itself by substantial charm or symbolical import; and as I shall discuss later some of the relations between fiction and biography, it will suffice to remark now that the highest praise that can be bestowed on the creations of fiction is that they are true to life. Achilles, sulking in his tent; Othello, maddened by jealousy; visionary Don Quixote, mistaking windmills for giants; Mephistopheles, Becky Sharp, Colonel Newcome, Silas Marner, and all the other immortals in the world of fiction live on by virtue of their lifelikeness. But life itself, and not its counterfeit, is the very stuff of biography.

BIOGRAPHY NOT MERE EULOGY

.One reason why biography dropped behind in the race for popularity with fiction is that it was taken for granted that the biographer must deal in eulogy only. His subjects were usually marvels—we may almost say monsters—of virtue. Most of us are so conscious of being a composite of good and bad that we are properly sceptical when we read of persons too pure and luminous to cast a shadow. We tolerate the pious fibs carved in an epitaph on a tombstone—the lapidary, as Dr. Johnson remarked, is not under oath; we discount the flattery of the avowed panegyrist, but when the epitaph or the eulogy is puffed out through a volume or two of biography, we balk and decline to read.

Lives of this kind are seldom written nowadays. They are too obviously untrue to deceive any one. Candidates for political or other office may connive at pen portraits of themselves which no more resemble them than Apollo; but these productions, like the caricatures of the day, are soon forgotten. In earlier times, even among English-speaking folk, laudation was the accepted tribute which the lower paid to the higher. Among monarchs, prelates, nobles, generals, poets, artists, or persons of the smallest distinction whatsoever, modesty could not be called a lost art, because it had never been found. And only recently a prime minister, equally cynical and subtly subservient, divulged that even he could not appease his sovereign's appetite for adulation. In general, however, it is now commonly the fashion to assume the virtue of modesty by those who have it not, and the professional flatterer finds fewer opportunities than formerly. Yet we need only glance at the biographies which have come down to us from the ages most addicted to artificial manners and speech in order to see that these, too, bear the stamp of sincerity. There is always the unconscious record, the expression or tone peculiar to the time, to betray them; and then, few writers have ever been cunning enough to dupe more than one generation—their own.

Nobody need forego the inestimable delights of biography from fear of being the dupe of some devious biographer. It requires no long practice to train yourself to sift the genuine from the false—a branch of intellectual detective work which possesses the zest of mystery, abounds in surprises, and can be carried on at your own fireside.

So inevitably does temperament register itself that it cannot be concealed even in autobiography, which some persons unwisely avoid because they suppose that those who write their lives set out with the deliberate purpose of painting themselves as more wise or virtuous, clever or courageous, than they really were. But though any special incident narrated by a Benvenuto Cellini cannot be verified, the sum of his amazing "Life"[1] reveals to us Cellini himself, that perfect product of the Italian Renaissance in its decline—versatile, brilliant, wicked, superstitious, infidel, fascinating, ready to kill himself toiling to perfect a medal, or to kill a neighbor for some passing whim. Even Goethe, who wrote the most artificial of autobiographies, recomposing the events of his childhood and youth so as to give them sequence and emphasis that belong to a work of fiction, even he, Olympian poseur that he was, could not by this device have hidden, if he had wished, his essential self from us.

We may well dismiss, therefore, the suspicion which has sometimes hovered over biography. The best lives are among the most precious possessions we have; even the

[1] *Harvard Classics,* xxxi; and cf. Lecture III, below.

mediocre, or those less than mediocre, can furnish us much solid amusement; and there are many biographical fragments which reveal to us the very heart of their subject, as surely as a piece of ore-bearing quartz the metal embedded in it.

THE PLEASURE OF BIOGRAPHY

The delights of biography are those of the highest human intercourse, in almost limitless diversity, which no one could hope to enjoy among the living. Even though you were placed so favorably that you became acquainted with many of the most interesting personages of your own time, were it not for this magic art, which makes the past present and the dead to live, you would still be shut out from all acquaintance with your forerunners. But, thanks to biography, you have only to reach out your hand and take down a volume from your shelf in order to converse with Napoleon or Bismarck, Lincoln or Cavour. You need spend no weary hours in antechambers on the chance of snatching a hasty interview. They wait upon your pleasure. No business of state can put you off. They talk and you listen. They disclose to you their inmost secrets. Carlyle may be never so petulant, Luther never so bluff, Swift never so bitter, but they must admit you, and the very defects which might have interposed a screen between each of them living and you are as loopholes through which you look into their hearts. So you may come to know them better than their contemporaries knew them, better than you know your intimates, or, unless you are a master of self-scrutiny, better than you know yourself.

The mixed motives which we seldom dissect in our own acts can usually be disentangled without difficulty in theirs. Through them we discover the true nature of traits, fair or hideous, of which we discern the embryos in ourselves; and however far they rise above us by genius or by fortune, we see that the difference is of degree and not of kind. The human touch makes us all solidaire. Were it not so, the story of their lives would interest us no more than if they were basilisks or griffins, phantasmal creatures having no possible relations with us.

Just now I mentioned at random some of the very great statesmen and leaders in religion and letters, access to whom in the flesh would presumably have been impossible, but with whom the humblest of us find many contacts in their biographies. Often we are surprised by a thought or feeling or experience such as we have had and scarcely heeded, but which at once takes on dignity from being shared with the illustrious man. Still, the touchstone of biography is not merely greatness, but interest and significance; and herein it coincides with its twin art, portraiture. The finest portraits, assuming equal skill in the technique of their painting, are not of kings and grandees, but those which embody or suggest character. Queen Victoria's face, though a Leonardo had painted it, could never rivet the world's attention or pique the world's curiosity as Monna Lisa's has done. In ten minutes one has revealed the uncomplex and uninspired nature behind it; while after four hundred years the other still fascinates us by its suggestive and perpetually elusive expression.

So the lives of persons who were inconspicuous, measured on the scale of international or enduring fame, are sometimes packed with the charm of individuality. Such, for instance, is "The Story of My Heart," by Richard Jeffries. You may not like it—one friend to whom I recommend it told me he found it so exasperating that he threw it into the fire—but you cannot deny, if you are reasonably sympathetic, that it is the genuine utterance of a genuine man. Solomon Maimon's biography is another of this sort, in which we see an unusual personality shackled by the cruelty of caste. John Sterling had talent, but he died too young to achieve any work of lasting note; and yet, thanks to Carlyle's exuberantly vital memoir of him—which reminds me of one of Rembrandt's portraits—Sterling will live on for years.

THE DIFFICULTY OF BIOGRAPHICAL WRITING

These examples will suffice to prove that a great biography does not require a great man for its original; but it does require a great biographer. For biography is an art, a very high art; and, if we judge by the comparatively small number of its masterpieces, we must conclude that the consummate biographer is rarer than the poet, the novelist, or the historian of similar worth.

The belief that anybody can write a life is one of the widespread fallacies. As if anybody could paint a portrait or compose a sonata! When some notable person dies, it is ten to one that his wife or sister, son or daughter, sets to work to compile his memoir. The result, at its best, must present a partial, family point of view, hardly more to be trusted than the official biographies of kings and queens.

It was the public relations of the gentleman that warranted writing about him at all; but from his wife—doting, perhaps —or from his child—spoiled, possibly—we shall hear of him chiefly in his rôle as husband or as father.

Personal affection, devotion even, may be and usually is a handicap, which the family biographer cannot overcome. The wise surgeon does not trust himself to perform an operation on his dearest; neither should a biographer.

Knowledge, sympathy, and imagination the biographer must possess; these, and that detachment of the artist which is partly intuition and partly a sort of conscience, against which personal considerations plead in vain. Thus, although Boswell, the master biographer among all those who have written in English, felt toward Johnson admiration little short of idolatry, yet, when he came to write, he was the artist striving to make a perfect picture, and not the worshiper hiding his idol in clouds of incense. Sir George Trevelyan was Macaulay's nephew, and therefore likely to be hampered by family reserves; but in him the quality of biographer so far surpassed the accident of nephew that he, too, was able to produce a biography which portrays Macaulay as adequately as Boswell's portrays Johnson.

Such exceptions simply prove the rule: detachment—which ensures fairness—and knowledge, sympathy, and imagination—uniting in a faculty which we may call divination—are indispensable.

CULTIVATING THE TASTE FOR BIOGRAPHY

The taste for biography, if it be not born in you, is quickly acquired. Many and many a person has had it first aroused in boyhood by Franklin's "Autobiography," [2] that astonishing book, which enchants you when you are young by its simplicity and its teeming incidents, and holds you when you are old by its shrewdness, its tonic optimism, its candor, its wisdom, its humor. Franklin has done for himself what Defoe did for the fictitious Robinson Crusoe; but his sphere was as wide as Crusoe's was confined. Follow his fortunes and you will soon be swept into the main currents of history, not in Philadelphia or the Colonies only, but in Europe. And after you have digested the information which Franklin provides so naturally, you will recall again and again the human touches in which his book abounds: his remarks on his marriage: his confession that, when he began to take an account of stock of his moral condition he found himself much fuller of faults than he imagined; his admission that he acquired the appearance of humility though he lacked the reality; the irony of his report of Braddock's conversation; —but to mention its characteristic passages would be to epitomize the book. Each reader will have his favorites and when he reaches the end of the fragment, with its unfinished sentence, he will regret to part from such a mellow companion. What a treat the world missed because Franklin died before he had narrated his experiences between 1775 and 1785, that decade when, we may truly say that, if Washington was the Father, Franklin was the Godfather of his country.

Perhaps, however, you were led into biography through other channels. The life of Napoleon or of Cæsar, of some painter, poet, man of letters, inventor, or explorer, may have been the first to attract you; but the outcome will be the same. You will feel that you have gained a new companion, as real as your flesh-and-blood intimates, but wittier, wiser, or more picturesque than they; a friend whose latchstring is always out for you to pull; a crony who will gossip when you desire, who will never desert you nor grow cold

[2] *H. C.*, i; and cf. Lecture IV, below

nor yawn at your dulness, nor resent your indifference. For
the relation between you is wholly one-sided. His spirit is
distilled in a book, like some rare cordial in a flask, to be
enjoyed or not according to your mood. He bestows his all
—himself: but only on condition that you supply the perfect
sympathy requisite for understanding him.

This relationship between the reader and the dead and
gone who have perpetuated themselves in literature is absolutely unique. In all other affairs there must be reciprocity,
the interplay of temperaments, the stress of moral obligation; but in this transaction the author gives all, and the
reader takes all (if he can) without thought of making
returns, and withouut incurring the imputation of being a
sponge or a parasite. If you are a free man, no inter-
mediary stands between you and the author who draws you
or repels you according to the subtle laws of affinity.
Rarely, rarely among the living is that condition for ideal
companionship realized.

THE VARIETY OF BIOGRAPHY

Because of the unique terms which exist between author
and reader, we associate with sinners not less than with
saints, and are unburdened by a sense of responsibility for
their acts. In daily life few of us, happily, come face to
face with perverts and criminals; but through biography we
can, if we will, measure the limits of human nature on its
dark side in the careers of such colossal reprobates as Cæsar
Borgia and his father; or monsters of cruelty like Ezzelino
and Alva; or traitors, spies, and informers, from Judas to
Benedict Arnold and Azeff; or of swindlers and more common scoundrels, George Law and Cagliostro and latter-day
"promoters," and that peculiarly offensive, brood—the pious
impostors.

In the long run, however, we make our lasting friends
among those who are normal but not commonplace, who
seem to carry our own better traits to a degree of perfection
which we have not attained, or who have qualities which we
lack but envy. Unlikeness also is often a potent element of
charm. I recall a frail little old lady, the embodiment of

peace, so gentle that she could not bear to have a fly harmed, who devoured every book about Napoleon and seemed almost to gloat over the details of his campaigns. Conversely, more than one great captain has concentrated his reading in one or two books of religion.

Having entered the realm inhabited by those who live through the magic of biography, we cannot dwell there long without meeting friends for whom we have sought in vain among our actual associates. In finding them we often find our best selves. They comfort us in our distress, they clarify our doubts, they give fresh impetus and straight aim to our hopes, they whisper to us the mystic word which unfolds the meaning of life; above all—they teach us by example how to live. Then we feel that our gratitude is barren and unworthy unless it spurs us to emulation. Unenviable indeed is he whose heart never

> ran o'er
> With silent worship of the great of old!
> The dead but sceptered sovereigns, who still rule
> Our spirits from their urns.

No matter what his creed may be, no man is so self-sufficient and original as not to be under the sway, whether he acknowledges it or not, of dead but sceptered kings; and biography brings them nearer to us and humanizes them, and thereby adds to the pertinence of their teaching. These are the supreme benefits conferred by biography; but as no healthy soul lives continuously in a state of ecstasy, so there are many moods in which we turn to other companions than the prophets. We require relaxation. Our intellect not less than our spirit craves its repast. Honest amusement is its own justification. Biography offers the widest possible choice for any fancy.

DR. JOHNSON AND HIS CIRCLE

One of the surest ways to secure unfailing pleasure is to naturalize yourself as a member of some significant group. Take, for instance, Dr. Johnson and his circle. Having disclosed to you the imperishable Doctor, Boswell will whet your curiosity as to the scores of persons, great and small, who figure in the biography. You will go in pursuit of Sir Joshua Reynolds and of Garrick, of Goldsmith and of Burke: and you will soon discover that a mere bowing acquaintance with any of these will not satisfy you. When Gibbon enters the scene, you will be drawn to his autobiography. Chatham and Fox, North and Sheridan, must all be investigated. You will wonder why the other members of the Club unite in declaring Beauclerk the peer of the best of them in wit; and after much digging, you will conclude that, for lack of other evidence, you must accept Beauclerk on the strength of their commendation. As your circle widens, it will take in Fanny Burney—whose memoirs are so much more readable now than her "Evelina"; Mrs. Thrale—that type of the eternal feminine, whose mission it is to cheer Genius by appreciating the man in whom it dwells; Mrs. Montague, the autocratic blue-stocking, who made and unmade literary reputations; and many others, from Paoli the vanquished patriot of Corsica to Oglethorpe the colonizer of Georgia.

The material for knowing Johnson's group is extraordinarily rich. It consists not only of formal biographies and histories, but of letters, recollections, diaries, anecdotes, and table talk which are often the very marrow of both history and biography. You cannot exhaust it in many seasons. Horace Walpole alone will outlast any fashion. Little by little you will come to know the chief personages in youth and in age, from every point of view. You can watch them develop, or trace the interactions of one upon the other. The minor folk also will become real to you—Lovett, the trusty servant, and the old ladies with whom the Doctor drank tea, the chance frequenters of the coffeehouses where he thundered his verdicts on books and politics, the pathetic derelicts whose old age he solaced with a pension. You will experience the pleasure of filling gaps in the *dramatis personæ* and the stage setting, or in discovering a missing link of evidence. And so at last you can mix with that company at will. No matter what the cares and torments of your day, at evening you can enter their magic city, forget your present, and follow in imagination those careers which closed in time so long ago, but live on with undimmed luster in the timeless domain of the imagination. And during all this delightful exploration, you have been learning more and more about human nature, the mysterious primal element in which you yourself have your being.

Instead of the province over which Dr. Johnson rules, you can choose from among many others. Take up the Lake School of poets—Byron, Shelley, and Keats—the mid-Victorian statesmen and men of letters—the founders of our Republic—Emerson and his contemporaries—and by the same method you will find your interest wonderfully enhanced. It is not the surface of life, but its depth and height that it behooves us to know; and we can get this knowledge vicariously from those who have soared highest or dropped their plummet farthest into the unfathomable deeps.

THE VALUE OF AUTOBIOGRAPHY

Autobiography is an important and often very precious product of biography. The common prejudice, that because it is egotistical it must be tedious, does not hold water. The impulse toward self-expression exceeds all others save the instinct of self-preservation. The artist blessed with great talent expresses himself through that talent, whether it be painting or sculpture, literature or eloquence. Let him strive never so hard to be impersonal, the tinge of his mind will color it; the work is *his* work. Men of pure science discover abstract laws by experimenting with material sterilized as far as possible from any taint due to a personal equation; but this does not lessen our interest in them as human beings. Far from it. We are all the more curious to learn how men, subject to our passions, contradictions and disabilities, have succeeded in exploring the passionless vastitudes of astronomy and the incomputably minute worlds of atoms and electrons.

We rejoice to find Darwin worthy of being the prophet of a new dispensation—Darwin, the strong, quiet, modest man, harassed hourly by a depressing ailment, but patient under suffering, and preferring truth to the triumph of his own opinions or to any other reward.

If self-conceit, or egotism, be rather too obtrusive in some autobiographies, you will learn to bear it if you regard it as a secretion apparently as necessary to the growth of certain talents as is the secretion which produces the pearl in the oyster. If a pearl results, the pearl compensates. And, after all, such conceit, like the make-believe of little children, is too patent to deceive us. It is the thought that they are trying to humbug us into supposing them greater than we know them to be that irritates us in the conceit of little men. But since conceited men have been great, even very great, although this blemish in them offends us, it ought not to blind us to their other positive accomplishments! And how much harmless amusement we owe to such unconscious humorists! When Victor Hugo grandly announces: "France is the head of civilization; Paris is the head of France; I am the brains of Paris," are we seized with a desire to refute him? Hardly. We smile an inward smile, too deeply permeating and satisfactory for outward laughter. So Ruskin's inordinate vanity in "Præterita" cannot detract from the iridescent beauties of that marvelous book; it seems rather to be the guarantee of truthfulness.

Whatever may be your prepossessions, you cannot travel far in the field of biography without recognizing the value, even if you do not feel the fascination, of autobiographies, of which in English we have a particularly rich collection. I have spoken of Franklin's, to which Gibbon's may serve as a pendant. It discloses the eighteenth-century cosmopolite, placid, rational, industrious, a consummate genius in one direction, but of tepid emotion; who immortalized in a single line his betrothal which he docilely broke at his father's bidding: "I sighed as a lover," he writes, "but I obeyed as a son."

Halfway between the man of pure intellect, like Franklin and Gibbon, and the man of sentiment, comes John Stuart Mill,[3] in whom the precocious development of a very remarkable mind did not succeed in crushing out the religious craving or the life of the feelings. Newman's "Apologia," largely occupied in the vain endeavor to transfuse the warm blood of the emotions into the hardened arteries of theo-

[3] *H. C.*, xxv; and cf. Lecture V, below.

logical dogmas, stands at the other extreme in this class of confessions.

Contrast with it John Woolman's "Journal," [4] the austerely sincere record of a soul that does not spend its time in casuistical interpretations of the quibbles propounded by mediæval theologians, but dwells consciously in the immediate presence of the living God.

Our only quarrel with Woolman is that, owing to his complete other-worldiness, he disdains to tell us facts about himself and about his time that we would gladly hear.

In other fields there is equal abundance. Many soldiers have written memoirs; enough to cite General Grant's, to parallel which we must go back to Cæsar's "Commentaries." Authors, poets, men of affairs, the obscure and the conspicuous, have voluntarily opened a window for us. From Queen Victoria's "Leaves from a Journal," to Booker T. Washington's "Up from Slavery," what contrasts, what richness, what range!

And in other lands also many of the pithiest examples of human faculty are to be sought in autobiographies. To Benvenuto Cellini's life I have already referred. Alfieri, Pellico, Massimo d'Azeglio, Mazzini, Garibaldi are other Italians whose self-revelations endure. The French, each of whom seems to be more conscious than men of other races that he is an actor in a drama, have produced a libraryful of autobiographies. At their head stands Rousseau's "Confessions," in style a masterpiece, in substance absorbing, by one of the most despicable of men.

THE RELATION OF BIOGRAPHY TO HISTORY

In the larger classification of literature, biography comes midway between history and fiction. One school of historians, indeed, unwilling to cramp their imaginations into so mean a space as a generation or a century, reckon by millenniums and lose sight of mere individuals. They are intent on discovering and formulating general laws of cosmic progress; on tracing the collective action of multitudes through long periods of time; on watching institutions

[4] *H. C.*, i, 177ff.

evolve. In their eyes, even Napoleon is a "negligible quantity."

I would not for a moment disparage the efforts of these investigators. Most of us have felt the fascination of moving to and fro over vast reaches of time, as imperially as the astronomer moves through space. Such flights are exhilarating. They involve us in no peril; we begin and end them in our armchair; they attach to us no responsibility. The power of generalizing, which even the humblest and most ignorant exercise daily, sheds upon us a peculiar satisfaction; but we must not value the generalizations we arrive at by the pleasurableness of the process. Counting by the hundred thousand years, individual man dwindles beyond the recall of the most powerful microscope. So we may well disregard an æon or two in speculating on the rate of progress between oligocene and neolithic conditions. But after mankind have plodded out of geology into history there is nothing more certain than that the masses have been pioneered by individuals. You can prove it wherever two or more persons meet—one inevitably leads.

As the race emerged from barbarism, the number and variety of individuals increased. Men in the mass are plastic; or, to change the figure, they are like reservoirs of latent energy, awaiting the leader who shall apply their force to a special work. In many cases the great man is far from being the product of his time, but he has some interior and unborrowed faculty for influencing, controlling, we may even say hypnotizing, his generation. It is idle to suppose that a Napoleon can be explained on the theory that he is the sum of a hundred, or ten thousand, of his average French contemporaries. He shared certain traits with them, just as he had organs and appetites common to all normal men; but it was precisely those uncommon attributes which were his and not theirs that made him Napoleon.

We may safely cultivate biography, therefore, not merely as an adjunct of history, but as one of history's mighty sources. In proportion as the materials concerning a given period or episode abound, it becomes easier to trace the significance of the great men who directed it—easier and most entrancing, for in this detective work we are shadowing

Destiny itself. We see how some apparently trivial personal happening—Napoleon's lassitude due to a cold at Borodino, Frederick the Second's seasickness on starting on his crusade, McDowell's cholera morbus at the first battle of Bull Run—was the hazard on which Fate hung the issue of history. We see, further, that men and women are not abstractions—that what we regard as laws in human evolution are the result of the motives and deeds—motives and deeds —of human beings; and that a flaw or twist in a single individual may break the current of development or deflect it into an unexpected channel.

The lives of state builders and of state preservers and pilots offer, accordingly, a double attraction: they show us history at those moments when, ceasing to be abstract and impersonal, it turns upon us recognizable human features and works through the heart and brain of highly individualized genius. They show us also biography, when individual genius becomes so powerful that it diffuses itself through multitudes, yet is never more truly itself than in this diffusion.

THE RELATION OF BIOGRAPHY TO FICTION

On the other hand, biography touches fiction at many points. Novelists discovered long ago the allure which any period except the present—for the present has always been Time's black sheep—exerts over the imagination.

The three-legged stool was only that and nothing more to our Puritan ancestors; now it is a piece of old Plymouth or old Salem, glorified by that association, and by the possibility that Governor Bradford or Priscilla Mullens may have sat on it. There lies the spell which historical novelists have cast with stupendous effect; and, having the environment, they introduce into it the historical personages who once belonged there.

The novelist, by his trade, may take or reject what he pleases; so that, if he finds the facts of history intractable, he may change or omit them. Or, since his deepest interest, like the biographer's, is in persons and the unfolding of character, he may achieve a lifelike portrait. At best, however, historical personages, as they appear in fiction, can never escape from the suspicion of being so far modified by the novelist that they are no longer real.

As to the larger question of the relative value of fiction and biography, we would not dogmatize. We would no more promote biography by abolishing fiction—if it were possible—than we would magnify sculpture by dwarfing painting. And yet, if talents equal to those of the foremost novelists had been or were devoted to writing biography, the popularity—at least among cultivated readers—of the two branches of literature might be reversed. As I have said, the utmost achievement for the novelist is to create an illusion so perfect that the characters in his books shall seem to be real.

In other words, so far as concerns reality, the novelist leaves off where the biographer begins. And if the novelist has an apparent advantage in dealing with unruly facts, he is under the immense disadvantage of being restricted in his choice of characters. So true is this that, if all other records except the novels of the past century were to be destroyed, posterity five hundred years hence would have slight means of knowing the men and women through whom human evolution has really operated in our age. In no art has the process of vulgarization gone so far as in fiction. The novelist to-day dares not paint goodness or greatness; his upper limit is mediocrity; his lower is depravity, and he tends more and more to exploit the lower.

An art which, pretending to mirror life, instinctively shuts out a large province of life—an art which boasts that it alone can display human personality in all its varieties and yet becomes dumb before the highest manifestations of personality—has no right to rank among the truly universal arts —painting and sculpture, the Elizabethan drama and biography.

All the myriad novelists writing in English since 1850 have not created one character comparable to Abraham Lincoln or to Cavour, nor have the romances imagined any hero to match Garibaldi. Or, to take contemporary examples, what novelist would venture to depict, even if his imagination could have conceived, a Theodore Roosevelt or a J. P. Morgan? For myself, if it were necessary, in a shipwreck, to choose between saving the Georgian novelists and Boswell's "Life of Johnson," I would unhesitatingly take Boswell.

THE ART OF BIOGRAPHY

Before concluding, let me recur to biography as an art. You cannot read far in this field without being struck by the great differences in the ability of biographers. One makes a brilliant subject dull, or a juicy subject dry; while a biographer of other quality holds you spellbound over the life story of some relatively unimportant person. Gradually you come to study the laws of the art; to determine how much depends upon the biographer and how much on the biographee; above all, to define just what portion of a given subject's life should be described. Remember that not a hundredth part of any life can be recorded. The biographer must select. But what? The significant, the individual, the revealing. How shall those be settled? By the judgment of the biographer. Selection and perspective are the sun and moon of all art, and unless they shine for him, his portrait will be out of drawing. When, for instance, the writer on Havelock devotes almost as much space to his piety as to his military achievement, you recognize the faulty selection; or when another describes General Grant's later misfortune as the dupe of a financial sharper as amply as his Vicksburg campaign, you have a fine example of bungled perspective. With practice, you will learn how to recover some of the true features of the victims of such distortions.

Comparison, the mother of Criticism, will help you to ampler pleasures. I have already suggested comparing Woolman's, Franklin's and Mill's autobiographies; but the process can be carried forward in many directions. You can investigate what matters were regarded as essential for a biographer to tell at any period. Plutarch, for instance, has left a gallery of portraits of ancient statesmen and soldiers.[5] Wherein would the method and results of a modern Plutarch differ from his? If Boswell, and not

H. C., xii, and cf. Lecture II, below.

Xenophon, had written the familiar life of Socrates, what would he have added? What do you miss in quaint Izaak Walton's lives of Wotton and Donne and Herbert?[6] Do we really know Napoleon better, for all the thousands of books about him, than we know Cæsar? How far does sameness of treatment in Vasari's "Lives" blur their individuality?

These and many other questions will stimulate you in any comparative reading of biography. They all refer to three deeper matters: differences in the skill of biographers; changes in the angle of curiosity from which the public regard celebrities; and, finally, the variation, slowly effectuated, in human Personality itself.

The outlook for biography never was brighter. Its votaries will practice it with a constantly increasing skill. The demand for veracity will not slacken. The public, grown more discerning, will read it with greater relish.

The fact that the persons and events whom the biographer depicts were *real* will lend to them an additional attractiveness.

Given life, the first impulse of life, the incessant, triumphant impulse, is to manifest itself in individuals. From the beginning there has never been a moment, or the fraction of a second, when the universe, or the tiniest part of it, became abstract. In the world of matter, not less than in the organic world of animals and plants, always and everywhere and forever—individuals! from atom to Sirius, nothing but individuals! Even in the protean transmutation of one thing into another, of life into death and death into life, individuality keeps pace with each changing stage.

Since the process of individualization is from lower to higher, from simple to complex, the acknowledged great men in history, or the persons who stand out from any mass, are endowed with unusual qualities, or with common qualities in an uncommon degree—an endowment which gives them more points of contact, more power, more interest, more charm. These are the men and women whom biography perpetuates. The master creations of fiction spring from the human brain; the subjects of biography are the very creations of God himself: the realities of God must forever transcend the fictions of man.

[6] *H. C.*, xv, 327, 377ff.

II. PLUTARCH

By Professor W. S. Ferguson

PLUTARCH was a kindly man, well educated in philosophy and rhetoric. He lived between 46 and 125 A. D. in little, out-of-the-way Bœotian Chæronea. He spent his days lecturing and in friendly correspondence and conversation with many cultivated contemporaries among both Greeks and Romans. He was fortunate in his age. "If a man were called to fix the period in the history of the world during which the condition of the human race was most happy and prosperous, he would," says Gibbon, "without hesitation, name that" in which Plutarch wrote. It was the twilight time of antiquity; and in the works of Plutarch[1] are clearly mirrored the charm and languor, the incentive to stroll and loiter, and the dimming of vision, characteristic of the hour before "the sun sank and all the ways were darkened."

PLUTARCH'S SUPERSTITION

His versatility is remarkable, and he has ever at hand an apt illustration for every situation; but his fertility tempts him to digress, and his learning is not matched by critical power. An admirable example of his mode of thought as well as an epitome of his natural philosophy appears in the following passage from his "Life of Pericles": "There is a story, that once Pericles had brought to him from a country farm of his, a ram's head with one horn, and that Lampon, the diviner, upon seeing the horn grow strong and solid out of the midst of the forehead, gave it as his judgment, that, there being at that time two potent ,factions, parties, or interests in the city, the one of Thucydides and the other of Pericles, the government would come about to that one of

[1] For a volume of selected "Lives," see *Harvard Classics,* xii.

them in whose ground or estate this token or indication of fate had shown itself. But that Anaxagoras, cleaving the skull in sunder, showed to the bystanders that the brain had not filled up its natural place, but being oblong, like an egg, had collected from all parts of the vessel which contained it, in a point to that place from whence the root of the horn took its rise. And that, for that time, Anaxagoras was much admired for his explanation by those that were present; and Lampon no less a little while after, when Thucydides was overpowered, and the whole affairs of the state and government came into the hands of Pericles. And yet, in my opinion, it is no absurdity to say that they were both in the right, both natural philosopher and diviner, one justly detecting the cause of this event, by which it was produced, the other the end for which it was designed. For it was the business of the one to find out and give an account of what it was made, and in what manner and by what means it grew as it did; and of the other to foretell to what end and purpose it was so made, and what it might mean or portend. Those who say that to find out the cause of a prodigy is in effect to destroy its supposed signification as such, do not take notice that, at the same time, together with divine prodigies, they also do away with signs and signals of human art and concert, as, for instance, the clashings of quoits, fire-beacons, and the shadows on sundials, every one of which things has its cause, and by that cause and contrivance is a sign of something else. But these are subjects, perhaps, that would better befit another place."

HIS CURIOSITY AND HIS PATRIOTISM

Plutarch was a widely read man. The world in which he lived was rather the world which his mind portrayed than that upon which his eyes looked. In other words, he lived in his past much more fully than in his present. For everything that had happened he had a gentle but persistent curiosity. Customs hallowed by time evoked in him the utmost tenderness; but his nature was without a vestige of fanaticism. To the hot, strenuous youth of his age, to zealots for preserving the old, and to harsh innovators alike he seemed probably a trifler and perhaps a bore. They must have turned with impatience from his universal charity; for he was a widely loyal man, loyal to his petty civic duties, his family obligations, his friends, his reputation, his race.

By his interest in, and profession of, practical morality Plutarch was called to be a biographer, but it is to his loyalty to his people that we owe his "Parallel Lives." In their composition he was guided by the desire to show the arrogant Romans and the later Greeks in whose midst he lived, that a great Hellenic man of affairs could be put in worthy comparison with every outstanding Roman general and statesman.

SCIENTIFIC AND PHILOSOPHIC BIOGRAPHY IN ANTIQUITY

Biography in antiquity was a branch of science and also a branch of philosophy. Scientific biography was interested in facts as such, in the collocation of miscellaneous information about persons. It laid claim to objectivity of details, but left free room for individuality to display itself in their selection. The principle of choice might be pruriency, political, class, or philosophic animosity, or mere love of scandal. Such biography might be with or without style, with or without painstaking: it was commonly without critical method. The precipitate of much lost scientific biography lies before us in the "Lives of the Twelve Cæsars" by Plutarch's contemporary, Suetonius.

In Plutarch's "Parallel Lives," we have, on the other hand, the precipitate of much lost philosophic biography. He stands for us at the end of a long development, in the course of which many contemporary, or approximately contemporary, biographies were produced, each to be superseded perhaps by its successor, as they all were finally superseded and destroyed by those of Plutarch. The plundering of the countless books and pamphlets, plays, and memoirs, cited in the "Parallel Lives," the culling of the multitude of anecdotes and *bons mots* with which they are set and enlivened, were by no means the personal work of Plutarch. Many, if not most, of them he found gathered for him by his name-

less predecessors. He was under no professional sense of
duty to look up and verify his references, and he regularly
omitted to do it. Mistakes abound in Plutarch's "Lives."
But even the historian finds them pardonable when he has
the assurance that the materials in conjunction with which
they appear were taken by men of greater patience and
leisure than Plutarch from works, many of them lost, reaching back over the centuries to the earliest Greek literature.

PLUTARCH'S OWN CONTRIBUTION TO HIS "LIVES"

The "Lives" of Plutarch are thus in a sense the product
of many ages and of many minds. But, like mediæval
cathedrals, they have unity of design and style. This is
not wholly the result of their origin in a community of philosophic biographers. It is in large part the result of Plutarch's own architectonic powers. He was far from being a
colorless and characterless compiler. His "Lives" seldom
seem "lumpy." They reveal, throughout, the quaint personality of the author. His philosophic standpoint is betrayed in almost every line of criticism they contain. His
mastery of literary technique is never wanting. The quiet
humor, unobtrusive and delicate, is unmistakably his.
Piquancy is a Greek trait, and Plutarch was a Greek. He
is never indecent, as his contemporaries understood that
term, but he never forgot the natural human interest in the
intimate relations of men and women. His dramatic sense
needs no more than mention: Shakespeare's debt to Plutarch in his "Julius Cæsar," "Coriolanus," and "Antony and
Cleopatra" speaks volumes on this point.

Yet, when everything has been said in praise of his fine
qualities, it is still true that his mind, like that of the philosophic biographers who preceded him, was an unfortunate medium for the great men of affairs of antiquity to
have to pass through on their way to us. They were all
sicklied over by the pale cast of ethical interpretation. Men
of flesh and blood, actuated by all the reasons and passions
of which human beings of diverse but distinguished endowments were capable, tend to appear as puppets ex-
emplifying laudable virtues and deterrent vices. Man whose

natures are truly revealed only in the work which they accomplished are isolated from their societies, and characterized by what they did or said at insignificant moments.
Trivialities serve Plutarch's purpose of ethical portraiture as
well as or better than the historic triumphs and failures of
his heroes.   Trite ethical considerations are made decisive for the formation of policies and the reaching of
decisions instead of the realities of each historical situation.
Hence one of the chief duties of modern historians and
modern historical biographers has been to murder "Plutarch's men," and put in their stead the real statesmen and
generals of ancient times.   The latter part of their task,
however, they could not even attempt without the materials
Plutarch furnishes to them.   As for the difficulty of the
former, it is well disclosed by the story Mahaffy tells of the
illiterate Irish peasant who said of a certain fortunate
neighbor that "he had as many lives as Plutarch."

III. BENVENUTO CELLINI

By Professor Chandler Rathfon Post

THE Italian Renaissance[1] produced many works, such as the polemics of the humanists upon subjects that have long since lost their significance, which are interesting rather as illustrations of cultural conditions than for their intrinsic value. Compositions like the pastoral romance of Sannazzaro, or the dramas based upon Senecan or upon Plautine and Terentian models, acquire importance as revivals of ancient literary types and as the seeds from which later great masterpieces were to be evolved. Much smaller is the number of works in which, as in the sonnets of Michelangelo, the absolute value preponderates over the historical. Still fewer, such as the writings of Machiavelli,[2] have the distinction of possessing an equal interest archæologically and in themselves, and to this class the "Autobiography" of Benvenuto Cellini[3] belongs. No other production of the period embodies more vividly the tendencies of the Renaissance or enjoys a more universal and enduring appeal. We can best appreciate it by considering it under these two aspects.

CELLINI AS A TYPE OF RENAISSANCE INDIVIDUALISM

Its great importance as a document for the study of contemporary Italian life is obvious to the reader, but its temper also is strikingly related to certain spiritual movements of the day. Of the two determinative characteristics of the Renaissance, humanism, or the devotion to antiquity, and individualism, or the devotion to self-development, Ben-

[1] See Professor Potter's lecture on the Renaissance in the course on History.
[2] *Harvard Classics*, xxxvi, 7ff; and xxvii, 381ff.
[3] *H. C.*, xxxi. The dates of his life are 1500-1571; the "Autobiography" was first published in 1568.

193

venuto emphasizes the latter. The very natural transition
from a study of self to the study of other personalities gave
rise to the *genre* known as biography, eminent instances of
which are Vespasiano da Bisticci's "Lives of Illustrious
Men," and Giorgio Vasari's more renowned "Lives of the
Most Excellent Painters, Sculptors, and Architects." Autobiography, however, is an even more pronounced manifestation of individualism, and as the composer of the first great
and definite example of this literary form in modern times,
Benvenuto stands forth as a brilliant exponent of his age.
It is possible, doubtless, for an author to exhibit in an autobiography little of his own individuality, confining himself
largely, like Trollope, to a narrative of events and a discussion of his books; but such was not the spirit of the six
teenth century, and Benvenuto even exceeds his time. He
strips to the very soul. Unblushingly he lays bare alike his
virtues and his vices, his public and his most private actions,
his loves and hatreds. He seems unconscious of modesty's
existence, and takes a palpable delight, which, by the magic
of his style, he causes the reader to share, in analyzing his
own passions and in recounting his own deeds and misdeeds; typical and widely varying examples are the affair
with the Sicilian girl, Angelica,[4] the terrible revenge for his
brother's assassination,[5] the celestial visions experienced in
his long and gruesome incarceration.[6]

THE CORRECTNESS OF HIS ESTIMATE OF HIMSELF

Hand in hand with this attitude struts an exalted opinion
of his own charms, prowess, and artistic superiority. In his
conceit (for it is only a heroic form of this defect), he embodies not only individualism but also the concurrent phenomenon of humanism, which resurrected from ancient Rome
such self-appreciation as appears so disagreeably in Cicero.
With his high estimate of his own art modern criticism does
not unqualifiedly agree. Of his labor as goldsmith so little
that is certainly authentic remains that judgment is difficult;
the chief extant example, the saltcellar of Francis I.[7] now

---

[4] *H. C.*, xxxi, 132-144.   [5] *H. C.*, xxxi, 102-110.
[6] *H. C.*, xxxi, 245, 252.   [7] See illustration facing p. 320, *H. C.* xxxi.

in the Imperial Treasury at Vienna, is unpleasant in composition and too ornate. In his few plastic works on a large
scale, one of which, the bronze bust of Bindo Altoviti,
America is fortunate enough to possess in the wonderful
collection of Mrs. John L. Gardner, Boston, he is perhaps
less affected than most of his rivals by the degeneration into
which Italian sculpture lapsed in the second and third quarters of the Cinquecento; but in comparison to the productions of the earlier Renaissance, or of his contemporary
Michelangelo, his profound affection and admiration for
whom form one of his noblest trains, he betrays too close a
dependence upon the antique, a tendency to excessive nicety
and elaboration, derived from his training as a jeweler but
unsuited to the broader manner of monumental statuary, a
leaning toward ostentatious and luxuriant decoration, and
a fatal predilection for sacrificing æsthetic considerations to
the display of virtuosity in composition and in processes.
All these characteristics are exemplified in what remains
from his work, and may also be read between the lines of
the "Autobiography." The inclination to a display of skill
is especially evident in the absorbing and famous description
of the casting of the Perseus.[8] Over his whole art, as indeed over most of the art of the later sixteenth century,
there broods a certain deadness and a sense of the perfunctory, which are strangely contrasted with the spontaneity that runs from his pen. The somewhat unjustifiable
braggadocio about this phase of his activity arouses sus-
picions as to the veracity of the tales about his courage and
other achievements. Some of the details, such as the worm
that he vomited forth after his long sickness,[9] or the sight
of the demons in the Colosseum,[10] seem hardly credible, but
it must be remembered that we are dealing with a man of a
high-strung, nervous temperament, whose imagination easily
materializes the visions of his mind. Other episodes, like
the various brawls and homicides in which he engaged, or
the escape from the Castel Sant' Angelo, are improbable
from our standpoint, but not in an epoch of extravagances
like the Renaissance or for one of those supermen of Cel-

[8] See frontispiece in *H. C.*, xxxi, and pp. 392-398.
[9] *H. C.*, xxxi, 178.   [10] *H. C.*, xxxi, 133.

lini's caliber, in which the period was so rich. Much of the "Autobiography" receives confirmation from contemporary documents, and its main fabric is certainly trustworthy, though highly colored, doubtless to increase its artistic worth and to set off to advantage the central figure of the writer.

I have spoken of Benvenuto as a superman, and herein, too, he is a result of the astounding development of the individual witnessed by the Renaissance. In his versatility he is second only to such giants of universal talent as Leon Battista Alberti, Leonardo da Vinci, and Michelangelo. He excels equally as musician, goldsmith, and sculptor; he is an adept with the sword and with the musket; his skill as a diplomatist is paralleled only by his merriness as a jester; a languishing lover one day, he is a fierce murderer the next; a part of his imprisonment he spends in devising a miraculous escape, and the rest in mystic religious trances; he can write you passable occasional sonnets and respectable treatises on art; and finally he bequeaths to the world what is probably the most remarkable autobiography in existence.

CELLINI'S MORALITY

Much of his activity is far from Christian. Benvenuto vies with Pietro Aretino for notoriety as an exponent of that Paganism which was a consequence, on one hand, of the indiscriminate acceptance of all that was ancient, even the license of decadent Rome, and, on the other, of the inevitable degeneration of self-development into self-gratification. The loose morals of the Renaissance have been much exaggerated by such writers as John Addington Symonds, who base their assertions too confidently upon the prejudiced Protestant accounts of the north and upon the short stories or *novelle* of the period, which magnify current abuses for humorous purposes. The ethical condition of Italy had still remained fairly sound in the fifteenth century, and it was not until now in the sixteenth that a debased humanism and individualism were developed to the bitter end with an effect that was baneful, but not so entirely fatal as is very commonly supposed. Almost every page of the "Autobiography," however, betrays the absence of any adequate moral standard. Cellini fathers an illegitimate child or cuts down an enemy as lightly as he sallies forth on a hunting expedition. There is little or no realization of sin; religion he has, but a religion which, however fervent, is divorced from morality and consists chiefly in an emotional mysticism and an observance of lovely and impressive ceremonies. He has shaken off the Christian curb upon the passions, and emulating the Paganism, not of the great days of antiquity, but of the Greek and Roman decline, he gives free rein to self.

VALUE OF THE "AUTOBIOGRAPHY"

The historical importance of the work, then, lies, not only in its painting of contemporary life, but also in its lively presentation of the individualism, the versatility, and the Paganism of the late Renaissance; its intrinsic value is proved by an almost unique and widespread popularity from among so much Italian literature of the sixteenth century that is forgotten or known only to specialists. Benvenuto has succeeded in transfusing it with the magnetism of his own personality. So intimate is the manner which he adopts that we seem to be, not readers, but a company of boon companions listening to good tales, half the attraction of which is afforded by the very force and charm of the speaker's genial character. The matter is often such as should be bruited only in this society; the style is distinctly that of an easy conversationalist, full of picturesque Tuscan idioms, colloquial to the last degree, frequently lapsing into the loose grammar that is permitted to the *raconteur*. Behind this apparent facility, however, is concealed the art of a supreme master of narrative, who knows how to choose the piquant episodes and details and to exclude the irrelevant; who dexterously avoids monotony by contrasts of high lights and shadows; who is all the greater because he nowhere reveals the methods of his craft, but appears always the clever and spontaneous entertainer.

IV. FRANKLIN AND WOOLMAN

By Professor Chester Noyes Greenough

IN ALL the literature of fact—as distinguished from the literature of fiction—hardly any kind of book surpasses a good biography in its power to interest and instruct. It combines the suspense of the novel with the actuality of history. It fills in the detail without which history would be too impersonal, and it shows us how people, not at all points unlike ourselves, have ordered their lives—what their guiding principles have been, and how principles have sometimes been modified to meet circumstances. Especially in the case of autobiography is all this true, for here we have the pleasure of feeling that the record is both authentic and intimate. The best of biographers, however learned, vivid, or philosophical, leaves between us and the past an interval which only a good autobiography can span. Such an autobiography may possess great historical value if its author was intimately connected with significant events and had some capacity to perceive their causes and their effects. But if the writer happens to be earnest about his career, free from self-consciousness, and blest with a good prose style, we have sufficient reasons for valuing the record of his life even though the historical importance of it may be quite secondary. Such is the basis of our permanent regard for autobiographies like those of Benjamin Franklin[1] (1706-1790) and John Woolman[2] (1720-1772).

THE BREAKING DOWN OF PURITANISM

Neither Franklin nor Woolman would have been at home among the makers of the literature which is most significant of America before their time. The latter as a Quaker, the former as a person whose general attitude may be indicated

[1] *Harvard Classics*, i, 5ff.   [2] *H. C.*, i, 177ff.

by his casually uttered remark[3] that he was usually too busy to go to church, would have been either punished or cast out (if not both) by most New England communities, who acquiesced in the banishment of some and the whipping or execution of others, in order that by uniform obedience to the theocratic ideal the purpose of the founders might be fulfilled.

But in the eighteenth century there began to be a change. The growing interest in science, the influence of such writers as John Locke, the rise of other learned professions than the ministry, the advance of the merchant class, the increasing concern about political relations with the mother country, the founding of other churches than the Congregational ones which hitherto had virtually constituted an Establishment—all of these influences make American life and letters in the eighteenth century radically different from the century of colonization. Strikingly unlike each other as Franklin and Woolman are in most respects, they agree in representing aspects of the American mind that could hardly flourish in American literature until in the eighteenth century that literature began to move out of New England and its intolerant church.

FRANKLIN'S METHODS IN LITERATURE AND SCIENCE

The career of Franklin well illustrates these changes. He finds himself cramped in Boston and moves to Philadelphia. He pays the most careful attention to the matter of writing well,[4] because he sees that it pays to consult the convenience of the reader. In his writing he employs the secular arts of humor and irony and takes particular care to "forbear all direct contradiction to the sentiments of others, and all positive assertions of [his] own."[5] He seeks the convenience of mankind also by various mechanical improvements and by the better organization of certain departments of the public service. His experiments in pure science mark him as patient, observant, and logical to an unusual degree. But most of his attention—in business, science, and public service—is given to matters of immediate utility.

[3] *H. C.,* i, 17.   [4] *H. C.,* i, 16, 17.   [5] *H. C.,* i, 91.

FRANKLIN IN POLITICS

In politics he was eminently successful, though probably
not entirely uncorrupt. He managed delicate affairs of
state with conspicuous coolness and skill. He was particularly useful to the colonies in explaining abroad the
actual condition and views of the average American. His
solid merits and unusual tact made him a great favorite in
France, where, as commissioner for the colonies, he attained
a personal popularity which was of the greatest advantage
to his country. In spite of some loss of reputation from
the suspicion that he had not always used his privileges un-
selfishly, Franklin returned to America to spend his last
years in a position of honor not much below that of Washington himself.

FRANKLIN'S MORALS AND RELIGION

Such eminence was not achieved without the most careful
management. Indeed, the fact that most strongly impresses
a reader of Franklin's "Autobiography" is the astonishing
degree to which he regulated his acts and developed his
character by a system of what, in the language of our day,
might almost be termed "scientific management." For example, he drew up,[6] as many others have done, a list of
virtues and of precepts for attaining them. Then, apparently untroubled by any suspicion that what he was doing
was at all funny, he kept a tabular record which showed,
week by week, how good a score he was making in the important game of living a moral life. His entire attitude toward life was of this prudential sort. Sins which would
have prostrated a Puritan in the fear of eternal torment are
to Franklin a matter of regret because of their expense and
their injurious effect upon his health. Virtue he seems to
have regarded chiefly as a means to the favor of man. The
favor of God, which the Puritan implored in fasts and
vigils, Franklin tranquilly expected as the outcome of a life
regulated by prudence and virtue. "Having experienced the
goodness of that Being in conducting me prosperously

[6] *H. C.,* i, 83ff.

through a long life," he wrote to President Stiles of Yale, "I have no doubt of its continuance in the next, though without the smallest conceit of meriting such goodness."

JOHN WOOLMAN'S RELIGION

Strikingly different in almost every respect are the life and aims of John Woolman. "There was a care on my mind," he writes, "so to pass my time that nothing might hinder me from the most steady attention to the voice of the true Shepherd."[7] This is the guiding principle of a life so inconspicuous in its outward circumstances and immediate rewards that we cannot possibly apply to it that somewhat worldly and dubious word "career," yet so steadily and unconsciously holy as to deserve our most affectionate regard.

Even as a young man Woolman began to be troubled by his own sins and by the dissolute life of many around him. Sometimes he felt moved to speak to others of their manner of life; oftener he concerned himself only with his own shortcomings and found that although "nature was feeble," yet "every trial was a fresh incitement to give himself up wholly to the service of God."[8] From the humility of Woolman's utterances one can hardly doubt that his own sins were less grave than he felt them to be, or that his warnings to others had no touch of the pharisaical about them, but came from a heart that unaffectedly desired the good of all men.

WOOLMAN AND SLAVERY

Having learned the trade of a tailor, and having perceived that large possessions are an unnecessary temptation and trouble, Woolman began to journey about and to "pursue worldly business no further than as truth opened [his] way."[9] He presently began to be much concerned about the evils of slavery, at that time practiced by Quakers as by others, and quietly set his face against an institution which he believed was destined to be "grievous to posterity."[10] To

[7] *H. C.*, i, 188.   [8] *H. C.*, i, 185.   [9] *H. C.*, i, 185.   [10] *H. C.*, i, 191.

act upon his convictions in this matter was not always easy
or profitable, as we see from the account[11] of his refusal to
write the will of a certain Quaker slaveholder. Woolman
felt regret at the loss of the employment and at the necessity of giving offence. But far more deeply he felt "that
acting contrary to present outward interest, from a motive
of Divine love and in regard to truth and righteousness,
and thereby incurring the resentment of people, opens the
way to a treasure better than silver, and to a friendship
exceeding the friendship of men." [12]

The temper shown in this incident is typical of the entire
journal, and it inclines one to believe that such beautiful
serenity and modesty as Woolman's are perhaps more rare,
as they are certainly more lovely, than mere avoidance of
sin. Woolman's care was not to be seen of men, but to be
prompted by "the pure spirit which inwardly moves upon the
heart." [13]   A man taught, as he was, "to wait in silence,
sometimes many weeks together," [14] until he hears God's
voice, is not likely to offend by an appearance of self-seeking
or self-praise.

Yet it would be a mistake to leave these two interesting
and instructive autobiographies with the feeling that one is
the record of a pure and exalted spirit, the other a story of
mere self-seeking. Woolman, though both in deed and in
temper, far above this world, wrought no small part of a
great practical reform. If Franklin's life seems earthy in
comparison, it should be remembered that, whatever his
motives, he did manage to confer upon his country such
benefits in science, in literature, diplomacy, practical arts,
and public welfare as should entitle him to a respect which
we may well deny to many of his rules for practicing the
art of life. We could spare the practical advantages of having had among us a man like Franklin only if it were necessary to do so in order that the inner light which guided
John Woolman might not be extinguished.

[11] *H. C.,* i 197.   [12] *H. C.,* i, 197.   [13] *H. C.,* i, 184.   [14] *H. C.,* i, 184.

V. JOHN STUART MILL

By Professor O. M. W. Sprague

THE first three chapters of the "Autobiography of John Stuart Mill,"[1] by far the most interesting part of the work, are concerned with the methods and results of his extraordinary education. Under the direct supervision of his father he began serious study with Greek at the tender age of three; at twelve he had covered the equivalent of the classical and mathematical requirements for graduation at the English universities, while in history and philosophy he had gone far beyond the requirements of those institutions of learning. Thereafter he continued his studies with unflagging industry, though along more special lines and in large measure independently, very much after the manner of scholarly graduates of the universities ten years his senior. Before he was twenty he had edited a ponderous legal treatise in a fashion which would have been highly creditable to any scholar in the full maturity of his powers. He was then, at twenty, clearly five, and perhaps ten, years in advance of that stage of intellectual acquirement which he would presumably have reached if he had received the education then, or, indeed, now, customary.

THE SUPPOSED ADVANTAGES OF PRECOCITY

By Mill himself this industrious childhood and youth was looked upon as an unmixed blessing. In the opening paragraph of the "Autobiography" he expresses the opinion that his experience shows that usually the early years of life are little better than wasted. But though no one can doubt that the rigorous mental discipline to which the younger Mill was subjected by his father was highly effective, educational methods fortunately have not been influenced by it in the

[1] *Harvard Classics,* xxv.

slightest degree. Contrasted with accepted methods, his education was superior in only one respect—it did save time. It enabled Mill to begin work as a mature writer at an unusually early age. But even so it does not follow that he was consequently able to do more or better work during his life than he would have otherwise accomplished. The addition of five or ten years at the outset of a life of normal length, and the work accomplished during those particular years, are not necessarily a net addition to its total achievement. Before drawing this conclusion we should need to be sure that physical strength and mental alertness were not prematurely lessened in consequence of the early training. After all, for continuous constructive intellectual work, the keeping of the mind open to new impressions and ideas is the one thing fundamentally important; and, while Mill was far superior to many of the world's great thinkers in this respect, this trait does not seem to have been due to the character of his education.

THE DEFECTS OF MILL'S EDUCATION

That he was deprived of the ordinary activities and pleasures of childhood and youth does not seem to have been an occasion of regret to Mill. As a philosopher and psychologist he might have been expected to recognize that his exclusive absorption in study during his early years must have narrowed the range of his knowledge of life and his capacity to act with and to lead other men. Mill's attitude toward life was always, and especially in the earlier years of his career, excessively intellectual. He exaggerated the force of reasoned conclusions as a factor in individual conduct and as a means of bringing about social improvement. One cannot but feel that the few years saved by Mill in the acquiring of knowledge from books involved some sacrifice of knowledge and understanding of the ordinary impulses and motives of men and women.

Still another defect in an education such as Mill received remains for consideration, though happily he escaped its threatened consequences. His father was one of the foremost of the utilitarian philosophers. He applied the principles of that school to the various problems of individual and of social improvement earnestly and with no lack of dogmatism. He impressed his views upon the mind of his son when he was far too young to subject them to critical analysis and to form an independent judgment regarding them through comparison with the opinions of other thinkers and from experience of life itself. Mill's early writings are, therefore, and quite naturally, little more than the expression of the views of his father with such acute modifications as might be expected from one gifted with his powerful intellect.

THE STARVING OF EMOTION

In the course of time the utilitarian philosophy, in the form, in which it had come to him from his father, ceased to satisfy the distinctly more emotional nature of the son. He became so completely disillusioned with the dry content of this philosophy that he became depressed, lost all joy in work and therewith the capacity for constructive intellectual effort.[2] Perhaps the most valuable part of the "Autobiography" is the account of this distressed and anxious period, and of the various influences which widened his horizon and humanized his views of life and its significance. Being a man of books, it was largely through a change in the character of his reading that he found solace. The poems of Wordsworth were the most potent single influence. It is altogether likely that a person born with less varied natural endowments would have remained content with and fixed in the cast of thought resulting from premature acquaintance with a single school of philosophy.

MILL'S CONTRIBUTION TO UTILITARIANISM AND LIBERALISM

This experience is reflected in the contribution made by Mill to utilitarian ethical theories. While adhering to the position that happiness is simply the sum total of pleasures, he made a distinction between higher and lower qualities of pleasure, regarding the higher as indefinitely more desirable

[2] See *H. C.*, xxv, 88-98.

than the lower. The criteria for making an exact classification of pleasures were, however, not fully and adequately worked out by Mill. Various branches of knowledge, in particular psychology and sociology, had not been developed sufficiently far for the purpose. On this, as on many other subjects, the work of Mill has been superseded, owing to fundamental differences in methods of approach even more than to the accumulation of additional data. Among influences of special far-reaching importance may be mentioned the evolutionary hypothesis, and what may be called, in contradistinction to the intellectual analytical psychology of Mill's time, the scientific psychology of the present.

The most influential of all Mill's writings has been "The Principles of Political Economy," published in 1848. In writing this treatise, Mill had two purposes in view. In the first place, he wished to bring together the many improvements which had been made in the principles of the subject since the appearance of "The Wealth of Nations"[3] in 1776 and, following the example of Adam Smith, to illustrate their practical applications. Here he was conspicuously successful. Many writers in recent years have set themselves the same task with no such measure of accomplishment. In the second place, he wished to relate economic principles and phenomena to his own social ideals and social philosophy. The character of these social ideals and the nature of his social philosophy are abundantly set forth in the "Autobiography,"[4] where particular attention is given to the influence upon his mind of his wife and of Auguste Comte, the father of the science of sociology. It can hardly be said that Mill was fully successful in this effort. The purely economic part of the treatise and the social philosophy are not fused together and at times are positively contradictory. Nevertheless, the treatise gained in human interest from the effort thus made, and at all events the way was indicated toward a broader treatment of social and economic questions than had been customary among economists since the time of Adam Smith.

The personality revealed in the "Autobiography" is one

[3] H. C., x, and see lecture on Adam Smith in the course on Political Science.
[4] H. C., xxv, 146-153.

that cannot fail to command respect and admiration. An ardent desire for social as well as individual progress is conspicuous both in the analysis of the growth of his own mind and in what is said about his own writings. Detailed consideration of the various reforms which he advocated in his writings is impossible within the narrow limits of a single lecture. In a general way it may be noted that Mill expected greater results from the removal of obstructions to freedom of thought and action[5] and from education than in fact have been realized. It is now more clearly evident that the removal of restrictions is often no more than an indispensable preliminary to positive means of improvement and that opportunities thus provided are by no means certain to be made use of. After making every qualification, however, the liberal movement of the nineteenth century surely made possible a long step forward in human progress. In this movement the writings of John Stuart Mill were a potent factor.

[5] See also the lecture on "The Idea of Liberty" in the series on Political Science.

PROSE FICTION

I. GENERAL INTRODUCTION

By Professor W. A. Neilson

I

WHEN the literary historian seeks to assign to each age its favorite form of literature, he finds no difficulty in dealing with our own time. As the Middle Ages delighted in long romantic narrative poems, the Elizabethans in drama, the Englishman of the reigns as Anne and the early Georges in didactic and satirical verse, so the public of our day is enamored of the novel. Almost all types of literary production continue to appear, but whether we judge from the lists of publishers, the statistics of public libraries, or general conversation, we find abundant evidence of the enormous preponderance of this kind of literary entertainment in popular favor.

EARLY FORMS OF FICTION

Though the instinct for a good story, on which the interest in fiction is based, is of immemorial antiquity, and may well be as old as human speech, the novel, as we understand it, is comparatively modern. The unsophisticated folk tale, represented by the contents of such collections as that of the brothers Grimm,[1] lacks the element of lifelikeness both in incident and character, and is too limited in scale to be regarded as anything but a very remote ancestor. The "Fables" ascribed to Æsop[2] are mere anecdotes with a moral. The myths[3] of both the Mediterranean and the Northern

[1] *Harvard Classics*, xvii, 51ff. [2] *H. C.*, xvii, 9ff.
[3] As contained, for example, in the "Odyssey," *H. C.*, vol. xxii, and the "Song of the Volsungs," xlix, 265ff.

nations are not primarily concerned with human life at all.
Epic poetry,[4] besides deriving from its verse a sustained
emotional elevation usually impossible in prose, finds its
central interest, not in individual personality or the passion
of love, but in some great national or racial issue.   The
romances[5] of the Middle Ages, though usually centering in
the fortunes of individuals and often dealing with love, are
superficial in treatment, loose in construction, and primarily
interesting as marvelous adventure.   The *fabliaux*[6] of the
same period, which, with the *novelle*[7] of the Renaissance,
belong to the ancestry of the short story of the modern
magazine, are concerned with single situations, and do not
attempt to display a whole phase of life in its subtlety and
complexity.   All these forms contain, in the imaginative
nature of their material, an element common to them and
the novel; but the negative statements which have been
made regarding each show how much they fall short or go
beyond our modern conception of prose fiction.

THE RISE OF THE NOVEL

Yet, though differing in these important and often fundamental respects from the modern novel, these earlier varieties of imaginative narratives contributed in a number of
ways to the making of the type dominant to-day.   In the
sixteenth century, for instance, we find appearing, first in
Spain and then in England, the so-called picaresque novel,[8]
a story told in the first person by a roguish servant, who
passes from master to master and exposes both his own
rascality and the seamy side of the more fashionable life of
his time.   Many of the episodes are of the kind narrated in
the *fabliaux* and *novelle,* but they are strung together by the
history of the rogue hero.   This type has persisted with
variations, especially the loss of the servant element, down

---

[4] For examples in *H. C.,* see "Odyssey," vol. xxii; "Æneid," vol. xiii;
"Paradise Lost" and "Paradise Regained," iv, 89ff. and 363ff.; and cf. the
lectures on Poetry.
[5] Cf., especially Malory, *H. C.,* xxxv, 107ff.
[6] Such as the Tales of the Miller and the Reeve in Chaucer's "Canterbury
Tales."
[7] Such as the stories in Boccaccio's "Decameron."
[8] The earliest English example is Nash's "Jack Wilton, or the Unfortunate
Traveller."

to our own time, and reached its highest pitch of art in English in Thackeray's "Barry Lyndon."

The Elizabethan romance, represented by such a work as Sir Philip Sidney's "Arcadia," is in respect of realism much farther from our novel than the picaresque tale. But in its abundance of sentiment and frequency of moral purpose, it has elements which the novel of roguery lacked. Characterization, which so far had rarely been a prominent feature in any form of fiction except the drama, was developed in the seventeenth century in a peculiar species of writing known as the *Character*,[9] outside of fiction altogether. The character was a short sketch of a typical figure of the time, used largely for purposes of social satire, apparently general in its application, but not infrequently written with an individual in view.

We find this form elaborated in a slight setting of situation and narrative in the De Coverley papers[10] contributed by Addison and Steele to the "Spectator"; and when the novel in the modern sense arose about a generation later, the practice in the analysis and presentation of typical human beings which the character had afforded proved of considerable service.

NOVEL AND DRAMA

Perhaps more contributive than either the older story of romantic adventure or the character sketch, was the drama. The seventeenth century had seen, especially in comedy, the drama descending from heroic themes of kings and princes to pictures of contemporary life in ordinary society, not highly realistic as we understand the term, yet reproducing many of the types and much of the atmosphere existing around the author. It had cultivated the sense of a well-knit plot, of effective situation, and of the interplay of character and action—all elements transferable to prose narrative. And when, in the middle of the eighteenth century, we find the novel beginning to take the place of the stage as the dominant kind of imaginative entertainment, it is easy

9 Among the best-known collections is that of **Overbury.**
10 *H. C.*, xxvii, 89ff.

to see how much the younger form owed to the elder. There had long been an interchange of material between the two species. In the time of Shakespeare, to go no farther back, the playwrights frankly dramatized familiar stories from history, romance, and *novella,* and occasionally the story of a popular play was retold in prose narrative. Both processes are familiar to-day. Many successful novels appear later on the stage, and not a few successful plays are "novelized." There are, of course, marked differences in the kind of thing that can be best told by narrative or action respectively, and the failure to recognize these differences accounts for the frequent ill success of this kind of translation. But, after all allowance for this has been made, many of the elements of effective story-telling remain common to both novel and play.

DEFOE AND RICHARDSON

The two chief claimants for the credit of founding the modern English novel are Daniel Defoe[11] and Samuel Richardson. Defoe's stories depend for their unity chiefly upon the personality of the leading character. They are usually series of episodes strung along the thread of the hero's or heroine's life. Many of them, from their pre-occupation with the criminal classes, approach the picaresque; and even "Robinson Crusoe," justly the most popular, is more an adventure tale than a novel. His most notable characteristic is a singular realism, achieved by a skillful selection of matter-of-fact details, which produces a circumstantial effect like that of a modern newspaper report. But the realism, clever though it is, is mainly external; and comparatively little in the way of insight into character or motive is to be found in most of his stories.

The great works of Richardson, "Pamela," "Clarissa Harlowe," and "Sir Charles Grandison," are novels without question. Not only does he achieve a large unity of action, building into a shapely structure round his central figure a complex of persons, motives, and social conditions, but he deals in detail with the inner life of his characters, and he gives to passion and sentiment the pervading importance

[11] *H. C.,* xxvii, 142.

that has now become traditional in this form of literature. Sentiment, indeed, with him often enough degenerated into sentimentality, and he dwelt on the emotional and pathetic elements in his narrative with a deliberation and an emphasis successfully calculated to draw from his readers the greatest possible lachrymose response.

FIELDING, SMOLLETT, STERNE, GOLDSMITH

It was largely this exaggeration of the pathetic, and the idealizing of the chief character in order to gain an opportunity for the pathetic, that led Fielding[12] to begin his first novel, "Joseph Andrews," as a parody of Richardson's "Pamela." Pamela had been pictured as a virtuous maid-servant, chastely resisting the approaches of her young master, and Fielding planned the story of Pamela's brother Joseph, placed in a corresponding position toward his mistress, to ridicule the absurdities of his predecessor's method. But he soon became interested in his hero for his own sake, and in this novel, and still more in his masterpiece, "Tom Jones," he treated human nature with a robust frankness that earned for him the famous compliment of his disciple, Thackeray, that he was the last English novelist who dared to draw a man.

Some of Fielding and perhaps more of Defoe is to be found in the sordid tales of Tobias Smollett; and in Laurence Sterne we have the sentimental tendencies of Richardson carried to the last extreme, but mingled in extraordinary fashion with a conscious humor that doubles back on the sentiment, the whole related in a style of remarkable individuality and brilliant wit. In the same period, Oliver Goldsmith produced his one novel, "The Vicar of Wakefield," a delicately drawn picture of a phase of contemporary society enriched with a group of characters, broadly typical, but delineated with an abundance of tender sympathy and gentle humor.

FICTION IN THE ROMANTIC MOVEMENT

Meantime, there had begun in England, as elsewhere, that complex reaction against the intellectualism of the eigh-

[12] *H. C.,* xxxix, 184.

teenth century known as the Romantic Movement. Among its more obvious phases was the revival of interest in remote places and periods, and especially in the Middle Ages. The extent to which this interest was ill-informed and merely sentimental is nowhere better illustrated than in the rise of the so-called "Gothic Romance." This variety of fiction is usually regarded as beginning with "The Castle of Otranto" of Horace Walpole, the son of the great Whig minister, Sir Robert Walpole, and the type of the fashionable dilettante of the London of his day. Walpole had no real understanding or sympathy for the spirit of the Middle Ages, but one of his fads was mediæval armor, furniture, and architecture, and out of this arose his curious half-sincere experiment in fiction. The real leader in the production of this sort of "thriller," however, was Mrs. Radcliffe,[13] who was followed by Clara Reeves[14] and scores of minor imitators. The novels of these ladies were set in a vaguely remote period of chivalry, their scenes were ancient castles, with concealed panels, subterranean passages, and family ghosts; their plots turned upon the usurpation of family estates by wicked uncles or villainous neighbors, and on the reparations and sufferings of missing heirs and heroines of "sensibility"; and their characters were the stereotyped figures of ordinary melodrama. A special development of this type appeared in the "School of Terror" headed by M. G. Lewis, whose nickname of "Monk" Lewis was derived from his novel of "Ambrosio, or the Monk," in which the terrifying and, it must be said, the licentious possibilities of the Gothic romance were carried to a high pitch.

This, on the whole, rather worthless species, which had been accompanied by many feeble attempts at a more definitely historical type of novel, culminated surprisingly in the romances of Sir Walter Scott. Scott, however, had in his training and in his vast reading a basis for historical and romantic fiction all his own. He stripped the Gothic type of romance of its sentimentality and absurdity, strengthened it with his great fund of historical and legendary information, gave it stability with his sanity and humor, and interest by

[13] For example, "The Mysteries of Udolpho."
[14] As in "The Old English Baron."

his creation of a great series of vigorous and picturesque creations. The art of fiction has gained in technical dexterity since Scott's day, stories now begin sooner and move more rapidly, conversation is reported with a greater lifelikeness, the tragedy in human life is more often given its due place; but the entrancing narratives of Scott, with all their deliberation, are likely to retain their charm, and his men and women still have blood in their veins. He created the historical novel, not only for Britain but for Europe, and all its writers since have been proud to sit at his feet.

GENTEEL REALISM—THE NOVEL OF MANNERS

In the time of Doctor Johnson, Fanny Burney, the daughter of a noted musician, and lady-in-waiting to the Queen, gathered out of her experience of London society materials for her "Evelina," a novel of manners shrewdly observed and acutely chronicled. She is the chief predecessor of Scott's contemporary and rival, Jane Austen, the daughter of a provincial clergyman, whose knowledge of the world was practically confined to the county in which she lived and the watering places, like Bath, where she spent an occasional vacation. But she had tact enough to confine her books[15] to the life she knew; and this life, with its squires, its curates, its old ladies, its managing mothers and eligible daughters, is pictured with a minuteness and fidelity that has scarcely been surpassed. She writes smoothly, with an evasiveness in her characteristic irony that makes her personality hard to grasp, while it prevents that personality from coming between the picture and the spectator. Limited in scope, commonplace in incident, and deliberately ordinary in type of characters, her novels have the exquisite finish and perfection of a miniature.

Parallel in some respects to Miss Austen's novels of English provincial life are Miss Edgeworth's,[16] dealing with the Irish, and Miss Ferrier's[17] with the Scottish field. Together these ladies stand at the head of that still vigorous branch of fiction which in America is mapping the life of the whole

---

[15] *E.g.*, "Pride and Prejudice," "Sense and Sensibility," "Emma." For a satire on the Gothic Romance, cf. her "Northanger Abbey."
[16] *E.g.*, "Castle Rackrent," and "The Absentee."   [17] *E.g.*, "Marriage."

country with sectional novels, like those of New England by Miss Jewett, Miss Wilkins, and Mrs. Riggs, of the South by James Lane Allen, George W. Cable, and Thomas Nelson Page, of the Middle West by Meredith Nicholson and Booth Tarkington.

THE GREATER VICTORIANS

Fifty years ago the world of readers was divisible into the partisans of two great novelists, who, despite their limitations, made more obvious by the development of fiction on the Continent, still rank among the highest. William Makepeace Thackeray, who went back, as has been said, to the work of Fielding for his models, devoted himself chiefly to the picturing of English society, in the more restricted sense of the word, from Queen Anne to Queen Victoria. Definitely and perhaps restrictedly English in his outlook on life, his view of the human scene is somewhat insular. His natural sentiment was tempered by an acute perception of the meaner elements in human nature to such a degree that his work has a strong satirical element, and some have even been misled into thinking him characteristically a cynic. Gifted with a superb style, with profound sympathy and insight into human emotion, and with a power of rendering the picturesque aspects of a society, Thackeray remains a great master.

The work of his contemporary, Charles Dickens, has had an even greater popular success. Dickens's early career gave him a knowledge of a much humbler grade of society than Thackeray pictures, and at the same time left him with a vivid sense of the wrongs under which the more unfortunate members of that society suffered. This led him to devote many of his works to the redress of social grievances, and connects him with the general humanitarian movements of modern times. Powerful as was Dickens's influence for reform in his own time, it seems clear that the very specific nature of the evils he attacked is bound to impair the permanence of his work, as it always impaired the artistic value. But we relish still his buoyant humor and geniality, the binding interest of his complex though sometimes confusing plots, and the charm of his immense throng of creations, typical to the point of caricature, but in their setting vital, appealing, and eminently memorable.

SCIENCE AND PHILOSOPHY IN THE NOVEL

In spite of the abundant humor in both Thackeray and Dickens, the novel with them had become a very serious form, the vehicle of important moral and social truths. In the hands of its more notable masters, serious it has remained. The prevalence of the scientific point of view, so marked since the promulgation of the theories of Charles Darwin, has left distinct traces on the history of fiction. The philosophical and scientific learning of George Eliot appears in her work in the emphasis on the reign of law in the character of the individual, and, although she too possesses a rich vein of humor, the charming playfulness in which her immediate predecessors permitted themselves to indulge is replaced by an almost portentous realization of the responsibilities of art and life. In Thomas Hardy, too, the scientific influence is plainly felt, the overwhelming power of environment and circumstance being presented with a force so crushing as to leave the reader depressed with a sense of the helplessness of the individual, without any compensating faith in a benevolence controlling the external forces which overwhelm him. Yet these writers display profound psychological insight, and make distinguished contributions to the progress of the art of fiction in its advance toward a more and more complete and penetrating portrayal of the whole of human life.

Less somber in tone, but no less brilliant in workmanship, are the novels of George Meredith. Hampered in regard to the greater public by a style at once dazzling and obscure, Meredith has been acclaimed by his fellow craftsmen as a great master. Beginning partly under the influence of Dickens, Meredith gained for himself at length a peculiar and distinguished position as perhaps the most intellectual of the English novelists, or, at least, the novelist who concerns himself most with the intellectual processes of his character. Yet he is far from impoverished on the emotional side, and there are few scenes in fiction more poignant in their tragedy than that which closes "The Ordeal of Richard Feverel."

Besides the influence of modern science, English fiction has latterly been much affected by foreign models, especially French and Russian. The tracing of these streams, however, would bring us to the consideration of men still writing, and involve us in a mass of production which cannot be characterized here, and on which we cannot hope to have as yet a proper perspective. The great amount of distinguished writing in the field of the English novel which has been revealed even in his rapid survey of its history will have suggested to the reader why it was found hopeless to try to represent it in The Harvard Classics. But these writers are easy of access, and this is the side of literature which the modern reader is least apt to ignore. Yet it is also the side which is most likely to be read carelessly, without consideration of purpose or method; so that it may now be worth while to try to come to some understanding as to its aim and the conditions of its excellence.

II

THE PURPOSE OF FICTION

In considering the purpose which works of fiction may be supposed to fulfill, it will be of interest and value to note what some of the more prominent writers have said with regard to their reasons for practicing the art. The more selfishly personal motives may be passed over quickly. Money and fame have been desired and welcomed by most authors, as by most men, but they help us little to an understanding of the purpose of literature. Yet there are some who have written with neither of these in view, like Jane Austen, who died leaving a considerable part of her work unpublished, and apparently without having sought to publish it. Since the motives of men are more usually complex than simple, it is a safe assumption that even those who have frankly written for a living, or who have acknowledged the lure of ambition, have had other things in view as well, and have not found profit or honor incompatible with deeper and more altruistic aims.

Of these last, the most commonly claimed is the moral improvement of the reader. No one has been more explicit about this than Richardson, whose preface to "Pamela" is characteristic enough to quote at length:

"If to divert and entertain, and at the same time to instruct and improve the minds of the youth of both sexes;

"If to inculcate religion and morality in so easy and agreeable a manner as shall render them equally delightful and profitable;

"If to set forth, in the most exemplary lights, the parental, the filial, and the social duties;

"If to paint vice in its proper colours, to make it deservedly odious; and to set virtue in its own amiable light, and to make it look lovely;

"If to draw characters with justness and to support them distinctly;

"If to effect all these good ends in so probable, so natural, so lively, a manner, as shall engage the passions of every sensible reader, and attach their regard to the story;

"If these be laudable or worthy recommendations, the editor of the following letters ventures to assert that all these ends are obtained here, together."

In similar vein his "Clarissa" is "proposed as an exemplar to her sex," and is made as perfect as is "consistent with human frailty," her faults being put in chiefly lest there should be "nothing for the Divine grace and a purified state to do."

Fielding, though less verbose, is no less explicit. He claims for "Tom Jones" that "to recommend goodness and innocence hath been my sincere endeavour in this history," and that he has "endeavoured to laugh mankind out of their favourite follies and vices." Of "Amelia" he says: "The following book is sincerely designed to promote the cause of virtue." The frequent satirical tone of Thackeray, as well as the nature of his analysis of human motive, testifies to his sharing Fielding's desire to drive men out of their follies and vices by ridicule and contempt.

Dickens characteristically combines the improvement of the individual with the reform of institutions. Of "Martin Chuzzlewit" he says: "My main object in this story was to exhibit in a variety of aspects the commonest of all the vices; to show how selfishness propagates itself, and to what a grim giant it may grow from small beginnings." Again, "I have taken every possible opportunity of showing the want of sanitary improvements in the neglected dwellings of the poor."

In contrast to such ethical claims as these, Scott's confession, "I write for general amusement," sounds more than humble. Yet he frequently repeats it. He hopes "to relieve anxiety of mind," "to unwrinkle a brow bent with the furrows of daily toil." At times he approaches the moral aim of his more serious brethren, "to fill the place of bad thoughts and suggest better," "to induce an idler to study the history of his country."

THE NOVEL WITH A PURPOSE

In contrast with these older statements of purpose is the assumption prevailing among the more serious of modern novelists that fiction is primarily concerned with giving a picture of life. This aim is set forth not only in explanation of their own work, but as a test of the value of that of others, irrespective of intention. By it is displayed the peculiar danger of "novels with a purpose," whether that purpose is moral or social. They point out that Richardson's method of "exemplars," whether of virtue to be imitated or vice to be shunned, is apt to result in creations snow-white or pitch black, which fail in truth because human nature, even in the best and worst, is a complex of good and evil; and which fail in effectiveness, because the reader finds no corroboration in his experience and remains unconvinced of their reality. Similarly the novelist with a theory to prove, of the stupidity or cruelty of bad poor laws, foul prisons, red tape and the law's delays, as in Dickens; of the rights of women, the falsity of Calvinism, the wickedness of commercial marriages, as in more modern writers, is likely to drive his point home by exaggeration, false proportion, some interference with the natural way of the world. The aim to recommend virtuous action by the display of "poetic justice" is open to the same objections. In both cases there results loss of both truth and effectiveness. The same may be true of both the satirical and the merely entertaining aims: in the first, the emphasis on the traits held up to ridicule runs the risk of going beyond the bounds of the normal; in the second, the curious, the marvelous, the mysterious, or the amusing may be sought for at the expense of the natural, with the result that the reader's skepticism prevents his submitting himself to the illusion of reality necessary for the enjoyment of the pleasure or the advantages to be derived from imaginative art.

KINDS OF REALISM

The zeal for true pictures of life which thus censures the older theories of "instruction and delight" is part of the modern tendency to realism, and is connected with the triumph of the scientific point of view. Indeed, its most extreme advocates are at times quite explicit about this: "We should work," says Zola, "upon characters, passions, human and social facts, as the physicist and chemist work with inorganic bodies, as the physiologist works with living organisms." On this theory he believed himself to have constructed his novels; and though he did not carry it out as rigorously as he supposed he did, the results of it are all too evident in the assembling in his pages of vast masses of almost statistical facts, set down without regard to taste, convention, or decency.

But not all modern realists interpret their creed in so mechanical a manner. Many have held to the belief in true pictures of life without committing themselves to the extreme view that the record should be untinged with the personality of the writer. And, indeed, it is now fairly well agreed that such absolute objectivity, is neither possible nor desirable. It is not possible for many reasons. All the facts concerning any human episode, not to say life, cannot be recorded in a book, so infinitely numerous and complex are they, linked to thousands of others which are necessary

to a full statement of them, and themselves involving a life
history and an immemorial ancestry. Thus in the most
severely realistic work selection is necessary, the selection
of what seems significant to the author; and with this selection the personal element has already entered. Again, the
sympathy of the author unconsciously determines questions
of relative stress and emphasis; and intimate qualities of
temperament and imagination affect the atmosphere in
which the most baldly reported incidents take place.

ARTISTIC *versus* LITERAL TRUTH

So we arrive at the important distinction between artistic
and literal truth. This is a distinction which everyone is
accustomed to recognize in daily intercourse, yet which even
professional critics are liable to muddle at times in the discussion of art. We all know how it is possible to report the
bare facts of an action or the actual words of a conversation so as to convey to the hearer a totally false impression.
On the other hand, an accurate view of what was done and
said, with the right implications as to character, motive, and
tone, may be conveyed without any reproduction of facts,
in the narrow sense, at all. The second method is clearly
that at which the artist should aim. His business is with
the typical, not the individual; the permanently characteristic, not the temporarily actual; the spirit, not the letter.

Most of us have heard discussions of a book in which a
critic has urged as an objection that a certain incident is
not lifelike, when a friend of the author has triumphantly
answered that that precise incident is *the* thing in the work
which actually happened. Supposing that the criticism was
just, we see at once that one of two things must have occurred; either the author did not understand what happened
in real life, failed to see its true causes and relations, and
so did not himself know the real facts; or else he reported
it out of its true relations, and so deprived the reader of
the means of knowing the real facts. An apparent third
possibility might also be mentioned; that the episode in
question was what might be called a "freak" happening, an
abnormal occurrence like the birth of an eight-legged calf,

which, while historically actual, is really out of the order of
nature, and not in itself fit to be a link in the chain of happenings which a true picture of life represents. Of course,
such an abnormality has a cause; but the obscurity of the
cause makes this possibility a special case under our first
explanation—it is not easily displayed in connection with its
true causes.

THE AUTHOR'S PHILOSOPHY OF LIFE

It is evident, then, that the recording of mere detached
fact, untouched by the author's personality, is not only impossible, but may, when attempted, lead to the violation of
actual truth. The door is thus opened to the exercise of
the artistic judgment, both in the selection of material and
in its manipulation and presentation. The background of
this judgment, as it were, is the general view of human
nature and of the world at large which the individual author
entertains. This view has been arrived at by the observation and meditation which he has practised throughout his
life; the conclusions which it involves affect the interpretation of everything that comes under his notice; and its first
effect on his art is in determining the choice of subjects to
be treated. Individual people and events will arrest his attention and suggest artistic treatment according as they are
happy illustrations of what he has perceived to be general
truths; and in his treatment he will not scruple to modify
them to make them more apt. He will choose what Bagehot
calls "literatesque" subjects, subjects fit to be put in a book,
as he calls picturesque subjects those fit to be put in a picture; and he defines both as those summing up in a single
instance the characteristics that mark the class as a whole
to which they belong.

DEFENSE OF THE NOVEL WITH A PURPOSE

Let us now compare this conclusion as to the legitimate
purpose of the novel with such a moral aim as that of
Richardson. As a matter of fact, the difference lies more
in his way of stating his theory than in his practice. So far
as his observation of life led him to believe that people of

the type of Pamela and Clarissa act in general as these
heroines do, and that their fortunes in general are determined by their character and their society in the manner he
represents, so far he is merely using them properly as
illustrations of the view of life of which experience has
convinced him.   So far, however, as he modifies their characters or careers to conform not to the way the world is,
but to the way he wants people to believe the world is, he is
artistically false, his picture fails in truth, and the modern
reader declines to be interested or convinced.   The whole
question turns on which the author puts first, artistic truth
or effect.   If he is more concerned with specific effects than
with truth, his "novel with a purpose" will deserve the contempt with which the phrase is usually employed.   If his
main concern is with truth, his "purpose," being merely a
special illustration of the truth with whatever practical result in mind, will do no harm, but may add greatly to the
zest with which he paints his picture.

THE VALUE OF FICTION

Assuming the correctness of the view that the novelist's
business is to give true pictures of life, we are met by the
question of the value of this result.   The answer to this is twofold: there is an intellectual value and an emotional value.

The amount and range of experience that comes to the
ordinary man is of necessity limited.   Most of us are tied
to a particular locality, move in a society representing only
a few of the myriad human types that exist, spend the majority of our waking hours attending to a more or less monotonous series of duties or enjoying a small variety of
recreations.   In such a life there is often no great range of
opportunity; and the most adventurous career touches, after
all, but a few points in the infinite complex of existence.
But we have our imaginations, and it is to these that the
artist appeals.   The discriminating reader of fiction can
enormously enlarge his experience of life through his acquaintance with the new tracts brought within his vision
by the novelist, at second hand, it is true, but the vivid
writer can often bring before our mental eyes scenes and

persons whom we can realize and understand with a greater thoroughness than those we perceive directly through our senses. The materials for the understanding of men and life are thus greatly increased, and at the same time the data for the forming of those generalizations which collectively make up our philosophy.

The basis of all sound altruistic activity is sympathy, and sympathy again depends on the imagination. We act tactfully and effectively for the relief of another's suffering when we are able imaginatively to put ourselves in that other's place. Now, familiarity with well-described characters in fiction not only makes us acquainted with a much wider variety of human beings and enables us to understand them, but it provides us with a kind of emotional gymnastic, increasing our capacity for putting ourselves whole-heartedly and clear-mindedly in the other man's place. Thus such familiarity is a corrective of both provincialism and selfishness, broadening the outlook and enlarging the emotional range through the development of the imagination. Here is an ethical result more effective by far than that indicated by the old formula of "exemplars," warnings, and poetic justice, and one that implies no forcing of the truth to bring its lessons home.

THE METHODS OF FICTION

In what has been said about fiction as a picturing of life, something has already been implied as to the methods involved. There remain, however, some other important questions of technic on which we may briefly touch.

However true a writer's picture of life, it is of little value if it does not impress itself on the reader. The question of effectiveness is thus of great importance, and with certain classes of authors it not infrequently absorbs them to the exclusion even of the question of truth.

The most comprehensive element of effectiveness is structure. A story that does not hang well together, in which the scenes are mere scattered episodes, which has no palpable thread, no climaxes, and no conclusion, is not likely to be read through, and, if it is, it rouses no deep interest, intellectual or emotional, and leaves no definite stamp on the memory. The factors which it lacks are those that give unity of structure. From this point of view, the problem of the novelist is to make as close-knit and thoroughly organized a plot as possible without violating natural probability in appearance or reality. This is the greatest of technical problems for the author, as the critical appreciation of structure is the last power to be acquired by the careless reader; yet no sound capacity for judging or enjoying fiction is possible to him who cannot thus view the work as a whole.

Somewhat similar faculties are required on a smaller scale in the handling of situation and incident. Many writers are able to present these effectively in isolation; but the great writer treats them not as beads on a string, but as stones in a great building.

Both plot and incident in turn must be vitally related to character. Not only must the persons stand out clearly described and recognizable as the people we know, but the things that happen and the kind of characters through and to whom they happen, must reciprocally explain each other. Much discussion has taken place with regard to the propriety of explicit analysis of character in the novel, some writers feeling bound to let a character's words and deeds alone explain him as they do in the drama, others feeling free to come forward in their own persons and explain frankly the motives and feelings of their creatures. Much naturally depends on the way it is done. Thackeray's friendly gossip with the reader behind the backs of his *dramatis personæ* is often so charming that we should be loath to lose it; and often the explicit statement of the author saves us much labor and prevents important misunderstanding. On the other hand, there is unquestionably great satisfaction in the drawing of our own inferences, and a considerable gain in the illusion of reality when the actors are allowed to exhibit their quality unaided by a talking showman.

The attempt has here been made to outline some of the main principles of the art of fiction without adopting the

HCL—8

partisan attitude of any one school. Within the limits of these principles there is room for a great variety of type, for realism and romance, for chronicles of the commonplace and annals of adventure, for stirring tales of action and subtle psychological analysis. The endless variety of human life supplies an equally endless variety of themes; and the nature of the theme will properly lead to emphasis now on the external, now on the internal, now on the ordinary, now on the extraordinary, with appropriate variation of the technical methods employed. But with all this variation the demand holds for truth to the permanent and essential traits of human nature and human life, and for vitality and interest in the presentation of this truth.

But what, the reader may ask, of the pleasure from novels? naturally, since the giving of pleasure is usually assumed as the main end of fiction. Well, pleasure largely depends on who is to be pleased: there are readers who could demand no greater pleasure than that sense of enlargement of personality, of the scope of experience and sympathy, which has been put down as the chief value of the novel. It may be claimed, also, that in the demand that fiction should impress vividly and hold the interest powerfully we have provided for the seekers after pleasure. The greatest pleasure is to live broadly and intensely, to feel oneself in a world significant at every point and palpitating in response to our activities, and this the greatest fiction surely tends to give. One of the finest of modern masters of the art, Mr. Henry James, has summed up the matter in an epigram as true as it is brilliant, that we are *entertained* by the novelist because we live at his expense.

II. POPULAR PROSE FICTION

By Professor F. N. Robinson

THE WORKS to be dealt with in the present lecture are widely separated in time and place. They include "Æsop's Fables," a collection which bears the name of a Greek slave of the sixth century, but is actually a growth of many generations before and after him; the "Arabian Nights," which contains Oriental stories of diverse origin; the sagas of mediæval Ireland, as represented by "The Destruction of Da Derga's Hostel"; and the folk origin; the sagas of mediæval Ireland, as represented by the Grimms or imitated by Hans Christian Andersen. In so broad a range of writings there is naturally great variety of matter and style, and there might seem at first to be few common characteristics. But all the works mentioned—or all except Andersen's tales—are alike in being popular prose fiction, and Andersen's collection is an artistic imitation of similar productions.

THE MEANING OF "POPULAR"

The term "popular" is here employed, of course, in a technical meaning, and does not have reference to vogue or popularity, in the ordinary sense. Popular works, in the stricter definition of the term, are anonymous and are held to be the product of many successive authors. They commonly pass through a long period of oral transmission before being committed to writing, and they are consequently cast in a conventional or traditional, rather than an individual, style and form. The exact nature and extent of popular composition is a matter of dispute. In the case of ballad poetry, with its dancing, singing throng, the process of communal authorship can sometimes be actually observed; but in the case of the prose tales no such opportunity exists for collective composition. Still even there the changes and additions introduced by successive narrators make of a story a common product, for which no single author is responsible. Popular works in both prose and verse show various stages of artistry; and just as in the Anglo-Saxon epic of "Beowulf," [1] there is evidence of the hand of a single poet of high order, so in the "Arabian Nights," [2] for example, one may suspect that the style and structure were largely molded by a single writer, or group of writers, of skill and literary training. There are many mooted questions as to the history of the whole type, or as to the exact nature of particular works, but there can be no doubt of the existence of a great body of literature which is in a real sense public property— popular somehow in origin and transmission, and thereby determined in its character. Both the verse and the prose of this popular sort are well represented in The Harvard Classics, the former by the traditional ballads and the latter by the works enumerated above.

THE MODERN TASTE FOR POPULAR LITERATURE

Writings of the kind under consideration would probably have had a less conspicuous place in a literary or educational collection a few generations ago. For interest in popular literature, or, at least, formal attention to it on the part of the learned and cultivated, is largely a growth of the eighteenth and nineteenth centuries. In earlier periods, and especially in those when classical standards prevailed, the study of literature meant primarily the study of great masterpieces of poetry, philosophy, or oratory, and the art of criticism consisted largely in the deduction of rules and standards from such models. The products of the people, if noticed at all by men of letters, were likely to be treated with condescension or perhaps judged by formal standards, as Addison praised the ballad of "Chevy Chase," [3] for conforming in great measure to the narrative method of the "Æneid." [4] But in more recent times the spirit of criticism has changed, and writers have even swung to the opposite

[1] *Harvard Classics,* xlix, 5ff.
[3] *H. C.,* xl, 94.
[2] *H. C.,* xvi, 17ff.
[4] *H. C.,* xiii.

extreme of adulation of all popular products. The part of the people in composition has been magnified, until the "Iliad" or the Beowulf" has been conceived as the actual production of a whole community. With this renewed admiration for popular literature in its highest forms has come an enthusiastic interest in all the minor products of popular or semi-popular composition, and vast numbers of scholars have devoted themselves to the collection and investigation of folk songs and folk tales from every corner of the world. Most interest has doubtless centered in the poetry, as most labor and ingenuity has been spent upon the great epics, such as the "Iliad" or the "Nibelungenlied." But the excellence of much popular prose narrative has also been recognized, and this also has been very extensively studied.

INFLUENCE OF POPULAR UPON ARTISTIC LITERATURE

Though popular fiction has not always occupied a dignified place in the works on literary history, it has long exerted an important influence on the more sophisticated forms of literature. In the ancient world, it is almost too obvious to point out, the myths upon which drama and epic turned were at the outset often popular tales of gods and heroes. The fable, as the embodiment of moral wisdom, has been, of course, the constant resource of speakers and writers, and in the hands of such poets as Marie de France in the twelfth century, or La Fontaine in the seventeenth, it has received the highest finish of art. Though the "Arabian Nights" collection, as a whole, is of recent introduction into European literature, Oriental tales of the sort which compose it circulated extensively in Europe from the time of the crusades and supplied much material for the fiction of the Middle Ages. In the last century, too, poets have found a rich storehouse in the traditions of the days of "good Haroun Alraschid." The folktales of northern Europe, again, as represented by Celtic and Scandinavian sagas or by the modern German collection of the Grimms, have been the source of much lofty poetry and romance. Many a great play or poem goes back in substance to some bit of fairy mythology or to a single tale like that of a

persecuted Cinderella, or of a father and son unwittingly
engaged in mortal combat. The splendid romances of King
Arthur[5] have derived many of their essential elements from
popular sagas not very different in character from the account of Da Derga[6] printed in this series. In the hands of
court poets or polite romancers the original stories were, of
course, often disguised beyond easy recognition. Their
motives were changed, and they were transferred to the
setting of a higher civilization. Oftener than not the
authors who treated them were wholly unaware of the history or meaning of the material. Yet a chief result of the
critical scholarship of the last hundred years has been to
show how the highest products of literary art are derived
from simple elements of popular tradition.

CHARACTERISTICS OF POPULAR NARRATIVE

From the historical point of view, then, popular fiction
has an important place in literary education. But in and
for itself also, without regard to historical standards, this
great body of writings possesses a direct human interest
not inferior to that of the literature of art. The works
selected for the present series illustrate very well the varieties of the type and the phases of life with which it may
be concerned. The collections of Andersen[7] and the
Grimms[8] offer, in general, the least complicated of narratives. The tales, or *Märchen* (as they have come to be
called in English as well as in German), deal with simple
episodes, localized, to be sure, but having for the most part
no marked national or personal character. They are universal in appeal, and almost universal in actual occurrence
wherever folklore has been collected. A very simple stage
of narrative is likewise exhibited by the Æsopic fable.[9] The
hero tale of Ireland, on the other hand, is a more complex
product. Here there is accumulation of episodes, with
something like epic structure; and definite characters, half-
historic and half-legendary, stand out as the heroes of the
action. The localization is significant, and the stories re-

---

[5] *H. C.,* xxxv, 107ff.   [6] *H. C.,* xlix, 211ff.   [7] *H. C.,* xvii, 237ff.
[8] *H. C.,* xvii, 51ff.   [9] *H. C.,* xvii, 9ff.

produce the life and atmosphere of the northern heroic age. Both the narrative prose and the numerous poems that are interspersed in the sagas testify to the existence of a distinct literary tradition, still barbaric in many respects, in the old bardic schools. Finally, the "Arabian Nights" presents a still more elaborate development in a different direction. The fundamental elements again are beast fables, fairy lore, and popular anecdotes of love, prowess, or intrigue; but they are worked up under the influence of a rich and settled civilization and depict, with something like historic fullness, the life and manners of the Mohammedan Middle Ages. The collection, like the works mentioned earlier, is of unknown authorship, and is plainly the product of many men through many generations. But the style gives evidence of a finished literary tradition; the nameless and numerous contributors appear to have been men of books rather than the simple story-tellers of an age of oral delivery. Though not in the stage of individual authorship, the "Arabian Nights" stands yet outside the range of the strictly popular and within the realm of literary composition.

Even in its most elaborate development, however, popular fiction remains something quite different from the customary modern novel or narrative poem. It commonly lacks a sustained plot, worked out with close regard to cause and effect. Still more characteristically it lacks the study of character and the intellectual analysis of such varied problems as occupy the fiction of the present age. The popular romances lay their stress chiefly on incident and adventure or simple intrigue, and set forth only the more familiar and accepted moral teachings. They represent, on the whole, an instinctive or traditional, rather than a highly reflective, philosophy of life. For all these reasons they have come to be regarded chiefly as the literature of children; a natural result, perhaps, of the fact that they originated largely in the childhood of civilization or among the simple peoples in more advanced ages. But it is noteworthy that they were not, in most cases, really intended for the young; and the man or woman who has outgrown them completely has one serious loss to set down against the gains of advancing years.

III. MALORY

By Dr. G. H. Maynadier

SIR THOMAS MALORY is unique among English writers. His famous "Morte Darthur," which came from the press of William Caxton, the first English printer, in 1485, he completed probably in 1470. Thus he wrote at a time when the printing press was beginning to make the various European languages less changeable than they had been when a gentleman's library might consist of but a single parchment manuscript; he was near enough to our own day to be the first English author whose work can now be read with enjoyment and yet without special study. Save for an occasional word which one must look up in a glossary—like the obsolete *wood,* meaning *frenzied*—a page of Malory, despite its archaisms of grammar and expression, is as intelligible as one of the latest magazines or novels. Nevertheless, when he wrote, the world of European civilization was still narrow materially and intellectually. The Atlantic was its bound to the west; the Sahara, to the south; the Far East was an almost mythical Cathay. The Renaissance had scarcely made itself felt beyond Italy; to all but a very few scholars, the old worlds of Greece and Rome and Palestine were known solely through stories from poetry and history so metamorphosed that King David, Julius Cæsar, and Alexander the Great wore mediæval armor and held splendid court like Capet and Plantagenet kings. In spirit Malory is as much of the Middle Ages as if he had died two hundred instead of two score years before Columbus set out to solve the mystery of the western seas. It is hard to believe that only half a century after his death. Englishmen should be reading Homer at Oxford and Cambridge, and Luther translating the New Testament into German; that a few years more, and the leading countries of Europe should be making plans for colonial empire which have resulted in the world-powers of the present. Thanks to his living in just the years that he did, Malory has left us in his "Morte Darthur" a work full of mediæval spirit with almost no mediæval difficulty of language, though with a very charming suggestion of mediævalism in style.

LEGEND AND ROMANCE

Even if the "Morte Darthur" had not this charm of style, it would be important in literature as giving the modern world the most easily intelligible mediæval version of what Tennyson called "the greatest of all poetic subjects." Of the several valuable contributions of the Middle Ages to the general store of European art and thought, none is richer than their mass of legend—stories of saints and martyrs, of many local champions of more or less fame, and of a few who attaining wider fame became great epic heroes of the world. In nearly every case, poetic fame has a basis of historical fact, but most of the superstructure, and all its adornment, is popular story. Such a hero is Siegfried,[1] now the typical representative of the Germanic hero-age, but at first no better known than half a dozen other warriors, like Dietrich of Verona, whose stories grew out of the unsettling migrations of the Germanic peoples in the fourth, fifth, and sixth centuries. Another is Charlemagne,[2] as colossal a figure in mediæval romance as in history is the monarch who was crowned Holy Roman Emperor on Christmas Day in the year 800. An even greater epic hero of the Middle Ages is Arthur, who is much better known to English readers than the others largely because of Sir Thomas Malory.

THE HISTORICAL AND THE LEGENDARY ARTHUR

The historical basis of the Arthur-legends is the Anglo-Saxon conquest of Britain. In the three centuries after the first settlement of the Germanic invaders in that island, the Britons were gradually driven into the moun-

[1] See "The Song of the Volsungs" in *Harvard Classics,* xlix, 265ff.
[2] See "The Song of Roland" in *H. C.,* xlix, 97ff.

tains of Wales and Cumberland and the peninsula of
Cornwall, or they fled across the Channel to turn
Armorica into Brittany. Meanwhile they suffered almost
uniform defeat. But for a while about the year 500 they
won victories that for nearly half a century checked the
Saxon advance. Their leader was Arthur, a good general,
but probably not a king. Now men much in the public eye
attract stories to themselves, as witness the countless anecdotes related of Abraham Lincoln. With peoples of slight
civilization, such stories are full of marvels and portents.
Thus hero-legends are made; thus the Arthur-legend grew up.
Probably immediately after Arthur's death, popular story
began to increase his fame. In the so-called chronicle of a
British monk, Nennius, written three hundred years after
Arthur's victories, we have our sole literary glimpse of the
romantic hero-legend in the making, for Nennius associates
several supernatural tales with the British leader. Presumably among Britons on both sides of the Channel—for
Arthur won his victories before the principal migration to
Armorica—similar association of marvel and adventure with
the national champion was common. By degrees these hero-
tales passed to the neighbors of the Britons. Because of
their interest and poetic charm they came to be known in
both France and England, though always purely popular—
"old wives' tales" beneath the notice of serious writers.

The Norman Conquest, however, had quickened tremendously interest in everything connected with Britain, even its
legendary heroes; and so, early in the reign of Stephen,
grandson of the Conqueror, the clerk, Geoffrey of Mon-
mouth, drawing on the store of British legend and altering
it freely, ventured to publish his "History of the Kings of
Britain," an alleged chronicle in Latin prose. Here we
have for the first time in literary form the story of Arthur,
King of Britain, of his wide conquests, and of his death at
the hands of traitorous Mordred. Soon other authors,
mostly Anglo-Norman or subject to Anglo-Norman influence, began to use material similar to Geoffrey's. They
celebrated Arthur's Round Table, and various knights whom
Geoffrey had not mentioned. By the beginning of the thirteenth century, the stories of Arthur and his knights had

become world literature, for Geoffrey's "Chronicle" and the
first French Arthurian romances had been translated or
adapted into every language of western Europe. Wherever
they went, these stories retained certain common traits. In
all was poetic wonder; in all was utter geographical confusion and historical inaccuracy; kings, knights, and ladies
were characters contemporary with the authors who wrote
about them; instead of the rough manners of the sixth century, there was the polish of mediæval chivalry. And with
the exception of Geoffrey's work, the first Arthur-stories
were in verse, and the adventures of different knights
formed the subjects of different romances.

In historical inaccuracies, mediæval authors did not
change. Nor, for that matter, did postmediæval authors;
Arthur and his knights remain for all time typical romantic
representatives of the age of chivalry. But early in the
thirteenth century, writers began to turn metrical romances
into prose. Then they began to combine the adventures of
one knight with another in one romance, till by degrees
there grew up vast jumbles of adventure which clumsily
tried to give something like comprehensive tales of the
adventures of Arthur and all his principal knights. Owing
to multiplicity of sources and mistakes of scribes, these
composite stories were sometimes contradictory and confusing in the extreme. A late copy of one of them seems to
have been Malory's principal source. Probably he modified
this source by information from other manuscripts, and by
independent judgment in putting materials together. However that may be, he has by no means brought order out of
chaos. Yet, taken as a whole, Malory's work has some
organic structure. It is the best and clearest comprehensive
story of "King Arthur and of his Noble Knights of the
Round Table" that the Middle Ages have left us.

THE HISTORY OF THE GRAIL LEGEND

Like the other principal Round Table stories, the story
of the Grail came from ancient folk-tales, if not from the
mythology, of the insular Celts. Both British and Gaelic
Celts knew tales of life-giving or healing vessels analogous

to the Grail; and they frequently associated with such a vessel a spear and sometimes a sword. There is even a tale of Irish fairies who had a caldron from which no man ever went away unsatisfied, a spear, a sword, and a "stone of fate" that is perhaps related to the stone "hoving on the water" from which Galahad draws his fated sword. Explanations of the way in which pagan talismans of old Celtic story changed into objects of Christian significance in mediæval story can probably never be more than conjecture. There is no doubt, though, that after the Grail story was incorporated in the great Arthur cycle about 1175, the tendency was to make it more and more significant of mediæval Christianity, perhaps because the mysterious vessel called Grail suggested the sacred mystery of the sacramental cup. So Percival, a good worldly knight, the first hero of the Grail, was superseded in the early thirteenth century by Galahad, invented by an unknown romancer for the sole purpose, apparently, of being an ideally ascetic hero. Already the Grail had become the cup from which Christ drank at the Last Supper, and symbolical of the Communion Cup. A long account had been written of its journey from Palestine to Britain, which is not included in the "Morte Darthur." Marvels in the story were explained after the fashion of the scriptural interpretation of dreams. Sir Lancelot, Galahad's father, was made to "come but of the eighth degree from our Lord Jesu Christ." And among the many monkish grafts on the old pagan tree was that so-called "wonderful tale of King Solomon and his wife," and their three spindles, and Solomon's ship, all of which is not so "wonderful" as senseless.

If Malory's version of the Grail legend is characteristic of mediæval romance in introducing the superstition and ignorance of mediæval Christianity, it introduces also its mystical beauty. Galahad in his incomprehension of human temptation may lack human sympathy, but he is a very fair picture of innocent youth when, led by "a good old man, and an ancient, clothed all in white," he comes to sit in the siege perilous, in red arms himself and a "coat of red sendal," and "a mantel upon his shoulders that was furred with ermine." He must be a very hard-headed agnostic or insensitive puritan who is not awed by the "alighting" of "the grace of the Holy Ghost" on the knights when the Grail appears miraculously at Arthur's court, and impressed by the celebration of the Mass at Carbonek and Sarras.

Also in secular ways, Malory's Grail chapters are typical of mediæval romance. The institution of "courtly love"— that is, a knight's unquestioning obedience to his lady, such as we see in Lancelot's devotion to Guinevere—the obligation to the vows of knighthood, with its ideals of frankness, chastity, courtesy, and service to all who are weak and suffering, and also the forgetting of these vows in the heat of human passion—all this may be found in Malory's chapters of the Grail, as in the rest of his "Morte Darthur." As Caxton[3] says in the oft-quoted words of his Preface to Malory's book: "Herein may be seen noble chivalry, courtesy, humanity, friendliness, hardyhood, love, friendship, cowardice, murder, hate, virtue, and sin." But the general impression of it all is of good rather than evil, "of many joyous and pleasant histories, and noble and renowned acts of humanity, gentleness, and chivalry."

[3] *H. C.,* xxxix. 21ff.

IV. CERVANTES

By Professor J. D. M. Ford

MIGUEL DE CERVANTES SAAVEDRA was born in the little Spanish university town of Alcalá de Henares, in 1547. His father was a poor physician with a large family and with somewhat nomadic propensities, haling his offspring about from Alcalá to various other cities, such as Valladolid, Madrid, and Seville. The chances are that Miguel did not receive a university training. It is conjectured, on fairly reasonable grounds, that he qualified for teaching and became a tutor in a school at Madrid. At all events, by 1569 he was attached to the train of the Italian prelate, Acquaviva, who had come to Spain as papal nuncio, and with the latter he went to Rome toward the end of that year.

He did not long remain there, for in 1570 he was a gentleman volunteer on one of the vessels which, under Don John of Austria, inflicted a crushing defeat upon the Turk at the battle of Lepanto. In the engagement Cervantes was wounded quite seriously in his left hand, which remained forever after somewhat crippled. Still, after a period of convalescence spent in Italy, he played a part in other campaigns. Wearying of warfare, he took ship for Spain in September of 1575, having first provided himself with letters of recommendation from his military superiors and the viceroy of Naples. These credentials, by means of which he had hoped to obtain preferment at home, proved to be his undoing, for his vessel was captured by Moorish pirates and he was carried off to Algiers, where, because of the terms of praise in which these letters spoke of him, he was deemed a person of high degree and held for an excessively large ransom.

As his family and his friends could not raise the exorbitant sum demanded for his release, he remained five years a captive at Algiers, passing through most varied experiences. Finally, as a result of a happy chance, he was liberated and could return to Spain. He has himself adverted to the manner of his life as a slave at Algiers in his play, "El trato de Argel," and in the episode of "El cautivo" in "Don Quixote," and tradition has even more to say respecting it. It would seem that he headed many attempts at escape on the part of the Christian captives and nevertheless was not subjected to the penalties for such attempts, of which empalement was the most usual. Possibly his captors regarded him as a madman and therefore, according to Mohammedan ideas, exempt from punishment for his offenses.

LITERARY ACTIVITY OF CERVANTES

Back in Spain, he may have engaged again in military service for a brief period, but, at all events, by 1584 he had entered seriously upon a literary career, for in this year he had completed his pastoral romance, "Galatea." This is a work of little merit, being as unnatural and tedious in its treatment of the life of shepherds and shepherdesses as are the many native and foreign works of its kind; yet, occasionally it does betray some real emotion, and it is thought to have brought to a happy termination his courtship of Catalina de Palacios. A man without private means, now facing the exigencies of married life, Cervantes conceived the idea of supplying his needs by providing plays for the Spanish stage, which was already entering upon its age of glory. The idea was a bad one, for of the more than a score of pieces composed by him at this time not one was either a dramatic or a financial success. Defeated in this purpose, he was fain to fall back upon the meager salary which he gained as a minor officer of the Royal Treasurer, for during some years after 1587 he was engaged in collecting provisions for the royal forces or in extracting taxes from reluctant subjects of the king.

The sober facts at our command would incline us to believe that Cervantes was leading a life of misery. No doubt he was, but in spite of this he was constantly producing lyric effusions in praise of one or another friend, or celebrating this or that event. Once for all be it said that as a lyric poet Cervantes occupies quite a minor rank; his verses are rarely imaginative or sprightly, and now and then, as when he strikes the solemn note, does he rise to any great poetic height. But Cervantes was not only versifying during all this time that he was meeting with misfortune in carrying out the duties of his humble public office; he was doing something vastly more important for us all; he was contemplating the composition of the "Don Quixote." Legend has it that he wrote the "Don Quixote" in prison, but the legend is based on an unjustifiable interpretation of a passage in the Prologue to that novel. Still, the first thought of it may have occurred to him in the enforced leisure of some one of his incarcerations, although the chances are that the actual writing of the First Part extended over some years of the last decade of the sixteenth century and through the first three or four years of the seventeenth. In 1605 the first edition of the First Part appeared, and the story met with an acclaim which called forth speedily new editions at home and abroad, and no few translations into foreign languages.

THE EXEMPLARY TALES

But eleven years more of life remained for Cervantes, and during these, in so far as our knowledge goes, he met with no more worldly prosperity than in the past; although it is possible that his pecuniary distress was alleviated somewhat by modest returns from his books, and by the bounty of his patron, the Conde de Lemos. In one of the chapters of the First Part of the "Don Quixote" Cervantes mentions by name a little tale of roguish doings, the "Rinconete y Cortadillo." This, his own composition, reappears with eleven additional short stories in the collection entitled "Novelas ejamplares," which was issued from the press in 1612. Had he written nothing but the "Exemplary Tales," his fame would be secure in the annals of Spanish literature. They were the best-framed short stories so far produced in Spanish; they are interesting and realistic, although at times brutally offensive to morality. One of the proofs of the interest that they excited abroad is to be found in the fact that English dramatists like Fletcher, Massinger, Middleton, and Rowley drew upon them for the plots of some of their plays.

While composing these dramatic pieces, Cervantes was carrying on apace a sequel to the First Part of the "Don Quixote." This Second Part and conclusion of the story of the adventures of Don Quixote and Sancho Panza he completed hurriedly and published in 1615, upon learning that a spurious Second Part had been put forth at Tarragona in Aragon in 1614 by a person who masquerades under the pseudonym of Fernández de Avellaneda, and whose identity remains an enigma. The days of Cervantes were drawing to their close, but he continued to labor to the end, and on his dying couch he put the finishing touches to a novel of love and adventurous travel, the "Persiles y Sigismunda." On April 23, 1616, Cervantes passed away at Madrid, nominally on the same day as Shakespeare, but not precisely so on account of the difference still existing between the Spanish and the English calendar. His remains are supposed to rest in a community house of the Redemptionists in the Spanish capital.

THE PURPOSE AND SIGNIFICANCE OF "DON QUIXOTE"

For the modern world at large, the "Don Quixote" is that one among the works of Cervantes which exercises a paramount claim upon attention, and this it does both because it is the greatest novel as yet produced in the literatures of civilization and because it is the sole work of cosmopolitan importance that Spain has given to the rest of humanity. But in giving it Spain gave a noble gift, one which has brought unfeigned delight to the hearts and the minds of millions of human beings peopling both the Eastern and the Western Hemisphere, and this delight remains ever fresh although three centuries have passed since Don Quixote made his first sally forth.

Cervantes began the "Don Quixote" with the intention of making it a satirical burlesque of the romances of chivalry, which for more than a century before had beguiled the

Spanish fancy with accounts of absurdly impossible deeds
of derring-do. Their influence served only to entrance the
Spanish mind, fascinating it with the glamour of aspects
of mediævalism that had long since ceased to exist, and di-
verting its attention from the real world with its serious
daily tasks. As a matter of fact, the sway of the chivalric
romances had begun to weaken even before the close of the
sixteenth century, but it was from the "Don Quixote" that
they received their death stroke, for no new work of their
kind appeared after the "Don Quixote" was published. How
did Cervantes achieve his purpose? Simply by adopting
the methods of the romance of chivalry and showing the
falseness of their application to modern life; in a word, by
demonstrating that they were out of date. But Cervantes
built a structure far more grandiose than at first he had
planned, for his work grew under his hand and, transcending the author's original intent, became a great modern
novel which may be read and is generally read with intense
interest by countless thousands who know not at all and care
not at all that it is an attack upon a literary genre. "Under
Cervantes's vagabond pen," says Morel-Fatio, a masterly
critic of the work, "governed only by the inspiration of the
moment, his 'Don Quixote,' issuing forth from a simple idea
[that of ridiculing the novels of chivalry], of which no great
development could have been expected, has become little by
little the great social novel of the Spain of the beginning of
the seventeenth century, in which all that marks this epoch,
its sentiments, passions, prejudices, and institutions, has
found a place. Hence the powerful interest of the book,
which, independently of its value as a work of the imagination, and as an admirable treatise in practical philosophy,
possesses in addition the advantage of fixing the state of
civilization of a nation at a precise moment of its existence,
and of showing us the depths of its conscience."

V. MANZONI

By Professor J. D. M. Ford

AT AS early a date in their literary history as the thirteenth century, the Italians began to evince a propensity for tale-telling, and they have continued to
indulge it unremittingly down to our own times. Until the
nineteenth century, however, they favored the short story
or tale, rather than the longer and more ambitious form of
narrative prose fiction called the novel or romance. If in
the fourteenth century Boccaccio wrote his "Fiammetta,"
if about the end of that century or at the beginning of the
next Andrea da Barberino compiled the "Reali di Francia,"
and if the fifteenth and sixteenth centuries saw the appearance of the pastoral romance (the "Arcadia"), and of novels
of adventure as well as others infused with the erotic, or the
sentimental, or the moralizing spirit, it must be admitted
that all these works are either of poor vein, or, as is the
case for the "Fiammetta," the "Reali di Francia," and the
"Arcadia" of Sannazaro, they are far more important in
other connections than as examples of prose fiction. The
seventeenth and eighteenth centuries present hardly anything of interest; with the early nineteenth century and the
publication of the "Lettere di Jacopo Ortis" of Foscolo
(1802) the true novel was inaugurated in Italian, and with
the historical romance, "I Promessi Sposi," of Manzoni, first
put forth in 1827, its lasting success was achieved.

LIFE OF MANZONI

Alessandro Manzoni (he never used his title of Count)
was born of a patrician family at Milan, on March 7, 1785.
His maternal grandfather was the noted publicist, the
Marquis Cesare Beccaria. In his early studies, pursued
mainly at Milan, he inclined naturally toward *belles lettres,*

and, reading assiduously by himself, he developed the seeds of genius within him. Toward the literary career his steps were guided also by his relations with the kindly Italian poet, Monti, whom he venerated. In 1805 his mother took him to Paris, where he frequented *salons,* the atmosphere of which was wholly rationalistic and Voltairean, and in which he imbibed doctrines of skepticism. These, however, were not to last with him. At this time there was formed his friendship with the French scholar and man of letters, Claude Fauriel, who now and for many years later helped to mold his mind. Back in Milan in 1808, he married there in that year the Protestant lady, Enrichetta Blondel. Two years later, she became a Catholic, and Manzoni, impelled by her example and by a deep-rooted love, hitherto latent, for the ancestral religion, followed her into the Church, to remain thereafter a sincere and devout communicant. Abiding in the Milanese region, he wrote there in 1821 his remarkable ode, the "Cinque Maggio," commemorating the death of Napoleon, and at about this same time he commenced the composition of "I Promessi Sposi." When it was fully published in 1827, he removed with his family to Florence, and for a while enjoyed the favor of the grand duke,—who decorated the walls of his palace with scenes from "I Promessi Sposi,"—and the society of leading statesmen and writers, such as Giusti, Capponi, Niccolini, and Leopardi. Returning ere long to Milan, he had the misfortune to lose (1833) his wife, as well as his daughter, Giulia, who was married to the novelist Massimo d'Azeglio. In the sorrow of this period he derived no little comfort from his friendship with the brilliant although impetuous philosopher Rosmini and the novelist Tommaso Grossi. He remarried in 1837. During the stirring days of 1848, he showed himself a sterling Italian patriot, and urged his three sons to fight valiantly against the Austrian arms then engaged in subjugating his native region of Lombardy. With the success of the Austrians he retired voluntarily to a villa on Lake Maggiore, but the liberation of Lombardy again in 1859 brought him prominently to notice. King Vittorio Emmanuele bestowed honors upon him and assigned him a pension, which to one in his straitened circumstances was very grateful. He was made a senator in 1860, and played a part in the Assembly which proclaimed the Kingdom of Italy. Shortly after, in 1864, he was one of the National Assembly that voted for the transference of the capital from Turin to Rome. The Holy City he never visited, but in 1872 he was elected an honorary citizen of Rome, and in the letter in which he thanked the mayor for the courtesy shown him he expressed his joy at the consummation of Italian unity. He died on May 22, 1873.

MANZONI AS A POET AND CRITIC

Among modern Italian poets Manzoni takes high rank. Besides some minor lyrics and other poems of an occasional nature he wrote the "Inni Sacri," hymns in which he gives poetical form to the noblest and highest manifestations of the Christian religion, emphasizing especially the principles of charity, hope, and eventual comfort for all human ills; the ode "Cinque Maggio," already mentioned; the ode "Marzo, 1821," dealing with the aspirations and endeavors of the liberal party in Piedmont; and the two-verse dramas, the "Conte di Carmagnola" and the "Adelchi." These tragedies figure among the best productions of the Romantic movement in Italy, and they are the first examples of the historical play in Italian. The "Conte di Carmagnola" is concerned with the story of the famous captain of free lances, Francesco Bussone, called Carmagnola, who in the fifteenth century was undeservedly done to death by his employers, the Venetians; the "Adelchi" turns upon events in Lombardy back in the time of its king Desiderius and his foe and conqueror, Charlemagne.

Noteworthy among the minor prose works of Manzoni are the documents in which he discusses the validity of the French system of unities as applied to dramatic composition ("Lettre à M. Chauvet" and the purposes of the Italian Romantic school ("Lettera al Marchese Cesare d'Azeglio sul Romanticismo"). In various writings he discusses the often-mooted question as to what is the true form of speech for Italian literary expression, and he ranges himself on the side of sanity by advocating the use of the Florentine vocabulary on the part of Italian authors from all parts of the peninsula.

I PROMESSI SPOSI

His masterpiece is, of course, "I Promessi Sposi,"[1] which, begun as we have seen in 1821, occupied Manzoni for some six years with its composition and its printing; yet, hardly had it appeared when, faithful to his belief that the Florentine speech was the correct language of cultured Italians, he set to work to eliminate the dialectisms and Gallicisms in it, and the result was that in pure Tuscan the novel appeared, after seventy-five reprints of the first edition had been made, in the perfected form of 1842. Its main plot is simple; for the central story is that of the long-deferred marriage of two peasants, Lorenzo and his beloved Lucia. A tyrannical local potentate, aided by the proverbial Italian bravos, forbids their nuptials, because his own evil fancy has fallen upon the girl, and her parish priest, whose duty it is to perform the marriage ceremony irrespective of all exterior influences, avoids doing so through terror of the tyrant, Don Rodrigo, and his bloodthirsty satellites. Eventually a pest carries away Don Rodrigo, and the union of the lovers is effected. They are married by their own timid parish priest, Don Abbondio, who has, in the meantime, been taught his duty by his noble superior, the saintly Cardinal Carlo Borromeo.

Following Sir Walter Scott, whom he expressly acknowledges as his model for his methods, Manzoni gave to his novel an historical setting, adapting it to the Romantic sentiments then dominating the literary world. He chose for the period of action the three years between 1628 and 1631, during the Spanish supremacy at Milan, when a terrible famine and pestilence made desolate that part of Italy, and he confined operations between Lake Como, which he knew so well, and the city of Milan. Before undertaking the writing of his great work he made a serious study of works dealing with the pestilence and with administrative affairs of the time in which it occurred. Then, with the intuition of the true artist, having the historical and social

[1] See *Harvard Classics,* vol. xxi.

conditions well in mind, and possessing the power to analyze the most delicate of human feelings, he assembled a number of characters of divers sorts, through the play of which he presents us with a vivid picture of Lombardy in the early seventeenth century.

Next to Dante and Ariosto, Manzoni is, perhaps, the greatest of Italian authors, the most universal in appeal. His worth was quickly acknowledged abroad, by Goethe in Germany, by Chateaubriand in France, by Scott in the British Empire, and the last named was proud to have provoked imitation on the part of a genius of so high an order.

CRITICISM AND THE ESSAY

I. GENERAL INTRODUCTION

By Professor Bliss Perry

NO ONE can turn over the pages of The Harvard Classics without realizing how much of the most delightful writing of the last three hundred years has taken the form of the essay. No literary form is more flexible than this, and no form except lyric poetry has touched upon a wider variety of topics. Yet there is one subject of enduring human interest to which essayists are perpetually turning, and upon which they always find something new to say. It is the subject of Books and Reading. In the essays which deal with this perennially interesting topic, there is a constant expression of literary judgments —judgments that convey racial and national convictions, the ruling ideas of a generation or a school, or the likes and dislikes of individuals. These judgments, properly collected and classified, become the material for a history of literary criticism. Indeed, a surprisingly large proportion of the epoch-making documents of criticism are really essays, both in form and mood.

IMPORTANCE OF THE ESSAY IN LITERARY CRITICISM

The significance of the essay in the formation and perpetuation of critical doctrine is also apparent if one turns to the formal histories of criticism. Systematic treatises on the theory of the fine arts, including literature, have appeared at intervals since the time of Aristotle. The science of æsthetics, as we know it, was developed in Germany during the latter half of the eighteenth century, and it forms an integral portion of the philosophical system of Kant and of many other philosophers. But these formal treatises upon the nature of beauty, involving as they do the analysis of the beautiful as it exists in the natural world and in works of art, appeal primarily to a few thinkers and scholars, and not to the general public. It is true that men of genius like Goethe, Schiller, and Burke have the faculty of discussing the philosophic basis of æsthetic theories in such a way as to make them interesting and highly instructive to the general reader. But as a rule the systematic treatises upon the nature and history of the fine arts, and of literature in particular, have been necessarily addressed to a limited audience. The discussions which have really caught the ear of the public have been the casual utterances of brilliant men in the act of attacking or defending a literary creed, of writing a preface to a book or a play, or of hazarding, in some dialogue, pamphlet, or essay, a new opinion about beauty, a new theory of poetry or of prose.

WHAT IS AN ESSAY?

To understand, therefore, the history of actual critical opinion, one must study the essay. It is a very variable, highly personalized literary form: resembling now a dinner-table monologue or dialogue, and now a letter to a friend. Here it is a mere sparkling fragment of some solid mass of philosophical theory, and there it is a tiny jewel of paradox interrogation, or fancy; here an echo of some great historical debate over tragedy or comedy, and there the first faint stirring of some new, living idea, which by and by will be tossed about with all the winds of doctrine. But however changeable this literary type may be, one who reads the various essays in The Harvard Classics can hardly fail to get a general notion of the nature of "the essay." The type will gradually make itself clear to him, as something different from the formal treatise, the dialogue or the letter or the magazine article. He will learn to watch the type emerge into clear outline with Montaigne[1] and Bacon.[2] He will see that it modifies itself under the influence of national traits or of the fashions of successive historical periods,

[1] *Harvard Classics*, xxxii, 5ff.   [2] *H. C.*, iii, 7ff.

that it differentiates itself into species and varieties, precisely as other literary types undergo variation and development under specific conditions. It will flourish in one age and decline in another, as do the drama and the lyric, although, like them, the essay represents a certain permanent mood which never goes wholly out of fashion.

THE CRITICAL ESSAY

The reader who is interested in literary criticism will soon find that the essay has been a particularly convenient form for conveying literary theories from one mind or age to another. The "critical essay," while conforming in general to the flexible laws of "the essay," is used for a specific purpose. It deals with the emergence, continuance, and disappearance of critical opinions; it records, in an informal but none the less effective manner, the judgment of Europe upon books. Let us take a specific example. Charles Lamb's "Essay on the Tragedies of Shakespeare"[3] is a singularly perfect specimen of "the essay" type. It is personal and casual. It opens with the sentence: "Taking a turn the other day in the Abbey, I was struck with the affected attitude of a figure, which I do not remember to have seen before, and which upon examination proved to be a whole-length of the celebrated Mr. Garrick"; and then Lamb passes, with apparent artlessness, from the affectations and tricks of actors to the profound question of the possibility of an adequate representation of the personalities of Hamlet and Lear upon the stage. This personal essay, with its odd whims and fancies, deepens page by page into a masterly critical essay, which makes a distinct phase of the attitude of the English mind toward England's greatest poet.

In similar fashion, Victor Hugo's preface to his drama "Cromwell"[4] is a capital example of a personal essay—an essay "rampant" in its defense of the author's own literary creed. But that creed as it happens, becomes also the triumphant creed of the young French Romanticists. They rallied around the preface to "Cromwell" as soldiers rally around a flag, and the essay became a concrete embodiment

[3] *H. C.*, xxvii, 313.   [4] *H. C.*, xxxix, 354ff.

of a new reaction against Classicism, a significant document in the literary history of modern Europe.

NATIONAL CHARACTER IN THE ESSAY

The two essays which have just been mentioned—personal in their immediate character, and yet even more significant as representing doctrines which came to be held by a generation or a school—may also serve to illustrate a third aspect from which essays may be regarded. One may study them, in chronological order, as successive indications of a national point of view. Thus the English critical essay, in the Elizabethan period, in the seventeenth century, or in any subsequent epoch, reveals the precise extent to which the English mind accepts, modifies, or rejects the main body of European critical doctrine. As affording material for such a chronological study, it is not essential that any particular English critical essay should be marked by personal distinction of style, or by special critical acumen. The undistinguished mass of book reviews, of gossip about writers, about the stage and other forms of contemporary art, is often the most valuable evidence of the instinctive working of the English mind. What does an average bookish Englishman, in a given decade, understand by the words "tragic," "comic," "heroic," "the unities," "wit," "taste," "humor," "Nature"? The historian finds the answer in a thousand casual expressions, each one of which bears the stamp of the period and the race. The Englishman interprets the general laws and phrases of European criticism in terms of his own neighborhood and time, and a collection of English critical essays thus illustrates the traits of the English national character.

THE HISTORY OF THE WORD "ESSAY"

Let us now turn from the broader relations of the essay with criticism, and endeavor to ascertain precisely what the word "essay" means. The older English form of the word is "assay," i. e., a trial or experiment. It is derived, through the French, from a late Latin word "exagium," which means a standard weight, or more precisely, the act of weighing. The word "examine" comes from the same Latin root. As defined by the "Century Dictionary," "essay" means 1, A trial, attempt or endeavor; 2, An experimental trial or test; 3, An assay or test of metal; 4, In literature, a discursive composition concerned with a particular subject, usually shorter and less methodical and finished than a treatise; a short disquisition. Dr. Samuel Johnson, who was himself one of the most famous essayists of his day, defines "essay" in his Dictionary as "A loose sally of the mind; an irregular indigested piece; not a regular and orderly composition." Possibly it was the Doctor's happy word "sally" which suggested to a recent writer, Mr. F. N. Zabriskie, the following excellent definition: "The essay is properly a collection of notes, indicating certain aspects of a subject, or suggesting thoughts concerning it; . . . not a formal siege, but a series of assaults, essays or attempts upon it." It is for this reason that Mr. Zabriskie calls the essayist the excursionist of literature, the literary angler, the meditator rather than the thinker; and he points out that the German mind is not adapted to the essay, since the Germans are not satisfied to make mere assaults upon a subject, mere excursions into it; they must go through a subject from end to end and leave it a conquered territory.

THE FIRST MODERN ESSAYISTS

Montaigne, who was the initiator of the modern essay (1580), laid stress upon its essentially autobiographic nature. He confesses that he writes "not to discover things, but to lay open myself." He thinks that an essay should be spontaneous and free from every artificial trammel. It should have the characteristics of open, varied, wide-ranging talk: "I speak unto paper as unto the first man I meet." Lord Bacon, whose first edition of essays appeared in 1597, is more orderly than Montaigne. He masses his material more closely, keeps to his topic, packs his sentences as full as they will hold. He is too austere for the leisurely, personal method of Montaigne; he imparts his concentrated worldly wisdom coolly, almost impassively; he loves the pregnant opening and close. "To write just treatises," he says, "requireth time in the writer and leisure in the reader, which is the cause that hath made me choose to write certain brief notes, set down rather significantly than curiously, which I have called *essays;* the word is late, but the thing is ancient. For Seneca's Epistles to Lucilius, if one mark them well, are but essays—that is, dispersed meditations." And finally, Addison, whose essays sum up in the early eighteenth century as completely as Montaigne and Bacon represent the late Renaissance, is quite as explicit as they are in emphasizing the informal character of this type of literature: "When I make choice of a subject that has not been treated on by others, I throw together my reflections on it without any order or method, so that they may appear rather in the looseness and freedom of an essay, than in the regularity of a set discourse."

THE ANTIQUITY OF THE ESSAY

"The thing is ancient"; there is no doubt of that. Analogies to the mood of the modern essay and to its urbane, free, flexible methods of discussion, may be found in the "Dialogues" of Plato,[5] in the "Lives"[6] and "Morals" of Plutarch, in the letters of Cicero,[7] Horace, and the younger Pliny,[8] in the gossipy "Attic Nights" of Aulus Gellius, in the talks of Epictetus,[9] and the Meditations of Marcus Aurelius.[10] There is nothing new under the sun; and there were Greek and Roman gentlemen quite as capable as Montaigne of writing with frankness, ease, quaintness, and an open-minded attitude of skeptical inquiry. But though they often revealed the spirit of the modern essayist, they were groping uncertainly after the appropriate literary form. Montaigne's great achievement was to hazard his fortunes in an unsurpassed series of "sallies," "assaults," "assays" upon a hundred entrenched topics, and always to come bravely off—so that his tactics became the model for all literary skirmishes. To think and feel and write like Montaigne was to produce the modern essay. Without his

[5] See, for example, *H. C.,* ii, 3ff.   [6] *H. C.,* xii, 5ff.   [7] *H. C.,* ix, 7ff.
[8] *H. C.,* ix, 195ff.   [9] *H. C.,* ii, 117ff.   [10] *H. C.,* ii, 193ff.

example, it is doubtful if we should have had the essays of Lamb, of Emerson, and of Stevenson.

EFFECT OF THE RENAISSANCE ON THE ESSAY

Supporting the whole theory and practice of Montaigne, undoubtedly, stood the Renaissance itself. This "re-birth" of the human mind, this new awakening of vital energies and intellectual powers, involved a new way of looking at the world. Nothing seemed quite the same as it had been. Church and empire and feudal system were apparently weakening; new nationalities, new languages were to be reckoned with; new continents were explored, new inventions altered the face of daily life; a new intellectual confidence, inquiry, criticism, supplanted the mediæval obedience to authority. There was a new "weighing," "assaying" of all things. The actual world was changing before men's eyes, and the inner world changed no less. There was universal curiosity about individual capacities and opinions, experiences and tastes. The whole "undulating and various" scheme of things—to use a favorite expression of Montaigne—was a direct provocative of the essay state of mind; and the essay form, in turn, in its looseness, vagueness, and range, was singularly adapted to the intellectual spirit of the period.

THE BOOKISH ESSAY

One type of Renaissance essay, for example, concerned itself with a casual survey of the fragments of the classical and mediæval world. Modern books like Taylor's "Classical Heritage of the Middle Ages," and "The Mediæval Mind," Einstein's "Italian Renaissance in England," Sir Sidney Lee's "French Renaissance in England," Spingarn's "Literary Criticism in the Renaissance," and Saintsbury's "History of Criticism" set before us, with abundance of detail, the kind and extent of knowledge of the past which was possessed by Renaissance essayists. Caxton's naïve Prologues and Epilogues[11] to the popular classical and mediæval

[11] *H. C.*, xxxix, 5ff.

books which he issued in English, Sir Philip Sidney's chivalrous "Defense of Poesy,"[12] and Edmund Spenser's explanation to Sir Walter Raleigh of the purpose of "The
Faërie Queene"[13] are good illustrations of the attitude of
typical Englishmen toward the imaginative life of the past.
Gregory Smith's collection of "Elizabethan Critical Essays"
affords a fairly complete view of the critical ideas which
sixteenth-century England had inherited from Europe.
The evolution of the English critical essay, during the three
hundred years which have elapsed since then, is mainly the
story of the preservation of these ideas and their modification or transformation under the successive impacts of new
intellectual forces, and of differing social and literary conditions.

THE ESSAY AS EXPRESSIVE OF CURIOSITY ABOUT LIFE

Another type of essay, originating in the Renaissance,
and a favorite with Montaigne, deals not so much with
books as with life itself. The new culture, the novel intellectual perceptions, altered at once the accepted theories
of man's duty and destiny. Montaigne does not dogmatize
about these matters: he asks questions, he suggests possible
answers. The speculative essay, the philosophical and
scientific essay, the social essay which draws its materials
from the ever-renewed revelation of the actual life of man,
all find their source in an awakened curiosity. The enthusiasm, the gusto, with which sixteenth-century men discussed every topic within their range of vision, has remained an integral element of the effective essay. A man
may set himself sadly and grimly to work upon his formal
treatise, and write it through to the end with disillusion in
his soul. But the born essayist, though knowing well
enough that his raids into unconquered territory must be
merely a perpetual series of sallies and retreats, nevertheless advances gayly to the assault. Like Lamb and Stevenson, he preaches without being a preacher; like Huxley and
Tyndall, he teaches when he means only to inform; so com-
municable and infectious is this gift of curiosity about life.

[12] *H. C.,* xxvii, 7ff.   [13] *H. C.,* xxxix, 64.

THE AUTOBIOGRAPHICAL ESSAY

There is a third type of essay, originating in the Renaissance emphasis upon individualism, and confidently asserting itself upon the pages of Montaigne,[14] Addison, Hazlitt, De Quincey,[15] Emerson,[16] Thoreau,[17] and a hundred other men. It is the autobiographic, "egotistic" essay—in which there is rarely any insolence of egotism, but only an insatiable curiosity about oneself, and an entire willingness to discuss that question in public. If you like the man who is talking, this kind of essay is the most delightful of all. But it betrays a great deal, and like lyric verse—the most intensely personalized mode of poetry—it sometimes betrays too much. When the right balance is struck between openness and conceit, or when, as with Emerson, the man is sweet and sound to the core, the self-revealing essay justifies itself. Indeed, it is thought by some critics that the subjective or lyrical quality of the essay is a part of its essential character. Thus Professor A. C. Bradley has asserted: "Brevity, simplicity, and singleness of presentation; the strong play of personality, the subjective charm, the delicate touch, the limited range of theme and of treatment, and the ordered beauty through exclusion of all disordered moods and fiercer passions—these flow directly from the presence and dominance of the lyrical element, and these are the constant features of the Essay."

One should add, perhaps, that all three of the essay types here touched upon—the "critical," the "ethical" or "philosophic," and the "personal"—were strongly colored during the Renaissance, as they have been at intervals ever since, by the spirit of nationalism. French criticism, in the sixteenth century as in the nineteenth, is very French. English criticism, in Dryden and Arnold, is very English; the moralizing of Milton's tractates and of Samuel Johnson's "Lives of the Poets," the personal assertiveness of Thoreau's essay on "Walking," and Lowell's essay on "Democracy"[18] bear the unmistakable accents of England and of America. Blood tells, in the essay as elsewhere.

[14] *H. C.*, xxxii, 5ff.   [15] *H. C.*, xxvii, 82ff., 281ff., 335ff.
[16] *H. C.*, v, 5ff.   [17] *H. C.*, xxviii, 407ff.   [18] *H. C.*, xxviii, 464ff.

ESSAYS AS HISTORICAL DOCUMENTS

In fact, one of the most interesting studies made available through The Harvard Classics is the survey of various national moods in successive historical periods. Take, for instance, the English essayists of the eighteenth century. Here are characteristic utterances of men so differently yet richly endowed as Addison and Swift, Steele and Defoe,[19] Sidney and Samuel Johnson, Hume[20] and Burke,[21] yet the student of the eighteenth century, whether he is reading Hume or Burke on Taste, or Johnson explaining the plan of his great Dictionary,[22] Defoe's ironical scheme for ridding the world of Dissenters, or Addison's delicately sentimental musings in Westminster Abbey, detects, beneath all the differences in style and varieties of personal opinion, the unmistakable traits of race, nation, and period. These essays are thus historical documents of high importance. One understands better, for reading them, the England of Marlborough and of Walpole, the England of the Pitts and the four Georges. Any one century, as Carlyle said long ago, is the lineal descendant of all the preceding centuries, and an intelligent reading of the English essays of the seventeenth, eighteenth, and nineteenth centuries is one of the best ways of learning that significant lesson.

ARISTOTLE AND THE CRITICAL ESSAY

Even if the reader of these essays has no special knowledge of English history, and has hitherto paid but little attention to the influence of one school of thought upon its successors, he cannot help discovering one difference between what we have called "the essay" and its more specialized form "the critical essay." "The essay" moves in a circle. Its orbit tends to return perpetually upon itself. One may even say that the type was already complete in Montaigne, and that since then it has made no real advance; that we have only a succession of essayists, doing, of course, with infinite personal varieties of pattern precisely what

[19] *H. C.*, xxvii, 97ff., 89ff., 143ff.   [20] *H. C.*, xxvii, 215.
[21] *H. C.*, xxiv, 11.   [22] *H. C.*, xxxix, 191ff.

Montaigne showed them how to do. But the critical essay advances, albeit by zigzag lines. It is obliged to tack, as the winds of doctrine shift and the tides of opinion ebb and flow, yet it is always steering, and not merely drifting. Take, for example, the most famous critical essay of the Greeks, the "Poetics" of Aristotle. It is an attempt to establish certain fundamental principles of æsthetic criticism, such as the laws of epic poetry and the nature of tragedy. It analyzed the structure of contemporary works of literary art, tested the psychological effect of poem and play upon the mind of the reader and spectator, and laid down some shrewd rules for the guidance of poets. It is an essay rather than an exhaustive treatise, but it is by no means the sort of essay which Montaigne would have written had he been a Greek. It is impersonal, analytical, scientific. And so logical is its matter, so penetrating its insight, that it became a model of sound critical procedure.

The "rules" of Aristotle, based as they were upon the facts of human nature and the character of the literature of his day, deserved the reverence with which they were treated by the men who rediscovered them in the Renaissance. Trouble came only when the attempt was made to apply them rigidly and mechanically to poems and dramas of a type different from anything that Aristotle had known. Yet out of this very confusion and necessity for readjustment came the "critical essay" as we know it. Aristotle had set up Truth as his beacon mark: Truth to the physical and psychological facts, to the laws of beauty which are also laws of the mind. When the critics of the Renaissance and of the age of Neo-Classicism in France and England, confronted as they were by new facts, tried loyally to adjust the Aristotelian formulæ to the writings of Tasso, Shakespeare, and Molière, they made queer work of it. They endeavored to keep in mind both "the polestar of the ancients" and the "rules of the French stage among the moderns," to say nothing of the cross currents of actual contemporary fact. It was a difficult course to sail, and it is no wonder that the history of the critical essay exhibits every variety of daring or faltering seamanship. But the beacon mark of Truth was there all the while, and though no navigator has

ever succeeded in beating quite up to it, it is reward enough
for the critical essayist if he seems to be making headway.

CRITICAL TRADITION AND THE ESSAY

The writer of the critical essay, in short, finds that his
course has been laid out for him by the very nature of the
task which he has undertaken. The mere essayist, as we
have seen, can sail in a circle, starting and ending with his
own fancies; but the man who uses the essay as the vehicle
of criticism must use chart and compass; must proceed from
a given starting point to a definite point of arrival. And he
cannot do this if he is ignorant of the efforts of his predecessors, and unaware of the general aims and methods of
critical procedure. If he is writing, for instance, on the
theory of poetry, he does not wish to leave the matter where
he found it: he desires to make, if he can, a contribution to
that branch of human knowledge. But he is not likely to
succeed unless he has a tolerably clear notion of just how
far the world-old discussion has proceeded at the point
where he himself takes up the debate. When Horace wrote
that clever versified essay on the poet's art, an essay which
has been irreverently termed "the business man's guide to
poetry," he had no intention of slavishly imitating the rules
of the Greek theorists. But after all, his father had sent
him to a Greek University, and the ghosts of his old professors were peeping over his shoulders as he wrote. And
when, long afterward, the Italian Vida and the Frenchman
Boileau came to write their own verse essays on the same
topic, the ghost of the clever Roman held their pens. Sidney
and Shelley, in composing their eloquent Defences of
Poetry,[23] had probably no conscious thought of continuing
the formal discussion of poetic theory which the Greeks
began and the Renaissance resuscitated; nevertheless, their
confessions of faith in poetry form an essential chapter in
the evolution of criticism. So with the prefaces of Wordsworth and Coleridge and Walt Whitman.[24] These men are
innovators in theory and practice of their craft, but, like
most of the successful innovators and "modernists" in art,

[23] *H. C.,* xxvii, 7ff. and 345ff.   [24] See Lecture III, below.

they possessed a fairly accurate knowledge of the ancient defenses which they were trying to carry by assault. Yet these assaults, no matter how brilliant, never really end the siege. The final truth escapes complete analysis and definition. The history of the critical essay shows only a series of approximations, a record of endeavors which must be constantly renewed.

TYPES OF CRITICISM

Out of all this variety of effort, however, three tendencies of criticism emerge. They are usually called the "judicial," the "interpretative," and the "impressionistic." The theoretical distinction between these tendencies of criticism is clear enough. "Judicial" criticism passes judgment upon established facts. It deals primarily with rules, with the "canons" of criticism, although it may, of course, examine the principles upon which these rules are based. Its estimates are likely to be dogmatic and magisterial. It says bluntly, in the voice of Jeffrey, that Wordsworth's "Excursion" "will never do"; that his "White Doe of Rylstone" is "the very worst poem we ever saw imprinted in a quarto volume." It declares, with Professor Churton Collins, that "Criticism is to literature what legislation and government are to states." The aim of "interpretative" criticism, on the other hand, is not so much to pass judgment upon a specific work, as to explain it. It seeks and establishes, if possible, correct texts; it makes clear the biographical and historical facts essential to an understanding of the work in question. It finds and reveals the meaning and beauty there contained. It points out the ethical and social significance of the literary product. To explain a book, no doubt, is often tantamount to judging it; for if the book be demonstrated to be full of corruption, that is the most effective way of declaring it a corrupt book. Nevertheless, the object of the "interpretative" or "appreciative" critic is primarily expository, and he prefers that the reader himself should pass ultimate judgment, in the light of the exposition which has been made. He puts the needful facts before the jury, and then rests his case. Sainte-Beuve[25] is a master of this sort of

[25] *H. C.*, xxxii, 109ff.

criticism, as Jeffrey is of the magisterial. The "impression-istic" critic, finally, does not concern himself overmuch with the canons. He leaves "universal considerations" and "the common sense of most" to his rivals. Textual criticism bores him. The examination of principles strikes him as too "scientific," the massing of biographical and historical details seems to him the work of the historian rather than the critic. He deals frankly in his own "impressions," his personal preferences, the adventures of his soul in the presence of masterpieces. He translates the sensations and emotions which he has experienced in his contact with books into symbols borrowed from all the other arts and from the inexhaustible stores of natural beauty. His rivals may call him a man of caprice rather than a man of taste, but they cannot really confute him, for such are the infinitely varied modes of physical and psychological reaction to the presence of the beautiful, that nobody knows exactly how the other man feels. We must take his word for it, and the words of impressionist criticism have often been uttered with an exquisite delicacy and freshness and radiance that make all other types of literary criticism seem for the moment mere cold and formal pedantries.

THE UNION AND MERGING OF TYPES OF CRITICISM

So much for the theoretical distinction between the three tendencies. But no one can read many pages of the masters of modern criticism without becoming aware that all three tendencies frequently reveal themselves in the same man, and even in the same essay. Some of the famous "im-pressionists," like Lamb, Stevenson, Lemaître, and Anatole France, know a great deal more about the "canons" than they wish at the moment to confess. They play so skillfully with the overtones of criticism because they know the funda-mental tones so well. Stevenson attempts "scientific" criti-cism in his essay on "Style," "historical" criticism in his essay on Pepys.[26] Jeffrey occasionally writes "national character" criticism quite in the expository method of Sainte-Beuve. Coleridge and Emerson, Arnold and

[26] *H. C.*, xxviii, 295ff.

Ruskin,[27] are too many-sided and richly endowed men to limit their literary essays to any one type of criticism.

The justification of this eclecticism of practice is found, as we have tried to show, in the nature of the essay itself. It is the most sinuous, varied, and individualized of all the forms of prose literature. The moment it begins to deal with critical theory, however, it is obliged to make its reckoning with some one or more of the processes of judgment which have been evolved in the history of the race; it tends then to become "historical," "scientific," "expository," "judicial"; it sails, as we have said, by the chart, instead of in the capricious circle of purely personal preferences. And it is in this relation of "the essay" to "the critical essay" that we discover something of the literary and social significance of essay writing. It meets a need of the individual, and performs at the same time a function for society. The individual reader turns to the essayists for delight, for stimulus, for consolation, for a fortification of the will. Cicero and Montaigne and Thoreau will talk to him about friendship and books and behavior. What more can he ask for? He finds in the essayists, as in the lyric poets, the reflection of his own moods, his own tastes, his own varied contact with experience. In their company, as in the company of every form of art, he becomes intimately aware of the fullness and richness of life. As for society at large, the essayists—and particularly those who have occupied themselves with criticism—have aided in the establishment of standards of judgment. These standards are impersonal and relatively stable. They alter somewhat, it is true, with the progress of civilization, and with the temper of successive historical periods in each of the civilized races of the world. But for any one generation the "norm" exists. The departures from it and the returns to it constitute the æsthetic and intellectual activity of that generation. Expansion and contraction, the study of mankind followed by the study of individual men and women; then a new series of generalizations followed by another series of concrete applications of ideas to life—that is the history of

[27] *H. C.,* xxviii, 95ff.

culture. And while "the essay" has from time to time
asserted the claims of liberty in all matters of the mind,
"the critical essay" has with equal persistence recognized
and maintained the claims of authority. One generation
needs, no doubt, that its literary skirmishes should fight
mainly on the side of freedom, and another generation will
need no less that they should rally to the defense of law.
There can be little doubt of the primary need of our own
generation in America. We shall find most profit in reading
those essayists who have a respect for literary standards,
who are on the side of law.

II. WHAT THE MIDDLE AGES READ

By Professor W. A. Neilson

THE HISTORY of English literary criticism may be said to begin with Sir Philip Sidney's "Defense of Poesy."[1] A few treatises on rhetoric and prosody preceded it, but it was with this book that there reached England the first important influx from the main current of the Italian and French criticism of the Renaissance. In the preceding centuries men had, of course, expressed opinions about books; but these were random and personal, backed by no theory, part of no system, the casual utterances of men who merely knew what they liked.

THE EVIDENCE AS TO MEDIÆVAL TASTE IN LITERATURE

But the taste of an age can be inferred from other sources than the formal judgments of official critics. The evidence of vogue, when it can be obtained, is more significant, for the obvious reason that a man's spending tells us more than his words of what he values. For the centuries when books circulated in manuscript only, the facts as to popularity are hard to get at, since the numbers of those that have survived are the residuum of a thousand accidents; but the introduction of printing in the latter part of the fifteenth century affords an opportunity of an exceptional kind to learn which of the works then in existence were judged most promising and most worthy of the wider publicity which the new process made possible. It is for this reason that William Caxton, the first of English printers, is really an important figure in the history of literary opinion; for not only did he preface the books he printed with quaint and ingenuous statements of his own

[1] *Harvard Classics,* xxvii, 7-55; and cf. Professor Bliss Perry's lecture on "Theories of Poetry" in this series.

reasons for thinking them important, but the mere fact of his choosing them is a valuable evidence of their popularity as estimated by a shrewd man of business.

THE PREPONDERANCE OF DIDACTIC LITERATURE

As a matter of fact, this evidence coincides remarkably with the inferences that literary historians have drawn from other data. The fables which pass under the name of "Æsop," [2] to begin with what is probably the most ancient of the works he issued, had been popular for many centuries, and the tangle of the relationships of the endless mediæval collections in various languages is one of the most puzzling problems left for the modern scholar to solve. Their value Caxton seems to take for granted, largely, we may presume, because the didactic purpose which he always looks for first lies upon the surface and did not need to be pointed out. Indeed, more than half of the publications of Caxton the Prologues and Epilogues of which are printed in The Harvard Classics are confessedly of that improving kind for which the Middle Ages had so insatiable an appetite. The "Dictes and Sayings of the Philosophers" [3] and the "Distichs" [4] of "Cato" were collections of aphoristic wisdom, the appeal of which is apparent, not merely from the number of copies made, but also from the frequency with which we find them quoted by all kinds of mediæval writers.

THE GOLDEN LEGEND

The "Golden Legend" [5] was more specifically pious. It is the best-known collection of those marvelous stories of saints which happily performed the double service of cultivating faith and of providing entertainment by their constant stimulation of the sense of wonder. It is only the former of those services, however, which is explicitly recognized by Caxton. "As gold is most noble above all other metals, in like wise is this legend holden most noble

[2] *H. C.*, xxxix, 18f.   [3] *H. C.*, xxxix, 10.
[4] *H. C.*, xxxix, 15.   [5] *H. C.*, xxxix, 14.

above all other works," he says, and he prays "that it profit to all them that shall read or hear it read, and may increase in them virtue, and expel vice and sin, that by the example of the holy saints amend their living here in this short life."

LITERATURE OF ENTERTAINMENT

Of Chaucer's works he prints the immortal "Canterbury Tales"; and in the "Proem"[6] to this book he expatiates in praise of Chaucer's style and substance, both because "he comprehended his matters in short, quick, and high sentences, eschewing prolixity, casting away the chaff of superfluity, and shewing the picked grain of sentence uttered by crafty and sugared eloquence"—a characterization of the first great master of English which few of his later critics have bettered. The whole tone of this "Proem" is of a singularly noble and elevated enthusiasm, and in its evident genuineness and warmth it makes us forget that we are reading one of the earliest of English publishers' advertisements.

THE TROJAN LEGEND AND THE ÆNEID

The story of Troy, as everyone is aware, was unknown to the Middle Ages in the Homeric version. Two Latin prose works purporting to be derived from Greek contemporary accounts by Dares the Phrygian and Dictys the Cretan formed the basis of the mediæval tradition. These were elaborated into a French metrical romance by Benoît de Sainte Maure in the twelfth century, and from him the Sicilian Guido delle Colonne derived the material for his Latin prose history of Troy. For the later Middle Ages Guido was the main source. It is to this tradition that Boccaccio's romance of "Filostrato" belongs, with Chaucer's expansion and paraphrase of it in his "Troilus." On Guido also depends that French priest Raoul le Feure,[7] whom Caxton translated in Bruges and Ghent, and "finished in Cologne, in the time of the troublous world," when England

[6] *H. C.*, xxxix, 19. For examples of the "Canterbury Tales," see *H. C.*, xl, 11-51.
[7] *H. C.*, xxxix, 5ff.

was torn by the Wars of the Roses, and there was little peace for letters at home. Under these circumstances it is perhaps little wonder that the chief justification he offers for his labor in translation is the hope that the destruction of Troy "may be example to all men during the world how dreadful and jeopardous it is to begin a war, and what harms, losses, and death followeth."

The Troy story he continued in his translation of a French version of the "Æneid"[8] of Virgil, "that noble poet and great clerk." In this work he tells us he stood in great doubt between those advisers who urged him to use language which could be understood of the common people and those who wanted him to use the most curious terms he could find. He chose a middle path, "forasmuch as this present book is not for a rude uplandish man to labour therein ne read it, but only for a clerk and a noble gentleman that feeleth and understandeth in feats of arms, in love and in noble chivalry."

CAXTON ON MALORY

Finally, we have his Prologue to the great book of "King Arthur"[9] compiled by his contemporary, Sir Thomas Malory. If the Troy story was the favorite classical tale in mediæval times, the romances connected with King Arthur were the most notable and the most widely diffused of more recent imaginative literature. Founded on a minute basis of old British history, the Arthurian legends had passed from the chronicles into romance, finding their most important artistic development in France, but spreading in translation and paraphrase into every country of western Europe. At the close of the Middle Ages, an English knight, Sir Thomas Malory, collected, chiefly from French prose versions, materials for a loosely organized compilation of all the more important adventures, and retold them in a style and spirit that make his book one of the great monuments of English prose. For this book Caxton had the warmest admiration; and, though here, if anywhere, we have a literature of en-

---

[8] *H. C.*, xxxix, 25. For a modern translation, see *H. C.*, vol. xiii.
[9] *H. C.*, xxxix, 21. For the story of the Holy Grail from Malory, see *H. C.*, xxxv, 109-226, and cf. Dr. Maynadier's lecture in the series on Prose Fiction.

tertainment, in it also Caxton finds a possibility of moral and spiritual improvement. Few of his words are better known than his worthy praise of Malory: "And I, according to my copy, have down set it in print, to the intent that noble men may see and learn the noble acts of chivalry, the gentle and virtuous deeds that some knights used in those days, by which they came to honour, and how they that were vicious were punished and oft put to shame and rebuke; humbly beseeching all noble lords and ladies and all other estates, of what estate or degree they be of, that shall see and read in this said book and work, that they take the good and honest acts in their remembrance and to follow the same, wherein they shall find many joyous and pleasant histories and noble and renowned acts of humanity, gentleness, and chivalry. For herein may be seen noble chivalry, courtesy, humanity, friendliness, hardyhood, love, friendship, cowardice, murder, hate, virtue and sin. Do after the good and leave the evil and it shall bring you to good fame and renown. And for to pass the time this book shall be pleasant to read in; but for to give faith and believe that all is true that is contained herein, ye be at your liberty. But all is written for our doctrine."

This last sentence sums up the chief points in the professional faith of the father of English printing. Edification was assumed by him as by his age as the prime, if not the only, justification for writing and publishing. Yet, in spite of this narrow assumption, Caxton and the authors he did so much to make accessible were clearly sensitive to the element of delight as well as of instruction in literature; and enough has been said of the contents of these Prologues to show how rich they are in indications not only of what the Middle Ages read, but why they read it.

As for Caxton's own motives, if we took him literally, we should suppose that he translated and printed mainly to save himself from the sin of idleness. Yet a more generous impulse is easily read between the lines; and it is no mere self-regarding purpose that finds utterance in the words he penned as he closed wearily his long labor on the "Recuyell of the Histories of Troy": "Thus end I this book, which I have translated after mine Author as nigh as God hath given me cunning, to whom be given the laud and praising. And for as much as in the writing of the same my pen is worn, my hand weary and not steadfast, mine eyne dimmed with overmuch looking on the white paper, and my courage not so prone and ready to labour as it hath been, and that age creepeth on me daily and feebleth all the body, and also because I have promised to divers gentlemen and to my friends to address them as hastily as I might this same book, therefore I have practised and learned at my great charge and dispense to ordain this said book in print, after the manner and form as ye may here see, and is not written with pen and ink as other books be, to the end that every man may have them at once."

III. THEORIES OF POETRY

By Professor Bliss Perry

AMONG the various critical essays presented in The
Harvard Classics no group is more interesting than
that which deals with the theory of poetry. Our
consideration of the literary form or quality of the essay
has already shown us that we should not expect from the
essayist an exhaustive treatise, but rather a free and
spirited and suggestive discussion of certain aspects of his
subject. To write adequately upon the general theme of
poetry, expounding its nature, its æsthetic and social significance, and its technique, would be an enormously difficult
task. But there are few poets who have not uttered at one
time or another some of the secrets of this craft, or some
phase of their admiration for it. Let us glance at the essays
of eight English and American poets, ranging in time from
the age of Elizabeth to the Victorian epoch: Sidney, Dryden, Wordsworth, Coleridge, Shelley, Poe, Whitman, and
Arnold. Four of this group, Dryden, Coleridge, Poe, and
Arnold, are acknowledged adepts in general literary criticism; while Sidney and Shelley, Wordsworth and Whitman,
have given expression to some of the most eloquent and
revealing things that have ever been written about their
own art of poetry.

SIR PHILIP SIDNEY

Sidney's "Defense of Poesy," [1] like Shelley's, is a reply
to an attack, but neither poet is very angry, nor does either
believe that his opponent has done much harm. Shelley's
antagonist was a humorously Philistine essay by his friend
Peacock. Sidney is answering somewhat indirectly a fellow
Puritan, Gosson, whose "School of Abuse" (1579) had attacked

[1] *Harvard Classics*, xxvii, 7ff.

the moral shortcomings of ancient poetry and the license of the contemporary stage. Yet Sidney's "pitiful defense of poor poetry," as he playfully terms his essay, is composed in no narrowly controversial spirit, but rather in a strain of noble enthusiasm. He brings to his task a sufficient learning, a knowledge of the poetics of Plato and Aristotle, and an acquaintance with the humanistic critics of Italy and France. He knows his Homer and Virgil, his Horace and Ovid, but he does not on that account despise the "old song of Percy and Douglas." The nobility of Sidney's tone and his beauty of phrasing are no less notable than the clear ordering of his thought. In one close-packed paragraph after another, he praises the poet as a teacher and creator, compares poetry with history and philosophy, and finds, as Aristotle has done before him, that it is nobler than either. He discusses the various types of poetry, testing their capacities for teaching and moving the reader. Then, after a skillful refutation of the current objections against poetry, he turns, like a true Englishman, to the poetry of his own race, which was just then beginning, though Sidney did not foresee it, its most splendid epoch. He condemns, for instance, as being "neither right tragedies nor right comedies," that type of tragi-comedy which Shakespeare was soon to make illustrious. This opinion is now reckoned, of course, a heresy, as is Sidney's other opinion that verse is not essential to poetry. Yet no one who loves Sidney can quarrel with him over this or that opinion. His essay has proved itself, for more than three centuries, to be what he claimed for the beautiful art which he was celebrating—a permanent source of instruction and delight.

DRYDEN AS CRITIC

One hundred years after Sidney's untimely death, the prince of English criticism was John Dryden. He made no pretense of actual government: he "follows the Rules afar off." He is full of contradictions, reflecting the changing hues of contemporary taste, compromising between the classic and the romantic, changing his views as often as he likes, always readable and personal, always, in the best

sense, "impressionistic," always, as Professor Ker has said
of him, "sceptical, tentative, disengaged." His early essay
"Of Dramatic Poesy" is full of youthful zest for Shakespeare and romance. Then he turns conformist, aiming "to
delight the age in which I live" and to justify its prevalent
neo-classic taste; but presently he comes back to his "incomparable Shakespeare," praises Longinus, and abandons
rhyme. In his next period he turns rationalist, and exalts
"good sense" and "propriety." In the last dozen years of
his life his enthusiasm for highly imaginative literature returns; he translates Juvenal and Virgil, and modernizes
Chaucer; he is "lost in admiration over Virgil," though at
heart he "prefers Homer." It is in this final stage of his
career as a critic that he writes the charming praise of
Chaucer, which is reprinted in The Harvard Classics.[2] It is
the perfection of essay writing. "Here is God's plenty," as
he exclaims of the elder poet, in whom he finds a soul con-
genial to his own. Dryden did not, it is true, quite understand Chaucer's verse, else he could never have found it
"not harmonious," yet he makes royal amends by admitting
that "there is the rude sweetness of a Scotch tune in it,
which is natural and pleasing, though not perfect." In his
earlier "Apology for Heroic Poetry" (1677) he salutes "the
deceased author of 'Paradise Lost,'" then three years dead,
and calls Milton's masterpiece "one of the greatest, most
noble, and most sublime poems which either this age or
nation has produced."

WORDSWORTH AND COLERIDGE

Dryden's best pages of criticism tempt one, in brief, to
agree with him in declaring that "Poets themselves are the
most proper, though I conclude not the only critics." The
critical writings of Wordsworth and Coleridge confirm us
in that opinion. Wordsworth is less facile than Dryden, and
he does not range so far. Coleridge, by natural endowment
one of the greatest of literary critics, is desultory and in-
dolent. But the two men, when focusing their masterly
powers upon the defense and interpretation of that mode of

[2] *H. C.*, xxxix, 160ff.

Romantic poetry in which their own creative energies were for a time absorbed, produced criticism which has affected the whole subsequent development of English literature. Coleridge's lecture on "Poesy or Art," [3] for instance, is full of those flashes of penetrative insight which reveal the born critic: Art "is the power of humanizing nature"; "passion itself imitates order"; "beauty is the union of the shapely with the vital"; "the subjects chosen for works of art should be such as really are capable of being expressed and conveyed within the limits of those arts." Wordsworth's "Preface" [4] to his epoch-making early poems should be read in connection with Coleridge's comments in the "Biographia Literaria," and in the light of the well-known fact as to the proposed division of labor between the two young poets in the composition of the "Lyrical Ballads." Coleridge intended to treat supernatural objects as if they really existed. Wordsworth wished to find in natural objects elements of novelty and surprise, that is, the romance of everyday experience. The two methods blended of course, like the colors at the extreme edges of the spectrum. Wordsworth's successive statements of his purpose emphasize now his use of "the language of conversation in the middle and lower classes," as if it were mainly a question of poetic diction; then he stresses the necessity of truth to "the primary laws of our nature," and debates the æsthetic question of "the association of ideas in a state of excitement"; finally, he qualifies his first utterances by pointing out that the diction should be a "selection of language really used by men," and that the incidents and situations treated by the poet should have "a certain colouring of the imagination." Such criticism as this, if accompanied by close study of the verbal alterations which Wordsworth made in the text of his poems as his theories changed, is in the highest degree stimulating and profitable.

PERCY BYSSHE SHELLEY

The influence of Coleridge is traceable throughout Shelley's "Defence of Poetry" [5] (1821). Shelley rides into the

[3] *H. C.*, xxvii, 269ff.   [4] *H. C.*, xxxix, 281ff., 307ff., 327ff.
[5] *H. C.*, xxvii, 345ff.

lists with as high a heart as Sidney, to repel the attack, not of the "moralists" but of the utilitarians. He is not conscious, like Sidney, Dryden, and Arnold, of the history of criticism. He has steeped himself, it is true, in Plato, but he writes with the enthusiasm of a new and personal vision. Poetry, to him, is primarily the expression of the imagination: "it redeems from decay the visitations of the divinity in man"; "it is the record of the best and happiest moments of the happiest and best minds"; "a poem is the very image of life expressed in its eternal truth"; poetry "acts in a divine but unapprehended manner, beyond and above consciousness"; "a poet participates in the eternal, the infinite, and the one." Though the student of poetical theory can easily claim that such sentences as these are post-Coleridgean, they are really timeless, like the glorious spirit of Shelley itself.

EDGAR ALLAN POE

Poe's essay on "The Poetic Principle," [6] written to serve as a lecture during the last year (1849) of his brief life, illustrates his conviction that "the truly imaginative mind is never otherwise than analytic." As applied to Shelley, this dictum is far from true, but it expresses Poe's idealization of his own extraordinary gift for logical analysis. He was a craftsman who was never weary of explaining the trade secrets of his art, and though his criticism is uneven in quality and uninformed by deep and accurate scholarship, he expounded certain critical principles with incomparable clearness.

In "The Poetic Principle," together with some popularization of Coleridge, and some admixture no doubt of that "fudge" which Lowell thought so inextricably compounded with Poe's "genius," there will be found the famous definition of the "Poetry of words as *The Rhythmical Creation of Beauty.*" Poetry, according to Poe, excites, by elevating the soul. But as all excitements, by psychological necessity, are transient, it is only short poems that are truly poems at all. Such brief and indeterminate glimpses of the supernal loveliness, "the creation of supernal beauty," is the poet's

[6] *H. C.*, xxviii, 383ff.

struggle—and despair. If Poe's formulation of the task and method of poetry lacks, as it doubtless does, universal validity, it is nevertheless a key to the understanding of his own exquisitely musical fragments of lyric verse.

WHITMAN ON AMERICA AND POETRY

Walt Whitman, like Poe and Coleridge, is mystic and transcendental in his theory of poetry. Unlike them, he is an arch-rebel in poetic practice. The Preface to "Leaves of Grass"[7] (1855) is not so much a critical essay as a manifesto. It is vociferous, impassioned, inconsecutive. Some paragraphs of it were later turned into verse, so rich was it in emotion. The central theme is the opportunity which the immediate age in America offers to the poet. The past has had its fit poetical expression, but the new world of democracy and science now demands a different type of bard. The qualifications are obdurately clear: he must love the earth and animals and common people; he must be in his own flesh a poem, at one with the universe of things; his soul must be great and unconstrained. He must perceive that everything is miraculous and divine. The poet is to be the priest of the new age, and of all the coming ages. Whitman does not enter, in the Preface, upon the discussion of the technique of his own unmetrical, rhapsodic verse. Yet this verse, which has challenged the attention of two generations, and which is slowly making its way toward general recognition, is scarcely to be understood without a knowledge of the theory of poetry which underlies it. The Preface states that theory, confusedly, if one tries to parse and weigh it sentence by sentence, but adequately, if one watches simply, as Whitman bids, the "drift" of it.

MATTHEW ARNOLD

"I do not contest Mr. Walt Whitman's powers and originality," wrote Matthew Arnold in 1866, but he adds this warning: "No one can afford in literature to trade merely on his own bottom and to take no account of what

[7] *H. C.*, xxxix, 409ff.

the other ages and nations have acquired: a great original literature America will never get in this way, and her intellect must inevitably consent to come, in a considerable measure, into the European movement." It is not the least useful service of Arnold's own essay on "The Study of Poetry" [8] that it takes us at once into this European movement. The essay was written as a preface to a collection of English verse—"one great contributory stream to the world river of poetry." Arnold insists throughout, in characteristic fashion, upon the necessity of developing a sense for the best, for the really excellent. He points out the fallacies involved in the purely historical and the purely personal estimates. He uses lines and expressions of the great masters as "touchstones" for detecting the presence or absence of high poetic quality. He takes Aristotle's remark about the "higher truth" and "higher seriousness" of poetry as compared to history, and tests therewith the "classic" matter and manner of English poets.

There are pitfalls, without question, lurking in the path of Arnold's apparently sure-footed and adroit method, but the temper of his performance needs no praise. He brings us steadily and serenely back to "the European movement," to the laws and standards that endure. But he also teaches that life and art are inexhaustible in their resources. "The future of poetry is immense"; that is the first sentence of Arnold's essay; and it will be also the confirmed final truth of any reader who has taken pains to acquaint himself with the utterance of poets about poetry. Walter Bagehot wrote long ago: "The bare idea that poetry is a deep thing, a teaching thing, the most surely and wisely elevating of human things, is even now to the coarse public mind nearly unknown. . . . All about and around us a faith in poetry struggles to be extricated, but it is not extricated. Some day, at the touch of the true word, the whole confusion will by magic cease; the broken and shapeless notions will cohere and crystallize into a bright and true theory." We are still waiting, no doubt, for that true and final word, but if it is ever spoken, it is likely to be uttered by one of the poets.

[8] *H. C.*, xxviii, 65ff.

IV. ÆSTHETIC CRITICISM IN GERMANY

By Professor W. G. Howard

GOETHE admonishes the artist to create in forms of beauty, not to talk about beauty, and it is certain that no man ever became a poet from the study of an "art of poetry." Language is abstract, and art is concrete, the understanding is slow and emotion is swift, the reason may be convinced, but the senses cannot be persuaded. There is no disputing about tastes. Nevertheless, we know that taste can be cultivated, and that understanding not only makes the taste more discriminating but also multiplies the sources of æsthetic pleasure. Artists as well as amateurs and philosophers have ever sought to further such understanding.

The sculptor or the painter, whose primary means of expression are forms and colors, assumes the secondary function of teacher when he places at the disposal of his "school" the results of his studies in technique or theory. The philosophical lover of art delights to speculate on the constituents of beauty, and the critic boldly formulates the laws upon the basis of which he judges and classifies. Poetry, probably the earliest of the fine arts, was first subjected to this æsthetic legislation; but music, dancing, sculpture, and painting were soon brought under the same dominion, and have long been regarded as sisters of one and the same household with poetry.

THE RISE OF ÆSTHETIC CRITICISM

Especially since the revival of learning in the fifteenth and sixteenth centuries, practice in the arts has been accomplished by a running commentary of theory. The men of the Renaissance, having before them not merely numerous examples of Greek sculpture and the epics of Homer and Virgil, but also Aristotle's "Poetics" and Horace's "Art of Poetry," and seeing in these products of antiquity the height of human achievement, attempted in various ways to apply the canons of ancient taste to the settlement of contemporary problems. Accordingly, we find in Italy and, following the Italians, in France, England, and Germany, many writers on æsthetics only gradually emancipating themselves from the constraint of certain axioms which, being ancient, are unhesitatingly received as authoritative. Thus, all of the fine arts are, with Aristotle, regarded as arts of imitation—imitation, not of real but of ideal nature, of beautiful nature, as the French call it; and this vague and elusive conception is usually left without any very illuminating definition. Similarly, a painting is thought of, after Simonides, as a dumb poem, and a poem as a speaking picture; and, repeating a misunderstood phrase of Horace, men confidently say, "Like picture, like poetry."

The tendency is, then, to assimilate or at most to compare the several arts, and few observations penetrate beneath the surface. Artists calculated proportions and devised elaborate rules of technical procedure; writers of poetics discussed diction and rhetorical figures; but in treatises on painting and poetry alike, three "parts"—invention, disposition, and coloring—furnished the traditional subdivisions. Intelligence and industry seemed competent, if not to vie with the ancient genius, at least to follow the paths that the ancients had trod. With all their formalism, however, the critics seldom failed to insist that the end of art is to arouse emotion; to instruct, indeed, but also, as Horace had said, to please. Now pleasure is a personal reaction. We may ask what it is that pleases us in a work of art, or what there is in us that makes us sensitive to æsthetic pleasure; and the principal advance that modern theory has made beyond the point reached by the Renaissance consists in a better answer to the second question. In other words, our theory has, or seeks, a psychological foundation.

LESSING

To be sure, that modern work in which the sharpest line is drawn between the fields of painting and poetry, Lessing's "Laocoön," appears to treat the two arts in their most objective aspect, and is, in fact, far more concerned with the means than with the purpose or the substance of artistic expression. Lessing argues that if the means of painting be lines and colors in space, and the means of poetry articulate words in time, then evidently painting most properly addresses itself to the treatment of stationary bodies, and poetry to the treatment of successive actions; so that the attempt, carried too far, to represent actions in painting and to describe bodies in poetry is a perversion of the legitimate means of painting and poetry. We should not forget the qualifications that Lessing made to this rigid principle, nor the fact that he published only the first part of his projected treatise. He referred the effect of painting as well as of poetry to the imagination. But his purpose was to establish boundaries determinable by the difference in artistic means; and his "Laocoön" is a rationalistic document based upon knowledge and observation of external facts, not upon a study of internal reactions.

BURKE

Among the many predecessors of Lessing in the realm of æsthetic speculation, two men, not philosophers by profession, are conspicuous for attention to the personal phenomena which he did not much consult; the Abbé Dubos in France and Edmund Burke[1] in England. Dubos recognizes differences in the arts conditioned by their symbols of expression; but he compares and rates the arts according to their effect upon the senses, and so prepares the way for a purely impressionistic criticism. Burke did not agree with the Frenchman's ratings, nor did he in any manner imitate his book, however much he respected it; but he was in substantial agreement with Dubos as to the operation of æsthetic causes; and just as Dubos saw in the desire of the mind to be stimulated by *something* the prime motive for

[1] *Harvard Classics*, xxiv, 11ff.

interest in the arts, Burke found in two of our strongest
passions, love and terror, a definition of the chief ends of
artistic endeavor, the beautiful and the sublime.[2] Burke was
not much affected by painting. This art, the aim of which is
to represent the beautiful, has, he says, little effect on our passions. But poetry, to which he was sensitive, and which, he
holds, does not depend for its effect upon the power of raising
sensible images, is capable of stirring the passions with a
vague sense of the sublime, and is, strictly speaking, not an art
of imitation.

DAUMGARTEN

Though reached by a different process, Burke's conclusion
as to the province of poetry is, in its negative aspect,
identical with Lessing's: words are ill adapted to the vivid
presentation of objects by means of detailed description.
And though crude and materialistic, his "Inquiry" is an excellent introduction to the study of æsthetics as a branch of
psychology. The real founder of this science, however, and
the philosopher from whom it derives its name, was a contemporary of Burke's in Germany, Alexander Gottlieb
Baumgarten.

Adopting the monistic system of Leibnitz and Wolf,
Baumgarten, a clear thinker and a lover of poetry, but no
connoisseur of the formative arts, undertook to fill the gap
left by his forerunners in the logic of the lower powers of
the soul, that is, the senses. His theory of the beautiful is
general; he defines beauty as the perfection of sensuous
perception; but clinging to the maxim, "Like picture, like
poetry," he does not, in his application of the theory, progress far beyond the treatment of poetry as the typical art,
rating it, like Burke, higher than painting. Poetry he defines as perfect sensuous speech. So Milton says that
poetry is more simple, sensuous, and passionate than prose.
And that perfection which is the definition of beauty and of
poetry is a set of harmonious relationships in the object,
and between the object and the sensitive soul, of which the
intellect may take cognizance, but of which, above all, the
senses make us conscious, being impressed with an extensive

[2] *H. C.,* xxiv, 29ff.

clearness separable from intensive distinctness; so that a poem is a poem not for the accuracy of any "imitation," nor for the loftiness of its idea, nor for the elegance of its forms, but for the fullness of its appeal to those functions which most immediately respond to man's contact with his material environment; that is to say, for intuitively perceptible reality.

SCHILLER

Baumgarten's doctrine was taken up by Lessing's friend, Mendelssohn; it furnished fundamental presuppositions for "Laocoön"; and it persisted to the time of Kant and Schiller. Kant, the analyst and rationalist, tended to separate the spheres of reason, sense, and morals, and to refer all three to subjective judgment. But Schiller,[3] his disciple, fired as he was by moral enthusiasm, wished to find an objective foundation for a theory of the beautiful that should make æsthetics a mediator between science and ethics, and should give to the beautiful the sanction of a perfecter of the mind, the heart, and the will. Not unlike Lessing, whose "Education of the Human Race"[4] meant a gradual liberation from leading strings and final reliance upon trained natural faculties, Schiller conceived æsthetic education as a process of freeing man from bondage to the senses and leading him through culture to a state of more perfect nature, in which, as of old among the Greeks, truth and goodness shall be garbed in beauty. Civilization has been won through specialization, division of labor; it is a gain for the community, but at the loss of harmonious development of powers in the individual life. The beautiful soul longs to restore the balance. If this be impossible in the world of actuality, it is attainable in the world of appearance. There the mind is free to follow the image of beauty and to endow this image with the wealth of all its knowledge and all its goodness —not for any ulterior purpose, but in obedience to a native impulse. And so the poet is the sole modern representative of perfect humanity, with all his powers, intellectual, sensuous, and moral, cooperating toward the realization of an ideal.

[3] *H. C.*, xxxii, 221ff.
[4] *H. C.*, xxxii, 195ff.   See also Goethe's "Introduction to the Propyläen," xxxix, 264ff, and Hume, "On the Standard of Taste," xxvii, 215.

V. THE COMPOSITION OF A CRITICISM

By Dr. Ernest Bernbaum

O F THE critical essays not discussed in the previous lectures the most important are those by Hugo, Sainte-Beuve, Renan, Taine, and Mazzini. As their doctrines are quite obviously related to those expounded in the foregoing pages, it seems desirable to consider here the manner in which their opinions are expressed. The critical essays published in this series are classics, not merely because they contain significant doctrines about literature but also because they are in themselves literary works. They confer pleasure as well as profit. What distinguishes them from the journalistic book review on the one hand, and the pedantic study on the other, is their artistic composition. By what methods are their artistic effects produced?

A DOMINANT IDEA

The title of a work cited by Sainte-Beuve suggests what a literary criticism should not be. It runs as follows: "Michel de Montaigne, a collection of unedited or little-known facts about the author of the Essays, his book and other writings, about his family, his friends, his admirers, his detractors." Sainte-Beuve, Taine, and the other masters never present us with a "collection." They marshal their numerous facts into a system, and dominate them with a thought which, however complex, is coherent. Most of us arise from the perusal of an author with a chaotic throng of impressions. But in the mind of a true literary critic the chaos becomes order. Renan, in his "Poetry of the Celtic Races," [1] "giving a voice to races that are no more," lets us hear not a con-

---

[1] *Harvard Classics*, xxxii, 143.

fusion of tongues but an intelligible unity of national utterance—sad, gentle, and imaginative. Hugo, surveying in his
"Preface to Cromwell" [2] the highly intricate romantic movement, sees therein the harmonious union of the grotesque
and the sublime. Sainte-Beuve answers his sweeping question, "What is a Classic?" with the succinct definition—a
work that reveals in a beautiful and individual manner an
eternal truth or emotion. Mazzini characterizes Byron as a
subjective individualist, and Goethe as an objective one.
Taine, prefacing his "History of English Literature," [3] un-
locks the riddle of literary growth with the keys "race,
environment, and epoch." The truth of these doctrines does
not for the moment concern us. What is important for us is
that each of these long essays may be summed up in a single
sentence; for in each a powerful mind grasps and expresses
a single idea.

When a critic has conceived the leading idea of his essay,
he is still in danger of obscuring its presentation. The more
richly informed he is, the more he is tempted to introduce
facts not strictly related to his dominant thought. But the
great critical essayists, resisting that temptation, subordinate
all details to the general design. Hugo, in sketching the
development of the world's literature, selects only those
phases which forecast the timeliness of romanticism. Sainte-
Beuve and Mazzini, in dealing with the lives of Montaigne [4]
and Byron, [5] which offer many opportunities for recounting
interesting but irrelevant incidents, mention only those
which illustrate their conception of the authors.

METHODICAL ARRANGEMENT

In the arrangement of the materials, the same conscious
art is observable. Each of the sections of the essays of
Taine and Renan is a firm and necessary foundation for
those that succeed it. Not until Renan has described the
secluded national existence of the Celts does he draw the
resultant national traits of character, which thereupon we
are ready to trace intelligently in the various branches of

[2] H. C., xxxix, 354.   [3] H. C., xxxix, 433.
[4] H. C., xxxii, 109.   [5] H. C., xxxii, 399.

Celtic literature. The method of Taine's essay is even more admirably logical. To understand the growth of literature, he tells us, we must know first "the visible man," next "the invisible man," then the race, environment, and epoch which determined his character, and finally the way in which those causes distribute their effects. Thus is our progress through unknown fields made easy: we are not asked to leap from point to point, or to retrace our way; our guide takes us step by step along the path of his discovery.

ILLUSTRATIONS

The sustained and methodically expounded idea which is the basis of every great critical essay would, however, like all abstractions, seem dull or unintelligible if it were not constantly and vividly illustrated. The logical must flower in the picturesque. This even the great critics occasionally forget: one or two passages in Mazzini's essay would be more convincing if more fully illustrated by references to Goethe's works; and the only pages of Hugo where our interest flags a little are those in which he describes, without examples, the character of romantic verse. But such lapses are highly exceptional. Taine, the most intellectual and least emotional of these men, makes it a rule to clothe the skeleton of his theory in flesh and blood. To show what he means by "the visible man," he clearly portrays a modern poet, a seventeenth-century dramatist, a Greek citizen, and an Indian Purana. Renan, to exhibit the Celtic love of animals and nature, tells the story of Kilhwch and Olwen; and to explain Celtic Christianity, recounts the legend of St. Brandan. Sainte-Beuve states his definition of classicism in a few lines, and devotes the rest of his essay to applying it to particular authors.

All these masters have the gift of happy quotation. Montaigne's "I commend a gliding, solitary, and silent life," quoted by Sainte-Beuve, and Goethe's "I allow objects to act tranquilly upon me," quoted by Mazzini, clarify and confirm out of the authors' own mouths those impressions which the critics wish to impart. The astonishing effectiveness of the close of Hugo's essay is due to his apt quotations from Aristotle and Boileau, which seem to bring over those great classicists to Hugo's romantic party.

The illustrations are not derived only from literary works. Taine, insisting upon the delicacy with which a literature records changes in national character, likens it to the sensitive instrument of a physicist. The similes of Hugo are exceptionally frequent and elaborate. "To make clear by a metaphor the ideas that we have ventured to put forth," he writes, "we will compare early lyric poetry to a placid lake which reflects the clouds and stars; the epic is the stream which flows from the lake, and rushes on, reflecting its banks, forests, fields, and cities, until it throws itself into the ocean of the drama. Like the lake, the drama reflects the sky; like the stream, it reflects its banks; but it alone has tempests and measureless depths." His poet "is a tree that may be blown about by all winds and watered by every fall of dew; and bears his works as his fruits, as the *fablier* of old bore his fables. Why attach one's self to a master, or graft one's self upon a model? It were better to be a bramble or a thistle, fed by the same earth as the cedar and the palm, than the fungus or the lichen of those noble trees." Mazzini begins his comparison of Byron and Goethe by contrasting an Alpine falcon bravely floating in the midst of a storm, with a tranquil stork impassive amid the warring elements; and Renan prepares us for his conception of Celtic literature by giving us at the outset the characteristic tone of the Breton landscape. What the intellect has firmly outined, fancy and imagination paint in lively colors.

COMPARISON AND CONFLICT OF OPINION

An essay which has by these means achieved clearness may be pleasant to read but still lacking in power. To give force to his ideas about an author or a literature, the masterful critic exhibits the peculiarity of his subject by the use of contrast. The brilliancy of Mazzini's essay proceeds largely from its striking antithesis between Byron and Goethe. Renan enforces his doctrine of the individuality of Celtic literature by emphasizing the differences between the French "Roland" and the Celtic "Peredur," between the gentle Isolde and the "Scandinavian furies, Gudrun and Chrimhilde." Hugo intensifies our conviction of the complex character of modern life by describing the simplicity of the ancients.

If a critic does not observe this principle, we may say of his essay: "These ideas are, to be sure, clear and enjoyable; but what do they matter?" The great critics do not leave us calmly indifferent; they are on occasion critics militant. Even the gentle Sainte-Beuve admonishes the "Montaignologues," who, he feels, do not understand the spirit of Montaigne. Taine manifests the novelty and importance of his method of criticism by mentioning the imperfections of the eighteenth-century method. Mazzini reproves the enemies and misinterpreters of Byron. Hugo above all shows the stimulating value of pitting one's ideas against those of others. He calls his essay his "sling and stone against the classical Goliaths"; and by making his opponents utter their arguments against him gives to his work the force of dramatic combat. Critical essays that thus add vigor to lucidity arouse and delight our minds. When we recognize how skillfully they fuse logic, imagination, and emotion, we perceive the superficiality of the distinction between so-called criticism and so-called creative literature. Good criticism is indeed creative, and its composition is a high art.

EDUCATION

I. GENERAL INTRODUCTION

By Professor H. W. Holmes

IN ALL profitable thinking about modern education one central fact is stated or assumed—the fact that education has become a public enterprise. To think of it as a matter mainly of private interest, to discuss it chiefly in terms of personal development, is to ignore the achieved conditions of civilized life and the clear trend of progress. The spread of public schools is but the obvious outward sign of a growing conviction concerning all educational endeavor. That conviction was long ago proclaimed and has now become a guide to action—the conviction that the community has a vital stake in the education of every child. Education is a common concern not merely because there are many children to be educated, but because there can be no significant outcome in the education of any child which is not of importance, not to him only, but also to others, immediately to many, more remotely to all.

THE SOCIAL NATURE OF THE MODERN IDEAL

This has always been true. Modern life, with cities and the inventions which belittle time and space, has only made it more apparent and action upon it more pressing. No one can think with penetration upon the results of education who does not come at last to a fuller vision of the interdependence of men. That men shall live less and less each for himself, more and more each for the common good, is not merely a consequence of increasing numbers on the earth, but an essential condition of human progress, in the individual as well as in society. It is a poor and meager culture

287

which does not end in greater power to serve. To become a man is to become capable of living effectively with others and for all, in the normal relationships of life—not in subservience to custom, but in devotion to a welfare larger than one's own, a welfare at least not incompatible, in the end, with the welfare of the world. It is not enough to say that the common interest is at stake in the education of every child; the very process of education is properly a training for effective membership in the common life.

Such is the reasoning behind the great outlay of public money on schools, libraries, museums, and other educational agencies. Civilized communities undertake education as a part of their proper business, not as a charity, but as a necessary public function. Schools are tax supported and education is compulsory. The state claims final authority to prescribe standards and to supervise even private educational ventures. It calls on all citizens for their full support in this task of conserving and developing human resources. It considers every taxpayer as much in duty bound to support ultimate social improvement through education as to direct social improvement through public enterprises of any other sort. Personal return cannot be taken into the account; the good to be achieved is primarily a public good, in which the childless also share. And the problems of education are problems of public policy, involving the whole theory of the state, of government, of the social order, and of civic progress.

All educational questions have thus become increasingly complex. The character of modern life makes even well-rounded personal development a matter of much difficulty, for the life of the individual child is in some ways narrower to-day than it was in simpler times. To secure for modern children the full exercise of body, intellect, imagination, sympathy, and will is in itself a task which calls for insight, energy, and cooperation, to say nothing of money. Yet to provide for the formal cultivation of personal capacities, faculties, and powers, is by no means to solve the problem of education, even for a given child. The results may happen to be good, but the problem has not been solved, for it has not been adequately stated.

THE EDUCATIONAL PROBLEM CONCRETE, NOT ABSTRACT

It happens, in the first place, that "body, intellect, imagination, sympathy, and will" are poor terms to use in the actual direction of teaching. They name abstractions which have induced more futile educational discussion and more useless educational effort than can ever be reckoned. No child is a collection of general faculties which can be trained for universal use. But even when we have discovered the special capacities with which the individual is actually endowed, and with which we may therefore profitably work, the problem is only in part before us. It is quite as important to consider what our child is to do with his capacities, what stuff he is to exercise them on. It is the content of education that gives it social direction and social importance; from the public standpoint it is the school, the course, the subject that mean most, for these determine the concrete character of the individual's later activities and interests. That ancient educational saw, "I care not what you study, if you study it well," is profoundly misleading—a mischievous piece of common sense which hides the truth in order to emphasize a part of it. No matter what "faculty" a subject "trains," it is the information, the ideas, the ideals, principles, points of view, methods, interests, enthusiasms, purposes, and sympathies it imparts that chiefly determine its educational value. It is the content of a man's education which helps most to fix his place in the community, his vocation, his avocations, and his availability for special service.

RELATIVE NATURE OF "THE FUNDAMENTALS"

Education presents not one problem, therefore, but many. In the earlier years, to be sure, all children need much the same intellectual experience, at least in school. "The fundamentals" are the subjects everybody ought to master. Thus at first there is only the complexity of meeting individual differences among children—the brilliant, the backward, the well nurtured, the neglected. Complexity enough! And even so, each subject presents, besides, its own problem of social interpretation: "What everybody ought to master" in arithmetic or in geography is by no means clear, and new definitions of the aim and scope of each subject are continually needed. Such definitions must be made from the standpoint of public service and the real demands of life, not from the standpoint of complete mastery of the subject. A social view of education demands selection and reorganization of the elements of knowledge. But beyond this is the fact that children cannot long be kept in the same educational highway. The need to separate arises at least as early as adolescence, the end of childhood and the gate of youth. Here differences of native endowment, economic condition, and conscious purpose force the first fundamental differentiation of schools, courses, and classes. Even if, in some millennium of social justice, the stern necessity of earning a living in the teens were to be done away, the social necessity for variety of schooling would remain. Society needs many kinds of thinkers and workers, just as there are many kinds of aptitude to be trained. There is no "general course" which can provide an "all-round education," in the sense of providing all that is really needful for anybody who knows what is good for him. To discover the best in education for one child or class of children, though with the public interest well in mind, is to answer but one of the questions the educator must hereafter always ask.

For the public interest goes far beyond the need of supplying to all a uniform minimum of schooling. Democracy means far more in education than the warding off of danger from illiteracy. It is a crude and at bottom a wholly mistaken view of public education which confines it to "the three R's," or to those admitted necessities and such other subjects as the common good may dictate for the common school. The public interest is not met by merely elementary education. It is met only when every prospective citizen may secure without undue sacrifice that extent and kind of education which will make him most efficient in his fundamental social relationships, including his vocation. The state needs knowledge, efficiency, insight, and idealism in industry, commerce, the arts, science, philosophy, religion, and family life as much as in citizenship more narrowly defined. The only logical result of the thoroughly social character of education is public support of every socially profitable kind of schooling, with commensurate public authority.

Democracy in education invites, to be sure, the evils of political control; yet education is one of the few permanent means of counteracting political evil. No one need fear to trust educational authority to a public aroused to the meaning and value of education, and this essential condition of public support depends on the slow growth of public conscience and public intelligence. In any case, private initiative will long have an honorable part to play in education, and the very policy of the state may often best be served by leaving the special and the higher schools in private hands: but there are a few communities in which the extension of public provision and public authority in education is not imperative.

Of that extension what must be the guiding conceptions? Before all else must come the honesty of an attitude at once scientific and ethical. Educators must face the facts, without abatement of their enthusiasm for ideals.

THE AIM OF EDUCATION SOCIALLY CONSIDERED

Teachers and school officers find before them not mere types of humanity, with abstract virtues and vices, general habits, faculties, and powers waiting to be cultivated for "life" as it may be philosophically defined; they have to deal with real and ever-varying human beings, whose impulses, emotions, and purposes reach forward to the actual challenge of the specific duties, interests, and rewards of the real world. To provide, for every normal individual, whatever his endowment, nurture, or experience, an opportunity to prepare himself for a part in the legitimate work of the world, a share in its proper pleasures, and an understanding of the meaning and value of the life he leads—this is the problem to be solved. What are the things men do in which the public interest calls for intelligence and efficiency such as may be got in schools? For the getting of such intelligence and efficiency in the doing of such things, what schools are needed? In these schools what subjects shall be taught and how?

These questions present the problem of education as it must be viewed from the standpoint of the common good—and the questions presented by education viewed from any other standpoint are far less important. No doubt we need, in the crash and strain of modern life, remembrance of the old ideal of personal distinction. Grace is worth too much to lose it beyond retrieving, even for efficiency. But how impoverished now appears that aristocratic ideal which made much of personal charm and little of social worth—for which the education of women could consist chiefly of dancing, French, and hand embroidery! Whatever its faults and dangers, it is a stronger age which approves for women schools of household economy, of nursing, or philanthropy, to say nothing of clerical training, medicine, or law. But he interprets the modern ideal too narrowly who would have it take no account of beauty, leisure, or reflection. The work of the world is fundamental, and in itself neither selfish nor undignified; but the world's play—its generous sport, its curious science, its philosophic speculation, its art, and its worship—is a region of enduring values. It is only the separation of work and play that belittles either. A social conception of the ends of education finds reason for folk-dancing and pageants in the public schools, but none for the exploitation of children through premature industrial training. The common good demands education for play no less than education for work, education for the larger efficiency of insight, breadth of view, and reflective intelligence no less than education for the narrower efficiency of habit. Democracy cannot perpetuate slavery through schools.

EDUCATION AND FREEDOM

But the essential conditions of freedom cannot be established through education; only the love of it, the understanding of it, and the power and will to use it for service can be gained from the most liberalizing of curricula. The possibility and the extension of freedom are the work of direct social and political reform. It is futile, meanwhile, to insist that liberal studies shall be all that schools shall offer. It is simple error to insist that a traditional range of studies—the classics, science, mathematics, even history, or English—provide the only possible culture for freedom. Schools must meet the need of the world as frankly and directly as they can, without squeamish prejudice against practical or vocational studies. Shopwork may afford more liberal culture to a given boy than Greek—and the problem of educational values is always thus specific. The only profitable distinction between liberal studies and vocational studies is one which looks out and forward to the life the individual is to lead. A man's calling, if it be of much difficulty, demands vocational training; his life in the family, the community, the state, and the church demands an education which may justly be called liberal; the worthy use of his leisure demands an education which may properly be called cultural. But what is vocational for the artist will be cultural for others; and a given subject may serve many uses in every normal life. A complete education will prepare for life in all its relationships, either by direct study of the problems they present, or by the study of subjects valuable in one of them or in all.

This conception of the ends to be attained is clear enough; it is the means that fail. And the failure of means is due less to public apathy than to inherent difficulty in finding them. New schools, new courses, new subjects must be created. A new interpretation of old subjects and a new method of teaching them must be worked out. Much of our traditional teaching, especially in high schools, academies, and colleges, goes quite astray; it is fruitless because its uses are not clear or because they are not made clear; and the "intellectual discipline" which is supposed to result from it either does not occur or is not carried over into the conduct of mature life. Mental and moral habits and ideals, such attitudes, tendencies, and principles of conduct as "thoroughness," "order," "concentration," "self-reliance," may be taught by precept and example in the work of any subject; in every case they must be generalized and held consciously in mind, practiced and renewed in vision if they are ever to permeate life. In this general training of the mind and will, the unconscious effect of one subject is little

better than that of another of similar complexity and scope.
Science is as good as Latin, and mechanical drawing may be
better than either. Much depends on the ethical enthusiasm, the insight, the sympathy, and the leadership of the
teacher; much on the methods of teaching and class management he employs. More depends on the traditions and the
administrative, disciplinary, and social policies of the school.
This is to say that these precious moral results of education
are chiefly matters of personal contagion, direct inspiration,
and experience in the common effort of work and play.
They are achieved as much in the home or on the play-
ground as in the school. It is the specific habits of attention, the special methods of observing, comparing, classify-
ing, and reacting on facts, the particular forms of skill, the
definite information, the peculiar outlook, the actual incentives which a given subject may possess that make it
serviceable in education. In these things subjects differ and
lend themselves to different uses. In these things history
differs from dressmaking, science from agriculture. And
in these things the same subject will differ as it is taught
for different purposes, to pupils of different ages and different capacities and motives. Literature cannot yield the
same fruit in a night school that it yields in a college.
Under a conception of education which demands preparation
for all the essential activities of life, in schools designed to
meet the needs of every age and class, subjects must be
evaluated and organized anew.

VOCATIONAL EDUCATION

The schools and courses now most needed are partly
known, partly to be conceived. Vocational education has
come to stay, but its various forms and alliances have yet to
be completely determined. The fear that vocational training will materialize and lower education is groundless, even
in theory. To train carpenters and printers in schools instead of by apprenticeship is not a threatening educational
revolution; doctors, lawyers, and engineers were once
trained by personal tuition under practitioners. Vocational
training has long existed in the higher professions; its estab-

lishment for industry and business is the result of social changes which have undermined apprenticeship; and the fact that this training is now given at public expense shows a new sense of the social importance of labor. In the life of the modern world artisans are no more to be neglected than artists, farmers than philosophers. Vocational education is a mighty step in advance, which offers inspiring opportunities for the extension of general education, as an accompaniment of technical training, to those who might otherwise have secured neither. Ought we not to rejoice at the retention of boys and girls in schools, where they can be under the disinterested influence of teachers, whereas they might have drifted from one shabby and depressing experience to another until they had been able, perhaps, to "pick up a trade," acquiring their views of life and their ethical principles and habits who knows how? The pressing problem of vocational training is not the problem of justification and defense, but of organization and extension.

The kind and number of vocational schools to be established must be settled partly by the economic return for special forms of vocational efficiency. In the long run the social need for efficiency in a trade or profession determines the legitimate rewards of success in that calling. The fact that people will pay well for medical skill is an indication of social need for it. It cannot be said, of course, that schools should be established to train men for every calling in which they may earn a good living. A school may be established as much to teach men the value of training for knowledge and power in a special form of service as to prepare individuals to profit by rendering that service; for it is only in the end that economic demand justly reflects true social need. Accordingly, the public interest calls upon the educator to define social need and correct social demand, no less than to meet it. To plan a system of schools requires vision of a new and better order, in which the wants of men, and their consequent willingness to pay for the satisfaction of them, are more reasonably founded in the general welfare. Yet in discussing the advisability of training for any occupation, the possibility of earning a living in it cannot be

ignored. If agriculture could not be made to pay we should
not have agricultural high schools or agricultural colleges.
Even a school of philanthropy finds added sanction in the
fact that trained social workers are paid for their services.
In vocational education, then, there is at least an obvious
basis for discussion concerning schools, courses, and curricula. The state must train its workers, and work for which
there is fundamental need is work which pays. Vocational
education presents problems of the most vexing sort, but its
rationale is clear.

THE NEED FOR GENERAL EDUCATION

It is the persistent need for general education that com-
plicates the issue. Economic demand may justify child
labor, but educational theory does not. A theory of education which finds no place for vocational education is antiquated and meager; but a theory which considers only the
requirements of work is meager and inhuman. No training
for special skill in a trade is conceivable in the elementary
school: manual training, gardening, sewing, cooking, and
agriculture have a place in childhood because children cannot learn by books alone, but need a training of body, hand,
and eye, of purpose, loyalty, and leadership which these subjects can provide. This need does not disappear with
adolescence, but generalized manual training—constructive
work on objects without economic value, the making of
childish jimcracks, of joints which join nothing, or of seams
which sew no garment—ceases early to have even an educational value. The purely educational worth of any form of
manual training comes gradually to depend on the economic
value of the ends for which the pupil works. Manual training as a part of the general curriculum of a high-school
pupil must be practical training in some form of manual
skill of actual value in the working world. Even a pupil
who intends to go to college may well take one or two
courses of handwork in the secondary school, for the broadening of his experience and outlook and the specific training he may thus secure: a course in the elements of many
occupations would be better still. But this is not vocational

education. True vocational education aims at efficiency in
a special field of work—it trains printers, stenographers,
dressmakers, carpenters, mechanicians, doctors, lawyers,
clergymen, journalists, engineers. It brings into play the
purpose to earn a living by what one learns—which President Eliot has called the "life-career motive." It narrows,
not unjustifiably, but inevitably. The difficulty is to educate
for citizenship, for the duties of parenthood and social living, for leisure, and for the interpretation of life—in spite
of the need for early specialization, when that need is
present.

That need does not arise altogether from differences in
wealth. After adolescence many pupils lack incentive for
an education that has no direct reference to a career. But
the demand for vocational training is so overlaid and en-
tangled with economic pressure that selection of candidates
for vocational schooling on the ground of individual aptitude and free choice is visionary. While our social system
permits comparative poverty to constrain the vast majority
of young men and women to go to work at the earliest possible age, we must face the necessity of early specialization
in training, whatever their capacity or need for further
general culture. Education can only emphasize the value of
liberal studies and strive to include in every curriculum as
many as possible, and in profitable form. It can also resist
the tendency to specialize too soon.

ECONOMIC PRESSURE IN EDUCATION

Education has thus to struggle, like government or philanthropy, beneath the burdens imposed by the injustice of
our economic order. We must make educational provision
for social conditions which ought not to exist—night schools
for illiterate foreigners, specialized vocational training for
factory workers and shopgirls who ought to have at least
the time for a much extended general education in addition
to their preparation for work. We must also be content to
see the high privilege of general education seized by boys
and girls whose easy lives make them careless of its value
and inconstant in its pursuit. These conditions schools

themselves cannot change. But by public provision and by
scholarships the opportunity for prolonged education may be
kept open to the able and ambitious. The spirit of teaching
and school administration may help to prevent the formation
of social caste. By precept and example democratic ideals
and the will to serve may be encouraged in those who are in
danger of losing them. And no academic bars need be
hastily and blindly set up—as in the narrow interpretation
of college entrance requirements or in failure to provide a
reasonable opportunity for higher education of some desirable sort—against those who seek further training after mistaken choice of a high-school course or the early disadvantages of having to earn a living. In a democracy the
educational system must at least guard jealously against the
perpetuation of special privilege. Schools must discourage
the advance of the unfit, not of the unfortunate.

Obviously there is need for wise guidance of individuals
into the kind of schooling which will best fit them for the
life they can best lead. Vocational guidance is but part of
the larger problem of "the redistribution of human talent"
(a phrase recently and aptly coined by Professor Carver)
and it is often best to be accomplished as a part of an educational guidance which takes account of the need for liberal
culture as well as for vocational training. Transcendent
ability is doubtless seldom obscured through lack of counsel
or of privilege; educational guidance will not discover many
a mute inglorious Milton nor send to schools of pharmacy
many a discouraged Keats. It may prevent, however, less
disastrous misfittings in a thousand cases, and therein is its
sufficient sanction. But guidance will be futile if there are
no proper paths to tread. The money now provided for
schools must be increased many fold, if schools are to become for all men the gates of opportunity and the highways
to service. We must remember, to be sure, that there are
many educational agencies besides schools; libraries often
do far more toward education. But any systematic education is schooling, and if the interests of society are to be
adequately met, all valuable forms of educational activity
must be organized, supported, and made available to the
individuals who seek to use them.

THE LINE OF ADVANCE IN EDUCATION

To increase the size of schools is not enough. Schools and classes are already far too large. System is not enough. More schools and courses, of greater variety; smaller schools and smaller classes, with greater opportunity for personal contact between teachers and taught; more teachers, of higher native capacity and better training—all these are needed. But these things we shall not have until the common conception of schools and teachers has suffered change. We still think of teaching too narrowly or too vaguely—too narrowly if we look upon teachers as purveyors of learning for its own sake, too vaguely if we think of them as taskmasters in a dubious abstract discipline of mind. The task of the teacher must be reconceived; we must think of him and he must become a guide to worthy living, teaching not only his subject but how to use it and what it is for, making clear its incentives and ideals, its methods and its values, and helping his pupils to interpret life more justly because they have seen it in a new light. This is the larger opportunity of every teacher, but especially of the teacher of a traditional subject in a traditional course. The teacher of stenography may more safely confine himself to skill and speed with dots and dashes than the teacher of Latin to exactness in the use of tenses. The first task of any teacher is to teach his subject well, but he cannot leave the social interpretation and application of education wholly to principals, parents, school pamphlets, and chance. If the public is to value the teacher's work more highly, he must make it more valuable.

To become more valuable, teaching must develop both a science and a philosophy of its own, teachers must study their problems as physicians study theirs and as statesmen theirs. For the problems of teaching are at once problems of efficiency and problems of destiny. The teaching of any subject calls for scientific study of methods and ethical study of ends. How shall we teach it well? depends for its answer in part on the answer to What shall we teach it for? These questions have not yet been answered with finality for any subject. With due change of wording they may be asked of any school or course: How shall we manage it well?

and, What shall we manage it for? All questions of educational practice are thus both scientific and philosophical.

(a) IN THE ELEMENTARY SCHOOL

In the elementary school we need better methods of drill —greater efficiency in the formation of habits, as for instance in arithmetic. To gain it we must turn to experiments in the psychological laboratory and to exact measurement of arithmetical progress in the school. It is only in the last few years that we have had an adequate knowledge of what arithmetical ability is. We do not yet know with much precision how it develops under different methods of instruction. The teaching of every subject suffers for want of accurate records of results. We lack standards, fundamental tests, and a sufficiently detailed knowledge of the psychology of the subjects we teach. But measurement and experiment apply in the main to memory work and the formation of habits. They will not quickly show us how to relate one subject to another or to the life outside school walls; they cannot yet help us to vitalize our subjects and make them yield opportunity for independence and cooperation on the part of our pupils. They will not soon teach us how to make learning a light to life. In the arithmetic of the elementary school we need a social philosophy to govern our selection of topics to be taught or omitted, to justify varying emphasis on logical conceptions, drill in calculation, or exercise with real problems. So in the teaching of every subject we need new study, both exact and broad.

(b) IN THE SECONDARY SCHOOL

In the work of the high school this double duty is even more apparent. We face the immediate necessity of extending the period of compulsory school attendance far into the period of secondary education. But we cannot lightly set aside both the need to earn and the impulse to work, and the demand for workers will not readily yield to the idealism of the educator who would ignore it in favor of general culture. Compromise must be the outcome, but also cooperation: we must have many forms of vocational training, and employers of young workers must aid the state to educate them through schemes of part-time schooling. Such schemes are already in operation and commend themselves as both efficient and humane. In this increased provision for schooling the purely technical subjects lend themselves readily to measurement of results and standardization of method; it is the subjects of larger social value, such as civics or English, that must be studied anew, in the light of clearer conceptions of their aims and closer observation of their effects. We have to learn how to use these traditional means of education (and such newer ones as the study of household sanitation or personal hygiene) under new and trying conditions and with new purposes, as the liberal adjuncts of many forms of vocational training.

Yet in the secondary school which aims wholly at general culture (or at preparation for college, which is not supposed to be an obstacle to general culture), the problems of aim and method in the teaching of traditional subjects are more pressing still. How shall a modern language be taught to some real purpose? For what purpose shall it be taught? The actual mastery of the tongue can be achieved very much more effectively than it is now achieved if methods of teaching can be based on fuller knowledge of the psychology of learning and completer tests of classroom work and home study. The fundamental values of the subject can be more clearly conceived and more directly pursued if we can shake ourselves free from the befogging belief in general discipline as the goal of teaching in this or any given subject. Ability to handle the language as an instrument of thought and expression—for the achievement of this aim we need a new analysis of the fundamentals and more accurate standards of progress: appreciation of the foreign civilization represented in its literature—for the achievement of this aim we need new selection of material and more vital reference to life. In this and in many traditional subjects teachers are constantly at work at this double adjustment, and from them as well as from psychologists and students of education we may look for progress and reform.

For scientific study of method, whether by experiment in the psychological laboratory, by classroom test, or by exact statistical record, can but provide the basis for constructive reorganization of teaching in any subject; discussion of aims by educational leaders can but define in general terms a new interpretation of material; the teachers in the schools must make effective or prove visionary the ideals thus achieved. If they cling to traditional conceptions and tried methods—as many do, especially in private schools—they block progress; and if by personal worth and the power of leadership they win respect and affect deeply the lives of their pupils, the weight of their conservatism is the harder to bear. But the hasty and ill-considered application of scientific generalization or social conception is an equal if a rarer fault. The teacher must master for himself the science and the philosophy of his subject and be critical practitioner as well. He must be open-minded, critical, constructive.

(c) IN THE COLLEGE

This attitude is more general among teachers and principals of elementary schools and among school superintendents than among teachers and masters of secondary schools; among public secondary-school teachers than among private secondary-school teachers; and least general among college teachers. Yet to these latter the call to professional study of the problems of their own work is loudest. They have greatest need to test their results and possibly revise their methods, to reconceive their aims and discover new ways to achieve them. In America the college stands perforce for culture; yet it clears itself with difficulty from the snares of technical specialization in chosen fields of knowledge—a specialization essentially vocational. College professors must be specialists—scholars in the full sense of the term; but college students do not for their part commonly intend or care to specialize in the same sense. To study one field with greater thoroughness than others; to gain from it a disinterested enthusiasm for learning; to approach in one direction the limits of achieved knowledge; to taste the joy of constructive intellectual effort; these are essential elements in a college student's curriculum. But this does not call for the methods or ideals of graduate specialization, even in the student's chosen field. The privilege of college study is the opportunity to reach safe ground, in all the more important fields of scholarship, for the exercise of reflective intelligence. With a view to providing this opportunity college teachers may well spare time from research for that close observation of methods and results and that unprejudiced discussion of aims which are needed in the teaching of all subjects everywhere.

II. FRANCIS BACON

By Dr. Ernest Bernbaum

WE HONOR Francis Bacon as the prophetic inspirer of modern science. In perusing the long list of the activities of that scientific establishment which is described in the closing pages of "The New Atlantis,"[1] we are astonished by again and again recognizing in its imaginary methods and achievements precise anticipations of what is actually being done in modern medicine, meteorology, engineering, aeronautics, etc. Bacon himself, to be sure, modestly protested that he was but "stirring the earth a little about the roots of science." He was indeed no great discoverer of data, and from Harvey to Huxley the scientific specialists have sneered at his rather futile experiments. Even his method, which he sincerely believed a new and rapid way to complete mastery of our environment, is now considered somewhat impractical. Yet the prefaces to his "Instauratio Magna,"[2] though no longer accurate guideposts, are revered as monuments in the history of scientific progress. They served an even nobler purpose than to show the scientist just where to go; they sent him forth to seek his way with a new and conquering spirit, the spirit of confidence and of cooperation. The works of Bacon instilled in his successors the faith that by united effort they would presently understand, and thus control, those physical forces which in the past had toyed with the life of man, and exposed him to poverty, disease, and all the accidents of circumstance. In this hope were undertaken the Royal Society and the French "Encyclopédie"—leading enterprises in advancing respectively the discovery and the dissemination of rational knowledge. "We shall owe most," says Diderot in his prospectus to the "Encyclopédie," "to the Chancellor Bacon, who threw out

[1] *Harvard Classics,* iii, 151ff.   [2] *H. C.,* xxxix, 122ff., 150ff.

the plan of a universal dictionary of sciences and arts at a time when, so to speak, neither sciences nor arts existed. That extraordinary genius, at a time when it was not possible to write a history of what was known, wrote one of what it was necessary to learn." Wherever experimental investigators are to-day discovering new laws of nature, and thus more and more subjecting the physical world to the welfare of man, the spirit of Bacon is fruitfully at work.

BACON NOT PREOCCUPIED WITH SCIENCE

Among writers on education, the very magnitude of Bacon's position in the history of science has tended to overshadow his influence in other respects. Yet he urged the development of science because in his day it was relatively the most neglected and chaotic department of human endeavor, and not because he thought it absolutely and forever the most important. Newman himself does not insist more strongly than Bacon on the truth that science, though great, is not the complete satisfier of human needs. In "The Advancement of Learning," the first part of the "Instauratio Magna," Bacon pleads for the discovery and application to life, not merely of pure scientific truth, but also of clear ideals of mental, moral, and spiritual well-being. Religion and the so-called liberal studies had his eloquent and loyal support. "The New Atlantis" presents us not only with the model of a public institution of scientific research, but also with ideals of social and personal character. His Utopia was not, as some mistakenly declare, a merely industrial civilization, but a Christian commonwealth which exalted the humane feelings, family life, and artistic beauty.

DISTINCTION BETWEEN HIS ESSAYS AND HIS OTHER WORKS

Both in the prefaces to the "Instauratio Magna" and in "The New Atlantis," Bacon is thinking of the world as he believed it should and would become. The assumption that he had a similar purpose in his famous "Essays" [3] unfortunately misleads many modern critics, and tends to obscure

[3] *H. C.*, iii, 7ff.

the peculiar merits of his most popular work. Yet Bacon himself tells us that in his opinion we already had enough books which enthusiastically described moral ideals, and that what we really needed were accurate observations on the extent to which those ideals were attainable, and on the methods by which, under the actual conditions of everyday life, they might be put into practice. What he wished to present in the essays was human life, not as it ought to be, but as it is. "Let us know ourselves," he said, "and how it standeth with us."

BACON NOT A CYNIC

The result is a portrait of mankind beneath which may be inscribed his characteristic sentence: "It is good to retain sincerity." So accurate and candid an observer of human life is instinctively disliked by persons of sentimental temperament, and they call Bacon cynical and heartless. Ignoring his realistic intention, they turn, for instance, to the essays on love and on marriage,[4] excepting eloquent praise of what love and marriage may be at the very best; and they are disappointed, perplexed, and sometimes disgusted with what they find. In their haste they exclaim: "What a cold and calculating creature! All he says of the love between husband and wife is 'Nuptial love maketh mankind!'" These accusations, which may substantially be found in one of the best known editions of the "Essays," are as inaccurate as they are typical. Any careful reader, not led astray by the usual misconception of Bacon's purpose, will observe that the kind of love which he discusses in his essay on that subject is "the wanton love which corrupteth and embaseth," the condemnation of which should hardly be considered objectionable. As for family life (which, as I have mentioned, he idealizes in "The New Atlantis"), it is true that he dispatches it briefly in the essay on love; but in the essay on marriage he does not estimate it as cynically as we are led to suppose. He points out, to be sure, that, as a matter of sober fact, marriage may interfere with extraordinary public ambition; but he gives it preference over a selfish single life, he scorns those who

H. C., iii, *22,* 28.

consider children mere "bills of charges" instead of "dearest pledges," and he calls matrimony a "discipline of humanity," that is, a school of kindness or a humane education. To study the comparative merits and defects of many conditions of human life, to mark the extent and the limitations of human faculties, and to do so with even handed justice, is his ruling purpose.

BACON AS A PRACTICAL ADVISER

To create an ideal of life is a noble task; but to penetrate some of the perplexing realities of existence is as difficult and at least as serviceable. This Bacon does with supreme success. A lawyer, judge, and statesman, he knew the vicissitudes of life and the varieties of human character. He observed his fellow men with the eye of a genius, pondered their motives with the thoughtfulness of a student, and recorded his observations with the precision of a scientist. Time has wrought superficial changes in some of the social and political conditions he examined; but human nature and human intercourse are essentially immutable, and the impressive truth of his judgments is enduring. To this day he guides his readers in the conduct of life; and if it be too much to say that those who heed his advice will make no mistakes, it is certain that they will blunder less frequently than does the average man who knows him not.

HOW BACON TRAINS THE MIND

Bacon does more than enrich us with practical maxims applicable to particular situations; he trains us to think more wisely in the face of any and all occasions. He begins by informing, he ends by educating. His essays, valuable as discussions of special topics, are precious as exercises in a peculiar way of approaching all aspects of life. This way is one unusual and not inborn; it runs counter to the ways of the untrained mind. Just as children are apt to regard a person as either "nice" or "horrid," many of larger growth tend to look on anything as wholly good or wholly bad. Bacon methodically weighs advantages and disadvantages, and seeks to discover which predominate. In many of his essays he reasons somewhat after this manner: "This thing is good in this respect, but bad in that; it is useful to this extent, but harmful beyond; it will aid this kind of person, but will hinder that sort." For example, in describing youth and age he assigns distinct superiority to neither, but points out the special strength and the special weakness of each. Innovation, to the radical pure delight, to the conservative mere destructiveness, is to him neither the one nor the other. "Discriminate!" is his motto: things that men call by the same name are really of different values; "some books are to be tasted, others to be swallowed, and some few to be chewed and digested." What he says about any given subject, we may forget; but by frequent recourse to him we shall form the judicious habit of mind.

HIS ESPECIAL SERVICE TO-DAY

Most of us can be judicious on a few occasions, especially on occasions in which we are not deeply interested; but to be so habitually has always been among the rarest of virtues. It probably never was more rare than in this country at this time. In approaching the intricate problems that confront us, we display boundless enthusiasm, aspiration, and self-confidence. The defects in human character, the fast-rooted evils in society, that have baffled the efforts of saints and sages from the beginning of history, we hope to dispel by the sheer energy of emotional fervor. We are too impatient to ascertain the exact facts that are to be dealt with, we heartily dislike those facts which disturb our preconceived notions; in plain words, we do not love truth and we distrust the intellect. To Bacon, the intellect was the indispensable aid to moral progress, whether of the individual or of society. He does not dry up enthusiasm, but he teaches us to make it effective by directing it into rational channels. In his day he helped to rescue science from superstition, and in our own he may save morality from sentimentalism.

III. LOCKE AND MILTON

By Professor H. W. Holmes

IN THE history of education the seventeenth century is a period of much interest and importance. It is a time of earnest thought, of noble expression, and of zealous and faithful effort; yet throughout the century educational progress is at best sporadic. For education, it is a century of preparation. That the reformers of the period were thus pioneers whose endeavor bore, for the most part, little immediate fruit, was an almost inevitable consequence of the circumstances of their day.

Theirs was an age of reorganization in religion, in political life, and in philosophy and science. The Thirty Years' War and the Civil War in England were conflicts in which the basis of modern religious toleration was laid in suffering and desolation. In America the Colonies were begun. In England the continued struggle with the House of Stuart resulted in the assurance of political liberty, to be secured at length by an evolution without the price of blood which the Continent, and especially France, had later on to pay. On the Continent itself, despotisms, big and little, were strengthened, often to the direct detriment of education. Meanwhile modern science had its birth in the work of many a courageous intellectual adventurer, from Kepler and Galileo, astronomers, to Harvey, physiologist.

Francis Bacon was herald and journalist of that revolt against scholasticism which attacked mediæval error and superstition by the new method of observation, experiment, and inductive reasoning. With the writings of Descartes and his contemporaries began modern philosophy. In a century of such spiritual and material disturbance, what wonder that there should have been much inspiration to educational effort, with but little fixed accomplishment?

A new world of knowledge had already been partly explored; but the schoolmasters had not entered it, and it was only years afterward that science became even meagerly available for school purposes. A new method had also been discovered, a method not more important in the search for truth than in the attainment of intellectual freedom; but the schoolmasters did not know it, or thought less of intellectual freedom than of more obvious results in linguistic proficiency. A new need for universal education had begun to be foreseen; but to the schoolmasters of the seventeenth century democracy was not even a Utopian promise. Schools remained, therefore, narrow in curriculum and authoritative in method, and education the opportunity of the privileged. Writers on practical school keeping, such as John Brimsley and Charles Hoole, were more concerned over improvements in the teaching of the classics than over fundamental changes in programs of study, in the spirit of instruction and discipline, or in the extension of educational opportunity.

COMENIUS AND "THE GREAT DIDACTIC"

To dream, therefore, in that time, of an educational system, state-administered, state-supported, compulsory, and hence democratic; a system serving the varying need of all individuals, yet aiming in the education of each at a socially valuable result; a system culminating in great academies of research and experiment, with parallel graduate schools for professional training, including the training of teachers; a system, finally, in which all subjects were to be taught and learned by the mind-freeing method of science, and all schools, classes, and subjects to be ordered and managed in natural yet effective ways: this was an achievement, even among reformers. This dream and a life of effort to realize it must be credited to the greatest educator of the century, who was neither John Locke nor John Milton, but the Moravian bishop, John Amos Comenius.

SCOPE OF THE TREATISES OF LOCKE AND MILTON

It cannot be denied that neither Locke's "Thoughts on Education"[1] nor Milton's "Tractate on Education"[2] is a

[1] *Harvard Classics,* iii, 245ff.   [2] *H. C.,* xxxvii, 9ff.

document of such historical importance as the chief work of Comenius, "The Great Didactic." Indeed we might well wish that both Locke and Milton had studied this treatise and had written in the light of it. Their minds, better trained, both of them, than that of the Moravian, and more highly endowed by nature, might have given more permanently profitable form to his far-reaching projects. As it is, Locke does not refer to Comenius's work at all, and Milton refers to it only slightingly, as by hearsay. Accordingly, although we have in the "Thoughts" an essay on the education of a gentleman's son at home, with the improvements on current practice suggested by the sound sense of one of the first modern psychologists and one of the most clear-headed of moral philosophers, and in the "Tractate" a scheme for the education of the better classes under requirements suggested by the vigorous mentality of a great poet and an ardent patriot, we can find in neither much sympathy with the new movement for science nor any forecast of democracy in and through education.

Yet these works of Locke and Milton are still readable and profitable English essays, whereas the "Didactica Magna" (which was first written in Czech and later translated by its author into Latin) is now to be remembered chiefly as an important document in the history of education.

The power of Milton's prose, his generous vision, and his place in English literature and English history lend an interest to the "Tractate" aside from any present pertinence in Milton's practical suggestions. Locke's place in English philosophy and the insight and consistency of his views, especially as to the government of children in the home, give to the "Thoughts" a permanent value. If we read Milton's essay for the vigor and dignity of its style and for its general inspiration, admitting the present inapplicability of most of its detailed proposals, it will well repay us. If we take into account the avowed limitation of scope in Locke's treatise and make due allowance for the conditions of life and schooling in his day, we may still find his advice worthy of careful study.

MILTON ON AIM AND METHOD IN EDUCATION

The aim of education set forth in the "Tractate" is majestic: "I call therefore a compleat and generous Education that which fits a man to perform justly, skilfully, and magnanimously all the offices, both private and publick, of Peace and War." It is plain that the complexity of modern life makes it hopeless for any individual now to realize this ideal. But it may be noted that Milton's conception of education agrees with the modern conception in that it is social. The individual is to be prepared for the duties of life, not cultivated merely for the possession of accomplishments or learning. Indeed the burden of the "Tractate" is that learning is to be put to use. Milton insists, therefore, that the first principle of that "better education in extent and comprehension far more large" for which he pleads, shall be emphasis on matter rather than on form. Education is to be primarily through literature and is to begin with Latin grammar—to this extent is Milton conventional; but it is to come rapidly to the place where the content and meaning of the books to be studied—"the substance of good things"—shall be chiefly the aim in view. This advice is as sound to-day as it ever was; and if it is less needed, it is still not without application. Abstractions and technicalities of form so easily encumber teaching that we may hardly expect ever to outgrow the warning not to give our pupils "ragged notions and babblements, while they expected worthy and delightful knowledge."

If, then, Milton's scheme of national academies wherein picked youths are to be brought to a mastery of every art, science, and profession be impracticable, we need not therefore fail to find in this brief but pithy essay an ideal to be cherished. It is a plea for sound learning. Learning to-day may be had from sources unknown to Milton, and many sources he esteemed highly are to-day quite unimportant; but sound learning, now as then, is learning which comes at the realities of life. The author of "Lycidas" and "Comus" can never be accused of forgetting the requirements of form. We may heed him the more, therefore, when he warns us against "intellective abstractions" for "young unmatriculated

Novices" and the learning of "meer words or such things chiefly, as were better unlearnt." Happily it is one effort of modern education, from the first teaching of reading and arithmetic to the highest studies of the university to make learning serve life and to make life illuminate learning.

LOCKE ON THE EDUCATION OF A GENTLEMAN

In Locke's "Thoughts" we have no such comprehensive scheme as is presented in the "Tractate." At another time Locke sketched in outline a national system of education; here he deals only with the home training of a gentleman's son. He scorns the schools of the day, and urges great care in the selection of a tutor. Since Locke's time schools have so improved that he might now revise his opinion on this point, as he might on others; for it must be confessed that Locke was not in the modern sense a student of child psychology, nor of mental and physical development in general. Thus his advice on the feeding of children, the general tenor of which is good, could hardly be followed with safety in detail. But for us the chief interest of Locke's essay is in his conception of the moral discipline of children by their parents and teachers; and since he was a man of keen observation, wide experience, clear principles, and much human sympathy, his remarks on this subject are worth careful study.

The gist of his counsel may be put thus: abandon the rod, except as a last resort; abandon scolding, threats, rules, rewards, arguments, and persuasion; train to right thinking and right action through the use of approval and affection, with all their normal accompaniment of benefits, when children behave properly, and of disapproval and coldness, with their natural consequences in the withdrawal of pleasures and companionship, when children misbehave. But above all, use this moral discipline morally—that is, with direct reference to your child's motives, to his *will* in the matter, not with reference merely to the outward effect of his actions. Locke urges, in reality, a steady, consistent, sympathetic, yet dispassionate moral pressure as the surest means of bringing children to good conduct. He would have them learn "to love what they ought to love and hate what they ought to hate" as a matter first of habit, to be approved by reason only as they mature: but from the beginning he would have children act not in mere conformity to external requirements, but with a willing adoption of standards always clearly revealed and, as time goes on, properly explained. He would use authority as a moral agent to induce purpose.

There is wisdom in Locke's words. Even under more modern conceptions of child nature, parents can hardly find general principles better than those he gives for guidance in the concrete exigencies of moral training in the home. All moral training is difficult, because it demands character and judgment: it is truly as much a "training of parents" as of children. But although there is much to be learned from modern writing on many an aspect of child life of which John Locke was wholly ignorant, he put in his way certain essential truths which have often been put since in different terms but to the same effect.

As to learning, Locke agrees with the fundamental point in Milton's "Tractate." In Latin, he decries overemphasis on grammar and would substitute for it extended reading. He would also combine with literary study a training in handicraft, which parallels Milton's scheme of learning from workers in the various fields of practical activity. But the contrast between Locke's point of view, which is individualistic, and Milton's, which is national, is brought out by the fact that Milton would have practical men teach his young academicians with a view to the serious use of their knowledge and skill in public affairs, whereas Locke looks upon a handicraft chiefly as a good gentlemanly avocation.

On one point Locke has been generally misinterpreted. He has been held to be a typical advocate of the "doctrine of formal discipline"—the doctrine which asserts that studies are to be chosen not because of their objective usefulness but because of their supposed efficacy in the training of some intellectual "faculty" or in the production of an obscurely defined (and in reality wholly mythical) "general power." The passage on the training of memory, § 176, is clear proof that Locke held no such views as have been imputed to him. He did insist, to be sure, on the necessity of intellectual and moral discipline, but only on such discipline of specific habits of mind and will as is generally admitted to be possible and desirable.

These two essays were written some three hundred years ago. They reflect many customs, standards, and traditions foreign to modern thought. They name men and books most modern readers never heard of. Their authors were not even imbued with some of the most forward-looking conceptions and ideals of their own day. But, these things admitted, we must also admit that the essays are essentially fresh and valuable still—and profit by their wisdom if we can.[3]

[3] The best single book on education in the seventeenth century is Adamson's "Pioneers of Modern Education," Cambridge University Press.

IV. CARLYLE AND NEWMAN

By Frank Wilson Cheney Hersey, A. M.

AMONG the great voices that stirred England in the early years of the Victorian era, none were more eloquent than those of Newman and Carlyle—the one a suave ecclesiastic who lighted again the candles of the mediæval church; the other a volcanic Scots peasant who set the Thames on fire. We may still hear the sound of their voices, and note the vast difference in their appearance, their manner, their tone and method, their appeal to their generation. Matthew Arnold's description of Newman at Oxford[1] remains forever in the memory:

"Who could resist the charm of that spiritual apparition, gliding in the dim afternoon light through the aisles of St. Mary's, rising into the pulpit, and then, in the most entrancing of voices, breaking the silence with words and thoughts which were a religious music—subtle, sweet, mournful? I seem to hear him still, saying: 'After the fever of life, after weariness and sickness, fightings and despondings, languor and fretfulness, struggling and succeeding; after all the changes and chances of this troubled, unhealthy state,—at length comes death, at length the white throne of God, at length the beatific vision.'"

Now the other man comes before us (noted by Caroline Fox in her journals):

"Carlyle soon appeared, and looked as if he felt a well-dressed London audience scarcely the arena for him to figure in as a popular lecturer. He is a tall, robust-looking man; rugged simplicity and indomitable strength are in his face, and such a glow of genius in it—not always smouldering there, but flashing from his beautiful gray eyes, from the remoteness of their deep setting under that massive brow. His manner is very quiet, but he speaks like one

---

[1] See Newman's description of Oxford in *Harvard Classics*, xxviii, 47-50.

tremendously convinced of what he utters, and who had much—very much—in him that was quite unutterable, quite unfit to be uttered to the uninitiated ear; and when the Englishman's sense of beauty or truth exhibited itself in vociferous cheers, he would impatiently, almost contemptuously, wave his hand, as if that were not the kind of homage which Truth demanded."

And this man flung forth such ringing words as: "Be no longer a Chaos but a World or even Worldkin. Produce! Produce! Were it but the pitifullest infinitesimal fraction of a Product, produce it, in God's name! 'Tis the utmost thou hast in thee: out with it, then. Up, up! Whatsoever thy hand findeth to do, do it with thy whole might. Work while it is called To-day: for the Night cometh, wherein no man can work."

NEWMAN AND THE OXFORD MOVEMENT

The careers of Newman and Carlyle were no more similar than their personalities. Newman spent his life in the heat of theological controversy. He was the leader and kindling spiritual force of the Oxford Movement, 1833-1845, often called the Tractarian Movement from "Tracts for the Times." This was a movement within the Church of England to revive the Catholic doctrines which had always been retained in the Prayer Book. These doctrines were the apostolic succession, the priesthood, the sacramental system, and the real presence of Christ in the Eucharist. The Anglican Church was sadly in need of zeal. "Instead of heroic martyr Conduct," said Carlyle[2] in 1831, "and inspired and soul-inspiring Eloquence, whereby Religion itself were brought home to our living bosoms, to live and reign there, we have 'Discourses on the Evidences,' endeavoring, with smallest result, to make it probable that such a thing as Religion exists." "Soul-inspiring eloquence" was just what Newman brought to the Movement. Sunday after Sunday, year after year, his sermons and tracts quickened the spirit of men. A mysterious veneration gathered round him. "In Oriel Lane light-hearted undergraduates would drop their

[2] *H. C.,* xxv, 352.

voices and whisper, 'There's Newman.'" In his eyes the Christian Church was "the concrete representative of things invisible." The pageant of ritual was necessary to bring home the symbolism of the Church to the imagination. Dogmas, far from being barnacles on Scriptural tradition, were defenses erected by authority to preserve the spirit of primitive Christianity against barnacles. Newman had defended the Church of England as the Via Media—the middle road—between the theology of the Church of Rome and the theology of Calvinism. But he and his younger followers gradually came to believe that the weight of authority and permanence was on the side of Rome. Tract 90, on the Catholic doctrines in the Thirty-nine Articles, the bulwarks of the Protestant Church, raised a storm of opposition in that church. And finally in a dramatic scene at the Convocation of February 13, 1845, the Oxford Movement was snuffed out. Newman at once left the Via Media for the Via Appia and entered the Roman Catholic Church. Several years later, in 1864, he became involved in a controversy with Charles Kingsley, during which he wrote his religious autobiography, the "Apologia pro Vita Sua."[3] This famous book, though it cannot be considered a convincing refutation of the charges which Kingsley brought against Rome, was a triumphant vindication of Newman's integrity and nobility of spirit.

CARLYLE AND HIS TEACHING

With Newman, Carlyle had little sympathy. "John Henry Newman," he said, "has not the intellect of an average-sized rabbit." Carlyle's own life[4] was spent in writing the histories of great movements such as the French Revolution, and of great men such as Cromwell and Frederick the Great. He thundered forth denunciations of the evils of society. The gospel he preached was of Books, Silence, Work, and Heroes. "In Books lies the soul of the whole Past Time." "Silence is the eternal Duty of a man." "Work while it is called To-day." "Universal history is at

[3] See George Moore's "Salve," chap. xv., for a vigorous attack on Newman's style.
[4] For a full account see H. C., xxv, 329.

bottom the history of the Great Men who have worked here."
These doctrines you will find summed up in the Inaugural
Address at Edinburgh.[5] "Carlyle," wrote George Meredith
in one of the most luminous estimates[6] of the Sage of
Chelsea, "Carlyle was one who stood constantly in the
presence of those 'Eternal verities' of which he speaks. . . .
The spirit of the prophet was in him. . . . He was the
greatest of the Britons of his time—and after the British
fashion of not coming near perfection: Titanic, not
Olympian: a heaver of rocks, not a shaper. But if he did
no perfect work, he had lightning's power to strike out
marvelous pictures and reach to the inmost of men with a
phrase."

THE DOCTRINE OF THE UNCONSCIOUS

Could men so apparently antipodal as these in temperament, utterance, and life have a thought or doctrine in common? Yet it was the great paradox of the Victorian era
that the heart of their mystery, the source and pivot of
their teaching, was the same dominating idea. The same
idea led one man to insist on the value of the oldest clothes,
and led the other to insist on getting rid of them. This
dominating principle was the "Doctrine of the Unconscious." [7]

Carlyle first expounded this doctrine in his essay
"Characteristics." [8] "The truly strong mind," he says, "view
it as Intellect, as Morality, or under any other aspect, is
nowise the mind acquainted with its strength; here as before the sign of health is unconsciousness. In our inward,
as in our outward, world what is mechanical lies open to us;
not what is dynamical and has vitality. Of our thinking, we
might say, it is but the mere upper surface that we shape
into articulate Thoughts; underneath the region of argument and conscious discourse lies the region of meditation;
here, in its quiet mysterious depths, dwells what vital force
is in us; here, if aught is to be created, and not merely

[5] *H. C.,* xxv, 375.
[6] See "The Letters of George Meredith," Vol. II, 332.
[7] For an extended account see Professor J. B. Fletcher's article "Newman
and Carlyle" in the "Atlantic Monthly," Vol. XCV, p. 669.
[8] *H. C.,* xxv, 333.

manufactured and communicated, must the work go on.
Manufacture is intelligible, but trivial; Creation is great,
and cannot be understood." What is intuitive and spontaneous should be our guide. "The healthy understanding is
not the Logical, argumentative, but The Intuitive." "The
characteristic of right performance is a certain spontaneity,
an unconsciousness; 'the healthy know not of their health,
but only the sick.' " On this idea Carlyle bases his doctrines
of Work and Heroes. By work the spontaneous self has a
chance to reveal itself. Heroes are those Great Men who
are spontaneous and sincere, those masters of their time
who draw up into themselves the thoughts of masses of
men.

Newman's belief in the power of the unconscious was equally
firm and thoroughgoing. In his sermon on "Explicit and Implicit Reason," he means by "implicit reason" "unconscious
meditation." "Reasoning is a living, spontaneous energy
within us, not an art." "Progress," he said later, "is a living growth, not a mechanism; and its instruments are
mental acts, not the formulas and contrivances of language."
"As each individual has certain instincts of right and wrong
antecedently to reasoning, on which he acts—and rightly—
so has the world of men collectively. God gave them truths
in His miraculous revelations. . . . These are transmitted
as the 'wisdom of our ancestors.'" It was Newman's
staunch belief in what is intuitive and instinctive that made
him accept the wisdom of the race as more trustworthy than
the reason of the individual. Consequently he believed that
Christian truth is preserved not by the reasoning of the individual but by the diversified powers, insight, and feeling
which are found in a long-continuing society. For Newman, therefore, the Catholic Church was the articulate voice
of the body of Christian believers in the past—"the concrete representative of things invisible." [9]

These two great men, who did not understand each other,
based their teachings on the same initial principle—the
"doctrine of the unconscious." However far apart they
were at the end, they insisted with graceful pleading or

[9] Readers interested in Newman should see the new "Life" by Wilfrid
Ward.

with tumultuous eloquence on these high moral truths: faith in what is spontaneous and sincere in one's own nature, and spontaneous and instinctive submission to those highly endowed men whose innate sincerity will redeem the world.

V. HUXLEY ON SCIENCE AND CULTURE

By Professor A. O. Norton

H UXLEY'S address on "Science and Culture"[1] was
delivered in 1880, at the opening of Mason Science
College in Birmingham, England. Like many academic addresses, it not only celebrates a local event, but
also deals with questions of the day, chosen to suit the occasion. Unlike most such addresses, however, it is of permanent value as a document in the history of a great epoch
in English educational progress. The event which it celebrates marks "a crisis in the long battle, or rather of the
long series of battles" which were fought over education
during the nineteenth century; the discussion concerns two
of the most significant educational reforms of that century;
the speaker was a great leader in the struggle which brought
those reforms to pass; the style of the address illustrates
the "strenuous and attractive method of exposition" which
characterizes all of Huxley's writings, and which was a
powerful means of winning public support for his views.

HUXLEY'S OPPONENTS: (1) THE BUSINESS MEN

The full significance of "Science and Culture" appears
only when it is placed in its historical setting. To-day Huxley's views seem commonplace, because to-day everyone accepts them. Who, nowadays, disputes his proposition that
the sciences are an essential element of modern culture?
And who denies that "the diffusion of a thorough scientific
education is an absolutely essential condition of industrial
progress"?

In England in 1880, however, these ideas seemed shock-

[1] *Harvard Classics*, xxviii, 217ff.

ingly radical to a very large majority of the people who were doing the thinking of the country and managing its affairs; and the advocates of scientific studies faced a powerful opposing party composed of two groups—the practical men of business, and the men of liberal education.

Scientific education was despised by practical business men because it seemed not only unnecessary, but actually harmful as a preparation for business. English industries had flourished amazingly without the aid of the sciences, and the captains of industry saw no reason to believe that "rule of thumb," by which they had succeeded, would not continue to suffice for their needs. They failed to see the importance of the connection between scientific education and the industries; but it was even then perceived in Germany, that "land of damned professors," with the result that Germany rose, in the next twenty-five years, from industrial insignificance to the position of England's leading industrial competitor.

A further result was a general outcry in England for the kind of training which Huxley advocated.

(2) THE CLASSICAL TRADITION

The entrance of the sciences into the circle of liberal studies also met powerful opposition. School and university men in general doubted, and most of them denied, that the sciences—physics, chemistry, biology, geology, and the like —were at all essential to culture. And Huxley's conviction that, "for the purpose of attaining real culture, an exclusively scientific education is at least as effective as an exclusively literary education" was as shocking to the academic world of that day as the advent of a band of shooting cowboys would have been to an English garden party. Huxley states very fairly the working ideal of culture which was held by "the great majority of educated Englishmen" of 1880, and which had shaped the whole course of liberal education during the three centuries preceding: "In their belief," he says, "culture is obtainable only by a liberal education; and a liberal education is synonymous, not merely with education and instruction in literature, but in

one particular form of literature, namely that of Greek and
Roman antiquity. They hold that the man who has learned
Latin and Greek, however little, is educated; while he who
is versed in other branches of knowledge, however deeply,
is a more or less respectable specialist, not admissible into
the cultured caste. The stamp of the educated man, the
University degree, is not for him." The best-trained university men undoubtedly took a more liberal attitude than
this, but schoolmasters in general, and university men of
mediocre quality, often maintained this position with
patronizing, not to say insolent, superiority.

(3) THE THEOLOGIANS

Another group of educated men also opposed scientific
studies—especially biology—on religious grounds. Since the
appearance of Darwin's "Origin of Species" in 1859 there
had been "endless battles and skirmishes" between scientists
and theologians over the doctrine of evolution. It is almost
impossible for readers of this generation to realize the bit-
terness of the feelings aroused over this doctrine, or the
violence with which, during the sixties and early seventies,
evolution and its champions were attacked. To clergy and
the devout laity alike it seemed to undermine theology and
to sap the very foundations of Christian belief. Scientists
who defended it—Huxley chief among them—were regarded as the deadly enemies of religion, as rationalists,
materialists, atheists beyond redemption. Naturally, scientific studies were opposed on the ground that they were
anti-religious in their effect, the breeders of atheism, and
the destroyers of faith. The stormiest period of the debate
had passed by 1880, but the feelings which it aroused were
still strong. And, although Huxley does not directly address these opponents in "Science and Culture," some remi-
niscences of the conflict may be traced in its pages.

Under these cirumstances, the address was hardly the
tame affair which it seems to readers of the younger generation. On the contrary, it was the challenging utterance of
a champion in the warfare of science, at the crisis of the
battle.

As above suggested, the two great reforms for which Huxley contended in this address, and elsewhere, were, first, the diffusion of scientific education as a benefit to industrial workers and an aid to the industries themselves; second, the revision of the program of liberal studies to include modern studies, especially the natural sciences, as well as the tradi-- tional Latin and Greek. Thus he confronted two of the three groups of opponents of scientific studies—the practical men of business, and the men of liberal culture.

HUXLEY'S APPEAL TO THE BUSINESS WORLD

The first thing to note in reading the address is the skill with which Huxley meets each of these antagonists. To the practical men he appeals in a practical way. His appeal, summarized, is this: I won't try to reason you out of your opposition to scientific education. But consider what Sir Josiah Mason, the founder of this College, has done. He is a practical man like yourselves, and yet he believes in scientific education enough to spend a great part of his fortune in providing it for young men and women who are to enter the industries of Birmingham. No one is better qualified to judge than he. This College is his practical answer to your practical objections. I can say nothing which will add to its force.

Toward the close of the address Huxley returns to the charge with evidence that the general sciences are of practical value to the industries, and with the further remark that considered as culture alone they are of practical value, for they both ennoble character and increase and improve in quality the variety of desires which are satisfied by the products of industry.

HIS APPEAL TO THE UNIVERSITY MEN

Huxley's method of dealing with the second group of antagonists is very different from this. Here his appeal is to reason. He begins with a definition of culture which hardly anyone could refuse to accept. Next, he points out that the real matter on which they disagreed is the answer to the

question, How is culture to be obtained? Why do we differ
so sharply on this matter? he asks. History tells us why.
The studies which have been supposed to give culture have
changed from age to age. In the Middle Ages theology was
the sole basis of culture, because it furnished the best
ideals and standards then available for the criticism of life.
In the fifteenth century the great body of classical literature
was revealed to western Europe. This in turn became the
basis of culture, displacing theology, because in many ways
it furnished better ideals and standards—especially in
literature, sculpture, and above all in the use of reason.
But since the fifteenth century vast new sources of culture
have developed—the modern literatures, modern music,
modern painting, and above all the great structure of
modern science, which gives us ideals and standards of
judgment drawn from a new field, the book of Nature herself. The reason why we differ is clear. You still live in
the views of the fifteenth century, and you take no account
of the vast changes in our knowledge since that time. But
if culture is to be an effective criticism of modern life—
as we agree—is it not clear that the ideals and standards
given by these new fields of learning must form a part of
any scheme of complete culture? Thus by clear definition,
and by reasoning based on the historic facts, Huxley drives
home his conclusion with telling power.

HIS STYLE AND PERSONALITY

The style of the address deserves notice. It is characteristic of all Huxley's writings. Perfect clearness and simplicity are its most obvious qualities. So clear and simple
is it, indeed, that one constantly forgets that the printed
page is before one. One seems to be looking directly at
the thought expressed rather than at the words themselves,
just as one looks through a clear window at a landscape.
At the same time, the style is never dry. The "bottled life"
which, according to a reviewer, Huxley always "infused
into the driest topic on which human beings ever contrived
to prose," is evident here as in all his writings. Forcible
and interesting, as he always is, Huxley also makes this

address pungent by picturesque phrases and keen thrusts at his antagonists.

A last word must be given to Huxley as a man. He was one of the most distinguished and striking personalities of his day in England. Hardly any character will better repay study. Let the reader turn to his "Collected Essays," and especially to the two volumes of his "Life and Letters," edited by his son. There he will find a portrait, sharply drawn. It is the portrait of a passionate seeker of truth, fearless in its defense against all odds, and at any cost to himself—a man ruggedly honest and straightforward, big of mind, broad of vision, the soul of simplicity, sincerity, and honor.

POLITICAL SCIENCE

I. GENERAL INTRODUCTION

By Professor Thomas Nixon Carver

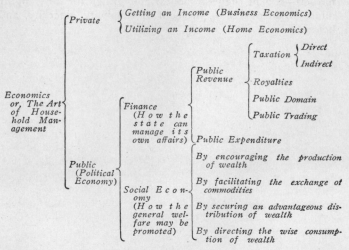

THE term Economics, as originally used by the Greeks, meant the art of household management, or the principles which govern the wise management of the household. Xenophon's treatise on this subject is a description of the management of a simple agricultural household where problems of revenue and expenditure, of business and home life, are not very sharply separated. In modern times, particularly in urban life, the business, or the source of income, is so sharply separated from the home, where the income is utilized, that we now have two distinct branches of the subject instead of one. To one branch we

328

now give the name business economics, business management, or business administration. The other is known by such names as home economics, household economics, household management, domestic science, etc. That these two branches are now so sharply separated as to seem unrelated is a commentary on how far we have departed from the simple conditions of the self-sufficing rural household, and how thoroughly we have divorced business from life.

Xenophon also wrote a treatise on the Revenues of Athens. While this cannot be regarded as a general treatise on public finance, it serves at least to show that he had some interest in that field, which may not inaptly be called public housekeeping. Every government, considered as a corporate body, has needs of its own apart from those of the people whom it governs. Whether it be a city, a state, or a smaller governing unit, it must solve the problems of revenue and expenditure just as a private household. Later writers applied the term economics mainly to this group of problems to which we now apply the name public finance, rather than to that group which in the diagram above are included under Private Economics. In a monarchy the providing of revenues for the king's household, and the expenditure of those revenues in the support of the household, may approximate very closely to the character of private economics, as when the chief source of revenue is the royal demesne, or to public economics when the chief source of revenue is taxation, and the king is regarded merely as a public official to be supported as other public officials are.

EARLY CONCEPTIONS OF PUBLIC ECONOMICS

In the mediæval and early modern period, the chief interest in economics had shifted from the private to the public aspects of the science, but was still centered mainly in problems of public revenue and expenditure, or, as we should now say, public finance. The chief students in this field were the finance ministers, who were charged with the office of raising revenue for the royal household and the enterprises both constructive and military of the king. It was soon apparent that the amount of royal revenue was strictly limited by the wealth of the people. If larger revenues were needed, the people must be made more prosperous in order that they might pay heavier taxes. From that time forward students gave increasing attention to the problems of national prosperity, until, at the present time, that is the primary object of interest, problems of public revenue and expenditure being strictly subordinated. That is to say, instead of trying to promote national prosperity in order that there may be more taxes and other forms of public revenue, the modern policy is to promote general prosperity for its own sake, and to raise revenue for the government only when, and to the extent that, it is necessary to do so in order to promote the general welfare.

MERCANTILISTS AND PHYSIOCRATS

Even when students began to focus their attention upon general economic prosperity, it took them some time to develop a really broad view of that problem. One school, known as the mercantilists, emphasized commerce, particularly foreign commerce, to such an extent as to make it seem that they identified prosperity with foreign trade. Writers of this school, for example, were accustomed to point out that an abundant supply of cheap labor was one factor in the development of foreign trade, because with cheap labor the country could compete with rival nations in international trade. This was obviously not intended to promote the prosperity of the laborers who were to supply the cheap labor. Another school, the physiocrats, emphasized the importance of agriculture as the industry which really produced a surplus over and above the cost of production.

Both these schools made the mistake of assuming an analogy between public prosperity and private prosperity. A private business which sells more than it buys, or takes in more money than it pays out, is said to be prosperous. The mercantile school assumed the same to be true of the nation at large, overlooking the fact that in the nation at large what is profit to one man may be cost to some one else, as in the case of the merchants who exported goods at a profit because they paid the laborers so little for their work. Again, a private business may be said to be prosperous when its products are greater than its costs. In agriculture there is the rent of land, which is not, strictly speaking, a cost, but a surplus income to the owner. This surplus income is the surplus value of the produce over and above the cost of producing it. Since very little rent was produced by the handicraft manufacturers of the day, the physiocrats assumed that these were not very profitable industries for the country at large, but that its main prosperity came from agriculture, where the main surplus, namely rent, accrued. Like the mercantilists, they overlooked the fact that this surplus might be the result, in part at least, of the poverty of the farm laborers. With a given efficiency, the cheaper they would work the lower the cost of growing crops and the higher the rent of the land.

It was not until Adam Smith's epoch-making work, the "Wealth of Nations,"[1] was given to the world that students began to take a really broad and comprehensive view of the problems of national welfare. Different students naturally have different special interests, but they generally realize the bearing of their specialties upon the larger problem. It has seemed at times that too many were focusing their attention upon production or exchange, and too few upon problems of distribution. For the last twenty-five years the problem of distribution has attracted more attention than all the others; but now the idea is beginning to dawn that consumption is the most important field of all, though it has been receiving the least attention of any.

THE MEANING OF WEALTH

Now that economics is definitely focusing attention upon problems of national prosperity, it is important that the student should understand clearly the leading concepts of the science before proceeding to study its literature. The leading concept is that of wealth, but this is a term with

[1] See *Harvard Classics*, x, and Lecture III in this Course.

two distinct but closely related meanings. In the first place, it is the name of a condition of well-being, in which sense it is not very different from the Saxon term *weal,* from which it is descended. In the second and more usual sense, wealth is the collective name for a category of goods. Goods are the means of satisfying desires, but not all goods are wealth. Only those goods are wealth upon which the satisfaction of desires depends in a very special and practical sense. People desire air, sunlight, and a number of other things which do not constitute wealth. But if they not only desire a thing, *but desire more than they have,* or more than there is to be had at once, then that thing is wealth. Their state of satisfaction is definitely affected by the question of more or less of this thing. More of it, more satisfaction; less of it, less satisfaction. Though we could not live at all without air, yet we do not ordinarily desire more than we have. There is enough to go around and satisfy every-body. We should not notice the difference if there were a little less. If special conditions should arise in any time and place where there was not enough air for everybody, so that people should desire more than they had, air would then and there be wealth.

Wealth may also be defined, tentatively, as the name of those goods upon which weal or well-being depends, in this immediate and practical sense. If our weal is increased by having more of a certain class of things, and decreased by having less of them, those things therefore constitute wealth. They become the objects of conscious and active human desire and therefore of conscious and active human en-deavor. More bread, more weal; less bread, less weal. Because we can say that, bread is wealth. Broadly speaking, everything to which we can apply that formula in any time and place is then and there wealth. Nothing is wealth which cannot be brought under that formula.

This statement calls for one qualification, namely, that men may not know upon what their weal or well-being de-pends. That upon which they *think* that their well-being depends they will *regard* as wealth. In other words, if they desire a thing, and desire more of it than they have, that indicates that they think their weal, or state of satisfaction, would be increased by having more of it. The fact that they want more, and try to get it, either by producing or purchasing it, indicates that they regard it as wealth, or as the means to well-being. Therefore it sometimes happens that the student is compelled to include some things under wealth which he regards as not only useless but deleterious and immoral—the means of satisfying vicious appetites, such as opium, tobacco, and alcohol. If one were to make much of this qualification, he would probably choose to divorce the word wealth from well-being, and define it as scarce means of satisfying desires.

Any of these definitions will be found to harmonize perfectly with another that has had some currency, namely, that wealth is the collective name for all goods which have value or power in exchange; for only those things which are desirable and scarce will have power in exchange, or value. In fact they are evaluated, bought and sold, solely because they are scarce and some one wants more than he has.

THE MEANING OF ECONOMY

The idea of scarcity as an essential to the concept of wealth suggests, next, the meaning of economy, which is another fundamental concept of the science of economics. Economy suggests the adjusting of means to ends, making a little go a long way, or, in the last analysis, choosing among one's desires and sacrificing the less important in order that the more important may be satisfied. This choice is forced upon us by the fact of scarcity, without which such choosing would be unnecessary, since we could, if everything were sufficiently abundant, satisfy all our desires without sacrificing any. It is in the utilization of those things which are scarce that economy is called for. These things which, being scarce, need to be economized in the interest of the largest satisfaction or well-being constitute economic goods, for which wealth is only another name. These are the things which have to be appraised, evaluated, and compared with one another with respect to their utility, in order that the limited supplies may be meted out and made to go as far as possible in the satisfaction of human desires, and in order that they may satisfy the greater rather than the lesser desires.

The economizing of scarce goods cannot be dissociated from such outstanding facts as production and exchange. The things toward which we must practice economy come to be esteemed or evaluated in a very direct and practical sense which is not true of anything else. When we desire a thing and desire more than we have, we not only try to get more, either by purchase or by production, but the more intensely we desire *more of it* the more we will give in exchange for a given unit of it, or the harder we will try to produce more of it. This process of evaluation gives such a thing power in exchange in proportion to its scarcity, or rather in proportion to the intensity of our desire for *more*. It also determines the direction in which the productive energies of society will be turned. Whether a given individual himself desires more of a thing or not, if there is somewhere in the community such a desire for more as will give the thing a high power in exchange, or a high value, that value will serve as effectively to induce the individual to produce it as though he desired the thing itself.

THE LAW OF VARIABLE PROPORTIONS

The process of production, in turn, calls for a new exercise of economy, because the means of production are scarce in some cases and abundant in others. In the last analysis, all industry consists in moving materials from one place to another. That is all that the moving-picture machine, or the human eye as a mechanical device, would reveal. But the mind sees plans, purposes, and laws back of this process of moving materials. One of the great generalizations of the scientific observer is that all this moving of materials is for the purpose of getting things together in the right proportions. Of course there are purposes back of all this, but the observed fact is that every industrial purpose is carried out by getting materials together in the right proportion. All this moving of materials which the eye sees is dominated by the law of proportionality, and the skill of the producer consists first in knowing the right proportions in which to combine materials, and, second, in his ability to bring them together.

This applies everywhere from a chemical experiment to the irrigation of a desert, from the work of the artist in his studio to that of the farmer in his field. The chemist, however, works under a law of definite proportions, under which chemical elements have to be combined in exact mathematical ratios, whereas the greater part of the work of production is under the law of variable proportions. In the irrigation of a piece of land, for example, there are variable quantities of water which may be used in the growing of a crop. One cannot say that an exact quantity of water must be applied, otherwise there will be no crop at all, or that the slightest variation either way would utterly ruin the crop. Within fairly wide limits of moisture a crop can be grown, though within these limits the crop will vary somewhat—but not exactly—according to the quantity of moisture provided.

Wherever the law of variable proportions holds, that is, wherever the law of definite proportions does not hold, the product may vary whenever any of the factors which are necessary to its production varies; but the product will seldom vary in exact proportion as any single factor is varied. Adding one-tenth to the quantity of moisture in the soil will seldom, and only accidentally, result in the increase of exactly one-tenth to the crop. The same may be said with respect to fertilizer, or to any single element of fertility, with respect to the labor of cultivation, or with respect to any other single factor which enters into the determination of the size of a crop. Moreover, all this can be repeated with respect to any productive plant, say a factory, and of the factors of production which have to be combined in it.

The work of assembling the factors of production in any productive establishment, whether it be a shop, farm, factory, or transportation system, calls for a degree of knowledge and care comparable with that of the chemist in the assembling of chemical elements, though, as stated before, the chemist must follow definite formulæ with mathematical precision, because of the law of definite proportions.

This law of variable proportions is difficult to state concisely, but the following formulæ may serve to give a fairly accurate notion as to its meaning and import. Let us assume that three factors, x, y, and z, are necessary to get a certain desirable product, which we will call p.

If 10 x with 20 y with 30 z will produce 100 p,

then 11 x with 20 y with 30 z will produce
- (1) more than 110 p;
- (2) 110 p;
- (3) less than 110 but more than 100 p;
- (4) 100 p;
- (5) less than 100 p.

If it should be found by experiment that the addition of one unit of x resulted in (1) more than 110 p, or (2) 110 p, that would indicate that the proportion of x to the other factors y and z was too low. Since an additional unit of x will result in such a large increase in the product, it is evident that more of x will be strongly desired, as compared with more of y and z, for if there is too little of x in the combination there must be too much of y and z. If, however, it were found that the addition of one unit of x resulted in (4) 100 p—that is, no increase at all—or (5) in less than 100 p—that is, less than was produced before—it is obvious that the proportion of x to the other factors is too high. Consequently, more of x will be little desired as compared with y and z, because if there is too much of x in the combination there must be too little of y and z. But if the increase in x results in an increase of five units of product proportional increase, in the product, then the factors are nearing the right proportions. Whether it is better to increase x by one unit will then depend upon the cost of x and the value of the increased product. Let us suppose that the increase in x results in an increase of five units of product (105 p). If one unit of x cost less than five units of p, it will be profitable to increase the factor x from 10 to 11; otherwise it will not.

Of course the formula and all that comes after it could be repeated with respect to y or z, as well as of x, if either were regarded as the variable factor. x, y, and z may represent labor, land, and capital in industry in general; they may represent different grades of labor in any industry;

they may represent nitrogen, potash, and phosphorus in the soil; or they may represent any group of factors anywhere combined to get any product. The essential thing to remember is that in any combination the scarcest factor is the limiting factor, and the product will vary more directly with that than with any other. Since the variation in the product follows more sharply the variation in this scarce factor than that of any of the more abundant factors in the combination, it is not uncommon to speak of the scarcest factor as having the highest productivity. Whether that be an accurate use of terms or not, there is not the slightest doubt that it will be most highly prized, will command the highest price, and will need to be economized most carefully. This formula and the remarks under it will serve to bring out the underlying physical fact of productivity upon which the law of supply and demand is based.

THE CONFLICT OF INTERESTS BETWEEN MAN AND MAN

That utility and scarcity, and these alone, are the factors which give value to a thing, whether its utility consists in its power to satisfy wants directly or indirectly, that is, whether it be an article of consumption or a factor of production, is now perhaps sufficiently clear. That the factor of scarcity creates the necessity for economy is also fairly obvious. That it is the source also of the conflict of human interests out of which most of our moral and social problems grow may not be quite so obvious, but the following considerations will show it to be true. The fact of scarcity means that man has wants for which nature does not spontaneously provide. This in turn implies a lack of harmony between man and nature, which it is the purpose of productive industry to restore.

That phase of the disharmony between man and nature which takes the form of scarcity gives rise also to a disharmony between man and man. Where there is scarcity there will be two men wanting the same thing; and where two men want the same thing there is an antagonism of interests. Where there is an antagonism of interests between man and man, there will be questions to be settled, questions of right and wrong, of justice and injustice; and these questions could not arise under any other condition. The antagonism of interests is, in other words, what gives rise to a moral problem, and it is, therefore, about the most fundamental fact in sociology and moral philosophy.[2]

This does not overlook the fact that there are many harmonies between man and man, as there are between man and nature. There may be innumerable cases where all human interests harmonize, but these give rise to no problem and therefore we do not need to concern ourselves with them. As already pointed out, there are many cases where man and nature are in complete harmony. There are things, for example, which nature furnishes in sufficient abundance to satisfy all our wants, but these also give rise to no problem. Toward these non-economic goods our habitual attitude is one of indifference or unconcern. Where the relations between man and nature are perfect, why should we concern ourselves about them? But the whole industrial world is bent on improving those relations where they are imperfect. Similarly with the relations between man and man; where they are perfect, that is, where interests are all harmonious, why should we concern ourselves about them? As a matter of fact we do not. But where they are imperfect, where interests are antagonistic and trouble is constantly arising, we are compelled to concern ourselves whether we want to or not. As a matter of fact, we do concern ourselves in various ways; we work out systems of moral philosophy and theories of justice, after much disputation; we establish tribunals where, in the midst of much wrangling, some of these theories are applied to the settlement of actual conflicts; we talk and argue interminably about the proper adjustment of antagonistic interests of various kinds, all of which, it must be remembered, grow out of the initial fact of scarcity—that there are not as many things as people want.

That underneath all these disharmonies there is a deep underlying harmony of human interests is the profound belief of some. But this belief, like that in a harmony between

[2] Cf. "The Economic Basis of the Problem of Evil," by T. N. Carver, in "Harvard Theological Review," Vol. I, No. 6.

man and nature, is not susceptible of a positive proof. It rests upon philosophical conjecture—and faith. To be sure, it is undoubtedly true that most men, even the strongest, are better off in the long run under a just government, where all their conflicts are accurately and wisely adjudicated, than they would be in a state of anarchy, where everyone who was able did what he pleased, or what he could if he was not able to do what he pleased. This might possibly be construed to imply a harmony of interests, in that all alike, the strong as well as the weak, are interested in maintaining a just government. But the argument is violently paradoxical, because it literally means that interests are so very antagonistic that in the absence of a government to hold them in check there would be such a multiplicity of conflicts, wasting the energies of society, that in the end everybody would suffer, even the strongest. This is an excellent argument in favor of the necessity of government, but it is the poorest kind of an argument in favor of the universal harmony of human interests.

Fundamentally, therefore, there are only two practical problems imposed upon us. The one is industrial and the other moral; the one has to do with the improvement of the relations between man and nature, and the other with the improvement of the relations between man and man. But these two primary problems are so inextricably intermingled, and they deal with such infinitely varying factors, that the secondary and tertiary problems are more than we can count.

THE CONFLICT OF MAN WITH NATURE

But whence arises that phase of the conflict with nature out of which grows the conflict between man and man? Is man in any way responsible for it, or is it due wholly to the harshness or the niggardliness of nature? The fruitfulness of nature varies, of course, in different environments. But in any environment there are two conditions, for both of which man is in a measure responsible, and either of which will result in economic scarcity. One is the indefinite expansion of human wants, and the other is the multiplication of numbers.

The well-known expansive power of human wants, continually running beyond the power of nature to satisfy, has
attracted the attention of moralists in all times and places.
"When goods increase, they are increased that eat them;
and what good is there to the owners thereof, saving the
beholding of them with their eyes?" is the point of view of
The Preacher.[3] It was the same aspect of life, obviously
throwing man out of harmony with nature, which gave point
to the Stoic's principle of "living according to nature." To
live according to nature would necessarily mean, among
other things, to keep desires within such limits as nature
could supply without too much coercion. Seeing that the
best things in life cost nothing, and that the most ephemeral
pleasures are the most expensive, there would appear to be
much economic wisdom in the Stoic philosophy. But the
pious Buddhist in his quest of Nirvana, overlooking the real
point—that the expansion of wants beyond nature's power
to satisfy is what throws man inevitably out of harmony
with nature and produces soul-killing conflicts—sees in desire itself the source of evil, and seeks release in the erad-
ication of all desire.

Out of the view that the conflict of man with nature is a
source of evil grow two widely different practical conclusions as to social conduct. If we assume that nature is beneficent and man at fault, the conclusion follows as a matter
of course that desires must be curbed and brought into harmony with nature, which is closely akin to Stoicism, if it be
not its very essence. But if, on the contrary, we assume
that human nature is sound, then the only practical conclusion is that external nature must be coerced into harmony
with man's desires and made to yield more and more for
their satisfaction. This is the theory of the modern industrial spirit in its wild pursuit of wealth and luxury.

Even if the wants of the individual never expanded at all,
it is quite obvious that an indefinite increase in the number
of individuals in any locality would, sooner or later, result
in scarcity and bring them into conflict with nature, and
therefore into conflict with one another. That human
populations are physiologically capable of indefinite increase,

[3] *H. C.,* xliv, 345.

if time be allowed, is admitted, and must be admitted by anyone who has given the slightest attention to the subject.
Among the non-economizing animals and plants, it is not the
limits of their procreative power but the limits of subsistence which determine their numbers. Neither is it lack
of procreative power which limits numbers in the case of
man, the economic animal. With him also it is a question
of subsistence, but of subsistence according to some standard. Being gifted with economic foresight, he will not multiply beyond the point where he can maintain that standard
of life which he considers decent. *But*—and this is to be
especially noted—so powerful are his procreative and domestic instincts that he *will* multiply up to the point where
it is *difficult* to maintain whatever standard he has. Whether
his standard of living be high or low to begin with, the
multiplication of numbers will be carried to the point where
he is in danger of being forced down to a lower standard.
In other words, it will always be hard for us to make as
good a living as we think we ought to have. Unsatisfied
desires, or economic scarcity, which means the same thing
are therefore inevitable. It is a condition from which there
is no possible escape. The cause lies deeper than forms of
social organization: it grows out of the relation of man and
nature.

THE INTERNAL CONFLICT OF INTERESTS

These considerations reveal a third form of conflict—
perhaps it ought to be called the second—a conflict of interests within the individual himself. If the procreative and
domestic instincts are freely gratified, there will inevitably
result a scarcity of means of satisfying other desires, however modest those desires may be, through the multiplication of numbers. If an abundance of these things is to be
assured, those instincts must be only partially satisfied.
Either horn of the dilemma leaves us with unsatisfied desires of one kind or another. We are therefore pulled in
two directions, and this also is a condition from which there
is no possible escape. But this is only one illustration of
the internal strife which tears the individual. The very
fact of scarcity means necessarily that if one desire is sat-

isfied it is at the expense of some other. What I spend for luxuries I cannot spend for necessaries; what I spend for clothing I cannot spend for food; and what I spend for one kind of food I cannot spend for some other kind. This is the situation which calls for economy, since to economize is merely to choose what desires shall be gratified, knowing that certain others must, on that account, remain ungratified. Economy always and everywhere means a threefold conflict; a conflict between man and nature, between man and man, and between the different interests of the same man.

THE PROBLEM OF EVIL

This suggests the twofold nature of the problem of evil. Evil in the broadest sense merely means disharmony, since any kind of disharmony is a source of pain to somebody. But that form of disharmony which arises between man and nature has, in itself, no moral qualities. It is an evil to be cold or hungry, to have a tree fall upon one, to be devoured by a wild beast, or wasted by microbes. But to evils of this kind, unless they are in some way the fault of other men, we never ascribe any moral significance whatever. It is also an evil for one man to rob another, or to cheat him, or in any way to injure him through carelessness or malice; and we do ascribe a moral significance to evils of this kind—to any evil, in fact, which grows out of the relations of man with man. But, as already pointed out, this latter form of evil—moral evil—grows out of, or results from, the former, which may be called non-moral evil. Any true account of the origin of moral evil must therefore begin with the disharmony between man and nature.

Let us imagine a limited number of individuals living in a very favorable environment, where all their wants could be freely and fully gratified, where there was no scarcity nor any need for economy. Under a harmony with nature so nearly perfect as this, there could arise none of those conflicts of interests within the individual, since the gratification of one desire would never be at the expense of some other; nor could there arise any conflict of interests among individuals, since the gratification of one individual's desire would never prevent the gratification of another's. There being no conflict of interests either within the individual or among different individuals, there could never arise a moral problem. That would be paradise. But suppose that wants should expand, or new wants develop; or suppose that, through the gratification of an elemental impulse, numbers should increase beyond any provision which nature had made. Paradise would be lost. Not only would labor and fatigue be necessary, but an antagonism of interests and a moral problem would arise. Human ingenuity would have to be directed, not only toward the problem of increasing the productivity of the earth, but toward the problem of adjusting conflicting interests. Questions of justice and equity would begin to puzzle men's brains.

It would be difficult to find in this illustration any suggestion of original sin or hereditary taint of any kind. The act which made for increase of numbers, instead of being a sinful one, for which punishment was meted out as a matter of justice, would, on the contrary, be as innocent of moral guilt as any other. But *the inevitable consequence* of it would be the destruction of the preexisting harmony, giving rise, in turn, to a conflict of human interests. Nor does the illustration suggest or imply any "fall" or change in human nature, but rather a change of conditions under which the same human qualities would produce different social results. Moreover, the illustration does not depend for its validity upon its historical character. That is to say, it is not necessary to show that there ever was a harmony between man and nature so nearly complete as the illustration assumes to begin with. The fundamental basis of conflict is clearly enough revealed by the illustration when it is shown to be inherent in the nature of man and of the material world about him.

This theory of the origin of evil is already embodied in a well-known story, which need not be interpreted as having a historical basis in order to have a profound meaning—more profound, probably, than its most reverent students have seen in it. Once upon a time there was a garden in which lived a man and a woman, all of whose wants were supplied by the spontaneous fruits of the earth. There was no struggle for existence, no antagonism of interests; in short, that was paradise. But the gratification of a certain desire brought increase of numbers, and increase of numbers brought scarcity, and paradise was lost. Thenceforward man was to eat his bread in the sweat of his brow. The struggle for existence had set in. Man had to contend against either natural or human rivals for the means of satisfying his wants, and every form of greed and rapacity had a potential existence. When his eyes were opened to these inherent antagonisms, that is, when he became a discerner of good and evil, of advantages and disadvantages, both near and remote, he became an economic being, an adapter of means to ends; a chooser between pleasures and pains. In short, the process of industrial civilization, of social evolution, had made its first faint beginning. The human race was caught in a network of forces from which it was never to extricate itself. It was adrift upon a current which set irresistibly outward—no man knew whither.

THE ORIGIN OF INSTITUTIONS

In this antagonism of interests, growing out of scarcity, the institutions of property, of the family, and of the state, all have their common origin. No one, for example, thinks of claiming property in anything which exists in sufficient abundance for all. But when there is not enough to go around, each unit of the supply becomes a prize for somebody, and there would be a general scramble did not society itself undertake to determine to whom each unit should belong. Possession, of course, is not property; but when society recognizes one's right to a thing, and undertakes to protect him in that right, that is property. Wherever society is sufficiently organized to recognize these rights and to afford them some measure of protection, there is a state; and there is a family wherever there is a small group within which the ties of blood and kinship are strong enough to overcome any natural rivalry and to create a unity of interests. This unity of economic interests within the group is sufficient to separate it from the rest of the world, or from other similar groups among which the natural rivalry of interests persists. Saying nothing of the barbaric notion that wives and children are themselves property, even in the higher types of society it is the desire to safeguard those to whom one is bound by ties of natural affection, by sharing the advantages of property with them, which furnishes the basis for the legal definition of the family group.

THE FUNDAMENTAL POSITION OF ECONOMICS

Closely associated with the right of property—as parts of it in fact—is a group of rights such as that of contract, of transfer, of bequest, and a number of other things with which lawyers occupy themselves. It would be difficult to find any question in the whole science of jurisprudence, or of ethics, or politics, or any of the social sciences for that matter, which does not grow out of the initial fact of economic scarcity and the consequent antagonism of interests among men. This reveals, as nothing else can, the underlying unity of all the social sciences, that is, of all the sciences which have to do with the relations between man and man; and it shows very clearly that the unifying principle is an economic one. Even the so-called gregarious instinct may very probably be the product of the struggle for existence, which, in turn, is the product of scarcity—the advantage of acting in groups being the selective agency in the development of this instinct. But that question, like a great many others, lies beyond the field of positive knowledge. This does not necessarily constitute economics as the "master science," with the other social sciences subordinate to it; but it does signify that, if there is such a thing as a master science, economics has the first claim to that position among the social sciences. The economic problem is the fundamental one, out of which all other social and moral problems have grown.

ECONOMIC COMPETITION

This conflict of man with man, when uncontrolled by society, either through moral codes or legal procedure, does not differ materially from the struggle for existence among brutes. But there is no human society which does not control the struggle in some way. In fact the one purpose for which organized society exists is that of controlling the struggle and directing it into productive channels. The self-interested individual cares nothing for *production* as such. What he is interested in is the *acquisition* of things which are scarce. If the easiest method of acquisition is that of production, then he will produce. If there is some easier way, he will pursue that way. The purpose of the law and government is to make it difficult and dangerous to acquire by any other method than that of production, or free and voluntary exchange of products, which means the same thing. In so far as the state succeeds in this attempt and thus forces all individuals to acquire by methods of production, it is justifying its existence.

When the struggle for existence is thus turned into productive channels, when every individual finds that he can acquire desirable things only by producing them, or by offering the producer something of equal value in exchange for them, then the brutal struggle for existence is transformed into economic competition. Perfect economic competition is merely a system under which each individual finds it most advantageous to acquire by productive or serviceable effort of some kind, and so, in Adam Smith's words, "to promote the public good while trying to promote his own."

When we consider that the individual's value to the rest of society is measured by the excess of his production over consumption, while his position in industry is determined by his rate of accumulation, which is merely his acquisition minus his consumption, we shall see how important it is that acquisition and production should be identified. This may be expressed by means of the following formulæ:

The value of a man=his production — his consumption.

His competing power=his acquisition — his consumption.

When acquisition=production

Then his value=his competing power.

The purpose of the state is to make acquisition=production.

II. THEORIES OF GOVERNMENT IN THE RENAISSANCE

By Professor O. M. W. Sprague

A VERY small number of books on political and social subjects have exerted a profound and continuous influence both upon the development of thought and upon the determination of the policies adopted regarding public questions. Aristotle's "Politics" and Adam Smith's "Wealth of Nations"[1] are notable works belonging to this exceptionally distinguished group. A much greater number of political writings had a potent influence at the time of their composition but now possess little other than historical significance.

Among such works may be mentioned Luther's "Address to the German Nobility" and "Concerning Christian Liberty,"[2] and Rousseau's "Social Contract." Machiavelli's "Prince"[3] and More's "Utopia"[4] do not fall exactly within either of these categories. They were not the starting points from which great and fruitful advance in knowledge has been made, and at no time have they been powerful factors in determining the legislation or policy of any nation. Both are indeed highly significant and characteristic products of the age in which they were written; compared with the writings of Luther, they were immensely less influential in shaping contemporary opinion; but they are quite as representative of the thought of the time and so possess great historic interest. Moreover, although the specific conclusions of Machiavelli and of More have never been followed closely in practice, they do exemplify in their work the two strikingly different attitudes, one or the other of which invariably appears in the methods and conclusions of writers upon political and social problems.

[1] *Harvard Classics*, x, 9ff.
[3] *H. C.*, xxxvi, 7ff.
[2] *H. C.*, xxxvi, 276ff., 353ff.
[4] *H. C.* xxxvi, 143ff.

THE RENAISSANCE SPIRIT IN MACHIAVELLI AND MORE

The "Prince" and the "Utopia" were both written in the second decade of the sixteenth century, at the time when those various influences which made the Renaissance period in history were being most completely exemplified in education, art, morals, and indeed in virtually every field of human activity and aspiration. In almost every direction the human spirit had freed itself from mediæval traditional limitations; political and social arrangements among others were subjected to philosophic analysis and investigation unrestrained by ancient concepts and regardless of the revolutionary conclusions that might be the outcome. Among the political writers of the period, Machiavelli and More exhibited in preeminent measure the working of the Renaissance spirit. Machiavelli subjected governmental machinery and policy to the test of facts. More subjected not only political but also social arrangements to the test of what he deemed ideally desirable. Both are in agreement that nothing in the social order is necessarily perfect even at the moment and certainly not for all time. Institutions and customs are to be judged by results, and all may be changed if something better can be devised. This is distinctly the modern point of view. It is quite as essentially the Renaissance point of view. Modern history begins with the Renaissance.

CONTRAST IN METHOD

In an age like the present, marked by swift advance in the exact sciences, the test of fact is apt to seem the one promising method of approach to the investigation of political and social problems. The test of the ideal exemplified in the "Utopia" has given the language an adjective, "Utopian," which connotes the impractical, the visionary, and even the fanciful. The test of fact exemplified in Machiavelli has also, however, yielded an adjective, "Machiavellian," of even more damning connotation. If the test of fact is to be a true test, all significant facts must be considered, and ideals are facts of vast importance in the development and maintenance of social arrangements.

Machiavelli's method was scientific in its general character; but his low estimate of human nature, founded as it was upon an assumption contrary to fact, rendered much of his analysis fundamentally inexact and unscientific.

MICHIAVELLI'S LIMITATIONS

Even within the field of the kind of facts to which he attaches significance, Machiavelli's analysis was far from being comprehensive. At the time he wrote, and indeed for a century and more before, Italy had been split up into a large number of political entities, most of which were in a chronic state of political instability not unlike that of many Central American countries to-day. Few Italian rulers were secure from either domestic or foreign foes. Machiavelli made much use of the comparative method in his analysis, and properly; but as he was mainly concerned with the means of securing and maintaining personal rule under conditions which at best could not provide a solid basis for governmental authority, his conclusions seldom possess general validity. They were not applicable to the centralized governments of large territorial areas then in process of development north of the Alps, where the ruling dynasties were already strongly entrenched in power. It is even more evident that his analysis affords little of practical value in the solution of modern problems of government. Possibly there is some analogy between the conditions described by Machiavelli and the struggle for political power carried on upon a low plane between rival bosses in misgoverned municipalities. One would, however, search the pages of the "Prince" in vain for a remedy for such ills of democratic government.

In the field of international politics, Machiavelli's analysis has undoubtedly been measurably in accord with practice in his own time and since. Ethical restraints have been relatively weak in the dealings of the nations one with another; and it is a significant fact that nowhere has Machiavelli found so many close readers as among those statesmen who have been mainly concerned with foreign affairs.

After making every qualification, it must still be recognized that in the "Prince" Machiavelli took a long step in advance toward the development of a sound method of analyzing political problems. His example was, however, not followed very generally by writers on government in his own and the two succeeding centuries. Questions of divine right and theories of natural rights and natural law rather than the facts of government absorbed the attention of most publicists. In the nineteenth century more exact methods have been adopted in this as in other fields of knowledge; but in bringing about this desirable change little or no direct influence can be attributed to the work of Machiavelli.

THE IMAGINARY COMMONWEALTH AS A FORM OF POLITICAL CRITICISM

With the exception of Plato's "Republic," the "Utopia" is the best instance of the use of the device of an imaginary society as a vehicle for analysis, and indeed arraignment, of social and political conditions. During the mediæval period, uniformity of ideals and conditions throughout Europe was too great to suggest writings of this character, but the discoveries in the New World disclosed the existence of societies which had never been in touch with the European world. The assumption of the finality of European arrangements was consequently somewhat weakened, at least for men of a reflective cast of mind. In placing his "Utopia" somewhere in the New World, More must have greatly heightened the imaginative effect of the work to readers of his own time. The sense of illusion thus given at the outset is remarkably well maintained throughout. No other creator of imaginary societies has been so successful in directly impressing the reader with the feasibility of his scheme of social betterment.

Later writers of Utopias have been commonly too anxiously concerned to put together a society which should meet the criticisms of experts in economics, sociology, and government. To attempt this, is to miss the true aim and lose much of effectiveness in this style of composition. It is certain that society will never be suddenly transformed into something quite different which may be worked out in advance by thoughtful investigators. Quite evidently also the exact course of social evolution in the distant future cannot be foreseen. Books like the "Utopia" are effective means of weakening the feeling of complete satisfaction with the existing social order, a state of mind which is neither helpful nor conducive to human betterment.

Effectiveness is far from being in direct ratio to the scientific possibilities of the imaginary society described. The imaginary society is simply the vehicle for satire and criticism of things as they are. In other words, it is as literature and not as a scientific treatise that ideal commonwealths should be considered. The possession of literary qualities has made a few of them effective. More's "Utopia" meets this test admirably and is, therefore, properly included among the Five-Foot Shelf of Books.

THE "UTOPIA" AND MODERN CONDITIONS

Some acquaintance with social conditions and politics in the time of More adds much to the significance and interest of the book; but society, and even more human nature, changes so slowly from age to age that much of it can hardly fail to prove full of stimulating suggestion even to readers familiar only with present conditions. Speaking generally, our own society is no nearer that depicted in the "Utopia" than was that of More's own period. In some respects it is further removed from Utopian conditions, notably in the greater relative importance of manufacturing and commercial as contrasted with agricultural activities. In some directions changes have taken place which all would agree are for the better, though they are contrary to the Utopian ideal. The government of "Utopia" was distinctly aristocratic. To a modern idealist the best of all conceivable societies would certainly be democratic in form and in practice. Slavery, though of an ameliorated sort, was an essential foundation of the Utopian polity. No better illustration may possibly be found of the difficulty experienced in getting away from the blinding influence of one's own environment, even when gifted with an exceptionally humane spirit and a powerful imagination One may hazard the hope, in this connection, that in the distant evolution of society a higher level of improvement may be reached than can now be foreseen.

III. ADAM SMITH AND THE "WEALTH OF NATIONS"

By Professor Charles J. Bullock

FROM 1752 to 1764 the author of the "Wealth of Nations" occupied the chair of moral philosophy at Glasgow College, and his writings were the natural outgrowth of the lectures delivered to his college classes. Following an unbroken tradition received from Greek philosophy, Smith conceived the province of moral philosophy to be as broad as the entire range of human conduct, both individual and social. "Wherein," says Smith, "consisted the happiness and perfection of a man, considered not only as an individual, but as a member of a family, of a state, and of the great society of mankind, was the object which the ancient moral philosophy proposed to investigate." Smith's own lectures followed substantially this plan of treatment.

THE UNDERLYING THEORY OF SMITH'S PHILOSOPHY

At Smith's hands, however, many of the traditional subjects received new treatment and development. In 1759, Smith published his "Theory of Moral Sentiments," a treatise on ethics which immediately won for him international fame as a philosopher. This work presented the doctrine that the moral judgment is, in the last analysis, an expression of impartial sympathy with the motives and result of human action. From sympathy Smith derives the sense of justice, which is "the main pillar of the social structure." Underlying the book is the common eighteenth-century theory of a beneficent natural order, by which it was held that a benevolent Creator had so ordered the universe as to produce the greatest possible human happiness. In this view of the matter the problem of philosophy, including politics and economics, is to discover the natural laws which make for the happiness of God's creatures. Of these laws the chief seems to be that Providence has commended the welfare of every man chiefly to his own keeping, not to that of others; and has so ordered things that men, in pursuing their own welfare within the limits set by justice, are ordinarily contributing to the general welfare. Upon this doctrine of a natural harmony of interests, Smith based his theory of natural liberty, according to which every man, "as long as he does not violate the laws of justice," is naturally free to pursue his own welfare in his own way.

Smith projected, but never published, a treatise on jurisprudence and government, subjects which in his lectures had naturally followed ethics. His "Wealth of Nations," which was published in 1776, treated of political economy which in his lectures had followed the subject of government.

HIS CONCEPTION OF WEALTH AND OF POLITICAL ECONOMY

The "Wealth of Nations"[1] combines a firm grasp of principles with a remarkable knowledge of the facts of economic life, derived from reading and personal observation. Smith's generalizations are usually supported by an appeal to the facts of economic life, and in this manner he gives the work an air of reality that is lacking in many economic treatises. He does not deal extensively with definitions. Without defining wealth he plunges directly into the causes of national opulence, but in the last sentence of his "Introduction" states, parenthetically, that "real wealth" is "the annual produce of the land and labor of the society." Even here he merely indicates that he considers the *annual income* of a society as its real wealth: whereas most economists prior to his time had conceived wealth as the *accumulated stock* of durable goods which a society possesses. Again Smith commences the treatise without offering a definition of political economy, and the nearest approach to such a definition is found in the first sentence of the fourth book: "Political economy, considered as a branch of the

[1] *Harvard Classics,* Vol. x.

science of a statesman or legislator, proposes two distinct objects: first, to supply a plentiful revenue or subsistence for the people, or, more properly, to enable them to provide such a revenue or subsistence for themselves; and secondly, to supply the state or commonwealth with a revenue sufficient for the public services. It proposes to enrich both the people and the sovereign."

PRODUCTION AND DISTRIBUTION

Captious critics have pronounced the arrangement of the "Wealth of Nations" unsystematic, but it is in fact well suited to Smith's purpose. The first book studies the process by which wealth is produced and then distributed among laborers, *entrepreneurs,* and landlords. It lays down the doctrine that the increased productivity of the industry of modern societies is due to division of labor. The discussion of this subject is an economic classic, and the reader should observe that Smith finds here an illustration of his cardinal doctrine that it is self-interest, not the action of government, that has brought about the improvement of economic conditions. Division of labor presupposes exchange, and so Smith naturally proceeds to consider money and price. His study of price leads to an investigation of its component parts—wages, profits, and rent; and thus Smith is led to consider fully the subject of the distribution of wealth. His theory of value at the hands of certain later writers becomes the classical cost-of-production theory; while, given another slant, it becomes the labor theory of Marx and the socialists. His theory of wages becomes, at the hands of later writers, the wage-fund theory of the classical English school. His theory of profits supplied much material for his followers, particularly concerning the difference of profits in the various employments of capital. His theory of rent, or rather his three different theories,[2] needed to be reconstructed by Ricardo before it could be added to our stock of economic principles.

[2] He first treats rent as the surplus product of land above the substance of the laborers. He also speaks of it as a form of monopoly income extorted by landlords; and again, in treating of the rent of mines, says that it varies with fertility and situation.

THE NATURE AND USE OF CAPITAL

The second book investigates the nature and employment of "capital stock," which is the force that sets laborers at work and puts industry in motion. Smith holds that capital originates in saving, that its function is to maintain productive labor, and that it may be either fixed or circulating.

Unproductive labor, the reader should observe, is not useless labor; it may, indeed, be very useful;[3] but it does not produce any durable material product, and for that reason Smith does not consider it productive. Parsimony, or saving, leads to an increase of the capital available for the employment of productive labor; while spending consumes funds which otherwise might have been given such employment.

Private frugality, due to the desire to better one's condition, is the cause of the growth of capital and the increase of national opulence; while government can do nothing more than protect the individual and allow him liberty to act in the manner he finds most advantageous. Finally Smith considers the different employments of capital. Agriculture gives more employment to productive labor than manufactures, and both are superior, in this regard, to transportation and trade. Domestic trade gives more employment than foreign, and foreign trade gives more than the carrying trade.

All these employments are useful; but a country with insufficient capital to engage in all of them will increase in opulence most rapidly if it employs its capital in agriculture first of all, then engages in manufactures and the home trade, and refrains from entering upon foreign commerce and the carrying trade until the natural increase of capital makes such a course advantageous. If governments merely withhold their hands, this is the course that industrial development will actually follow under the free play of individual self-interest. Smith's argument at this point is exceedingly important, for it lays the foundation for his doctrine of freedom of trade.

[3] See "Wealth of Nations," *H. C.*, x, 271.

HIS THEORY OF TRADE

After examining in the third book the various policies of restriction and preference adopted by the countries of Europe, Smith in the fourth book launches into the famous polemic against the so-called mercantile system of political economy. Smith shows that the restrictive measures of the mercantilists tended rather to prevent men serving each other than to promote public opulence. He assailed the theory of the balance of trade, much as David Hume had done. Everywhere he vindicated the system of natural liberty, and maintained that prosperity is not manufactured by governments but comes from "the natural effort of every individual to better his own condition." After disposing of the mercantilists, Smith treats of the "agricultural system" of political economy, which held that the net produce of the land is the sole source of national opulence. Since economists of this school had maintained that perfect liberty is the only policy that can raise this annual produce to a maximum, Smith considered their doctrines "the nearest approximation to the truth that has yet been published upon the subject of political economy."

PUBLIC FINANCE

The fifth book treats of public finance. His chapter upon the expenses of the sovereign is the first philosophical investigation of this important subject. The second chapter presents a noteworthy treatment of the subject of taxation, and lays down the celebrated maxims which, perhaps, have been quoted oftener than any other paragraphs in economic literature. Smith was especially successful in correlating his theory of taxation with his theory of the production and distribution of wealth, while on the practical side he proposed reforms many of which were later adopted. The chapter on public debts, while unduly pessimistic, criticizes forcibly the unwise financial policies pursued by Great Britain and other countries during the eighteenth century. In his theory of the essential nature of a public debt Smith was undoubtedly correct.

The "Wealth of Nations" achieved instant success, went

through five editions in the author's lifetime, and was soon translated into French, German, Italian, Spanish, and Danish. In the United States it began to be quoted by statesmen before the end of the Revolution, and an American edition was published at Philadelphia in 1789. Alexander Hamilton's state papers show the clearest evidence of his indebtedness to Smith's masterpiece. In time the book began to influence legislation, and to contribute powerfully to the removal of obsolete restrictions on industry and commerce. Its place as an economic classic is secure, and the lapse of time seems to detract nothing from its eminence.

IV. THE GROWTH OF THE AMERI-
CAN CONSTITUTION

By Professor W. B. Munro

IF HISTORY is to perform properly its function as an agency of instruction, it must be careful to record human events fairly and with accuracy, otherwise the lessons which it asks posterity to draw from the past are sure to be misleading. Now the most reliable sources of information concerning all that has happened in the public life of past generations are of course the contemporary records, the writings of those who had a hand in the events themselves and the public documents which set new historical landmarks. The makers of history are the men most competent to write about it; they are the ones best qualified to interpret their own experience.

These writings are the piers upon which the historian builds his long bridge of narrative, and the historical structure can be no stronger than its foundations. American history is well supplied with them, for it spans a period of only three centuries—three modern centuries in which men have written much concerning the outstanding events of their own day. Due allowance must of course be made for human shortcomings even in the records left to us by the wisest and most open-minded of writers. But the fact remains that contemporary materials afford the only sure basis on which to build our knowledge of what has gone before. The history of America, accordingly, may be best studied in the chronicles of early explorers, in the narratives of those who first made their homes on this side of the Atlantic, in the colonial charters and later State laws, in the messages and decrees of presidents, the treaties with foreign nations, the decisions of courts, the correspondence of public men, or, to put it broadly, in the great mass of official and unofficial writings which constitute the public literature of the New World.

THE BEGINNINGS OF AMERICAN GOVERNMENT

The English settlements in America, during the century and a half of their existence as colonies, encountered many difficult problems. In the earlier years of this period there were troubles with the Indians; in the later years there were almost incessant bickerings with the French colonists to the north. But in due time the redskins were humbled and France was expelled from her American territory. Then there were religious troubles which at times rent the English colonies in twain. Some of these settlements, it is true, had been founded as a protest against ecclesiastical bigotry at home.; but that did not make them tolerant of heresy within their own borders. Those who failed to make outward compliance with the established religious practices were in some cases harried out of the land, and a rigid enforcement of this policy in Massachusetts led to the founding of Rhode Island and Connecticut as separate colonies.

Another difficult problem was that of providing a satisfactory frame of civil government. Every colony had its own series of experiments embodied in charters,[1] fundamental laws[2] and bodies of liberties.[3] At this historical distance these quaint documents make instructive reading, for they portray with great fidelity the earliest political ideals of the American people. Despite the rigor with which these codes attempted to regulate the daily walk and conversation of citizens, one can nevertheless trace in every line a firm loyalty to the principle that governments should be of laws and not of men. The faith in constitutional guarantees of civil liberty goes back to the very origins of American government.

THE BREACH WITH ENGLAND

But the most difficult of all colonial problems was that of determining proper political relations with the motherland.

[1] First Charter of Virginia, *Harvard Classics*, xliii, 51-61.
[2] The Fundamental Orders of Connecticut (1639).
[3] The Massachusetts Body of Liberties (1641), etc., *H. C.*, xliii, 63ff.

While the colonies were weak and exposed to external dangers these relations gave rise to no acute controversies; but after 1760, when America's economic interests had grown greatly in importance, and when the treacherous arm of France had been removed from the northern frontiers—then it was that serious estrangements began. Matters which might have been easily adjusted under earlier conditions became sources of open friction and ill-feeling; the breach widened and active resistance to the authority of the home government ensued.

It is to be borne in mind, however, that the causes of the American Revolution were neither superficial nor few. The Declaration of Independence catalogues the colonial grievances as the colonists saw them, and their name is legion.[4]

The thirteen revolted colonies could not very well manage their struggle for independence as a joint enterprise without some form of central government, and a congress of delegates, sitting at Philadelphia, was established to meet this necessity. With no legal basis during the early years of its existence, this congress eventually framed and secured the adoption of the Articles of Confederation which served as a working constitution for the body of States during the next decade.[5] These articles gave very little power to the central government and while they served a useful purpose in their time, facilitating the settlement of matters at the close of the war, it was realized everywhere that they could not afford a permanently satisfactory basis of union.

THE FEDERAL CONSTITUTION

Two outstanding defects in the Articles of Confederation were the failure to give the central government an assured annual revenue and the lack of any provision for securing uniformity in the regulation of commerce. The urgent necessity of strengthening the articles on these points inspired the calling of a constitutional convention at Philadelphia in the spring of 1787. Most of the leaders of public opinion were members of this convention, among them Washington, Madison, Hamilton, and Benjamin Franklin.

[4] *H. C.*, xliii, 160-165.   [5] *H. C.*, xliii, 168-179.

It was deemed impracticable to secure the desired ends by merely amending the Articles of Confederation; so an entirely new constitution was prepared. The task occupied the entire summer of 1787, and when the document was finished it went to the thirteen States for their approval.[6] In some of them the issue of adoption was doubtful, for many provisions in the new constitution were bitterly attacked. But its friends were as active in its defense; Hamilton and Madison wielded their pens to good purpose in a publicity campaign, and in the course of time all thirteen States gave the document their indorsement. These letters of Hamilton and Madison in advocacy of the new constitution, subsequently published as "The Federalist," form a notable treatise on the principles of federal government.[7] The new central government began its career forthwith; and in his first inaugural Washington called upon the representatives of the people "to lay the foundations of national policy" in a way that would "command the respect of the world."[8]

STRENGTHENING THE UNION; TERRITORIAL EXPANSION; AND FOREIGN POLICY

Three outstanding features marked the trend of American political history during the first thirty years after the nation became welded into a federal unit. The first of these was the steady extension of those powers which the Constitution had intrusted to the new central government. A dozen years after the establishment of the United States Supreme Court the post of Chief Justice was given to John Marshall and was occupied by him with firmness and dignity until 1835. Marshall was a believer in an efficient central government; he was sure that this was what the framers of the Constitution had meant to establish; and for thirty-four years he devoted his great powers to the work of assaying from the nation's organic law all the jurisdiction it could yield to the authorities of the union. It was under his leadership that the court took the epoch-marking step of declaring that the Constitution gave to the Federal Govern-

[6] H. C., xliii, 192-211.   [7] H. C., xliii, 212-221.   [8] H. C., xliii, 243.

ment not only express but implied powers, and that where the Constitution gave a power to Congress it intrusted to that body a choice of the means to be used in carrying its authority into practical operation. "Let the end be legitimate, let it be within the scope of the Constitution, and all means which are appropriate, which are plainly adapted to that end, which are not prohibited, but consist with the letter and spirit of the Constitution, are constitutional." [9] When Marshall put aside his robes of office in 1835, the Constitution had been securely anchored in its station as the supreme law of the land and the Washington government, chiefly through his masterly legal skill, had been brought to a dominating place in the national life.

These three decades covered, in the second place, an era of territorial expansion, the successive steps of which have been traced in another lecture. [10]

In the third place the relations between the United States and European powers were placed on a better footing during the first quarter of the nineteenth century. The withdrawal of France and Spain from contiguous territory removed a source of possible danger. The war with England (1812-1815) cleared the international atmosphere of some noxious features, and in the era of better feeling which followed its conclusion came the virtual neutralization of the Great Lakes—a stroke of great and statesmanlike prudence. [11] Within a few years came the promulgation of the Monroe Doctrine with its unfaltering enunciation of American diplomatic policy in relation to the lands of the New Hemisphere. [12] In the twenty years intervening between 1803 and 1823 the Republic has cleared her boundaries to the south, removed a possible menace from her boundaries to the north, and frankly made known the fundamentals of her future policy as respects all surrounding lands.

[9] Opinion of Chief Justice John Marshall in the case of McCulloch *vs.* the State of Maryland, *H. C.*, xliii, 222-240.
[10] See Professor F. J. Turner in the lecture on "The Territorial Development of the United States," History, V.
[11] Arrangement as to the Naval Force to be Respectively Maintained on the American Lakes, *H. C.*, xliii, 283-285.
[12] The Monroe Doctrine, *H. C.*, xliii, 296-298.

V. LAW AND LIBERTY

By Professor Roscoe Pound

FOR what end does the legal order exist? What do we seek to achieve through the political organization? What is the ultimate purpose in lawmaking, that is, in the selection and formulation of the standards for the public administration of justice which organized society establishes or recognizes? These are the first questions in legal and in political philosophy. The history of juristic thought and of political thought is chiefly a history of the way in which men have answered them.

THE AIM OF LAW (1) IN PRIMITIVE SOCIETIES

In primitive societies the answers are that the legal order exists simply to keep the peace, that men seek through the legal order to avert individual self-redress and prevent private war, and that the purpose of lawmaking is to establish rules by which controversies may be adjusted peaceably. Accordingly, whereas to-day we seek, as we say, to do justice, seeking to preserve the peace and to adjust controversies peaceably simply as means thereto and incidents thereof, primitive legal systems make peace the end. Where to-day we think of compensation for an injury, primitive law thinks only of composition for the desire to be avenged. Where to-day we seek to give to each what he ought to have or the nearest possible equivalent, primitive law seeks only to give him a substitute for vengeance in case he is wronged.

(2) IN GREECE AND ROME

Greek philosophy and Roman law soon passed beyond the crude conception of the end of the legal order in primitive society. Instead, they gave these answers: The legal order exists to preserve the social *status quo;* men seek through the legal order to keep each individual in his appointed groove, and thus to prevent the friction with his fellowmen which primitive law sought only to mitigate. This is brought out very clearly in Greek political philosophy. Thus, in Plato's ideal state the state is to assign everyone to the class for which he is best fitted and the law is to keep him there, in order that a perfect harmony and unity may prevail. St. Paul's well-known exhortation (Eph. v, 22ff. and vi, 1-5) in which he calls on all the faithful to exert themselves to do their duty in the class in which they find themselves, proceeds upon the same conception. The Roman lawyers turned this idea of political philosophy into law. In the great institutional book of Roman law, the Institutes of Justinian, we are told that the precepts of law come to three; to live honorably, not to injure another, and to give to everyone his due. The idea here is that the state and the law exist to maintain harmoniously the existing social order. What the interests of another are, which one is not to injure, what makes anything another's due, so that it is to be given him, are matters which are left wholly to the traditional social organization.

(3) BEFORE AND AFTER THE REFORMATION

On the downfall of the Roman empire the Germanic invaders brought back for a season the primitive ideas of buying off vengeance and keeping the peace through arbitrary peaceful solution of disputes by mechanical modes of trial and hard and fast rules. But during the Middle Ages these conceptions gradually yielded to the classical idea of the legal order as a means of preserving the social *status quo,* the more since the latter was fortified by the unassailable authority of texts of scripture and of the Roman law. Moreover, from the thirteenth century on, philosophers more and more sought to sustain authority by reason, and in this way they prepared the way for a new conception which developed in the seventeenth century. For by that time two events of capital importance had compelled a complete revolution in legal and political philosophy. In the first place the Reformation had divorced the philosophy of law and of politics from theology and had set them free from the authority of the church. This was the work of the Protestant jurist theologians of the sixteenth century.[1] Secondly, following the nationalist movement which resulted from the breakdown of the unifying and universal authorities of the Middle Ages, the church and the empire,[2] the Germanists overthrew the idea of the binding authority of the Roman law in modern Europe. Accordingly it became necessary to find new bases for legal and political authority, and those bases were found in reason and in contract, or the consent and agreement of the individual.[3]

REASON AND NATURAL RIGHTS

In the seventeenth and eighteenth centuries reason was made the measure of all obligation. Seventeenth-century legal and political philosophers considered that law existed in order to produce conformity to the nature of rational creatures. In practice, however, though they had broken with authority as such, they accepted the Roman law as embodied reason and essayed very little that did not have authority behind it. In consequence the Roman maxim— not to injure another and to give to everyone his own—was taken to express the nature of rational creatures, and respect for personality and respect for acquired rights remained the two cardinal principles of justice. But these principles raised two obvious questions: (1) What is there in personality that makes aggression an injury, and (2) what is it that makes anything one's own? The answer was sought in a theory of natural rights, or of certain qualities inherent in individual human beings and demonstrated by reason to which society, state, and law were bound to give effect. According to this theory, justice is the maximum of individual self-assertion; it is the function of the state and of the law to make it possible for the individual to act freely. Hence the sphere of law is limited to the minimum of restraint and coercion necessary to allow of the maximum of self-assertion by each, limited by the like self-assertion by all.

[1] See *Harvard Classics*, xxxvi, 353.
[2] For this nationalist idea see *H. C.*, xxxvi, 7.   [3] *H. C.*, xxxiv, 319.

This purely individualist theory of justice culminated in the eighteenth century in the Declarations of the Rights of Man and Bills of Rights which are so characteristic of that time.[4]

At the close of the eighteenth century the foundations of the seventeenth and eighteenth century theory were shattered by Immanuel Kant.[5] But he furnished a new metaphysical foundation for the conception of justice as the maximum of individual self-assertion and in consequence it survived for about a hundred years and was given complete logical development in the political, economic, and juristic writing of the nineteenth century, although the actual law began to break away from this idea in Europe by the middle of the century and was definitely breaking away in America in the last decade thereof.

In the nineteenth century, then, legal and political philosophers were agreed that the end of the legal order, the purpose of political organization and purpose of lawmaking, were to secure and maintain individual liberty. The historian found in history the unfolding of this idea in human experience. The philosophical jurist postulated free will as the fundamental principle and deduced therefrom an ideal system of principles of liberty to which law ought to conform. The utilitarian legislator took individual liberty for the one sure means of producing human happiness and so made it the goal of all lawmaking. Mill's treatise "On Liberty"[6] is the best example of a thoroughgoing exposition of this nineteenth-century idea of abstract liberty. Moreover, it is much more tempered and reasonable in its attitude toward what we now call social legislation, so far as it restrains an abstract liberty of action whereby under pressure the weak barter away their actual liberty, than most contemporary or even subsequent writing from the same standpoint.

THE MODERN SOCIAL POINT OF VIEW

To-day the social-philosophical school has given us a new conception of the end of the legal order. Instead of the maximum of individual self-assertion consistent with a like self-assertion by all others, we are now putting as the end

[4] *H. C.,* xliii, 70, 157, 160.   [5] *H. C.,* xxxii, 323.   [6] *H. C.,* xxv, 203ff.

the maximum satisfaction of human wants, of which self-assertion is only one, even if a very important one. Hence juristic and political theory to-day thinks of interests, that is of claims which a human being may make, and of securing or protecting the greatest number of these interests possible with the least sacrifice of other interests. Moreover there are public interests, or claims which the organized political society may make, and social interests, or claims of society at large. Ultimately all interests, individual and public, are secured and maintained because of a social interest in so doing. But this does not mean that individual interests, the details of which the nineteenth century worked out so well, are to be ignored. On the contrary, the chiefest of social interests is the moral and social life of the individual, and thus individual interests become largely identical with a social interest. In securing them because of the social interest in the moral and social life of the individual, however, and in recognizing that individual self-assertion is only one human want, which must be weighed with others in a finite world where all wants cannot be satisfied, a governmental paternalism or even maternalism may become proper, which would have seemed intolerable to thinkers in the last century. In this connection, Mill on Liberty has a permanent value, despite the entire change in our views as to the end of law and of the state. Just as in the seventeenth century an undue insistence upon public interests, thought of as the interests of the sovereign, defeated the moral and social life of the individual and required the assertion of individual interests in Bills of Rights and Declarations of Rights, there is a like danger that certain social interests will be unduly emphasized and that governmental maternalism will become an end rather than a means and will defeat the real purposes of the legal order. Hence, although we think socially, we must still think of individual interests, and of that greatest of all claims which a human being may make, the claim to assert his individuality, to exercise freely the will and the reason which God has given him. We must emphasize the social interest in the moral and social life of the individual, but we must remember that it is the life of a free-willing being.

DRAMA

1. GENERAL INTRODUCTION

By Professor George Pierce Baker

RARE is the human being, immature or mature, who has never felt an impulse to pretend he is some one or something else. The human being who has never felt pleasure in seeing such a pretending is rarer still. Back through the ages of barbarism and civilization, in all tongues, we find this instinctive pleasure in the imitative action that is the very essence of all drama. The instinct to impersonate produces the actor; the desire to provide pleasure by impersonations produces the playwright; the desire to provide this pleasure with adequate characterization and dialogue memorable in itself produces dramatic literature. Though dramatic literature has been sporadic, dramatic entertainment by imitative action has been going steadily on since we first hear of it in connection with the Bacchic festivals of early Greece; and the dramatic instinct has been uninterruptedly alive since man's creation. We do not kill the drama, we do not really limit its appeal by failing to encourage the best in it; but we do thereby foster the weakest and poorest elements. In 1642 the English Parliament, facing war, closed the theatres and forbade all plays. Yet, though the years following were so troublous as not to favor drama, it was necessary in 1647 to repeat the edict, because surreptitious and garbled performances of plays formerly popular had been given, and because vulgarized excerpts from comic portions of past plays had been given at fairs and other public gatherings. Clearly, so strong was the instinct, the craving for drama, that if the public could not get new plays, or even its old plays as wholes, it would accept far less worthy entertainment rather than go without. Even in this country, far more recently, in many communities where theatres were regarded at least with hesitation, the panorama was popular, and local branches of the G. A. R. gave to enthusiastic audiences "The Drummer Boy of Shiloh." To-day, many who will not attend the theatre do attend the moving-picture show. One cannot annihilate an instinct of the races old as time: to legislate against it is to risk repressing only the better part; what is necessary is to make the undesirable unattractive.

THE DRAMA AND PUBLIC TASTE

The only sound basis for this result is a widespread taste in the public for good drama. While it is not true, as George Farquhar wrote, that "Plays are like suppers, poets are the cooks," there is yet truth in Samuel Johnson's saying that "The drama's laws the drama's patrons give." He who serves his dramatic meal, cooked and seasoned exactly for what he takes to be the tastes of his public, merely writes plays: he does not create drama. To try to hit public taste in the drama is like trying to hit the bull's-eye of a rapidly shifting target on a very foggy day. On the other hand, the public speaker who should try to present his subject to a public knowing nothing of it, and to a public of which he knows nothing, must skillfully interest them by finding in his subject some appeal of a general nature. In similar fashion works the dramatist. He cannot write comedies and farces for a community lacking in humor. He can do little in grim story play or tragedy with a laughter-loving public. Granted a public fond of the theatre, he is sure of a hearing and probably an appreciative one; but the fuller and the more accurate his public's knowledge of good drama in the past, the greater his chance for an attentive and comprehending hearing when he writes what should be good drama to-day.

HOW TO READ A PLAY

In reading plays, however, it should always be remembered that any play, however great, loses much when not seen in action. As John Marston wrote in 1606: "Comedies are writ to be spoken, not read; remember the life of these things consists in action"; or, as Molière put it: "Comedies are made to be played, not to be read." Any play is so planned that it can produce its exact effect only with its required scenery, lighting, and acting. And that acting means the gesture, movement, and voice of the actor. Above all, it means the voice, the instrument which conveys to the audience the exact shade of meaning of the author and, like music, opens up the emotions. Drama read to oneself is never drama at its best, and is not even drama as it should be. Usually, too, just because readers do not recognize the difference between drama and other forms of fiction, they lose the effects they might gain even in reading. Closer attention than with a novel or short story is required. The dramatist does not guide us by explanations, analysis, and comment in our visualizing of his figures. Instead, he depends on a few stage directions as to their movements, and on the rightness of his chosen words in the dialogue. Unfortunately, many a reader, accustomed to hasty reading of the sketchy stories so common in the magazines, does not piece out what is given him but sees only just what the words of the text force him to see with no effort on his part. He is not active and cooperative. No play read in this way yields its real value. First, see in your mind the setting as described. Then, reading sympathetically, thoughtfully, and slowly if need be, visualize the figures as they come and go. The lines of any good play mean more than appears at a hasty glance. They have been chosen not simply because they say what the character might have said, but because what is said will advance the plot, and, because better than some half dozen other phrases considered by the author, they will rouse the emotions of the audience. Keep the sympathetic, not the critical mood, to the fore. Reading to visualize, feel because you visualize, and feel as fully as you can. Then when you close the book, moved and admiring, and then only, let your critical training tell you whether you have done well to admire. Don't let prejudices, moral or artistic, cause prejudgments: keep an open mind as you read. A writer may so treat a subject for which you have

never cared as to make you care for it. He may so treat a
subject you have regarded as taboo as to make it acceptable
and helpful. Don't assume because a play is different from
the plays you have known that it is bad. As the general
editor has said: "It is precisely this encounter with the
mental states of other generations which enlarges the outlook and sympathies of the cultivated man." When a play
of a different nation or period at first proves unattractive,
don't assume that it will remain so. Rather, study the conditions of stage and audience which gave it being. Usually
this will transmute a seemingly dull play into a living, appealing work of art. In any case, when you have finished
reading, judge with discretion. Say, if you like, "This play
is not for me—for a person of my tastes," but not, "This is
a bad play for all," unless you are able to explain why what
is poison for you should be poison for the general public.
In all the great periods of the drama perfect freedom of
choice and subject, perfect freedom of individual treatment,
and an audience eager to give itself to sympathetic listening, even if instruction be involved, have brought the great
results. If a public widely read in the drama of the past and
judging it as suggested would come to the acting drama of
to-day in exactly that spirit, almost anything would become
possible for our dramatists.

THE ESSENTIALS OF DRAMA

But what is drama? Broadly speaking, it is whatever by
imitative action rouses interest or gives pleasure. The
earliest of the mediæval plays, the trope of the church in
which the three Marys go to the tomb to find that Christ has
risen, and make their way thence rejoicing, does not differentiate one Mary from another. The words, which were
given to music, have only an expository value. Here, as
through the ages succeeding, it is action, not characterization however good, not dialogue for the sake of characterization or for its own sake, which counts. Of course, this
very early drama is too bald and too simple to have value as
literature. As the trope in the tenth to the thirteenth centuries adds to the episode of the Resurrection or the Nativity

preliminary or continuing Biblical material, so story develops around the original episode. Almost inevitably, in order to make these differing episodes convincing, characterization appears, for, unless the people are unlike, some of the episodes could not occur. The dialogue ceases to be merely expository and begins to characterize each speaker. Later it comes to have charm, amusingness, wit, that is, quality of its own. When the drama attains a characterization which makes the play a revelation of human conduct and a dialogue which characterizes yet pleases for itself, we reach dramatic literature.

So, too, as times goes on, there develop the play of story, the play mainly of characterization, the play in which dialogue counts almost as much as plot or character, and the great masterpieces in which all these interests, plot, character, and dialogue are blended into a perfect whole. "The Duchess of Malfi" [1] of Webster is a story play which illustrates a change in public taste. For a modern reader, probably more interested in the character of the Duchess than in the story itself, the last act doubtless lacks the interest it had for its own public. In Jonson's "Alchemist" [2] it is character mainly which interests us. In Sheridan's "School for Scandal," [3] as in Congreve's "Way of the World," dialogue counts as much as character. In "Hamlet," "Lear," and "Macbeth" [4] there is a perfect union of story, characterization, and dialogue.

THE NATURE OF TRAGEDY

Once the idea was widespread that tragedy and comedy differ essentially in material. Dryden maintained that tragedy must deal with people of exalted rank in extraordinary situations, expressing themselves in speech befitting their extraordinary circumstances. This idea, first stated by Aristotle in his "Poetics" as a result of his observation of the Greek Tragedy—which the definition perfectly fits— was fostered and expanded by critical students of dramatic theory till it found expression in the exaggeration of the

---

[1] *Harvard Classics,* xlvii, 721ff.   [2] *H. C.,* xlvii, 521ff.
[3] *H. C.,* xviii, 105ff.   [4] *H. C.,* xlvi, 87, 203, 305.

Heroic Drama in England and the dignified if somewhat
cold tragedies of Corneille and Racine.[5] The coming of the
Sentimental Comedy in England in the first thirty years of
the eighteenth century, the related "Drame Larmoyante" of
France, and the "Bürgerliche Drama" in Germany, showed
that tragedy may exist in all ranks from high to low, from
educated to uneducated.

What then is tragedy? In the Elizabethan period it was
assumed that a play ending in death was a tragedy, but in
recent years we have come to understand that to live on is
sometimes far more tragic than death. Nor is the presence
of tragic incidents in a play sufficient reason for calling it a
tragedy, for many plays that end happily have in them profoundly moving episodes. Why, then, is it that we are so
agreed in calling "Hamlet," "The Duchess of Malfi" and
"The Cenci"[6] tragedies? Because in them character clash-
ing with itself, with environment, or with other temperaments, moves through tragic episodes to a final catastrophe
that is the logical outcome of what we have observed. By
"logical" I mean that the ending is seen to grow from the
preceding events in accordance with the characters. That
is, it conforms with human experience as known to us or as
revealed to us by the dramatist in question.

MELODRAMA

Suppose, however, that we have tragic circumstance not
justified by the characterization of the figures concerned.
For instance, in some play on Cleopatra the special scenes
may move us even if they do not put before us a character
whose willfulness and exacting love seem great enough to
bring about the final catastrophe. Then what have we?
Melodrama in the broadest sense of the word. Melodrama
in this sense of plays insufficiently motivated in characterization has existed from the beginning of drama. Technically, the word came into England early in the nineteenth
century to designate an importation from France of sensational scenes with frequent musical accompaniment. As
this particular combination disappeared, the name remained

[5] *H. C.*, xxvi, 71, 125.   [6] *H. C.*, xviii, 281ff.

for plays of sensational incident and inadequate characterization.

THE STORY PLAY

Between the two—melodrama and tragedy—both perhaps
sensational in episode, but only the second justifying its
episodes by perfectly motivated character, lies the story
play. In this the light and the serious, the comic and the
tragic, mingle, though the ending is cheerful. "The Merchant of Venice," regarded as Shakespeare regarded it as
the story of Portia and Bassanio, is clearly not a tragedy
but a story play. If, however, we sympathize with Shylock
as modern actors, especially by their rearrangement of the
scenes, often make us, is it not a tragedy? There lies the
important distinction. There is no essential difference between the material of comedy and tragedy. All depends on
the point of view of the dramatist, which, by clever emphasis, he tries to make the point of view of his audience.
The trial scene of Shylock perfectly illustrates the idea: to
the friends of Bassanio, as to most of the Elizabethan
audience, this Jew-baiting was highly delightful; to Shylock
it was torture and heartbreak. The dramatist who presents
such material so as to emphasize in it what would appeal to
the friends of Bassanio, writes comedy. He who presents
it to an audience likely to feel as Shylock felt, writes
tragedy.

HIGH COMEDY, LOW COMEDY, AND FARCE

Comedy divides into higher and lower. Low comedy
concerns itself directly or indirectly with manners. "The
Alchemist" of Jonson busies itself directly with manners by
means of characters varying from types of a single aspect
to well-individualized figures. Comedy of intrigue, centering about a love story, deals in complicated situations arising
therefrom, but indirectly paints manners as it characterizes.
"The Shoemaker's Holiday" [7] may perhaps stand as a specimen of this type, though Fletcher's "Wild-Goose Chase" is
a better example. High comedy, as George Meredith
pointed out in his masterly "Essay on Comedy," deals in

[7] *H. C.*, xlvii, 447ff.

thoughtful laughter. This laughter comes from the recognition, made instantaneously by the author, of the comic value of a comparison or contrast. For instance, in "Much Ado About Nothing" it is high comedy at which we laugh when from moment to moment we contrast Benedick and Beatrice as they see themselves and as we see them in the revelatory touches of the dramatist.

Farce treats the improbable as probable, the impossible as possible. In the second case it often passes into extravaganza or burlesque. "The Frogs"[8] of Aristophanes illustrates farcical burlesque. In the best farce to-day we start with some absurd premise as to character or situation, but if the premises be once granted we move logically enough to the ending.

SOCIAL BACKGROUND OF DRAMA

Yet, even if one understands these differences, one may find it difficult at first to appreciate the drama of a past time. Modern drama from 980 A. D. onward passes from the simple Latin trope, already described, by accumulation of incident, developing characterization, and a feeling for expression for its own sake, to similar work in the vernacular, be it English, French, or German. Then slowly it gains enormously in characterization till some of the miracle and morality plays of the late fifteenth century equal or surpass any English drama up to Marlowe. But what lay behind all this drama of miracle play and morality was an undivided church. With the coming of the Reformation and its insistence on the value and finality of individual judgment, the didactic drama gave way to the drama of entertainment—the interludes and the beginnings of the five-act plays. Yet, fine as are some of the plays of the days of Elizabeth and James I, we find in them a brutality of mood, a childish sense of the comic, a love of story for mere story's sake that make them oftentimes a little hard reading. Moreover, their technique—their frequent disregard of our ideas of unity, their methods of exposition by chorus, soliloquy, and aside—frequently appears to us antiquated. Except for the greatest of these plays—mainly by Shakespeare—the Elizabethan

[8] *H. C.,* xviii, 419ff.

drama seems strange to us at a first reading. Only coming to know the conditions from which it sprang can give us its real values.

Even the great dramas of Æschylus, Sophocles, and to a less extent of Euripides, because he is more modern, are best read when we know something of the Greek life around these dramas and of the stage for which they were written. To these plays a great audience of perhaps 10,000 brought a common knowledge of the myths and stories represented, akin to our universal knowledge a generation ago of Biblical story. The audience brought also memories of successive and even recent treatments of the same myth by other dramatists, taking delight, not as we do in something because it seems new, but in the individual treatment of the old story by the new dramatist. The same attitude held for the Elizabethan public which delighted in successive versions of "Romeo and Juliet," "Julius Cæsar," and "Hamlet." In judging the drama of Greece or Elizabethan England this fact must be kept constantly in mind.

As one turns from Greek and Elizabethan drama, written for the delight and edification of the masses, to the work of Corneille and Racine, one faces plays written primarily for the cultivated, and worked out, not spontaneously by individual genius, but carefully according to critical theory derived not so much from study of classic drama as from commentators on a commentator on the Greek drama—Aristotle. From him, for instance, came the idea as to the essentiality of the unities of time, action, and place, themselves the result of physical conditions of the Greek stage. By contrast, then, this French tragedy of the seventeenth century is a drama of intellectuals.

Then as the spirit of humanitarianism spread and men shared more and more in Samuel Johnson's desire "with extensive view" to "survey mankind from China to Peru," the drama reflected all this. No longer did the world laugh at the selfish complacency and indulgence of the rake and fop, but it began to sympathize with his wife, fiancée, or friend who suffered from this selfishness and complacency. Illustrating that the difference between tragedy and comedy lies only in emphasis, Restoration comedy turned from thoughtless laughter to sympathetic tears. But such psychology as the sentimental comedy shows is conventional and superficial. It is in the nineteenth century that the drama, ever sensitive to public moods and sentiment, undergoes great changes. In France and Germany it breaks the shackles of the pseudoclassicism which had for centuries held the drama to empty speech and a dead level of characterization. Goethe, Schiller, Hugo, Dumas père, and Alfred de Vigny reveal a new world of dramatic romance and history. In turn this romance leads to realism with an underlying scientific spirit which takes nothing at its old values.

MODERN PSYCHOLOGY AND SOCIOLOGY IN THE DRAMA

This searching scrutiny of accepted ideas of personality, conduct, right, wrong, and even causation in general, is seen in Ibsen and all his followers. Planting themselves firmly on the new and developing science of psychology, guided by the most intense belief in individualism, demanding its passports from every accepted idea, the dramatists of the last half century have steadily enlarged the scope of their art. From mere story-telling they passed to ethical drama. Convinced by practice that it is difficult for a play in its limited time—two and a half hours at the most—to do more than state a problem or paint a set of social conditions, they have taken to merely drawing pictures or raising questions rather than attempting even to suggest an answer. As we have seen, in the eighteenth century the writer of sentimental comedy painted social conditions, but with a psychology purely intuitional. To-day we have swung to the other extreme. Recognizing the limited space of the dramatist, confused by contrasting psychological theories, puzzled by the baffling intricacies of the human soul, convinced that the great questions raised cannot be settled in a breath, or with any ready-made panacea, many a dramatist to-day merely pictures an evil condition, waiting for others to find its exact significance or, better still, a solution. "Justice" of Mr. Galsworthy, like "La Robe Rouge" of M. Brieux, offers no solution, yet both led to changes in the conditions portrayed—in the former, conditions of prison life; in the latter, evils attending the life of the petty judiciary of France.

THE MENACE OF VAUDEVILLE AND MOVING PICTURES

A veritable passion for the theatre is shown by the younger generation to-day in the United States. It crowds the theatres—if we use the word to include not only places giving performances of legitimate drama but also vaudeville houses and picture shows—as in this country it never has crowded them before. To go to a theatre of the older type one must usually travel some distance and often one must save beforehand. Vaudeville and picture shows cheap enough for almost any purse are provided at our very doors. The difficulty is that what they offer is sometimes as low in art as in price. Yet surely, it may be said, there is good vaudeville, and surely proper legislation ought to dispose of what is poor or dangerous in it or the picture show. Granted, but there are inherent dangers which legislation cannot reach. In the first place, the balcony and galleries of our theatres are far less filled than they used to be before vaudeville and the picture show provided at much less expense and with greater comfort entertainment to many as satisfactory as the theatre itself. This decrease in attendance at the theatres naturally jeopardizes the chances of many a play which can be produced only if the manager feels reasonably sure of large houses or a public more general than usually frequents the orchestra. Vaudeville, too, like the collections of short stories we read in the train, is usually a mere time killer, making the least possible demand on our application and attention. In vaudeville, if something grips our interest we pay attention; if one "turn" does not interest us we simply wait for the next. Sooner or later, without any effort on our part, something will win our absorbed attention. Now drama that has literary value demands, when read, as I have pointed out, concentration, an effort to visualize. Acted drama requires surrender of one's self, sympathetic absorption in the play as it develops. These absolutely essential conditions grow less possible for the person trained by vaudeville. The moving picture show, too, is at best drama stripped of everything but motion. The greatest appeal of all, the voice, except in so far as the phonograph can reproduce it, is wanting. But can any combination of mechanical devices such as the cinematograph and the graphophone ever equal in human significance, in reality of effect, in persuasive power, the human being— most vividly seen and felt in drama at its best? A combination of the cinematograph and the phonograph can be at best only a dramatic Frankenstein's automaton. Dramatic literature is really threatened by the picture show and vaudeville.

THE DRAMA IN MODERN EDUCATION

All this would be discouraging were not these conditions somewhat counteracted by drama as we find it in our schools, colleges, and social settlements. As far back as the sixteenth century in England and on the Continent the value for pronunciation, enunciation, and deportment of acting by school children was recognized. Ralph Radcliffe, a schoolmaster of Hitchen in Hertfordshire, wrote many plays for his scholars. Nicholas Udall, successively a master of Eton and Westminster schools, left us one of the early landmarks of English drama, "Ralph Roister Doister," a mixture of early English dramatic practice and borrowings from the Latin comedy. On the Continent, fathers and mothers gathered often, fondly to watch their boys in similar Latin or vernacular plays. In like manner to-day, all over this country, in grammar and high schools, wise teachers are guiding their pupils in varied expression of their dramatic instinct. Many a high school to-day has, as part of its equipment, a small stage on which standard plays of the past, plays selected from the best written to-day, and, occasionally, even plays written by the students themselves are given. From participation in such performances more results than a mere gain in enunciation, pronunciation, and deportment. The standards of a youth who associates often with the best in dramatic literature must improve. Inculcate thus pleasantly right standards of drama, and the lure of vaudeville and picture show is weakened. But the training must be broad: our youth must know the best—comedy,

tragedy, farce, burlesque—in the drama of to-day and
yesterday.

No such training of our youth can ever be complete if in
the home there is no real understanding, at least from reading, of what the best in drama has been. Otherwise how
can the elders sympathize with this natural demand of the
young, for probably they will not recognize either the worthiness or the permanence of the appeal which the drama properly makes. While youth inevitably seek entertainment in
the theatre, their elders must see to the kind of entertainment provided. That is a fair and natural division.

Year by year we receive at Ellis Island people from all
over the world, people little fitted for the responsibilities of
a citizenship that was planned for a people relatively homogeneous and trained for centuries in a growing political
power which rested on the responsibility of the individual.
How shall we reveal to this immigrant what this great
varied American life means and thus assimilate him into the
body politic? Seeking an answer to this problem, the settlement houses have found one of their most effective means
in the drama. The southern or southeastern European,
filled with emotion, loves to act. In the settlement house,
through carefully selected plays, he learns our language and
gains the ideals of the land in which he is to live.

HOW THE LEVEL OF DRAMATIC ART IS DETERMINED

Responsive to all this widespread interest of the people at
large, men and women all over the country are busied with
the difficult art of the dramatist. In turn responsive to their
needs, our colleges are developing courses in dramatic composition, though ten years ago not one existed. But to these
playwrights comes sooner or later the question: "Shall I
write so as surely to make money, but pandering to the lower
artistic and moral taste of my public; or shall I keep to my
inculcated and self-discovered standards of dramatic art till
I win my public to them?" For the latter result there must
be a considerable part of the public which so understands
and loves the best of the drama of the past that it can
quickly discover promise in the drama to-day. Out of the

past come the standards for judging the present; standards
in turn to be shaped by the practice of present-day dramatists into broader standards for the next generation. The
drama possesses a great literature growing out of an eternal
desire of the races. The drama is a great revealer of life.
Potentially, it is a social educative force of the greatest
possibilities, provided it be properly handled. You cannot
annihilate it. Repressing it you bring its poorer qualities to
the front. How, then, can any so-called educated man fail
to try to understand it? But to understand it one must read
closely, sympathetically, and above all widely.

For such results a collection like this must be but the fillip
that creates a craving for more. Here is only a little of all
the Elizabethan and Jacobean drama. Here it is possible to
represent only by a few masterpieces the vast stores of the
drama in France, Germany, England, Scandinavia, Italy,
Spain, and Russia in the nineteenth and twentieth centuries.
To-day, English drama, with only a few exceptions better
than any written since the seventeenth century, comes often
to the stage. From month to month the drama is making
history. In England and the United States to-day it is wonderfully alive, independent, ambitious, seeking new ways of
expression on an infinite variety of subjects. Yet it is often
crude, especially in this country. It will never know how
crude till its public forces it to closer, finer thinking, more
logical characterization, and stern avoidance of mere
theatricality. Back of any such gains must stand a public
with a love for the drama, gained not merely from seeing
plays of to-day but from wide reading in the drama of different periods and different nations in the past.

THE INFLUENCE OF THE STAGE ON THE DRAMA

No drama, however great, is entirely independent of the
stage on which it is given. In a great period the drama
forces its stage to yield to its demands, however exacting,
till that stage becomes plastic. At a time of secondary
drama plays yield to the rigidities of their stage, making life
conform to the stage, not the stage to life. Consequently,
just as different periods have seen different kinds of drama,

they have seen different kinds of stage. In the trope the monks acted in the chancel near the high altar, to come out, as the form developed, to the space before the choir screen under the great dome of the cathedral where nave and transepts met. In that nave and in the adjoining aisles knelt or stood the rapt throng of worshipers. Forced by numbers who could not be accommodated in the cathedral and by other causes, the monks, after some generations, brought their plays out into the square in front of the cathedral. That all might see them to the best advantage they were ultimately given on raised platforms. Certainly by the time these plays passed from the hands of the churchmen to the control of the trade guilds, they were on pageant cars, a construction not unlike our floats for trade processions except that they contained two stories, the lower high enough to use for a dressing room. These pageant cars the journeymen drew, between daylight and dark, from station to station across a city like York or Chester. At each station people filled the windows of the houses, the seats built up around the sides of the square, and even the roofs. The very nature of this platform stage forbade scenery, though elaborate properties seem to have been used. By contrast, on the Continent, especially in France, constructions resembling house fronts, city gates, or walls could be freely set up on the large, fixed stage for miracle plays which was built in some great square of the city. To this one place flocked all the would-be auditors. The point to remember is that down to the building of theatres the stage meant a platform, large or small, movable or stationary, in some public place. Simply treated, as was the case when it was movable, it would have a curtain at the back, shutting off a space where costumes could be changed and where the prompter could stand: scenery was out of the question. Elaborately treated, when it was stationary, constructions suggesting houses, ships, town walls, etc., might be shown at the back or side of the stage, but they seem never to have been shifted from the beginning to the end of the performance. Such houses, walls, etc., were used when needed, but when not in use were treated as nonexistent.

In the sixteenth century when playing passed from the

hands of the guilds to groups of actors, the latter sought refuge from the noise and discomforts of the public square in the yards of inns. In those day galleries like the balconies of our theatres were on all four sides of such an inn yard, sometimes two and sometimes three. The players, erecting a rough platform opposite the entrance from the street, hung a curtain from the edge of the first gallery to their stage. In the room or rooms behind this they dressed. Thus they gained a front stage; a rear stage under the first gallery to be revealed when the curtain was drawn; an upper stage in the first balcony representing at will city walls, a balcony for Romeo and Juliet, or an upper room. High above all this one or more galleries rose which could be used for heavens in which gods and goddesses appeared. In the yard stood the pittites; in the side and end galleries sat the people who paid the higher prices.

DEVELOPMENT OF THE MODERN STAGE

When, in 1576, London saw its first theatre just outside Bishopsgate, it was circular, in imitation of existing bullbaiting arenas. So far as a stage projecting into the pit, the rear stage underneath the balcony, and the use of the first balcony itself were concerned, the actors merely duplicated conditions to which they had grown attached in the old inn yards. As under the older conditions, scenery was impossible except as painted cloths might be hung at the back of the balcony or under it. Hence the care of the Elizabethan dramatists to place their scene by some hint or description in the text. Moreover, a play lacking the stage settings of a century later must be given atmosphere, reality, and even charm from within. More and more, however, influenced by increasingly elaborate performances at court of the masks, the public pressed the theatre manager as far as possible to duplicate their gorgeous and illusory settings. But such settings at the court were on stages behind an arch like our modern proscenium. Consequently by 1660 the stage of 1590 to 1642 had shrunk behind a proscenium arch. Then follow two centuries of very elaborate staging by painted drops at the back, side flats set in grooves, and painted borders. It should be remembered that till the second half of the sixteenth century public performances were given by daylight, largely because of the difficulty in using flaring and unsteady links or cressets for artificial light. When evening performances became the vogue, candles gave the light till the discovery of illuminating gas made a revolution in theatrical lighting. About 1860, the so-called box set, a means of shutting in the whole stage, replaced for interiors a back drop and painted side flats. Undoubtedly, some of the splendid and imaginative settings of Macready, Charles Kean, and Sir Henry Irving, seemed the last word on the subject. Steadily, however, producer and dramatist have worked together to make the stage as illusive as possible. On the one hand, realism has strained it to the utmost; on the other, poetic and fantastic drama have forced it to visualize for us the realms of imagination. Responding to all this, modern science and invention have come to the aid of drama. Electricity has opened up ways of lighting not even yet fully explored. At present, particularly in Germany, most ingenious devices have been invented for shifting scenery as quickly as possible. There and elsewhere, especially in Russia and England, skill and much artistry have been shown in quickening the imagination of the audience to the utmost by suggestion rather than by representation of minute and confusing detail. Frequently to-day the elaborate scenery of the past is improved upon by a stage hung about with curtains, with some properties here and there or a painted drop at the back to give all the suggestion needed. Alert and responsive, the stage of to-day at its best, in sharpest contrast with the bare stage of the sixteenth century, is calling on architects to make it flexible, on physicists and artists to light it elusively, on great designers to arrange its decorations. In brief, the stage throughout its history, longing always and trying always to adapt itself to the demands of the dramatist, is to-day, as never before, plastic.

THE COSMOPOLITANISM OF MODERN DRAMA

Nor has the drama changed merely in these respects. Once the drama was almost wholly national. Then just because a play smacked so of its soil, it could not be intelligently heard elsewhere. In the seventies, as far as the American public was concerned, this was true of the plays of Dumas fils and Augier. Now, increased travel and all the varied means of intercommunication between nations make for such swift interchange of ideas that the dramatic success of Moscow, St. Petersburg, Stockholm, Paris, London, or Madrid is known quickly the world over. With the drawing together of the nations more common interests have developed, so that intellectual and moral movements are not merely national but world-wide. All this makes any national treatment of a world question widely interesting: it even makes the world interested in local problems. Most marked change of all, this free intercommunication of ideas tends to make even the humor of one nation comprehensible by another.

To-day, then, the drama has become cosmopolitan. Broadway sees Reinhardt's Berlin productions: Paris and Berlin see "Kismet." Broadway knows Gorki, Brieux, and Schnitzler; English and American plays have a hearing on the Continent. For two generations the drama has been fighting to take for its motto "Nihil mihi alienum." It has won that right. Sensitive, responsive, eagerly welcomed everywhere, the drama, holding the mirror up to nature, by laughter and by tears reveals to mankind the world of men.

II. GREEK TRAGEDY

By Professor Charles Burton Gulick

THE word "drama" is Greek, and means action—or, as the Greeks limited its use, action that goes on before our eyes. In this way they distinguished the product of the theater from the action of epic poetry and the action of history, both of which, as understood and written by the Greeks, had highly dramatic qualities.

Three centuries roughly coincide with the three periods of development into which the history of the Greek theater naturally falls. The sixth century B. C. is the time of preparation. The fifth witnessed the full flowering of Athenian genius. In the fourth the so-called New Comedy, largely inspired by the realism of Euripides, took shape in the comedy of manners, the portrayal of domestic life, and the foibles of society.

THE ORIGIN OF DRAMA IN GREECE

A superficial glance at any play contained in The Harvard Classics will at once reveal the prominence of the chorus. To understand this, a swell as other features in the structure of a play, we must inquire into the origin of tragedy and comedy.

This inquiry, slight though it must be, is the more essential because it was the constructive genius of the Greeks that discovered and developed the drama as all countries and ages have since known it.

The drama is founded in religion. In the Greek consciousness it had its spring in the worship of Dionysus, who in one of his aspects was a god of the underworld, latest comer into the Greek Pantheon, whose religion had evoked much opposition, and whose story was full of suffering as well as triumph and joy. He represented the life-giving forces of nature; he was god of the vine and of wine, and at the vintage festival the country folk celebrated him in dance and song. They smeared their faces with wine lees and covered their bodies with goatskins, to imitate the goat-like attendants of the god, who were called satyrs. Thus their song, *tragoedia,* was the "song of the goats," *tragoi,* and many years elapsed before it became dignified. Toward the end of the seventh century B. C, the poet Arion of Corinth adapted this folksong to his own purposes and gave it, under the name of dithyramb, something like literary distinction. It was capable of great variety in form and matter, but maintained its characteristic pathos throughout. The chorus gave expression to cries of joy or ejaculations of pity and terror as the story of the god unfolded itself. A refrain, in which the same words were repeated, was a constant element.

The dithyramb remained purely lyric; but during the sixth century, we know not how or through what personality, it underwent a modification of profound importance. Some genius, perhaps Thespis, conceived the idea of impersonating the god or some hero connected with his myth, in the presence of his chorus of worshipers. He wore a mask and carried other properties appropriate to his nature, and with the leader of the chorus interchanged a dialogue which was interrupted from time to time by the comments of the chorus, accompanied by dancing and gestures.

Thespis, whose name has become familiar in all the literatures of Europe, was a native of Icaria, a village in Attica, at the foot of Mt. Pentelicus. The region, excavated by American explorers some years ago, is still known as Dionysos. It lies in a valley which leads to Marathon, and the scanty ruins, hidden among olive groves and vineyards, betray no sign that it is the birthplace of European drama. Thespis exhibited here during the latter half of the sixth century.

None of his works have survived. They were probably merely sketched, not written out, and still followed the method of improvisation which, Aristotle says, was in vogue in the early steps of the drama.

THE FIRST THEATER

The fifth century begins with authentic names and shows more positive progress toward an imposing achievement. By this time the country festivals of Dionysus had been taken up by the city. As early as the middle of the sixth century the god had been brought in pomp to Athens, and a precinct was consecrated to him at the southeast slope of the Acropolis. Beside his temple the ground was smoothed and laid out in a great dancing circle—*orchestra*—with an altar in the center. The spectators, or *theatron,* were ranged on the slope of the Acropolis. Opposite at some distance from the circle, was the temple, and beyond that Mt. Hymettus made a distant background. There was no scenery except what nature had thus provided, but a convention soon arose whereby it was understood that an actor entering from the right of the spectators came from the city or the immediate vicinity, whereas one coming from the left came from some distant country.

The early composers of tragedy—for the author composed music, invented dance steps, and trained the chorus to sing —were content with one actor who by changing mask and costume in a neighboring booth (*skênê*) could take different rôles. The chorus leader was his interlocutor and bore the most difficult part, if we may judge from the plays of Æschylus. Among the earliest poets was Phrynichus, noted for his lofty patriotism, for the sweetness of his lyrics, for vigorous inventiveness—which dared on one occasion to employ a historical theme, "The Fall of Miletus"—and for the introduction of female rôles among those assigned to the actor. The progress, as Aristotle emphasizes, was slow and tentative, and it is clear that the audience did not willingly allow any wide departure from the limits imposed by the religious origin and occasion of the performance. More than once the conservative complaint, "This has nothing to do with Dionysus," would restrain an author from breaking too hurriedly with tradition, and the high purpose and seriousness of tragedy was due not so much to any latent germ at its beginning—for comedy had the same popular origin in the vintage festival—as to the serious intent and deep religious conviction of the poets of the time, whose minds were also impressed by the gravity of the coming conflict with Persia.

ÆSCHYLUS, THE FATHER OF TRAGEDY

Æschylus was thirty-five years old when he fought at Marathon. Born at Eleusis, near the Greek sanctuary where the Mysteries of Demeter, Persephone, and Dionysus (here worshiped as Bacchus) were celebrated, his soul was charged with influences which affected his plays and explain why religious problems, like that of sin and the justice of God, are so prominent in his thought. Externally, the gorgeous vestments of the Eleusinian priests inspired him with the idea of perfecting the costume of his players; but it was his own genius which led him to take the step that entitles him to be called the Father of Tragedy. This was the introduction of a second actor, which made it possible to portray two contrasted characters, two sets of emotions or purposes, and to bring before the sympathizing chorus and spectators a conflict of ideals which, according to Hegel, is the essence of tragedy.

The dithyramb was a comparatively short piece; hence an early tragedy was short. When, as the constructive faculty increased, it became evident that a theme could not be worked out within the limits of a single play, the custom arose of treating it in a group of three plays, to which was added, in deference to the festival, a satyr play, wherein the chorus took the part of satyrs, as in the ancient time. Thus the great theme of the commission, transmission, and re-mission of sin has its beginning, middle, and end in the "Agamemnon," "Libation-Bearers," and "Furies,"[1] the only trilogy that is extant. Even this lacks the satyr play which once made the group a normal tetralogy. The "Prometheus Bound,"[2] is obviously incomplete. We have lost the part of the trilogy in which the reconciliation between the rebellious Titan and his enemy, Zeus, was effected, and the justice of Zeus vindicated.

[1] For the complete trilogy see *Harvard Classics*, viii, 5ff.
[2] *H. C.*, viii, 156ff.

All the Greek plays contained in The Harvard Classics
belong to the period of Athenian expansion following the
successful fight against Persia. Poets, painters, sculptors,
joined in celebrating the achievement of Greece, due mostly
to Athens, in ridding Europe for centuries from the fear of
Oriental despotism. Exploration and commerce brought
new wealth into Attica, which now controlled the sea, and
the outburst of lyric and dramatic genius has had no parallel except in England after the destruction of the Spanish
Armada.

SOPHOCLES

Sophocles,[3] the tragedian who represents the purest type
of the classical Greek, was in his teens when the Battle of
Salamis was won. Beautiful in person and clear sighted in
intellect, he was the first to use the new Greek art in the
theater. For he introduced scene painting. Heretofore
even Æschylus had been content with only the altar in the
orchestra and a few statues of gods on the outer edge away
from the audience. Sophocles now erected a scene building,
the front of which showed to the audience the façade of a
temple or palace, pierced by a single door. The two side
entrances were retained. Æschylus adopted the innovation
readily, and thus we find the scenery of the "Agamemnon,"
simple as it is, far advanced from the earlier conditions.
Sophocles also enlarged the chorus from twelve to fifteen
singers, securing greater volume of tone and variety of motion and gesture. But from this time onward we note a
steady diminution of the choral parts and the greater prominence of the actors, whose number Sophocles increased to
three.

EURIPIDES

In Euripides we have the boldest innovator, both in the
resources of dramaturgy and in the moral problems which he
treats. Even he cannot break entirely with tradition, and
it is a curious chance that the latest play of this great period,
the "Bacchae,"[4] harks back to the theme of the earliest
tragedies, the savage triumph of Dionysus over his per-

[3] *H. C.*, viii, 197.   [4] *H. C.*, viii, 349.

secutors. But the method of Euripides leads him to devices
for which he was bitterly criticized. His characters are no
longer gods, the motive power in his plots no longer divine.
They are men and women, often moved by sordid and trivial
causes, yet none the less pathetic. To Aristotle he is the
most tragic of the three, and his appeal to sympathy is
strong because his personages are human. The effects of
tragedy, pity and terror, become more vivid because the
sufferers are made of the same stuff as the audience. In
plot he is less skillful than Sophocles at his best, and he
sometimes has recourse to the *deus ex machina* to cut the
complicated knot of his own tying. Yet even here the appearance of the god, as at the end of the "Hippolytus," [5] is
justified by its spectacular effect.

[5] *H. C.*, viii, 287.

III. THE ELIZABETHAN DRAMA

By Professor W. A. Neilson

W HEN the great European movement known as the Renaissance reached England, it found its fullest and most lasting expression in the drama. By a fortunate group of coincidences this intellectual and artistic impulse affected the people of England at a moment when the country was undergoing a rapid and, on the whole, a peaceful expansion—when the national spirit soared high, and when the development of the language and the forms of versification had reached a point which made possible the most triumphant literary achievement which that country has seen.

THE DRAMA BEFORE SHAKESPEARE

Throughout the Middle Ages the English drama, like that of other European countries, was mainly religious and didactic, its chief forms being the Miracle Plays, which presented in crude dialogue stories from the Bible and the lives of the saints, and the Moralities, which taught lessons for the guidance of life through the means of allegorical action and the personification of abstract qualities. Both forms were severely limited in their oportunities for picturing human nature and human life with breadth and variety. With the revival of learning came naturally the study and imitation of the ancient classical drama, and in some countries this proved the chief influence in determining the prevalent type of drama for generations to come. But in England, though we can trace important results of the models given by Seneca in tragedy and Plautus in comedy, the main characteristics of the drama of the Elizabethan age were of native origin, and reflected the spirit and the interests of the Englishmen of that day.

THE CHRONICLE HISTORY

Of the various forms which this drama took, the first to reach a culmination was the so-called Chronicle History. This is represented in The Harvard Classics by the "Edward II." [1] of Marlowe, the greatest of the predecessors of Shakespeare; and Shakespeare himself produced some ten plays belonging to the type. These dramas reflect the interest the Elizabethans took in the heroic past of their country, and before the vogue of this kind of play passed nearly the whole of English history for the previous three hundred years had been presented on the stage. As a form of dramatic art the Chronicle History had many defects and limitations. The facts of history do not always lend themselves to effective theatrical representation, and in the attempt to combine history and drama both frequently suffered. But suprisingly often the playwrights found opportunity for such studies of character as that of the King in Marlowe's tragedy, for real dramatic structure as in Shakespeare's "Richard III," or for the display of gorgeous rhetoric and national exultation as in "Henry V." These plays should not be judged by comparison with the realism of the modern drama. The authors sought to give the actors fine lines to deliver, without seeking to imitate the manner of actual conversation; and if the story was conveyed interestingly and absorbingly, no further illusion was sought. If this implied some loss, it also made possible much splendid poetry.

ELIZABETHAN TRAGEDY

Closely connected with the historical plays was the early development of Tragedy. But in the search for themes, the dramatists soon broke away from fact, and the whole range of imaginative narrative also was searched for tragic subjects. While the work of Seneca accounts to some extent for the prevalence of such features as ghosts and the motive of revenge, the form of Tragedy that Shakespeare developed from the experiments of men like Marlowe and Kyd

[1] *Harvard Classics*, xlvi, 5ff. For "Doctor Faustus" see Professor Francke's article below.

was really a new and distinct type. Such classical restrictions as the unities of place and time, and the complete
separation of comedy and tragedy, were discarded, and there
resulted a series of plays which, while often marked by
lack of restraint, of regular form, of unity of tone, yet gave
a picture of human life as affected by sin and suffering
which in its richness, its variety, and its imaginative exuberance has never been equaled.

The greatest master of Tragedy was Shakespeare, and in
Tragedy he reached his greatest height. "Hamlet," [2] "King
Lear," [3] and "Macbeth" [4] are among his finest productions,
and they represent the noblest pitch of English genius. Of
these, "Hamlet" was perhaps most popular at the time of its
production, and it has held its interest and provoked discussion as perhaps no other play of any time or country has
done.

This is in part due to the splendor of its poetry, the
absorbing nature of the plot, and the vividness of the drawing of characters who marvelously combine individuality
with a universal and typical quality that makes them appeal
to people of all kinds and races. But much also is due to
the delineation of the hero, the subtlety of whose character
and the complexity of whose motives constitute a perpetual
challenge to our capacity for solving mysteries. "King
Lear" owes its appeal less to its tendency to rouse curiosity
than to its power to awe us with an overwhelming spectacle
of the suffering which folly and evil can cause and which
human nature can sustain. In spite of, or perhaps because
of, its intricacy of motive and superabundance of incident,
it is the most overwhelming of all in its effect on our emotions. Compared with it, "Macbeth" is a simple play, but
nowhere does one find a more masterly portrayal of the
moral disaster that falls upon the man who, seeing the light,
chooses the darkness.

Though first, Shakespeare was by no means alone in the
production of great tragedy. Contemporary with him or
immediately following came Jonson, Marston, Middleton,
Massinger, Ford, Shirley, and others, all producing brilliant
work; but the man who most nearly approached him in

[2] *H. C.*, xlvi, 87ff.　　[3] *H. C.*, xlvi, 203ff.　　[4] *H. C.*, xlvi, 305ff.

tragic intensity was John Webster. "The Duchess of Malfi" [5] is a favorable example of his ability to inspire terror and pity; and though his range is not comparable to that of Shakespeare, he is unsurpassed in his power of coining a phrase which casts a lurid light into the recesses of the human heart in moments of supreme passion.

ELIZABETHAN COMEDY

In the field of comedy, Shakespeare's supremacy is hardly less assured. From the nature of this kind of drama, we do not expect in it the depth of penetration into human motive or the call upon our profounder sympathies that we find in Tragedy; and the conventional happy ending of Comedy makes difficult the degree of truth to life that one expects in serious plays. Yet the comedies of Shakespeare are far from superficial. Those written in the middle of his career, such as "As You Like It" and "Twelfth Night," not only display with great skill many sides of human nature, but with indescribable lightness and grace introduce us to charming creations, speaking lines rich in poetry and sparkling with wit, and bring before our imaginations whole series of delightful scenes. "The Tempest" [6] does more than this. While it gives us again much of the charm of the earlier comedies, it is laden with the mellow wisdom of its author's riper years.

"The Alchemist," [7] representing the work of Ben Jonson, belongs to a type which Shakespeare hardly touched—the Realistic Comedy. It is a vivid satire on the forms of trickery prevailing in London about 1600—alchemy, astrology, and the like. The plot is constructed with the care and skill for which its author is famous; and though its main purpose is the exposure of fraud, and much of its interest lies in its picture of the time, yet, in the speeches of Sir Epicure Mammon, for instance, it contains some splendid poetry. Dekker's "Shoemaker's Holiday" [8] in a much gayer mood, shows us another side of London life, that of the respectable tradesfolk. Something of what Jonson and

[5] H. C., xlvii, 721ff.
[7] H. C., xlvii, 521ff.
[6] H. C., xlvi, 379ff.
[8] H. C., xlvii, 447ff.

Dekker do for the city, Massinger does for country life in his best known play, "A New Way to Pay Old Debts,"[9] one of the few Elizabethan dramas outside of Shakespeare which have held the stage down to our own time. Massinger's characters, like Jonson's, are apt to be more typical embodiments of tendencies, less individuals whom one comes to know, than Shakespeare's; yet this play retains its interest and power of rousing emotion as well as its moral significance. The "Philaster"[10] of Beaumont and Fletcher belongs to the same type of romantic drama as "The Tempest" —the type of play which belongs to Comedy by virtue of its happy ending, but contains incidents and passages in an all but tragic tone. Less convincing in characterization than Shakespeare, Beaumont and Fletcher yet amaze us by the brilliant effectiveness of individual scenes, and sprinkle their pages with speeches of poetry of great charm.

The dramas of the Elizabethan period printed in The Harvard Classics serve to give a taste of the quality of this literature at its highest, but cannot, of course, show the surprising amount of it, or indicate the extreme literary-historical interest of its rise and development. Seldom in the history of the world has the spirit of a period found so adequate an expression in literature as the Elizabethan spirit did in the drama; seldom can we see so completely manifested the growth, maturity, and decline of a literary form. But beyond these historical considerations, we are drawn to the reading of Shakespeare and his contemporaries by the attraction of their profound and sympathetic knowledge of mankind and its possibilities for suffering and joy, for sin and nobility, by the entertainment afforded by their dramatic skill in the presentation of their stories, and by the superb poetry that they lavished so profusely on their lines.

[9] *H. C.*, xlvii, 819ff.   [10] *H. C.*, xlvii, 639ff.

IV. THE FAUST LEGEND

By Professor Kuno Francke

THE Faust legend is a conglomerate of anonymous popular traditions, largely of mediæval origin, which in the latter part of the sixteenth century came to be associated with an actual individual of the name of Faustus whose notorious career during the first four decades of the century, as a pseudoscientific mountebank, juggler, and magician, can be traced through various parts of Germany. The "Faust Book" of 1587, the earliest collection of these tales, is of prevailingly theological character. It represents Faust as a sinner and reprobate, and it holds up his compact with Mephistophiles and his subsequent damnation as an example of human recklessness and as a warning to the faithful to cling to the orthodox means of Christian salvation.

THE ELIZABETHAN "DOCTOR FAUSTUS"

From this "Faust Book," that is, from its English translation, which appeared in 1588, Marlowe took his tragedy of "Dr. Faustus"[1] (1589; published 1604). In Marlowe's drama Faust appears as a typical man of the Renaissance, as an explorer and adventurer, as a superman craving for extraordinary power, wealth, enjoyment, and wordly eminence. The finer emotions are hardly touched upon. Mephistophiles is the mediæval devil, harsh and grim and fierce, bent on seduction, without any comprehension of human aspirations. Helen of Troy is a she-devil, and becomes the final means of Faust's destruction. Faust's career has hardly an element of true greatness. None of the many tricks, conjurings, and miracles, which Faust performs with Mephistophiles's help, has any relation to the deeper mean-

[1] *Harvard Classics,* xix, 199.

ing of life. They are mostly mere pastimes and vanity.
From the compact on to the end hardly anything happens
which brings Faust inwardly nearer either to heaven or hell.
But there is a sturdiness of character and stirring intensity
of action, with a happy admixture of buffoonery, through it
all. And we feel something of the pathos and paradox of
human passions in the fearful agony of Faust's final doom.

THE LEGEND IN GERMAN POPULAR DRAMA

The German popular Faust drama of the seventeenth century, and its outgrowth, the puppet plays, are a reflex both
of Marlowe's tragedy and the "Faust Book" of 1587, although they contain a number of original scenes, notably
the Council of the Devils at the beginning. Here again
the underlying sentiment is the abhorrence of human recklessness and extravagance. In some of these plays the
vanity of bold ambition is brought out with particular emphasis through the contrast between the daring and dissatisfied Faust and his farcical counterpart, the jolly and
contented Casperle.

In the last scene, while Faust in despair and contrition is
waiting for the sound of the midnight bell which is to be
the signal of his destruction, Casperle, as night watchman,
patrols the streets of the town calling out the hours and
singing the traditional verses of admonition to quiet and
orderly conduct.

To the sixteenth and seventeenth centuries, then, Faust
appeared as a criminal who sins against the eternal laws of
life, as a rebel against holiness who ruins his better self and
finally receives the merited reward of his misdeeds. He
could not appear thus to the eighteenth century. The
eighteenth century is the age of Rationalism and of Romanticism. The eighteenth century glorifies human reason and
human feeling. The rights of man and the dignity of man
are its principal watchwords. Such an age was bound to see
in Faust a representative of true humanity, a champion of
freedom, nature, truth. Such an age was bound to see
in Faust a symbol of human striving for completeness of
life.

THE VERSION OF LESSING

It is Lessing who has given to the Faust Legend this turn. His "Faust," unfortunately consisting only of a few fragmentary sketches, is a defense of Rationalism. The most important of these fragments, preserved to us in copies by some friends of Lessing's, is the prelude, a council of devils. Satan is receiving reports from his subordinates as to what they have done to bring harm to the realm of God. The first devil who speaks has set the hut of some pious poor on fire; the second has buried a fleet of usurers in the waves. Both excite Satan's disgust. "For," he says, "to make the pious poor still poorer means only to chain him all the more firmly to God"; and the usurers, if, instead of being buried in the waves, they had been allowed to reach the goal of their voyage, would have wrought new evil on distant shores.

Much more satisfied is Satan with the report of a third devil, who has stolen the first kiss from a young, innocent girl and thereby breathed the flame of desire into her veins; for he has worked evil in the world of spirit, and that means much more and is a much greater triumph for hell than to work evil in the world of bodies. But it is the fourth devil to whom Satan gives the prize. He has not done anything as yet. He has only a plan, but a plan which, if carried out, would put the deeds of all the other devils into the shade— the plan "to snatch from God his favorite." This favorite of God is Faust, "a solitary, brooding youth, renouncing all passion except the passion for truth, entirely living in truth, entirely absorbed in it." To snatch him from God—that would be a victory over which the whole realm of night would rejoice. Satan is enchanted; the war against truth is his element. Yes, Faust must be seduced, he must be destroyed. And he shall be destroyed through his very aspiration. "Didst thou not say he has desire for knowledge? That is enough for perdition!" His striving for truth is to lead him into darkness. With such exclamations the devils break up, to set about their work of seduction; but, as they are breaking up, there is heard from above a divine voice: "Ye shall not conquer."

GOETHE'S EARLIER AND LATER TREATMENTS

It cannot be denied that Goethe's earliest Faust conception, the so-called "Urfaust" of 1773 and 1774, lacks the wide sweep of thought that characterizes these fragments of Lessing's drama. His Faust of the Storm and Stress period is essentially a Romanticist. He is a dreamer, craving for a sight of the divine, longing to fathom the inner working of nature, drunk with the mysteries of the universe. But he is also an unruly individualist, a reckless despiser of accepted morality; and it is hard to see how his relation with Gretchen, which forms by far the largest part of the "Urfaust," can lead to anything but a tragic catastrophe. Only Goethe's second Faust [2] conception, which sets in with the end of the nineties of the eighteenth century, opens up a clear view of the heights of life.

Goethe was now in the full maturity of his powers, a man widely separated from the impetuous youth of the seventies whose Promethean emotions had burst forth with volcanic passion. He had meanwhile become a statesman and philosopher. He had come to know in the court of Weimar a model of paternal government, conservative yet liberally inclined, and friendly to all higher culture. He had found in his truly spiritual relation to Frau von Stein a safe harbor for his tempestuous feelings. He had been brought face to face, during his sojourn in Italy, with the wonders of classic art. The study of Spinoza and his own scientific investigations had confirmed him in a thoroughly monistic view of the world and strengthened his belief in a universal law which makes evil itself an integral part of the good. The example of Schiller as well as his own practical experience had taught him that the untrammeled living out of personality must go hand in hand with incessant work for the common welfare of mankind. All this is reflected in the completed *Part First* of 1808; it finds its most comprehensive expression in *Part Second,* the bequest of the dying poet to posterity.

Restless endeavor, incessant striving from lower spheres of life to higher ones, from the sensuous to the spiritual, from enjoyment to work, from creed to deed, from self to humanity—this is the moving thought of Goethe's completed

[2] *H. C.,* xix, 7ff.

"Faust." The keynote is struck in the "Prologue in Heaven." Faust, so we hear, the daring idealist, the servant of God, is to be tempted by Mephisto, the despiser of reason, the materialistic scoffer. But we also hear, and we hear it from God's own lips, that the tempter will not succeed. God allows the devil free play, because he knows that he will frustrate his own ends. Faust will be led astray—"man errs while he strives"; but he will not abandon his higher aspirations; through aberration and sin he will find the true way toward which his inner nature instinctively guides him. He will not eat dust. Even in the compact with Mephisto the same ineradicable optimism asserts itself. Faust's wager with the devil is nothing but an act of temporary despair, and the very fact that he does not hope anything from it shows that he will win it. He knows that sensual enjoyment will never give him satisfaction; he knows that, as long as he gives himself up to self-gratification, there will never be a moment to which he would say: "Abide, thou art so fair!" From the outset we feel that by living up to the very terms of the compact, Faust will rise superior to it; that by rushing into the whirlpool of earthly experience and passion his being will be heightened and expanded.

And thus everything in the whole drama, all its incidents and all its characters, become episodes in the rounding out of this grand, all-comprehensive personality. Gretchen and Helena, Wagner and Mephisto, Homunculus and Euphorion, the Emperor's court and the shades of the Greek past, the broodings of mediæval mysticism and the practical tasks of modern industrialism, the enlightened despotism of the eighteenth century and the ideal democracy of the future—all this and a great deal more enters into Faust's being and is absorbed by him. He strides on from experience to experience, from task to task, expiating guilt by doing, losing himself, and finding himself again. Blinded in old age by Dame Care, he feels a new light kindled within. Dying, he gazes into a far future. And even in the heavenly regions he goes on ever changing into new and higher and finer forms. It is this irrepressible spirit of striving which makes Goethe's "Faust" the Bible of modern humanity.[3]

* For further critical comments on Goethe, see General Index, H. C., 1.

V. MODERN ENGLISH DRAMA

By Dr. Ernest Bernbaum

THE modern English drama is represented in The Harvard Classics by two comedies of the eighteenth century and by four tragedies of the seventeenth and the nineteenth. Since literary fashions change from age to age, and since the authors of these plays were, even when contemporaries, men of markedly different tastes, it is natural that the six dramas should be more or less conspicuously dissimilar. Each is great because it follows an ideal; each is great in a different way because its ideal is not that of the others. Which of these ideals is absolutely the best, is a question that critics have much debated, sometimes acrimoniously: Dryden has been pitted against Shakespeare, Goldsmith against Sheridan, Shelley against Browning, and so on. Interesting as such contentions may be, they tend to obscure rather than enlighten the mind of him who approaches these plays simply with the desire to enjoy each to the full. To him comparisons are odious because, instead of leading him to appreciate many plays of many kinds, they may confine his enjoyment to those of one school. Yet, though he may set aside the vexatious question of the relative worth of the purposes that inspired these dramatists, he will not gain the greatest possible delight from them until he understands what each of them was trying to do.

GOLDSMITH AND "SHE STOOPS TO CONQUER"

Genial Goldsmith[1] delighted in the kind of humor that is characteristic of "the plain people" and that is spontaneously enjoyed by them. The accidental predicaments into which all of us stumble, to our embarrassment and the amusement of bystanders; the blunders of well-meaning but untrained

[1] *Harvard Classics*, xviii, 203.

servants; the practical jokes, without malice, that ever delight youth; the shy awkwardness of lovers; even the clownish tavern jest and joviality; these are in Goldsmith's merry eyes sources of wholesome laughter. It troubles him not that Young Marlow continues to believe a country house an inn, and the host's daughter a maidservant, nor that Mrs. Hardcastle mistakes her own garden for a distant heath; he ignores the improbability of such situations as arouse instinctive laughter. It is the unsophisticated human beings who blunder in and out of these straits that he wishes to depict; and he draws simple folk like Mr. and Mrs. Hardcastle, Tony Lumpkin, and Diggory, with extraordinary zest, fidelity, and kindly yet shrewd humor.

SHERIDAN AND "THE SCHOOL FOR SCANDAL"

Sheridan, the statesman, orator, and wit, wrote of the fashionable world, and for it. In conformity with its conventional existence, and its taste for regularity, he admitted no improbabilities into the plot of "The School for Scandal." [2] As men and women of fashion tried to be elegant, witty, or epigrammatic in speech, he aimed to bestow like graces upon the dialogue of his personages—to make Joseph Surface sententious, Charles sprightly, Lady Teazle invincible in repartee. To a society that was too fastidious to be entertained by naive simplicity, rude manners, and boisterous merriment, Sheridan wanted to reveal the comic aspects of its usual life. He laughed at the scandal mongers who, after tearing others' reputations to tatters, departed without a shred of their own, at the foolish though innocent young wife who was fascinated by the perilous pleasures of a fast set, and at the affected young hypocrite whose devious schemes undid him. He was not without kindliness of heart, as the humor of the final scene between Sir Peter and Lady Teazle shows; but satire was his aim.

DRYDEN AND "ALL FOR LOVE"

Like most tragedies, Dryden's "All for Love," [3] shows the pitiable outcome of a struggle between good and evil.

---

[2] *H. C.,* xviii, 105.   [3] *H. C.,* xviii, 21.

Among the innumerable manifestations of this eternal strife there are some which attract by their singularity, but these were not of interest to Dryden. To him the really important tragic conflicts were those which are frequent in human life, such as that between duty and passion. He chose the theme of Antony and Cleopatra, not because it was new or extraordinary, but because it was a noble illustration of a normal dilemma of human existence. He knew of course that the defeat in the decisive battle of Actium of the last kingdom of the Grecian empire by triumphant Rome was epoch making,[4] and offered superb opportunities for historical and scenic contrasts; but he did not wish to write a "world drama." When he raises the curtain, Actium has already been fought and the destiny of nations decided; what remains is the personal fate of Antony and of Cleopatra, the former vainly though nobly endeavoring to reanimate his former manhood and loyalty, the latter trying amid the wreck to save her domination over him, and each tortured by lack of true faith in the other. Their emotions in the brief final crisis of their lives Dryden sought to trace with clearness and truth to nature, and to express with majestic simplicity.

SHELLEY AND "THE CENCI"

When Shelley in his preface to "The Cenci"[5] speaks of "teaching the human heart, through its sympathies and antipathies, the knowledge of itself," he expresses intentions not widely different from those of all dramatists, including Dryden; but when he mentions his desire to "make apparent some of the most dark and secret caverns of the human heart," he indicates his own predilection. This he followed in choosing as his subject a "dark and secret" crime, the situation into which the monstrous Cenci forces Beatrice being unspeakable and abnormal. As suitable backgrounds, Shelley selects a sinister banquet, a gloomy castle at night, and a prison with instruments of torture. Yet he wishes not to fix attention upon physical horrors, but to use them to

---

[4] "Lectures on Dr. Eliot's Five-Foot Shelf of Books," History, p. 7.
[5] H. C., xviii, 281.

call forth in his characters extreme revelations of vice and virtue. He feels that only under such dread circumstances can the deepest potentialities of human nature be displayed. The very extremity of Beatrice's plight lays bare the core of her womanhood, revealing to the full the sensitiveness of chastity and the courage of innocence.

BYRON AND "MANFRED"

Byron, like Shelley, sought what lay beyond the commonplace, but found it in another aspect of life. His "Manfred"[6] succumbs not to man or society, but in a solitary struggle with the mysteries of Nature. From her he has wrested secrets, her forces he has learned to command; but his proud knowledge and power have been gained by stifling the social feelings of humanity, and his life is now a penitent search for oblivion, in which science, philosophy, and religion can give him no consolation. "I was," he laments, "my own destroyer, and will be my own Hereafter!" Byron's temperament enabled him to fathom a lonely soul like Manfred's, and urged him to express its passions with fiery vigor. The subject offered almost insuperable obstacles to dramatic treatment, since most of the forces that acted upon Manfred were either abstractions or inanimate objects. Byron, however, felt, and used all the energy of his imagination to make us feel, that these physical phenomena and laws were not vague or dead things, but that earth and air, mountains and cataracts, were to the distracted wanderer real personalities, and exercised upon him an influence more intimate than that of any fellow man.

BROWNING AND "A BLOT IN THE 'SCUTCHEON"

With Browning's "A Blot in the 'Scutcheon"[7] we return to the kind of tragedy that arises amid normal conditions of life. Yet here again a peculiar aspect of the tragic is emphasized. Both Dryden's Antony and Shelley's Cenci know clearly that they are committing wrong. Browning perceived that there are tragic cases in which a character acts

[6] H. C., xviii, 403.   [7] H. C., xviii, 357.

in accordance with his highest moral standard, and comes too late to realize that his standard is false or inapplicable. The personages in "A Blot in the 'Scutcheon" are of admirable nobility, and among them Thorold is not the least scrupulously conscientious, but the code of honor which he loyally obeys becomes an instrument of fatal cruelty. The very intensity with which he looks up to a splendid ideal blinds his judgment regarding the apparent dishonor of his beloved sister, so that he fails to see "through the surface of crime a depth of purity unmovable." It is thus a subtle as well as a natural course of events that Browning aims to trace, and only a rich and pregnant style could express the complex thoughts and feelings of so highly cultivated and exquisitely sensitive beings as his Thorold, Mildred, and Guendolen.

The reader of these six dramas who understands their main purposes will surely admire the conscientious manner in which those aims are carried out. He will perceive that the plot, characterization, and dialogue of each are designed with remarkable skill to conform to its dominant ideal. In fact, the chief reason why these plays are among the very, very few dramatic masterpieces of their time is that their authors clearly knew what they wanted to do, and came about as near to doing it as human limitations permit. The different means they had to employ interestingly exhibit the varieties of dramatic technique; and the diverse views of human life that they held serve to enlarge the bounds of our sympathy with many sorts and conditions of men.

VOYAGES AND TRAVEL

I. GENERAL INTRODUCTION

By Professor R. B. Dixon

For to admire and for to see,
For to behold this world so wide.

IT IS probable that from the very earliest times the spirit of these familiar lines has been a potent factor in human history. One might be led, because of the marked development of curiosity in monkeys and apes, to suppose that, even before the complete development of the human type had been attained, our precursors were tempted to explore beyond their customary haunts. Be that as it may, it seems certain that the first spread of the human race over the face of the globe must have been preceded by more or less conscious exploration and travel. As population grew and began to press upon the food supply and available hunting grounds, and the need for expansion and emigration was recognized, the relative availability and attractiveness of the country in different directions must have been investigated, and movement have taken place toward the most favorable. This would, of course, not hold true where movement was due to war or the pressure of conquest, but much of this earliest movement of peoples must have been largely voluntary. Travel has thus in these primitive scouts and explorers its earliest exponents, and the history of travel is seen to be as old as the race.

PREHISTORIC TRAVEL

This primitive travel was moreover in the truest sense exploration, for these travelers were the first to penetrate into lands wholly unknown and previously untrodden by the feet of man. Once the greater part of the world was over-run, however, the need for travel was by no means at an end. Intensive exploration in the search for the best hunting grounds and fishing places, or, with the advent of agriculture, for suitable and fertile soils, must have continued for generations. During the long period in which human civilization has been developing it is clear, moreover, that in the shifting of populations, which has constantly been going on, the same areas have thus been explored again and again, now by this people, now by that. Of these countless travels and travelers, little definite trace of course remains, and it is only with the beginning of the historic period that records of travel become available.

Although of this prehistoric travel we can find no accounts, yet we can gain some idea of its character from observation of the savage and barbarous peoples of the world to-day. Now, as then probably, there are sedentary, stay-at-home peoples, contented to live and die within a narrow horizon, people whose individual radius of travel may in a whole lifetime not exceed a score of miles, and whom neither commerce nor conquest can tempt beyond their own small sphere. Now, as then, there are other peoples in whom the spirit of travel is strong, in whom is a great restlessness, an inborn tendency to wander in quest of food or trade or conquest. The radius of travel of a single individual in such a tribe may, as for example in the case of certain Eskimos, reach as much as a thousand miles. But such extensive wanderings are, on the whole, rare among savage peoples, and we may well admire the courage and skill of those old Polynesian travelers who, according to tradition, dared in their small canoes to push their search for new lands far to the south beyond their sunny seas, until they reached the fogs and drift ice of the Antarctic.

THE MOTIVE OF THE TRUE EXPLORER

Leaving this period of early and unrecorded travel, however, and turning to historic times, two facts force themselves upon our attention, first that the volume of travel has apparently been constantly increasing, and, second, that the motives which induce men to travel are of many kinds; that there are indeed many sorts of travelers.

First by right comes the true explorer, for whom travel is not a means, but an end in itself. For others religion, commerce, science, may be the goal, the "long trail," with all its beauties, its hardships, and its dangers, mere incidents along the way. Not so for the true explorer. Impelled by an inborn curiosity, an intense craving to see new lands, new peoples, and driven by an incurable restlessness of spirit, he penetrates to the remotest corners of the earth, braving every danger, surmounting every difficulty, and asks but little of the world in the way of tangible returns. For him the life of the trail, the triumph over obstacles, the thrill of danger, are things in themselves desirable and beyond price; his reward lies not in the attainment, but in the quest. There may be few indeed for whom no other motives enter, but it is nevertheless true that for most great travelers, however much they may deceive themselves into thinking that they follow other and, as they believe, higher calls, it is the master motive.

THE MOTIVE OF CONQUEST

A different force, but one which has at all times been effective, is that of war or conquest. To the explorer enrichment of experience, not increase of possessions, is the aim; he does not care to whom the world belongs if only he may be free to travel therein. The conqueror, however, demands possession, and the lust for it and for revenge has, in the case of savage and civilized alike, led men into distant lands and among strange people. From the Iroquois who, sometimes alone, sometimes in company with a handful of others, went from the Hudson a thousand miles westward to the Mississippi to strike a blow at the hated Sioux, to Attila and the other leaders of those hordes which poured their thousands into mediæval Europe from the farthest East; from Alexander and his conquest of most of the old world to Cortez and Pizarro and their conquest of much of the new, in varying degree and at different times war has made of the conqueror a traveler. To such as these it is not the beauty but the wealth of a country that makes it desirable, and interest in its people lies more in their exploitation than in any other field.

THE MOTIVE OF RELIGION

Another very potent incentive to travel has been religion. From its influence have developed the pilgrim and the missionary, types which have furnished some of the greatest travelers of historic times. Pilgrims, led by the desire to visit the holy places of their faith, often undertake journeys of great length and difficulty. Singly or in companies they traverse their hundreds or thousands of miles, their eyes fixed always on the distant goal, and too absorbed in anticipation of the things to be to take notice of the things about them as they go. Treading the same paths which generations before them have trod, whose ups and downs, whose hardships and dangers have become a matter of tradition, they follow like sheep in each other's footsteps. So they have journeyed and still journey in their thousands, century after century; in early times from China and other parts of Asia to the sacred places of India; from the uttermost parts of Europe to Jerusalem in the Middle Ages; from every corner of the Mohammedan world to Mecca to-day. Each and all are seeking for salvation, for all the reward is of the spirit; we may not blame them, therefore, that they do not heed the world through which they pass.

In one sense pilgrim travel may be said to be centripetal, in that it draws the traveler by known roads to some great center of his faith; missionary travel on the other hand may be said to be centrifugal, in that it leads away from these centers, by untraveled paths into the unknown. Thus the missonary, far more than the pilgrim, has been an explorer; and whether it be the early Buddhist monks who brought their faith from India to much of eastern and southeastern Asia; or Christians who have preached their doctrines in every clime; or fierce followers of the Prophet, who with the sword in one hand and the Koran in the other carried Islam alike to Spain and the Spice Islands of the East—all alike have journeyed far and faithfully, led always by the fire of their zeal. They had no foreknowledge of what they might expect, for them new vistas opened as they went; Mohammedans excepted, their lives were spent, their journeys were made, not for their own but for others' sake; and their interest or pity was aroused in no small degree in the strange peoples whose souls they went to save. It is not surprising, therefore, that they should show a keener interest in what they saw, or that they should have left far more of record than the pilgrim has.

THE COMMERCIAL MOTIVE

Great as has been the influence of conquest and religion upon travel, a greater impulse and one leading to even wider results has been that of trade and commerce. In earlier times in search of foreign commodities and products, in modern days of new markets to which to export the products of home manufacture, men have penetrated to the ends of the earth, and to this commercial impulse is attributable most of the great travels and explorations from the thirteenth century to the beginning of modern scientific exploration at the end of the eighteenth. To the merchant traveler, even more than to the missionary, observation of the country and its products, its peoples and their needs, is important. The easiest and safest roads by which his merchandise may be transported, new materials, new sources, new markets, are the basis of his success; and the character and customs of the people are of vital import in the prosecution of his work. A new and shorter road gives him an advantage over his competitors, and it was this search for new ways to reach the Indies which led to the greatest fifty years in the whole history of travel—a period in which the area of the world as known to civilized Europe was far more than doubled.[1]

THE SCIENTIFIC MOTIVE

Although purely scientific curiosity became an important element of travel only toward the end of the eighteenth

[1] See *Harvard Classics*, xliii, 22, 29, 47; xxxiii, 133, 207, 237, 271, 321; and the lecture below on "The Elizabethan Adventurers."

century, there were in earlier times a few for whom this was a great incentive. To seek for knowledge for its own sake, to be fired with the desire to extend, if only by a little, the limits of the known, is not wholly a modern trait; but before this could be in large measure an important factor, the extraordinary widening and development of scientific interest characteristic of the last century and a half was necessary. Each has, however, contributed to the advance of the other, and the vast additions to knowledge gained by scientific exploration have in large degree provided the materials from which the present structure of science has been built. As once for religion, so now for science men plunge into the unknown; now as then they strive, not for themselves, but for an ideal.

Travel is then, as we have seen, as old as the human race, and of travelers there are and have been many kinds, according to the motives which induced them to fare forth. The records of these many travelers form a body of literature whose interest is undying, for besides the facts which they have gathered, and the additions to our knowledge which they have made, they give us often a clear and vivid picture of the character of the travelers themselves, their courage in the face of danger, their patience in overcoming every kind of obstacle; and heroism and self-sacrifice of the truest and highest types have been exemplified again and again in their lives. Of all these many travelers but a part have left a record, and, as might be expected, the earlier have left far less than those of later times. From the historical point of view, the records fall into several fairly definite groups or periods, each differing from the other not only in time, but also to a considerable extent in the character of the motive which was dominant.

THE FIRST PERIOD OF RECORDED TRAVEL

The first or early period may be said to begin about the fifth century B. C. with Herodotus,[2] who in his travels in Egypt, Babylonia, and Persia gives us our first accurate accounts of those countries, and seems to be one of the earliest

[2] *H. C.*, xxxiii, 5ff.; and lecture on "Herodotus on Egypt," below.

of scientific travelers. He traveled widely, gathered information assiduously both as to the actual condition and the history of the countries he visited, and seems to have been an accurate and painstaking observer. The bold explorations of the Carthaginian Hanno, at about this same time, along the west coast of Africa possibly as far as the Gulf of Guinea, were designed to extend the growing commerce of this great mercantile people, and show how, even at this early date, trade was one of the most potent incentives to travel. It is perhaps of interest to note that on this expedition gorillas were seen apparently for the first time, being described as hairy men of great ferocity and strength. Several of them were captured, and Hanno attempted to carry them back to Carthage alive, but was forced to kill them because of their violence, and so brought back only their skins. A century or so later, the expedition of Alexander, while primarily actuated by the desire for conquest, was also in part exploratory, and resulted not only in bringing back the earliest authentic accounts of India, but demonstrated the feasibility of reaching that country by sea. With the rise of the Roman Empire, this early period came to an end, and from then on until the fourth or fifth century is a time of relative quiescence, during which the attention of the Mediterranean world was devoted to the intensive occupation of the world as already known, rather than to exploration beyond those limits.

THE SECOND PERIOD—PILGRIMS AND MISSIONARIES

With the fourth century, however, the second period begins and lasts for some seven or eight hundred years. Perhaps the most characteristic feature of travel during this time was the prominence of the religious motive, for the travelers were largely pilgrims and missionaries, or, toward the latter end, those who, making religion their war cry, journeyed as Crusaders to wrest Jerusalem from the Saracen. The pilgrim, as already pointed out, was, although a traveler, usually an unobservant one; his interest was centered in his goal and in the spiritual benefits which were to accrue from his long and perilous journey, so that for the incidents of the day he had little care. To a large extent, also, the pilgrims were humble folk, illiterate, unlearned, and so left as a rule no records of what they saw. There were, of course, exceptions, and many persons of high rank as well as some scholarly attainment were to be found among the throngs who from all parts of Europe made the journey to Palestine. Not all the pilgrims, it should be noted, were men, for both during the early as well as the later portions of the period many women performed the arduous trip.[3] Such, for example, was Sylvia of Aquitaine, apparently a woman of rank, who about 380 not only visited Jerusalem and the usual sacred places, but went on into parts of Arabia and Mesopotamia, and has left brief but interesting accounts of her years of travel. She may thus be considered one of the first great woman travelers. In the seventh and eighth centuries the volume of pilgrim travel seems to have increased, or at least we have more abundant records of it; and in the accounts left by Willibald, a man of rank apparently from Kent, we have one of the earliest stories of English travel. This pilgrim gives us an interesting incident of his return journey from Palestine. It seems that he wished to bring back with him to England a supply of a certain balsam, but feared that this would be taken from him by the customs officials whose duty it was to see that none of this precious substance left the country. Accordingly he devised an ingenious smuggling scheme. Taking a reed which was of a size such that it exactly fitted the mouth of the calabash in which the balsam was contained, he plugged up one end and filled the tube thus formed with petroleum. This he carefully inserted into the opening, cutting off the end flush with the mouth of the calabash and inserting a stopper. On arriving at Acre the customs officials searched his luggage, found the calabash and opened it, but seeing and smelling only the petroleum, suspected nothing and allowed him to pass. From this it is clear that travelers of old as well as modern times were more or less at the mercy of customs regulations, and that then as now they took such means as they could to evade the laws.

[3] Cf. The Wife of Bath in Chaucer's Prologue to "The Canterbury Tales," H. C., xl, 24.

Although in Europe the records of pilgrim travel are not only meager but generally disappointing in their brevity and lack of detail, conditions were somewhat different in far-away China. There, although the number of pilgrims was much smaller, the records which they left were of much greater value. The names of two of the Chinese pilgrims stand out as of particular importance, those namely of Fa Hian and of Hiuen Thsang. Journeying to India from northern China to visit the places made holy by the life and death of Gautama, the Buddha, and to consult and copy some of the sacred writings, they have left us records which are not only of the greatest interest as stories of travel, but which are of quite inestimable value as giving practically the only information to be had in regard to the condition of India and the life of its people at this time. Both pilgrims journeyed to India by way of Turkestan and across the Pamirs, and the former returned, after nearly fifteen years of travel, from Ceylon by sea to his home. Both give very full and detailed accounts of all that they saw and heard, and both show far more than the European travelers of the time an appreciation of the beauties of the scenery through which they passed. That travelers then as now, and of other races as well as our own, felt at times their loneliness and yearned to return, is shown by an incident related by Fa Hian. He had then been absent from his home living among strange people in strange lands for nearly fifteen years, when one day in Ceylon he saw in the hands of a merchant a small Chinese fan of white silk which had found its way thither. The sight of this, he says, brought back to him so keenly thoughts of his home that he was able to endure his exile no longer, so soon after set out on his return journey, and after many perils by the way ultimately reached his native place.

The poverty of record which characterizes the pilgrim travel of Europe at this time is even more marked in the case of those who were led by missionary zeal. The two directions in which missionary enterprise seems to have been most marked at this period were south to Abyssinia, and east to China and India. Of the former we have but the slightest record, of the latter practically none at all.

That missionary activity was great throughout India, Central Asia, and China, however, we know from various sources. The Nestorian missions which were thus founded between the seventh and the ninth centuries are known to have been abundant, and the missionaries must have been great travelers for they seem to have penetrated throughout much of China and widely along the Indian coasts, but of records they left nothing. Indeed their names are not even known for the most part, although two, Olopan and Kiho, are given in the Chinese annals. Curiously enough, it is at the opposite end of the world that the other missionary travelers of the time are found, namely in Ireland. Here there are a few accounts of explorations northward to the Faroes and Iceland during the eighth century, but little information of value was recorded.

MOHAMMEDAN PROPAGANDA

Another and very important group of travelers during this period were the Arabs. With the rise of Mohammedanism in the seventh century a strong impulse, in part due to missionary fervor, in part to a desire for conquest, was given to Arab travel. For some time previous to the Hegira, merchants and others from Arabia had visited Ceylon, India, and the African coast, but with the rapid spread of Islam this trade was greatly stimulated, as the militant forces of the faith carried the banner of the Prophet with unexampled rapidity not only to Central Asia, China, and the east African shores, but into western Europe as well. The missionary conquerors themselves have left little in the way of record of their journeys, but the traders and travelers who followed in their wake have. We have thus a case in which the religious impulse, combined with that of conquest, impelled many to travel, and also prepared the way for a host of others whose journeyings would not have been made had not the former paved the way. Perhaps the best known of these early Arab travelers are Soleyman and Masoudi; the first a merchant who in the course of his business journeyed as far as the Chinese coast; the second more a geographer-traveler, who not only visited and described the Far East, but also the African coasts as well. Both, and particularly the latter, have left voluminous records of their travels, and give us many interesting glimpses into the life and conditions of their day. In many ways of greater interest were the numerous less known travelers, for on some of their accounts, now in part lost, the familiar voyages of Sindbad the Sailor[4] in the collection known to us as the Arabian Nights were based. It is possible to identify with a fair degree of accuracy many of the places referred to in those well-known exploits; India, Ceylon, Madagascar, and China are all among the localities visited by that redoubtable sailor; his accounts of the gathering of camphor represent the actual process as employed in the Indian Archipelago; and without much doubt the famous Old Man of the Sea refers to the orang-utan of Sumatra and the adjacent regions. Not only did the Arabs themselves thus become great travelers, but they also supplied the means by which in large measure the great development of travel in the fifteenth and sixteenth centuries was made possible. From their contact with the Chinese the Arabs learned the use of the compass, and from them it passed to the sailors of the Mediterranean, thus bringing to European navigators one of the means which enabled them to prosecute those long sea voyages, resulting among other things in the discovery of the New World.

THE VIKINGS AND THE CRUSADERS

Although religion and religious motives were thus directly or indirectly the dominant features of the travel of this period, they were not the only ones, and if the spirit of exploration was almost dormant in the lands about the Mediterranean, it was very much alive in northern Europe. Beginning at first in piratical raids to the southward along the rich coasts of France and Spain, the Vikings, the "men of the fiords," after a time turned their attention westward, and in the spirit of true discovery pushed out into the unknown Atlantic. Here they first reached Iceland, then Greenland, and at last in the eleventh century the northern

[4] *H. C.,* xvi, 242-309.

shores of America. In the sagas the records of many of these voyages are preserved, and in the Saga of Eric the Red[5] we have the first account, albeit a meager one, of the New World.

Following close upon this activity of the Norsemen in the north of Europe there begins a new period, in which there is a great revival of interest in travel among the nations farther south. This was in part a continuation of the religious travel of the previous period, now transformed into the militancy of the Crusaders; in part due to political events occurring far away in China; and in part to a great and rapid development of trade. So far as the Crusaders are concerned they may be considered largely as military pilgrims who sought to drive the Moslem conqueror from the holy places of their faith. Like the peaceful pilgrims of an earlier age, they were inflamed by a great purpose which kept their eyes and thoughts upon their goal. They have left, it is true, considerable in the way of record, but as travelers their importance falls far behind others of a different type.

THE EXTENSION OF THE MONGOL EMPIRE

One of the most important, perhaps the most important, event of the thirteenth century was the sudden rise of the great Mongol power in eastern Asia under Genghiz Khan. Once secure in the East, the Mongols turned their attention toward the West, swept through all Central Asia, and invaded Europe. Although they were repulsed at the battle of Liegnitz in 1241, Europe feared for the future, and accordingly a diplomatic mission was sent by the Pope to the capital of the Great Khan. Of these ambassadors the most important was the Franciscan, John of Plano Carpini. Two years were occupied by him on his mission, and he returned with a glowing account of the countries and peoples he had seen. Others followed, part diplomat, part missionary, such as Rubruquis, and as a result Europe for the first time began to realize the greatness and the wealth of this kingdom of Cathay. Merchants and traders were not slow to respond, and as Venice was then the leader in the eastern trade, it was not unnatural that her merchants should attempt to make use of the route to this rich market made known by the papal envoys. It was under these circumstances, then, that Marco Polo began his famous travels toward the end of the century.

For twenty years he was absent from his home, traveling during this time through most of Central Asia, China, and Tibet, and voyaging to Java and India from the China coasts, in large part as an appointed official of the Mongol Empire, which at this time under Kublai Khan was the greatest the world had ever seen. Returning at last to Europe, he fell into prison, and his wonderful story was only saved to the world by the interest of one of his fellow prisoners, who wrote it down from his lips. Polo's account is on the whole remarkably accurate, but as much cannot be said for some of the other travelers, merchants, or others of the time. Many showed great credulity in reporting all sorts of marvelous things, and on some of these accounts the famous but wholly mythical travels of Sir John Mandeville were based. This, in its day, most popular book seems to have been written by an obscure physician of Liege who, so far as is known, never left his native town. Thus the fabrication of travels is not by any means a wholly modern accomplishment. Great as were the achievements as travelers of Polo and other Europeans, their records are equaled or even surpassed by some of the Arabs who still showed until the fifteenth century great activity in this field. The greatest of these and of all Arab travelers was Ibn Batuta, a physician of Tangier. For twenty-five years he traveled uninterruptedly, visiting not only every part of the East and the Indian Archipelago, but the steppes of southern Russia, the east African coast as far as the equator, and crossed the Sahara to Timbuktu and the valley of the Niger on the west.

THE ROUTE TO THE INDIES

With the fifteenth century a sudden impetus was given to travel by the recently greatly developed trade with the Indies. The introduction of the compass had greatly stimu-

lated sea travel, and the closing of the overland routes to
the East, due to political conditions of the time, forced
Europe to seek for new routes by sea. From Portugal first,
under the influence of Prince Henry the Navigator, there
sailed a long series of travelers and explorers who sought a
way around Africa to the Indies. Little by little they edged
their way south along the western coast, until, six years
before Columbus[6] started on his great voyage, Diaz discovered and rounded the Cape of Good Hope, and eleven
years later was followed by Vasco de Gama who, passing
around the Cape, continued on to India. Three years later,
Cabral, bound for the same goal but steering too far to the
west, reached the Brazilian coast and established the claim
of Portugal to a great section of the southern New World.

While Portugal thus can claim for her travelers the discovery of most of southern Africa, to Spain falls the greater
honor of the unveiling of the New World. The discoveries
of the great Genoese were the signal for a host of other
explorers to follow, such as Vespucci,[7] who, sailing first for
Spain, discovered Venezuela, and later for Portugal, explored the South American coast as far as the La Plata.
The goal of all these travelers was the Indies and the discovery of a trade route thither, but it was not until the
second decade of the sixteenth century that Magellan, another Portuguese, although sailing in the service of the
Spanish king, at last succeeded in the quest. Far to the
south he found a passage through the wall that had stood
between Europe and the tempting markets of the East, and,
first to cross the great Pacific, reached the Philippines in
1521, only to be killed there in a skirmish with the natives.
Although he himself did not live to complete the remainder
of the voyage, one of his ships with a part of the original
crew returned to Spain by way of the Cape of Good Hope,
these men being thus the first to travel around the world.

THE EPOCH OF AMERICAN EXPLORATION

The first fifty years of the sixteenth century were so
crowded with explorations and conquests of new lands that

[6] *H. C.,* xliii, 22ff.   [7] *H. C.,* xliii, 29ff.

they may well be regarded as the most wonderful years in the whole history of travel. Not only were further great discoveries made by sea of new lands, but travelers such as Coronado in North and Orellana in South America, explored great areas and journeyed thousands of miles in the interior of the new continents—the latter traveler being the first to cross South America and to descend the Amazon. Cortez in Mexico and Pizarro in Peru, although led by somewhat different motives, traveled far and wide in their conquests of these, the two greatest and most cultured of the countries of the New World.

Although so great a mark was made during this period by Italian, Portuguese, and Spanish travelers, the nations of northern Europe soon entered the lists. England, France, and Holland began to take their part, and such names as Cabot, Cartier, and Hudson attest their prowess in the field. Raleigh's ill-fated expedition to Guiana,[8] and Drake's great achievement in circumnavigating the globe,[9] supply records of great interest, and bear witness to the part played by Englishmen in these stirring times. Drake and the sea rovers of the Elizabethan period[10] were largely actuated by the desire to attack and pillage the rich commerce of Spain in the New World; Raleigh, Gilbert,[11] and others, on the contrary, sought more the settlement and colonization of the new-found lands; yet the older impulse of the search for a shorter trade route to the East was still a factor, as one can see from the attempts by Frobisher, Davis, and others, to find the ever-elusive Northwest Passage.

With the beginning of the seventeenth century France supplies the names of many who deserve to rank among the great travelers of all time. Champlain, La Salle, Marquette, Verendrye, and many others both lay and cleric, were the pioneers in the exploration of New France, and the story of their journeys and lives forms a record of which any traveler might well be proud.

While France was thus engaged in America, the Dutch were no less bold explorers at the Antipodes. Although Australia had first been seen by the Spaniards in the middle

[8] *H. C.*, xxxiii, 321ff.   [9] *H. C.*, xxxiii, 207ff.
[10] See Lecture III, below.   [11] *H. C.*, xxxiii, 271ff.

of the previous century, the Dutch now, as the Portuguese before them had done in the case of Africa, began to push south along the western coast, their travels culminating in the expedition of Tasman, who not only showed that Australia was an island, but also was the first to see New Zealand.

THE PERIOD OF SCIENTIFIC TRAVEL

The last great period in the history of travel may be said to begin with the voyage of Captain Cook, who in 1768 sailed from England on what was virtually the first purely scientific expedition. The primary object was for the observation at the newly discovered Society Islands in the southern Pacific of the transit of Venus, an astronomical phenomenon in which the men of science of the time were much interested. Several scientists were among the members of the expedition, which was further charged with the duty of making collections and surveys. From this time on, in ever-increasing numbers individual travelers and great expeditions have scoured the world in order to observe and collect for scientific purposes. One after another the great nations of the world have taken up the task, until to-day the volume of scientific travel is immense. Darwin's famous voyage in the *Beagle*,[12] and Wallace's years of travel in the East Indies have revolutionized much of the science of our times, and show how great may be the outcome of travel when directed toward a purely ideal end. As part and parcel of this growth of science as an inspiration to travel, we have the splendid records of the search for the Poles. Here the goal was also an ideal, the price was shorn of any practical value, and trade and commercial motives were wholly barred; yet generation after generation men strove against tremendous odds, and faced suffering and death a thousand times in their attempts to reach these, the last strongholds of the unknown. The light that led them was, however, not alone the cold flame of ideal science, although for many this may indeed have burned with pale but steady glow; for them, perhaps as much as for any men, it was the fiercer flame which burns in the hearts of all true

[12] *H. C.*, xxix, 11ff.

explorers, for whom the doing is more than the deed, who go because in very truth they *must*.

Such a hasty glance at the history of travel from earliest times can do little more than suggest the vastness and the interest of the field. In so wide a prospect only the larger features of the landscape can be seen, and if we have, so to speak, had only glimpses of the higher mountain peaks, it does not follow that there is less of interest in the valleys that nestle at their feet. We have of necessity considered only the great travelers, the great journeys, but those more humble and of lesser compass are not therefore to be despised. Of such more modest travelers, whose little journeys lay in narrower fields, there are a host; and from the best, with their intimate local knowledge, their keen and critical observations, their sympathetic descriptions, we may gain great pleasure and be stimulated perhaps to make all the use possible of the opportunities which come to us to see more thoroughly and with a more observing eye the country and the people round about.

METHODS OF TRAVEL

No one can read the records of the travelers of different periods without being struck by the differences in the character and method of travel which they reveal. Although reference to the comfort, the rapidity, and the safety of modern travel, at least along the great highways of the civilized world, is a commonplace, yet the contrast of the present conditions with those that formerly obtained is none the less noteworthy. The earlier travelers had frequently to go alone, sometimes disguise was their only hope, and they were, far more than at present, subject to hardship, suffering, and danger. They made, indeed were able to make, little in the way of special preparation for the journey; they carried with them little in the way of special outfit; and they traveled as a rule very slowly, often halting or being obliged to halt long on the way. Dependent for guidance frequently on the information of suspicious or unfriendly folk, they often went astray, and lacking regular or direct means of communication, they had often to journey

by very roundabout routes to reach their goal. To-day the
conditions have vastly changed. The lonely traveler or the
elaborately organized expedition alike are spared much of
the hardship and danger, and both may secure all sorts of
cunningly devised special equipment and supplies, which not
only add enormously to comfort and safety, but to the certainty of success. Travel away from the beaten track or exploration in untraveled regions is still and of necessity slow
compared with what it is in civilized lands, but the traveler
and explorer in remote places to-day has at least this inestimable advantage, that he is able to reach quickly and
easily the actual point of departure into the unknown.

THE PLEASURES AND PROFITS OF TRAVEL

Of the advantages and of the pleasures of travel there is
little need to speak—they are too obvious. New lands, new
peoples, new experiences, all alike offer to the traveler the
opportunity of a wider knowledge. He may add almost
without limit thus to his stores, although in this field as in
most others it must be remembered that "he who would
bring back the wealth of the Indies must take with him the
wealth of the Indies"—in other words he will gain just in
proportion to the knowledge and appreciation which he
brings. But greater than any knowledge gained is the influence which travel exerts or should exert on habits of
thought, and on one's attitude to one's fellow man. A
wider tolerance, a juster appreciation of the real values in
life, a deeper realization of the oneness of mankind, and a
growing wonder at the magnitude of the achievements of
the race—these are some of the results which travel rightly
pursued cannot fail to produce. Quite apart, moreover,
from any or all of these things, desirable as they are, is
the pleasure of travel in and for itself. It has been already
pointed out that this is for some the main, and for many
at least an important if unadmitted, motive. To the real
traveler there is no joy which is keener, no pleasure more
lasting, no call more imperious, than that of travel. There
is fatigue, hardship, perhaps suffering, to be endured—for
him this is of small moment, for they will soon pass; the

recollection even of them will fade away—all these will be forgotten, while the memory holds with almost undiminished clearness the wonder and the beauty of the past. For him the colors of old sunsets glow with undimmed splendor, in his ears the winds of other days still make their music, and in his nostrils is still the perfume of flowers that long passed away.

We cannot all be travelers; there are many who must be content to do their traveling in an armchair. Rightly read, however, the records of others' journeys may bring to the reader much not only of value but of pleasure. He may play consciously the part which for the traveler memory plays unconsciously, and from the mass of experience select and hold only the best. For him thus the patience, the heroism, and the indomitable perseverance revealed in the lives and deeds of great travelers may serve as an inspiration; and from their description of the wonder and the beauty of the world he may gain some understanding of and sympathy with those who have in all ages set their faces toward the unseen; whose spirit has been that put into the mouth of Ulysses:

> my purpose holds
> To sail beyond the sunset, and the baths
> Of all the western stars, until I die.[13]

[13] Tennyson's "Ulysses," *H. C.*, xlii, 1007.

II. HERODOTUS ON EGYPT

By Professor George H. Chase

HERODOTUS is called "the father of history." The phrase goes back to Cicero, and its justice has been universally recognized, for Herodotus was the first writer in the course of European literature to use the word "history" with the meaning in which it has since been used, and to exemplify this meaning by the composition of a history in the modern sense of the word. Before his time there was a literature which in certain ways resembled history, the writings of the so-called logographers, consisting of "logoi" or "tales" which treated, in a manner closely resembling the epic, the stories connected with the foundation of the Greek cities, or the genealogy of single families, or the marvels of remote regions. Herodotus himself shows the influence of this earlier sort of writing; his history is full of "logoi," and he shows great interest in the geography of distant lands and the manners and customs of foreign peoples. But what distinguishes him from his predecessors and gives him a unique place in the history of literature is the fact that he was the first writer to undertake the narration of a series of events of world-wide importance upon a comprehensive plan and to trace in those events the relations of cause and effect.

THE SUBJECT OF THE HISTORY OF HERODOTUS

The theme of the History of Herodotus is the struggle between the Persians and the Greeks, which, more than any other single event, determined the later history of Europe. There are many digressions, but the main subject is never lost sight of through all the nine books into which the work was divided by later grammarians. The earlier books trace the gradual growth of Persian power, the conquest of the Lydian Empire, of Babylon, and of Egypt,[1] and the Persian expeditions to Scythia and Libya; with Book V we come to the Ionian revolt and the burning of Sardis—events which led up to the Persian attacks on Greece; Book VI describes the punishment of the Ionian cities and the first invasion, ending with the glorious victory of Marathon; and the remaining books record the great invasion of Xerxes.

Herodotus's inspiration came largely, no doubt, from the time in which he lived. He was born early in the fifth century, and so was of the next generation to those who took part in the Persian struggle. He must have known and talked with many men who had fought at Marathon and Salamis. His own native city, Halicarnassus in Caria, was subject to Persia, so that he must early have learned to know and to fear the Persian power. Fate and inclination seem to have combined to make him a traveler. He was twice exiled from his native city, and was for many years "a man without a country," until at last he obtained citizenship in the town of Thurii in southern Italy, a sort of international colony which had been established by the Athenians in 443 B. C. on the site of the old city of Sybaris. He certainly spent some time in Athens, where he enjoyed the friendship of Sophocles, and doubtless of others of that brilliant group of writers and artists whose works have made the "Age of Pericles"[2] a synonym for the "great age" in Greek literature and art. There are traditions that he gave public readings at Athens, Olympia, Corinth, and Thebes; and he speaks with first-hand knowledge of many other places in Greece.

THE RANGE AND PURPOSE OF HIS TRAVELS

But the journeyings of Herodotus were not confined to Greece and its immediate neighborhood. From his own statements we learn that he had traveled through the Persian Empire to Babylon, and even to distant Susa and Ecbatana; had visited Egypt and gone up the Nile as far as

[1] *Harvard Classics*, xxxiii, 5ff.   [2] *H. C.*, xii, 36ff.

Elephantine; had gone by sea to Tyre and to Libya; and had made a journey to the Black Sea, visiting the Crimea and the land of the Colchians.

He seems also to have traveled through the interior of Asia Minor and down the Syrian coast to the borders of Egypt.

The purpose of these travels presents an interesting problem. The simplest and most natural supposition would be that they were undertaken simply as a means of preparation for writing the History. But many other theories are possible. It has been thought that Herodotus was a merchant and that his journeys were primarily business undertakings. Against this it may be urged that the History shows no evidence of a commercial point of view, and that Herodotus speaks of merchants as he speaks of many other classes, with no suggestion of special interest. Again, it has been maintained that the journeys were made simply to collect evidence about foreign lands, with no direct reference to the History. Those who hold this theory believe that Herodotus was a professional reciter, like the rhapsodes who recited the Homeric poems, only that he took as his subject, not the great events of the heroic age, but the description of distant countries and their inhabitants—that he was, in short, a sort of ancient Stoddard or Burton Holmes. To such a belief the tradition that he read parts of his work at different places in Greece and the amount of space devoted to the aspect of foreign countries and the ways of foreign peoples in the History itself lend a certain amount of color. Finally, it is possible that some of the journeys had a political significance. Most of the countries which Herodotus visited were regions of which a knowledge was of great importance to the Greek statesmen of the fifth century, especially to Pericles, with his well-known scheme for founding an Athenian Empire, and it is pointed out that the large sum of ten talents (over $10,000) which Herodotus is said to have received from the Athenian Assembly can hardly have been paid simply for a series of readings, but must have been a reward for political services. All these theories suggest interesting possibilities, but none of them can be proved. Herodotus himself merely states that his History was written "that the deeds of men may not be forgotten, and that the great and wondrous works of Greek and barbarian may not lose their name." In any case, the fact remains that he did at last put his materials into the form in which we have them and thus established his fame as the first writer of history.

THE VERACITY OF HERODOTUS

The fitness of Herodotus for the task that he undertook is another question which has been vigorously debated. Even in antiquity the History was violently assailed. Plutarch wrote an essay "On the Malignity of Herodotus," and a late grammarian, Aelius Harpocration, is said to have written a book entitled "The Lies in the History of Herodotus." In modern times, the judgments passed upon the work have often been severe, and even the greatest admirers of the historian are forced to admit that it shows many serious defects. Like most of his contemporaries, Herodotus knew no language but his own, and he was therefore forced to rely on interpreters or on natives who spoke Greek. He himself is perfectly frank about the matter, and usually tells the source of his information. "This is what the Persians say," "Thus the priests of the Egyptians told me," are types of expressions which recur again and again. Even when Greek matters are involved, he seems usually to have relied on oral tradition, rather than on documentary evidence; he rarely mentions an inscription as the source of his information. It is not quite fair to call him entirely credulous and uncritical, for he often questions the truth of the statements he records and tries to weigh one theory against another, as when he discusses the inundation of the Nile. But in him, as in the majority of his contemporaries, the critical faculty was not developed, and his work suffers in consequence. He was, moreover, an inveterate story-teller, and it often seems as if he recorded stories for the mere love of telling them. Not a few of the tales he tells, like the story of the treasure chamber of Rhampsinitos, belong rather to the realm of folklore than to that of history.

THE RELIGIOUS ELEMENT IN HERODOTUS

Another quality in Herodotus which resulted disadvantageously for his History was his strong religious bent. His was still the age of faith, when men saw the hand of the gods revealed in all human affairs, and Herodotus was deeply imbued with this belief. In the History, therefore, much attention is paid to oracles and signs, and the chapters that treat of foreign lands are filled with attempts to correlate the gods of the barbarians with the gods of Greece. The Second Book, with its constant striving to prove an Egyptian origin for many of the Greek divinities, is only the most striking example of a general tendency.

Regarded as history, therefore, the work of Herodotus suffers from grave defects, and it is not to be wondered at that ancient and modern critics have vied with one another in pointing them out. The attitude of many of these critics is well expressed by an Oxford rhyme:

> The priests of Egypt humbugged you,
> A thing not very hard to do.
> But we won't let you humbug us,
> Herodotus! Herodotus!

Yet it must be said that in spite of much adverse criticism, few people have been led to believe in any bad faith on Herodotus's part. The defects which his work betrays are defects of his race and his time; and to offset them he has many merits. Few Greeks of any age showed themselves so fair-minded in dealing with barbarian nations. He is as ready to praise what seems good in the customs of foreign races as he is to praise the customs of the Greeks. If he is too fond of stories to be a good historian, at least he is a prince of story-tellers. His style is lucid, simple, and straightforward, showing everywhere the "art which conceals art"—a wonderful achievement, when one considers that this is the first literary prose that was written in Europe. Finally, few writers of any age have succeeded so well in impressing on their work the stamp of personality. As we read the pages of the History, the picture of the author rises vividly before us. We can almost see him as, tablet and stylus in hand, he follows the interpreter or the priest through the great cities of the Persian Empire or the temples of Egypt, eagerly listening and questioning, quick to notice differences from his own Greek way of doing things, courteous, sympathetic, always on the watch for the story that will adorn his narrative. Quite apart from its value as a record of facts, the History of Herodotus is intensely interesting as a human document, as a record of the beliefs and the impressions of a remarkable member of a remarkable race at the period of its highest development.

III. THE ELIZABETHAN ADVENTURERS

By Professor W. A. Neilson

AMONG the many manifestations of the spirit of intellectual inquiry which marked the Renaissance in Europe, the new impetus toward geographical exploration is one of the most notable. The discovery of the New World by Columbus in 1492 had given this a fresh start, and not many years had passed before Spain had followed it up by large settlements and annexations of territory, chiefly in Central and South America. Spain was in the sixteenth century the leading Catholic power in Europe, and after England under Elizabeth had definitely and finally broken with Rome, her position as leading Protestant power added a religious motive to that of political ambition to lead her to seek to share with her rival the wealth and dominion of the Americas. Further, there was a powerful commercial interest in this rivalry. The peaceful development of England under the great Queen led to a need for wider markets, and besides the hope of plunder and the settlement of colonies, the Elizabethan merchant adventurers were seeking to build up a large commerce overseas. Curiosity, piety, patriotism, and trade were, then, the leading motives that led these daring "sea dogs" on their perilous voyages to the ends of the earth.

THE EXPANSION OF ELIZABETHAN ENGLAND

The diversity of routes traversed in these quests is not always realized. It was not merely the Spanish Main to which these men looked for profit and adventure. Seeking a northeastern route to China in 1553, English sailors found themselves in the White Sea and made their way to the

Court of the Czar, thus establishing a trade route to Russia which rendered them independent of the Baltic route previously blocked by the jealousy of the Hansa league. They pushed into the Mediterranean, sending expeditions to Tripoli and Morocco, and trading with the Greek Archipelago. Others cultivated intercourse with Egypt and the Levant, and, penetrating Arabia and Persia, carried their samples overland to India, while still others reached the same goal by way of the Persian Gulf or round the Cape of Good Hope. Here they came into competition with the Portuguese; and in 1600 was founded the East India Company, and with it the beginning of the British Empire in India.

THE SPANISH MAIN

But it was in the regions where they came into conflict with the Spaniards that those exploits occurred which most touched the imaginations of their contemporaries, and of which we have preserved the most picturesque accounts. The three voyages of Sir Francis Drake,[1] Sir Humphrey Gilbert's "Voyage to Newfoundland,"[2] and Sir Walter Raleigh's "Discovery of Guiana,"[3] all printed in The Harvard Classics, are good representative records of the manner and results of these expeditions, partly scientific and religious, but more patriotic and piratical. Few narratives are more absorbing than these, with their pictures of courage against terrible odds, of endurance of the most frightful hardships on sea and land, of generosity and treachery, of kindliness and cruelty. Drake was still young when he first voyaged to the west, and in 1572 he made the expedition against Nombre de Dios in which they all but secured the contents of the great King's Treasure House. "By means of this light," says the narrator, "we saw a huge heap of silver in that nether room; being a pile of bars of silver of, as near as we could guess, seventy feet in length, of ten feet in breadth, and twelve feet in height; piled up against the wall," each bar was between thirty-five and forty pounds in weight"—altogether over 360 tons, as it turned out. This

---

[1] *Harvard Classics*, xxxiii, 133, 207, 237.   [2] *H. C.*, xxxiii, 271.
[3] *H. C.*, xxxiii, 321.

vast treasure, with as much more in gold, they left untouched, however, preferring to save the life of their
wounded captain.[4] How they plagued the Spaniards in
spite of this abstinence may be judged from the summary
statement at the close of the narrative: "There were, at
this time, belonging to Cartagena, Nombre de Dios, etc.,
above 200 frigates . . . the most of which, during our
abode in those parts, we took; and some of them twice or
thrice each; yet never burned nor sunk any unless they were
made out men-of-war against us, or laid as stales to en-
trap us."[5]

CONTRIBUTIONS TO GEOGRAPHY

To the narratives of these adventurers we owe much of
our early knowledge of America and its aborigines. The
information they give, it is true, is not always to be taken
at its face value, and often is more of the nature of travelers' tales than scientific geography. But it has value, and,
reflecting as it does the inflamed imagination of the time,
vast entertainment. Thus in an account of one of Hawkins's
voyages we read of the crocodile: "His nature is ever, when
he would have his prey, to cry and sob like a Christian
body, to provoke them to come to him; and then he
snatched at them! And thereupon came this proverb, that
is applied unto women, when they weep, 'Lachrymae Croco-
dili': the meaning whereof is, that as the crocodile when he
crieth goeth then about most to deceive; so doth a woman,
most commonly, when she weepeth." The wondrous properties of tobacco are thus described in the same narrative:
"The Floridans, when they travel, have a kind of herb dried,
who with a cane and a earthen cup in the end, with fire and
the dried herbs put together, do suck through the cane the
smoke thereof; which smoke satisfieth their hunger, and
therewith they live four or five days without meat or drink.
And this all the Frenchmen used for this purpose; yet do
they hold opinion withal, that it causeth water and phlegm
to void from their stomachs." The potato is hardly less
glorified: "These potatoes be the most delicate roots that
may be eaten; and do far exceed our parsnips or carrots.

[4] H. C., xxxiii, 143, 145.   [5] H. C., xxxiii, 203.

Their pines be of the bigness of two fists, the outside whereof is of the making of a pine apple, but it is soft like the rind of a cucumber; and the inside eateth like an apple, but it is more delicious than any sweet apple sugared."

Besides descriptions of plants and animals, these stories of travel and conquest contain much interesting information, though colored by fancy, of the native tribes encountered and of their habits of life. Especially is the reader struck by the vast riches in gold and pearls ascribed to the Indians, such description as that of El Dorado, quoted by Raleigh in his account of the Emperor of Guiana,[6] sounding like a fairy tale. Not content with kitchen utensils of gold and silver, the Emperor was believed to have adorned his pleasure gardens with flowers and trees of the same precious metals.

BEHAVIOR OF THE EXPLORERS

These stories, as the reader is not likely to forget, are all told from the English point of view. Religious animosity and political and commercial rivalry whetted the English hatred of Spain, and produced accounts of Spanish cruelty to the natives and to English prisoners which must be taken with much modification. For the English adventurers themselves were no saints. Many of them were nothing more than pirates, and many were engaged in the slave trade between Africa and the Indies. At times our admiration for their intrepid courage and persistence, and for their loyalty to one another and to the Queen, is overcome by the evidence of their inhumanity in the treatment of their human cargoes, and their lack of all consideration of the rights of negroes as men. They contracted for the delivery of African slaves to the West Indies precisely as if they were cattle or hides, and in case of danger at sea they lightened their ships of these miserable wretches with apparently little less compunction than if they had been mere bales of merchandise.

Yet, amid all the horrors induced by lust of gold and conquest, one finds often enough incidents of striking generosity to enemies, of tender affection to their own peo-

[6] *H. C.,* xxxiii, 328-329.

ple, and of a code of honor and an adherence to the rules of the game as they understood it, which go far to brighten the picture.

THE STYLE OF THE NARRATIVES

Nothing was farther from the minds of the writers of these voyages than the production of literature. The glorification of their captains and their country, the inciting of their fellow citizens against the enemy, and the fondness of the returned traveler for narrating his adventures, these were the main motives which induced them to write; and they told their stories with no thought of style or ornament. They have thus almost the flavor of actual conversation, and reveal, none the less truly because unconsciously, the temper of the writers and the spirit of the time. It was a time of great enthusiasms and boundless ambitions, of undertakings conceived under the influence of an almost fantastic imagination, and carried out with absolute unscrupulousness, but with complete devotion and invincible courage. The modern world has largely outgrown the temptation to many of the vices which beset these buccaneers, but our blood is still stirred by the spectacle of their magnificent energy, and our imaginations are roused by those

> heroic hearts,
> Made weak by time and fate, but strong in will
> To strive, to seek, to find, and not to yield.

IV. THE ERA OF DISCOVERY

By Professor W. B. Munro

WITH the close of the fifteenth century the Dark Ages came to an end. The great mediæval institution of feudalism was everywhere losing its hold, for the growth of monarchical power and the rise of standing armies made the feudal system no longer necessary. Small states were being consolidated into nations—Castile and Aragon had become the kingdom of Spain; the various provinces of France were now welded together under the House of Bourbon; while England had settled her internal quarrels and was now safely unified under the dominant Tudor dynasty. With this consolidation and unity came national consciousness and a desire for territorial expansion. The revived study of geography, moreover, and the adaptation of the compass to marine use were features which led mariners to proceed more boldly away from the shores, so that when the Turkish conquests shut off the old trade routes between the Mediterranean ports and the Orient, the time was ripe for venturesome voyages out into the western ocean.

THE VOYAGES OF COLUMBUS

It was altogether appropriate that the first successful expedition of discovery into the New Hemisphere should have been under the guidance of a Genoese navigator in the service of the Spanish crown. Genoa was one of the first commercial cities of the Mediterranean; Spain was one of the most powerful and progressive among European monarchies. Columbus had the maritime skill and daring of his own race together with the financial backing of a nation which from its location had much to gain from western discoveries The story of his thirty-three-day voyage to the new Indies his reception by the natives, and his glowing accounts of the new lands are known to every American schoolboy; but never can it be better recounted than in the discoverer's own words.[1] It is true that the honor of having been the first to touch upon the shores of the New World has been claimed by others. Nearly four centuries before Columbus set sail from Palos, some Norse navigators under the leadership of Leif Ericson, son of Eric the Red, are said to have sailed from the Norse colony in Greenland and to have reached the coasts of Wineland the Good. Whether this Wineland was Labrador or Nova Scotia or New England is something upon which historians have never agreed; but the general drift of opinion at present is that Leif and his followers in all probability never came south of Labrador, if, indeed, they proceeded so far.[2] But in any event these Norse forays never led to any permanent colonization; the planting of a new nation was reserved to those who followed where Columbus led the way.

The return of Columbus with his news concerning the wealth and resources of Hispaniola made a profound impression upon the imagination of all Europe. The Spanish Court hastened to follow up its advantage by sending Columbus on further voyages in order that the entire fruits of the discovery might be monopolized. The navigators of other nations also bestirred themselves to get some share of the New World's spoil. Among these was the Florentine sea captain Amerigo Vespucci, who made his way across the Atlantic in 1497, and on his return presented the geographical information which led the map makers of Europe to name the new continent after him.[3] Likewise the Cabots, father and son, sailed from Bristol in the same year under the auspices of King Henry VIII, and by their explorations along the Labrador coast laid the basis of later English claims to great regions of North America.[4] France, for her part, sent Jacques Cartier on his errands of discovery and in due course established French claims to the valley of the St. Lawrence in this way.

[1] The Letter of Columbus to Luis de Sant Angel announcing his discovery, in *Harvard Classics*, xliii, 22-46.
[2] The Voyages to Vineland, *H. C.*, xliii, 5-21.
[3] Amerigo Vespucci's Account of his First Voyage, *H. C.*, xliii, 29-46.
[4] John Cabot's Discovery of North America, *H. C.*, xliii, 47-50.

PLANTING NEW NATIONS IN AMERICA

But to get secure possession of the new territories it was necessary that European nations should do more than discover. They must make settlements and colonize. Spain, being first in the field, directed her energies to those regions which seemed to constitute the largest prize, that is to say, the West Indies, Central America, and the western slopes of the South American continent. In the Indies there was a fertile soil which could be made to yield its increase without much labor; on the mainland there were great areas of gold and silver ore. Portugal, coming hard on the heels of her peninsular neighbor, went still further to the south and took as her patrimony the sea coast of Brazil, a region which also promised a rich tribute in precious metals. England, being rather slow to follow up the beginnings made in her behalf by John and Sebastian Cabot, was forced to be content with territories north of the Spanish claims—the coast from Florida to the Bay of Fundy—where there were no great stores of mineral wealth to attract the adventuresome. In the long run, however, this selection proved to be the most prudent of them all. France, coming last into the field, found herself pushed still farther northward to the regions of Acadia, the St. Lawrence and the Great Lakes. Other countries of Europe, Sweden, and the Netherlands, were also in the race and both managed to get a precarious foothold in the new territories, the former on the Delaware and the latter on the Hudson. But both were in due course dislodged and these colonies passed into English hands. So did the territories of France after a century of conflict.

VIRGINIA AND NEW ENGLAND

In the region along the Atlantic seaboard which England claimed for her own, two settlements were made at dates not far apart. Early in 1607 a group of about one hundred settlers established at Jamestown in Virginia the first permanent Anglo-American colony, and through the inevitable hardships of a pioneer community managed to hold the settlement on its feet. With them they had brought a royal charter couched in the legal diction of the time, and in due course established their own system of local self-government with its boroughs and its House of Burgesses reproducing in miniature the old English administrative system.[5] Farther to the north unsuccessful attempts to found settlements had been made near the mouth of the Kennebec as early as 1607; but it was not until 1620 that the Mayflower Pilgrims made their landing at Plymouth and laid the foundations of New England. The Pilgrims had gone first from England to Holland, but finding that they were being drawn into the vortex of an alien environment, reached a decision to set forth for a new land where they could create their own surroundings. Before they went ashore the Pilgrims made a political compact among themselves whereby they created a "civill body politick" and covenanted each with each to enact just laws for the welfare of the new community.[6] The early years of this settlement were passed in great hardship and the population grew very slowly. Ten years after the disembarkation at Plymouth Rock it numbered but three hundred in all. The first economic and social system was communistic, but in due course this was abandoned and by dint of persistent effort the colony rounded the corner on the road to prosperity.

A more important settlement in New England, however, was that made by John Winthrop and his followers on the shores of Massachusetts Bay. In 1630 Winthrop brought to Salem a body of nearly a thousand settlers, and these, during the ensuing two years, founded a half-dozen towns, including Boston. The colonies of Plymouth and Massachusetts Bay continued a separate existence for more than a half-century after their foundation; in 1690 they were amalgamated into the province of Massachusetts.

By 1630, therefore, Englishmen had firmly established their outposts on the Atlantic seaboard both to the north and to the south; their next enterprise was to dominate the interval between. From Massachusetts the settlers, driven forth in some cases because of their refusal to observe

---

[5] First Charter of Virginia, *H. C.*, xliii, 51-61.
[6] The Mayflower Compact, *H. C.*, xliii, 62.

stringent religious requirements, moved southward into the Rhode Island and Connecticut territories. William Penn, Lord Baltimore, and others proved ready to undertake colonization as a private enterprise and, being favored by the Crown in their ambitions, laid the foundations of Pennsylvania and Maryland. The Swedes on the Delaware and the Dutch on the Hudson were overpowered and their lands brought under English control. Then having possessed herself of the whole region from Virginia to Massachusetts it was England's next task to expel France from her menacing position still farther above.

INTERIOR EXPLORATION AND TRADE

This colonizing movement went hand in hand with the exploration of the interior. During the seventeenth century the Great Lakes and the Mississippi were traversed by the French voyageurs, while the hinterlands of the New England colonies were penetrated by the English fur traders. Missionaries followed in the footsteps of the traders and in due course the two chief colonizing powers of North America were using both as agents for enlarging their respective spheres of influence. Even before the earliest settlements were made to the westward of the Alleghenies, the initial skirmishes of a long struggle for the possession of these territories were taking place. The French colonists, though inferior in numbers and in material resources, were far more daring, more enterprising as explorers and as *coureurs-des-bois,* and more persevering than their southern neighbors—that is why the task of securing and enlarging the English frontiers proved so difficult. But in the end sheer numerical superiority determined the issue, and England, for the time being, became master of the whole area from the Atlantic to the Mississippi.[7]

[7] For a sketch of the subsequent movements, see section on History: V. "Territorial Development of the United States," by Professor F. J. Turner, in this course.

V. DARWIN'S VOYAGE OF THE BEAGLE

By Professor George Howard Parker

HAD Charles Darwin never published more than "The Voyage of the Beagle,"[1] his reputation as a naturalist of the first rank would have been fully assured. Even before the close of that eventful circumnavigation of the globe, the English geologist Sedgwick, who had probably seen some of the letters sent by the young naturalist to friends in England, predicted to Dr. Darwin, Charles Darwin's father, that his son would take a place among the leading scientific men of the day. As it afterward proved, the voyage of the *Beagle* was the foundation stone on which rested that monument of work and industry which, as a matter of fact, made Charles Darwin one of the distinguished scientists not only of his generation but of all time.

The conventional school and university training had very little attraction for Darwin. From boyhood his real interests were to be found in collecting natural objects; minerals, plants, insects, and birds were the materials that excited his mind to full activity. But it was not till his Cambridge days, when he was supposedly studying for the clergy, that the encouragement of Henslow changed this pastime into a serious occupation.

THE OCCASION OF THE VOYAGE

About 1831 the British Admiralty decided to fit out the *Beagle,* a ten-gun brig, to complete the survey of Patagonia and Tierra del Fuego begun some years before, to survey the shores of Chili, Peru, and some of the islands of the Pacific, and to carry a chain of chronometrical measure-

[1] *Harvard Classics,* xxix.

ments round the world. It seemed important to all concerned that a naturalist should accompany this expedition; and Captain Fitz-Roy, through the mediation of Professor Henslow, eventually induced Charles Darwin to become his cabin companion and naturalist for the voyage. Henslow recommended Darwin not as a *finished* naturalist but as one amply qualified for collecting, observing, and noting anything worthy to be noted in natural history.

The *Beagle,* after two unsuccessful attempts to get away, finally set sail from Devonport, England, December 27, 1831; and, after a cruise of almost five years, she returned to Falmouth, England, October 2, 1836. Her course had lain across the Atlantic to the Brazilian coast, thence southward along the east coast of South America to Tierra del Fuego, whence she turned northward skirting the seaboard of Chili and Peru. Near the equator a westerly course was taken and she then crossed the Pacific to Australia whence she traversed the Indian Ocean, and, rounding the Cape of Good Hope, headed across the South Atlantic for Brazil. Here she completed the circumnavigation of the globe and, picking up her former course, she retraced her way to England.

When Darwin left England on the *Beagle,* he was twenty-two years old. The five-year voyage, therefore, occupied in his life the period of maturing manhood. What it was to mean to him he only partly saw. Before leaving England he declared that the day of sailing would mark the beginning of his second life, a new birthday to him. All through his boyhood he had dreamed of seeing the tropics; and now his dream was to be realized. His letters and his account of the voyage are full of the exuberance of youth. To his friend Fox he wrote from Brazil: "My mind has been, since leaving England, in a perfect *hurricane* of delight and astonishment." To Henslow he sent word from Rio as follows: "Here I first saw a tropical forest in all its sublime grandeur —nothing but the reality can give you any idea how wonderful, how magnificent the scene is." And to another correspondent he wrote: "When I first entered on and beheld the luxuriant vegetation of Brazil, it was realizing the visions in the 'Arabian Nights.' The brilliancy of the scenery throws one into a delirium of delight, and a beetle hunter is not likely soon to awaken from it when, whichever way he turns, fresh treasures meet his eye." Such expressions could spring only from the enthusiasm of the born naturalist.

THE TRAINING OF A NATURALIST

But the voyage of the *Beagle* meant more to Darwin than the mere opportunity to see the world; it trained him to be a naturalist. During his five years at sea he learned to work, and to work under conditions that were often almost intolerable. The *Beagle* was small and cramped, and the collections of a naturalist were not always easily cared for. The first lieutenant, who is described by Darwin in terms of the highest admiration, was responsible for the appearance of the ship, and strongly objected to having such a litter on deck as Darwin often made. To this man specimens were "d—d beastly devilment," and he is said to have added, "If I were skipper, I would soon have you and all your d—d mess out of the place." Darwin is quoted as saying that the absolute necessity of tidiness in the cramped space of the *Beagle* gave him his methodical habits of work. On the *Beagle*, too, he learned what he considered the golden rule for saving time, i. e., take care of the minutes, a rule that gives significance to an expression he has somewhere used, that all life is made of a succession of five-minute periods.

Darwin, however, not only learned on the *Beagle* how to work against time and under conditions of material inconvenience, but he also acquired the habit of carrying on his occupations under considerable physical discomfort. Although he was probably not seriously ill after the first three weeks of the voyage, he was constantly uncomfortable when the vessel pitched at all heavily, and his sensitiveness to this trouble is well shown in a letter dated June 3, 1836, from the Cape of Good Hope, in which he said: "It is lucky for me that the voyage is drawing to a close, for I positively suffer more from seasickness now than three years ago." Yet he always kept busily at work, and notwithstanding the more or less continuous nature of this discomfort, he was not inclined to attribute the digestive disturbances of his later life to these early experiences.

The return voyage found his spirits somewhat subdued. Writing to his sister from Bahia in Brazil where the *Beagle* crossed her outward course, he said: "It has been almost painful to find how much good enthusiasm has been evaporated in the last four years. I can now walk soberly through a Brazilian forest." Yet years after in rehearsing the voyage in his autobiography he declared: "The glories of the vegetation of the Tropics rise before my mind at the present time more vividly than anything else."

PRACTICAL RESULTS OF THE VOYAGE

Darwin's opinion of the value of the voyage to him can scarcely be expressed better than in his own words. In his later years he wrote: "The voyage of the *Beagle* has been by far the most important event of my life," and again: "I have always felt that I owe to the voyage the first real training or education of my mind; I was led to attend closely to several branches of natural history, and thus my powers of observation were improved, though they were always fairly developed." And finally in a letter to Captain Fitz-Roy he said: "However others may look back on the *Beagle's* voyage, now that the small disagreeable parts are well nigh forgotten, I think it far the most fortunate circumstance in my life that the chance afforded by your offer of taking a naturalist fell on me. I often have the most vivid and delightful pictures of what I saw on board the *Beagle* pass before my eyes. These recollections, and what I learned on natural history, I would not exchange for twice then thousand a year."

But the voyage of the *Beagle* was not only training for Darwin, it was the means of gathering together a large and valuable collection of specimens that kept naturalists busy for some years to come, and added greatly to our knowledge of these distant lands and seas. In the work of arranging and describing these collections, Darwin was finally obliged to take an active part himself, for, to quote from his "Life and Letters," it seemed "only gradually to have occurred to him that he would ever be more than a collector of specimens and facts, of which the great men were to make use. And even of the value of his collections he seems to have had much doubt, for he wrote to Henslow in 1834: 'I really began to think that my collections were so poor that you were puzzled what to say; the case is now quite on the opposite tack, for you are guilty of exciting all my vain feelings to a most comfortable pitch; if hard work will atone for these thoughts I vow it shall not be spared.'" Thus the collections made on the *Beagle* served to confirm Darwin in the occupation of a naturalist and brought him into contact with many of the working scientists of his day.

SPECULATIVE RESULTS OF THE VOYAGE

Darwin, however, not only brought back, as a result of his work on the *Beagle,* large collections of interesting specimens, but he came home with a mind richly stored with new ideas, and one of these he put into shape so rapidly that it forms no small part of "The Voyage of the Beagle." During much of the latter part of the journey he was occupied with a study of coral islands and his theory of the method of formation of these remarkable deposits was the first to gain general acceptance in the scientific world. In fact, his views gained so firm a foothold that they are to-day more generally accepted than those of any other naturalist. But coral islands were not the the the only objects of his speculations. Without doubt he spent much time reflecting on that problem of problems, the origin of species, for, though there is not much reference to this subject either in the "Voyage" itself or in his letters of that period, he states in his autobiography that in July, 1837, less than a year after his return, he opened his first notebook for facts in relation to the origin of species about which, as he remarks, he had *long* reflected.[2] Thus the years spent on the *Beagle* were years rich in speculation as well as in observation and field work.

[2] For Darwin's conclusions on this subject see "The Origin of Species" in *H. C.,* xi.

Doubtless the direct results of the voyage of the *Beagle* were acceptable to the British Admiralty and justified in their eyes the necessary expenditure of money and energy. But the great accomplishment of that voyage was not the charting of distant shore lines nor the carrying of a chain of chronometrical measurements round the world; it was the training and education of Charles Darwin as a naturalist, and no greater tribute can be paid to the voyage than what Darwin himself has said: "I feel sure that it was this training which has enabled me to do whatever I have done in science."

RELIGION

I. GENERAL INTRODUCTION

By Professor R. B. Perry

THERE are two ways of reading the documents of religion. In the first place one may read the book of one's own faith, as the Christian reads his Bible. In this case one reads for instruction or education in some source to which one attributes authority, and finds there the familiar and well-loved symbols of one's own belief and hope. Such a relation between a man and a book is only possible under peculiar conditions. It is the work of time and tradition and social experience. A book does not become a man's "bible" unless it has been the principal quickening influence in his spiritual life and the source of his illumination, so that he returns to it when he needs to reanimate his purposes or confirm his belief. A "bible" is the proved remedy to which a man confidently resorts for the health of his own soul. It becomes associated in his mind with all that he owes to it, and all that he hopes from it; so that it is not only an instrument, but a symbol. The sacred book of any racial or historical religion is, of course, more than such a personal bible, by as much as a race is more than an individual or history than a lifetime. But it is the personal relation, that between a man and the book that has become *his* sacred book, that I want here to emphasize. It is evident that in such a relation the reader's attitude will be unique; it will differ from his attitude to any other book. Religious documents are usually and normally read in this way. Each man reads his own bible. And it is only when a document is somebody's bible in this sense that it is a religious document at all.

OTHER MEN'S BIBLES

But there is a second way in which such documents may be read, and it is this 'second way that must be adopted by those who wish to read religious literature with any comprehensiveness. One may read *another man's bible*. Now this requires a quite different attitude, and one that may need to be cultivated. It will not do to look for the same value which one finds in the book of one's own religion; or to judge by one's own peculiar spiritual standards. For then the other man's bible will seem cold, repugnant, superstitious, or heretical. Nor will it do to read another man's bible as so much secular literature, for then it will appear curious, fantastic, or at best poetical. It is necessary to bring one's self by imagination and sympathy to an understanding of the other man's outlook and needs. The outward aspect of Mohammedanism is to the Christian traveler only a curious local custom. But, "I would have you," says H. Fielding in his "Hearts of Men," "go and kneel beside the Mohammedan as he prays at the sunset hour, and put your heart to his and wait for the echo that will surely come." It is in the inward value of this outward posture that its religion lies. And the same is true of any sacred writings. Their religious meaning is relative to the believer whom they exalt, stir, comfort, enlighten, or strike with awe. And no one can apprehend that meaning who cannot bring himself at least for the moment into the believer's attitude.

Perhaps this seems to ask too much. How can one convert oneself in turn into a Buddhist, a Mohammedan, a Christian, a Brahman, and a Confucian? There is, however, a saving possibility. May there not be some attitude common to all believers? May one not divest oneself of what is peculiar to one's own religion and yet retain a something which is in all religion, and by this come to a better understanding of each religion? An Englishman may understand a Frenchman by becoming less English and more human. Similarly it is possible that a Christian may understand Mohammedanism by becoming less Christian and more religious. "No matter where you go," says Fielding, "no mat-

ter what the faith is called, if you have the hearing ear, if
your heart is in unison with the heart of the world, you will
hear always the same song." There is, in other words, a
sameness in all religion, which is the link between one
special cult and another; and by coming to know and feel
this common religion one may pass beyond the limits of
one's native religious province.

There is a danger that this important truth should be misunderstood. Some years ago a Parliament of Religions was
held in connection with the World's Fair at Chicago. It
was a spectacular and impressive event which no doubt did
much to liberalize and broaden religious opinion in America.
But it encouraged the mistaken opinion that because all religions are equally religious they must be equally good or
true. It would be equally reasonable to argue that because
all forms of political organization are equally political, one
must be as sound or equitable as another. All polities arise
in response to the same fundamental need for order and
justice, and in so far as they are accepted and persist, they
must to some extent satisfy that need. And to understand
a foreign polity I must see how it accomplishes in its way
and for its place and time what my polity accomplishes in
another way for me. But it does not follow that the two are
equally sound in principle, or that the one might not be cor-
rected in the light of the other. Similarly religion arises in
response to the same fundamental need, a need that is world-
wide and for all time. But one religion may meet that
need more genuinely and permanently than another;
it may be based on a truer notion of man or God,
and so deserve preference in a comparative and critical
study.

It is also important to avoid the error of supposing that
religions should lose their individuality and retain only what
they have in common. A religion which consisted only of
what it had in common with all other religions would probably be no religion at all. There are peculiar needs as well
as common needs. A religion must satisfy the concrete
community or individual, and not the abstract man. Perhaps, in all strictness, there must be as many religions as
there are believers or worshipers. But this is quite con-

sistent with the important truth that there is one constant factor in life from which all religions spring, and which makes of religion a common necessity. And if one is to study the forms or read the literature of a religion that is not one's own, one must see them in this light. One must become for the purpose simply religious; one must become alive not only to one's peculiar needs, but to that deeper and identical need from which all religions have sprung.

I have suggested that this attitude requires cultivation. This is doubtless the case with the great majority even of enlightened readers of the present day, and is very apparent in the history of European thought. By a curious working of the laws of habit and imitation we are for the most part blind to the meaning of our commonest social practices. How many men who obey law and authority, or who are loyal to the peculiar political institution under which they live, reflect upon the utility of government? Most men take government for granted, or fail to think of it at all; and merely assert their factional differences or personal griev-ances. Similarly for most men religion as a general fact, as a human institution, does not exist. They are conscious only of their particular religious differences; or they identify religion so thoroughly with a special religion that they can think of alien religions only as irreligion. For the vast majority of Christians to be religious means the same thing as to be Christian; not to believe as they believe means the same thing as to be an "unbeliever." Nevertheless a great change has taken place in the course of the last three centuries, and it will be worth our while briefly to trace it.

NATURAL *versus* POSITIVE RELIGION

As everyone knows, modern thought arose as a protest against a tendency in the Middle Ages to take too many things for granted. Reason was to be freed from authority, tradition, and pedantry. But this meant, at first, only that man was to exercise his reason in the fields of physics and metaphysics. It was supposed in the seventeenth century that he could do this and yet not question the authority of the state, the church, and the established ethical code. The man of reason was to be internally free, but externally obedient. Institutions, in short, were still to be taken for granted. But in the eighteenth century the liberated reason was directed to institutions themselves, and there arose a rational ethics, a new political science, and a theory of "natural religion." Hobbes, a century earlier, was the forerunner of this movement, and so the original author of all modern social revolutions in so far as these arose from ideas and not from immediate practical exigencies. Of religion Hobbes wrote as follows: "In these four things, opinion of ghosts, ignorance of second causes, devotion toward what men call fear, and taking of things casual for prognostics, consisteth the natural seed of 'religion'; which by reason of the different fancies, judgments, and passions of several men, hath grown up into ceremonies so different, that those which are used by one man are for the most part ridiculous to another." This passage appears in the "Leviathan," [1] published in 1651. In 1755 Hume wrote a treatise bearing the title "The Natural History of Religion," in which he contended that polytheism is the original form of religion, and that "the first ideas of religion arose not from a contemplation of the works of nature, but from a concern with regard to the events of life, and from the incessant hopes and fears which actuate the human mind." Agitated by "the anxious concern for happiness, the dread of future misery, the terror of death, the thirst of revenge, the appetite for food, and other necessaries . . . men scrutinize, with a trembling curiosity, the course of future causes, and examine the various and contrary events of human life. And in this disordered scene, with eyes still more disordered and astonished, they see the first obscure traces of divinity." Both of these passages represented a manner of regarding religion which was revolutionary and offensive to the conservative opinion of the time. They meant that in a certain sense Christianity must be regarded as on a par with the most despised superstitions, since all spring from the same seed in human nature, or from the same general situation in which all men find themselves. It is man's fear of fortune,

[1] See *Harvard Classics*, xxxiv, 323ff.

his hope of controlling the deeper forces of nature for his own good, from which his religion has sprung, and all religions alike may be judged by their power to dispel this fear and fulfill this hope. So there arose the difference between "natural religion," religion conceived as springing from the constitution of man and the common facts of life, and positive religion, which consists in some specific institution, tradition, and dogma. One now has a new standard by which to judge of religion. Just as one may compare monarchy and democracy with reference to their utility as instruments of government, so one may compare Christianity and Buddhism with reference to their fulfillment of the general religious need. Which is the better religion, in the sense of doing better what a religion is intended to do? And quite apart from the question of comparative merits there is a new field of study opened to the human mind, the study of religion as a natural historical fact.

COMPARATIVE RELIGION

Hume's "Natural History of Religion" has developed in two directions. First, the emphasis in the nineteenth century on history and evolution, the interest in the sources and manifold varieties of all growing things, promoted the development of what is now called "Comparative Religion." Missionaries, travelers, and in recent years students of anthropology and ethnography have collected the religious literature and described the religious customs of India, China, and Japan, as well as of primitive and savage peoples in all parts of the globe. Ancient religions have been made known through the development of archæology. Most important of all for the recovery of the past has been the increased knowledge of languages. The knowledge of Sanskrit opened the way to an understanding of the sources of the ancient Indian religions; the translation of hieroglyphics and cuneiform characters has brought to light the ancient religions of Egypt, Babylonia, and Assyria. More refined methods have shed a wholly new light upon Greek and early Semitic religions. The possession of this wealth of material has made possible new generalizations concerning the generic character of religion, or concerning its origin and evolution.

The work of Tylor, Spencer, Max Müller, Andrew Lang, and Frazer may be said to signalize a genuinely new branch of human knowledge in which religion as a universal human interest or aspect of life is made an object of dispassionate and empirical study.

THE PSYCHOLOGY OF RELIGION

Second, toward the close of the nineteenth century a great impetus was given to the science of psychology, and this is reflected in another extension of Hume's "Natural History of Religion," in what is called "Psychology of Religion." There is the question of the genesis of the religious consciousness from instincts and sentiments such as fear and reverence. There are psychological types of religion such as James's "sick soul" and "religion of healthy mindedness." There is the elaborate analysis of the mystical experience, with its "rhythm," its "disconnection," and its characteristic stages. Special psychological importance attaches to religious crises, such as "conversion," and their relation to physiological conditions such as adolescence. Certain religious states border upon hysteria and belong to the domain of abnormal psychology, others illustrate the play of the great social forces of imitation and suggestion. Professor James's great book has given currency to its title "Varieties of Religious Experience," and these varieties are being collected, described, and catalogued by an ever-increasing body of observers.

But both Hobbes and Hume, as we have seen, attempted to name the generic essence of religion. What amid all its varieties external and internal, amid its bewildering manifoldness of ritual, dogma, and mental state, is its common character? Were these authors correct in tracing all religion to man's fear of the influence of the deeper causes of nature on his fortunes? This question is still the interesting question which vitalizes the patient empirical studies in comparative religion and the psychology of religion, and constitutes the problem of philosophy of religion.

To what universal fact does religion owe its existence? Is it perchance a fact concerning human nature? It has often been taught that man possesses a distinct and original faculty called "the religious consciousness" by which he forms the idea of God. All men, possessing the same mental constitution, will thus agree in conceiving of a God. But this view is based upon an obsolete psychology. It is now generally believed that a man is born with instincts and capacities which enable him to cope with his world, but which do not predetermine his ideas. These result from experience, from the interaction between his instincts and capacities and the environment in which he is called upon to exercise them. As respects religion in particular it has become fairly evident that it calls into play various factors of human nature, such as the instincts of fear or of curiosity, no one of which is in itself peculiarly religious. The religious consciousness, in other words, is complex and derived rather than original; a product of experience rather than an innate possession of the mind. How then is the universality of religion to be accounted for? There is a second possibility. Perhaps God, the object of religion, is a common and familiar object, like the sun—so palpable, so ubiquitous that no man can fail to acquire a notion of it. But if one sets aside all preconceived ideas and looks out upon one's world with the eye of a first discoverer, or of a Martian just arrived upon earth, one does not find God. God is not an evident fact in any ordinary sense. Herbert Spencer attempted to trace religion to a belief in ghosts founded upon the experience of dreams. To one who interprets dreams naively it is doubtless a fact that persons "appear" after death and seem to speak and act where their bodies are not. But in so far as a ghost is such a commonplace and evident fact it is not a God. It is merely one sort of curious creature that inhabits this teeming world. And the religious man finds objects of worship in what is most substantial and least ghostlike. It is a forced and farfetched hypothesis that would have us explain the worship of the sun, or the sea, or the Creator, by supposing that man has projected into nature the substances of his dreams. God is not a substance. He is not more vaporous or incorporeal than he is liquid or solid, except in sophisticated theologies. And it is certainly only in a careless or figurative sense that God can be said to be manifest in his works, in the splendor or terrors of nature. He may be inferred or interpreted from these, but he is not perceived as literally present in their midst. "The heavens declare the glory of God; and the firmament sheweth his handiwork," but not to the eye of the mere observer of fact even though it be placed at the end of a telescope.

There seems to me to be only one alternative left. We must, I think, conclude that in so far as religion is universal it arises from *the conjunction of man and his environment*. Its seed is the situation in which man finds himself, a situation made up of two interacting parts, man and his world. Let us see if we can describe this situation so as to see the inevitableness of religion.

Life may be broadly described as *seeking something under given circumstances*. Man is impelled toward ends, and limited by an existing situation. If we view our world dramatically, and assign to man the rôle of hero, the fundamental fact is his dependence on environment. He exists, as it were, despite the environment, which, though it has given birth to him, is ever threatening to devour him; and whatever he gains must be wrung from that environment. Life must be conducted, in short, on terms dictated by its environment. But before religion we must suppose life to have already conquered something of nature and made it its own. When man finds himself, there is already much that he can control. He can move about freely on the surface of the earth; he can manipulate physical objects and so procure himself food and shelter; and through individual prowess or through combination he can control other men. Within certain limits, then, man has the upper hand, and may make his fortune as he wills. But these limits are narrow. They are, of course, most narrow in the early stages of human development. But there has been no time in which they have not been pitifully narrow. Man may deceive himself. He may so magnify his achievements or be so preoccupied with his affairs as to enjoy illusions of grandeur and self-sufficiency. But it is a question if our Western, modern, and "civilized" boastfulness does not betoken a more imperfect sense of proportion than that consciousness of dependence which was once felt more keenly and is still felt wherever man finds himself in the immediate presence of the unharnessed energies of nature. In any case man is periodically reminded, if he is not perpetually mindful, of the great residual environment that is beyond his control. Man proposes, but after all something beyond him disposes. Floods, droughts, pestilence, rigors of climate, subjection, error, failure—these are the facts that teach and drive home the lesson of dependence. The most impressive and unanswerable fact is death. The whole fabric of personal achievement. woven by innumerable painstaking acts, all the fruits of struggle and of growth—possessions, power, friendship—are apparently annihilated in an instant, and with an ease that would be ridiculous if it were not so deeply tragic.

Now how shall man profit by this bitter lesson? He must not despair if he is to live; for to live is to hope for and to seek a way out of every predicament. To live in the consciousness of finitude and dependence means to look for help. If the forces that man cannot control do actually determine his destiny, then he must seek to win them over, or to ally himself with them. Here, I believe, is the root of religion: the attempt of man, conscious of his helplessness, to unite himself with the powers which do actually dominate. Religion is a *sense of need,* a conviction of the insecurity of any merely worldly advantage that he may gain for himself, and a *way of salvation* through coming to terms with that which controls his destiny. Religion is both founded on fear and consummated in hope.

It will perhaps seem strange that one should thus have attempted to describe religion without referring to deity. But the reason for the attempt lies in the fact that deity is not the cause of religion, but the product of religion. God is not, as we have seen, a manifest fact among facts; but is an object invoked to meet the religious need. Let us consider briefly the various types of deity to which religion has given rise.

TYPES OF DEITY

The commonest of all objects of worship is some prominent aspect of nature, such as the sky, sun, moon, and stars, the earth, the sea, rivers, winds, the seasons, day, and night. Before the development of science man cannot control the operations of these phenomena. Whether they shall favor him with moderate rains, fertility, a calm passage and temperate weather, or torture and destroy him with drought, flood, storm, and the extremes of heat and cold, he can neither foretell nor predetermine. He can only wait and tremble, hope and pray. That he should hope and pray is inevitable. It is the instinct of any living thing toward that which is to decide its fate and which it is impotent otherwise to control. The sun thus regarded as able either to bless or to destroy, and therefore an object of importunity, already begins to be a god. But there is lacking a factor which if it be not absolutely indispensable to deity, is almost invariably present. I refer to what is commonly called "personification." What is worshiped is the "spirit" in the sun, or the sun construed as spirit. But this factor, too, arises, I believe, directly from the practical situation and not from any metaphysics on the part of the worshiper. It is the sequel to the familiar fact that we impute interest or will to any agency that helps or hurts. I do not mean that there is any express judgment to that effect, but that our emotional and practical response is similar to that which we accord to other living individuals. The animal will exhibit rage toward the rod with which he is prodded, the child will chastise the blocks which "refuse" to stand up, as his father will revenge himself upon the perverse golf stick by breaking it across his knee. Similarly it is natural to love, eulogize, caress, or adorn any object to which one owes pleasure or any other benefit. These responses are equivalent to imputing *an attitude* to their objects, an attitude of malice or hostility when the effect is hurtful, and one of benevolence when the effect is helpful. This, I believe, is the root of religious personification. The sun, in so far as its effects are good, is an object of gratitude for favor shown; in so far as its effects are bad, it is an object of solicitous regard in the hope that its hostility may be averted and its favor won. The sun so regarded or worshiped is the sun god. The extent to which the will or intent, and the power over man, are divorced from the visible and bodily sun and regarded as a "spirit" is of secondary importance; as is also the extent to which such a god has a history of his own apart from his treatment of man. For the exuberant imagination of the Greeks the sun god becomes an individuality vividly realized in art, poetry, and legend. But for practical people like the Chinese, "it is enough," as Professor Moore points out, "to know what the Gods do, and what their worshipers have to do to secure their favor, without trying to imagine what they are like."[2]

A second type of deity is the ancestor; the actual human ancestor, as worshiped by the Chinese, the mystical animal ancestor of totemism, or any deity adopted as ancestor, as the Christian God is claimed as Father by his believers. The idea of kinship with the object of worship is very widespread, and its motive is clearly intelligible in the light of what has been said above. Kinship implies alliance, the existence of friendly support and the right to claim it. One's departed ancestors belong to that world beyond from which emanate the dread forces that one cannot control. Their presence there means that there are friends at court. Man is not surrounded by indifferent strangers, but by beings bound to him by nature and inseparable ties, partisans who are favorably inclined.

A third type of deity is the tutelary god, conceived *ad hoc* to render some special service. He may be the personal, tribal, or national protector; or the good genius of some human or social activity, such as is the god who presides over husbandry, war, or navigation, or the homely household god of the hearth and the "cooking furnace." Here the insistent need invents and objectifies its own fulfillment.

All three notions of deity may be united in a local tribal deity, "who on the one hand has fixed relations to a race of men, and on the other hand has fixed relations to a definite sphere of nature," so that "the worshiper is brought into stated and permanent alliance with certain parts of his

[2] G. F. Moore: "History of Religions," p. 22.

material environment which are not subject to his will and control." [3]

There is one further notion of deity that demands recognition in this brief summary, the notion, namely, of *the supreme deity*. As men develop in intelligence, imagination, and in range of social intercourse, it is inevitable that one god should be exalted above all others, or worshiped to the exclusion of all others. Such a religious conception arises from the experience of the unity of nature or of the unity of man. There is an evident hierarchy among the powers of nature; some are subordinated to others, and it is natural to conceive of one as supreme. Most evident to sense is the exultation of the heavens above the earth and the intermediate spaces. So we find Heaven to be supreme God among the Chinese, and Zeus among the Greeks. On the other hand, there is a hierarchy among tutelary and ancestral gods. As the patron gods of individuals, of special arts, or of tribes and provinces are subordinated to the national god, so the national god in turn is subjected to the god of a conquering nation. Allied with the idea of universal conquest is the idea of an all-dominant god, the god of the ruling class. Or a tutelary god may be universal in proportion to the universality of the activity over which he presides. The gods of the same activity though belonging originally to different cults may come to be identified; so that there arises the conception of a god that shall be universal in the sense of presiding over the common undertaking in which all men are engaged. And similarly the god from whom all men are descended will take precedence of the gods of families, tribes, and nations. Thus there are several more or less independent motives which may lead to a universal religion, such as Christianity, whose god is a god of all men, regardless of time, place, race, or station.

Deity, then, in the generic sense common to all religions, high and low, is some force beyond the range of man's control, potent over his fortunes, construed as friendly or

[3] W. Robertson Smith: "Religion of the Semites," p. 124.

hostile, and so treated as to secure, if possible, its favor and support. It is important in the next place to point out two different motives in worship, connected with two different ways in which the worshiper and his god may be brought into unison. To put it briefly, one may propose to have one's own way, or surrender to the god's way. This is the religious application of the fact that there are two ways to obtain satisfaction and peace of mind; to get what one wants, or to want what one gets. Religion may be said always to lie somewhere between these two extremes. It is natural and reasonable to try the former method first. And this is undoubtedly the earlier motive in worship. Man wants food, and long life, and victory over his enemies, and he seeks to gain the deity's support in these undertakings. But there is never a time when he does not recognize the necessity of making concessions. He pays sacrifices, or observes taboo, or adopts the code of conduct which his god prescribes. And it is the common religious experience that the conditions of divine favor become more exacting, while the benefit is less evident. Thus there arises what philosophers call the problem of evil, of which the classic Christian expression is to be found in the Book of Job,[4] who "was perfect and upright, and one that feared God, and eschewed evil," and nevertheless was visited with every misery and disaster. In so far as Job solved this problem he found the solution in entire surrender to the will of God. "Naked came I out of my mother's womb, and naked shall I return thither: the Lord gave, and the Lord hath taken away; blessed be the name of the Lord." Nevertheless in the end "the Lord gave Job twice as much as he had before." Certainly a religion of utter renunciation would be no religion at all. There would be no motive in worship unless one were in some sense blessed thereby. The tendency in the evolution of religion is to substitute for the carnal or worldly blessing for which one had at first invoked divine aid a new and higher good which one learns to find in the mode of life which religion prescribes. Religion becomes thus not merely instrumental, but educative. From it one learns not so much the way to satisfy one's natural and secular wants, as

[4] *H. C.*, xliv, 73ff.

the way to despise those wants and set one's heart on other things. It is this mingled self-assertion and self-surrender in religion that makes reverence its characteristic emotion. God is both the means by which one realizes one's end, and also a higher law by which one's end is reconstructed.

THE RELIGION OF RENUNCIATION

The religion in which entire renunciation is most closely approximated is the philosophical or esoteric religion of India. All the varieties of this religion reflect one fundamental attitude to life, the feeling that no good can come of persistent endeavor. The attempt to fulfill desire is hopeless. The Indian does not abandon himself to despair; but he differs from his occidental brother in this, that whereas the latter hopes by divine aid, or in the distant future, to achieve either personal happiness or the perfection of what he calls "civilization," the former regards the whole attempt as founded on error. Its inevitable failure does not signify real failure, but the adoption of a wrong standard of success. According to the teaching of the "Upanishads" even separate individuality is an illusion perpetuated by desire.

> When all the passion is at rest
> That lurks within the heart of man
> Then is the mortal no more mortal,
> But here and now attaineth Brahman.[5]

In Brahman, the deeper unity of the world, the individual has his true being and is saved.

The importance of regarding the conception of God, not as the root of religion, but as the product of religion, appears when we come to the consideration of Buddhism.[6] For Buddhism is, in fact, a godless religion, paradoxical as that may seem. It is true that Buddha himself has come like Confucius to be an object of religion. Every founder of a religion is almost inevitably deified by his followers. But Buddha did not deify himself. He taught men to regard even the soul itself as a transient and illusory experience. Suffering is the universal law of existence. Existence

[5] Quoted by G. F. Moore, op. cit., p. 270.
[6] See lecture by Professor Lanman, below.

is the penalty of desire, a rebirth owing to *Karma,* the dispositions and desert which are the precipitate of a previous existence. There is a fatal recurrence of existence, for life tends ever to create the conditions of its own reincarnation and continuance. Salvation means not successful existence, the realization of actual desires, but escape from existence, through the conquering of desire. In such a religion there is no god, for there is no ulterior power in or through which man is to fulfill his positive longings. But it is nevertheless religion, in that it is a release of man from his predicament. *Nirvana* is perhaps from all other points of view equivalent to annihilation; but from the point of view of man, conscious of his helplessness and failure, it means salvation. It is a philosophy of life, an accord between man and his world by which he wins the greatest good that he can conceive.

In order to understand the general scope of religious literature it is not sufficient that one should grasp the general principle of religion. One must know something of the forms which religion assumes in human life; and especially important is it to know something of its relations to science on the one hand, and to art and poetry on the other hand.

RELIGION AND SCIENCE

By science let us understand knowledge founded on fact or rigorous reasoning. How far is one to construe religious literature as science, that is, as the work of man's theorizing and cognizing faculties? There is probably more confusion in this matter at the present time than there has ever been in the past. The increase of doubt, the scientific refutation of beliefs once authorized by religion, have led to various attempts to retain these beliefs by a sheer act of "faith," or on account of their subjective and imaginative values. Since the ascendency of Catholic orthodoxy in the fourteenth century there has been a steady tendency to regard one Christian teaching after another, the story of Jonah and the whale, the account of creation in Genesis, and now even the miracles of the New Testament, as fictions which are to be valued as symbols, tradition, poetry, or as parts of a system of faith which as a whole is to be judged not by reference to historic fact but by its comforting or regenerating effect upon the believer. But if we recall to our minds that original human need in response to which religion arises, it is unmistakably evident that there must be a nucleus of truth in a religion if it is to meet that need at all. In religion man seeks to relate himself profitably *to things as they are.* He seeks to save his soul by adopting the course that is consistent with the deeper reality. If he is misled as to the nature of reality, then his whole plan is founded on error and is foredoomed to failure. If the forces of nature have no power, or are not to be influenced by human importunity, then it is folly to worship them. If there be no deeper cause that guarantees the triumph of righteousness, then the Christian's hope is illusory, and his prayer and worship idle. In short, every religion is at heart a belief in something as true, and if that something be not true, then the religion is discredited.

Nevertheless, although there is a scientific nucleus in every religion, that nucleus is but a small fraction of it. In the first place religion differs from science proper in that it deliberately adopts a view of things according to which man is the central fact of the universe. Religion is interested in cosmic affairs only in so far as they bear upon human fortunes. Hence it finally expresses itself not in judgments of fact, but in emotion, such as hope, fear, confidence, despair, reverence, love, gratitude, or self-subjection. Its object is the cosmos or some ulterior cosmic agency, construed as helpful or hurtful, colored by the worshiper's solicitude. Hence much religious literature, such, for example, as the Psalms,[7] or St. Augustine's Confessions,[8] are essentially expressions of the religious emotions, characterizations of deity not by the use of cold scientific formulas, but by the use of epithets that signify the feelings and attitude of the worshiper himself.

A second non-scientific factor in religion is that contributed by the imagination and by social tradition. Religion differs from theory in that it comes after and not before

[7] *H. C.,* xliv, 147ff.   [8] *H. C.,* vii, 5ff.

belief. Religion is not effective, does not do its work, until after some interpretation of cosmic forces has been adopted by an individual and has become the accepted basis of his life. Buddhism begins as a religion when the individual enters upon that course of discipline by which he hopes to attain *Nirvana;* and Christianity begins when the believer actually follows the way of salvation by prayer, obedience, and good works. And in all important historical religions the underlying dogmas are assimilated not only to personal but also to social life. They are commonly and collectively believed, and have become the unconscious presuppositions of a community worship. The office of the religious imagination is in making these scientific presuppositions vital and effective. A religion of hope is not a series of propositions concerning the favorable bearing of cosmic forces, but a *vivid realization* of the purport of such propositions, a hopefulness translated into emotional buoyance or confident action. By the imagination religious truth is made impressive, so that it evokes the affections and motivates action. The social counterpart is found in tradition and symbolism, which secures the continuity and solidarity of religious feelings and practices. In brief, then, we may expect to find in all expressions of religion, such as religious literature, certain underlying assumptions which are capable of being converted into scientific propositions; but these will be overlaid and obscured by an imaginative and symbolic representation in which their meaning is emotionally and practically realized.

There is another important respect in which religion differs from science, namely, in its proceeding beyond the limits of evidence. There never was and never will be a religion which possesses the same verification that is demanded in the case of a scientific theory. Religion is a leap in the dark. The reason for this is evident. For practical purposes it is necessary to conclude matters that for strictly theoretical purposes one would postpone in the hope of further light. Life is an emergency, a crisis, or as William James has said, a "forced option." [9] One must make up one's mind quickly, or live altogether at random. What

[9] "Will to Believe," p. 3.

shall one make of this world, and what shall one do to be saved? The decision cannot be postponed; and yet the evidence is, strictly considered, inconclusive. Faith means to believe what seems probable, and to believe it not half-heartedly, but with conviction. For if one believes half-heartedly, one cannot *proceed* according to one's belief, or attain salvation by it. The element of sheer faith may be more or less, according to the degree of critical and philosophical power which the worshiper possesses. But in every case there will be some basis in experienced fact and in inference, and also some "will to believe" or reliance on authority. And we shall consequently find in religious literature a note of dogmatic certainty and of willfulness, which is as inevitable in such a context as it would be intolerable in science.

RELIGION AND MORALITY

There is one further topic to which even so brief an introduction as this must allude. What is the relation between religion and morality? Are we to regard ethical teachings such as those of the "Book of Proverbs" or the "Sayings of Confucius" [10] as religious? To answer this question, we have only, I think, to bear clearly in mind the generic meaning of religion. A mode of life becomes religious only when it is pursued under certain auspices; only when it is conceived as sanctioned by the general nature of the cosmos, and as constituting a way of salvation. If justice be prized as a means of social welfare, it is ethical; if it be adopted as a means of winning the favor of God, or as a means of achieving *Nirvana,* it is religious. The moral life takes on a religious character when it is in some way connected with the cosmic life. In the so-called "ethical religions" the mode of life prescribed by religion tends to coincide with that prescribed by the moral consciousness, and righteousness is conceived as the way of salvation. Needless to say, such a contraction of morality greatly enhances its impressiveness and appeal. In all ethical religions that are inspired with hope, religion adds to a good conscience the sense of ascendency or

[10] *H. C.,* xliv, 5ff., and lecture by A. D. Sheffield, below.

victory over nature. Right living takes on the aspect of ultimate reality. To sheer duty is added confidence, inspiration, the expectation of limitless and durable achievement. Even in pessimistic religions of the ethical type, morality acquires prestige as having supreme importance for escape from the misery of existence. And from the religious consciousness as such, irrespective of its special claims and beliefs, morality acquires a certain dignity and reinforcement. For religion encourages man to look at life roundly and seriously. It frees him from the obsession of passion and the circumscription of immediate interests. It keeps alive the cosmic imagination, and invites attention to the problem of life as a whole in all its bearings, internal and external.

Thus it is fair to conclude that religion is universal in two senses. On the one hand it springs from a universal need. On the other hand, it possesses a universal value, and cannot fail, however much of error or blindness there may be in it, to elevate and dignify life. True religion is better than false, but it is not less certain that religion is better than irreligion.

II. BUDDHISM

By Professor C. R. Lanman

THE life of Gotama, the Enlightened One or Buddha, a life of eighty years, is divided into two parts, one of thirty-five years and one of forty-five, by the event of his Enlightenment or Bodhi. This seeing of a new light is to a Buddhist the one supreme event of the incalculably long æon now current, just as is the birth of Jesus in Occidental chronology. Those first thirty-five years are again divided into two parts, the period of his life as a prince or the time from his birth until (at the age of twenty-nine[1]) he forsook the world to struggle for the Supreme Enlightenment, and the period of the six years of that struggle. Of these thirty-five years we have elaborate accounts.[2] Of the last forty-five, tradition has little to say in the way of entertaining story, but very much by way of reporting "the Teacher's" teachings. These teachings as laid down in the canonical scriptures of Buddhism are in very deed his life in the truest sense.

THE BIRTHS OF BUDDHA

The belief that a man must be born and live and die, only to be born and die again and again through a weary round of existences, was widespread in India long before Buddha's day. And accordingly the "biography" of a Buddha must include an account of some of those former "births" or existences. The story of Sumedha[3] is one of these. The "Jātaka," the most charming of all Buddhist story books,[4] contains the narrative of not less than 547 former existences

---

[1] *Harvard Classics.* xlv, 657.   [2] *H. C.*, xlv, 617-661.
[3] *H. C.*, xlv, 591-616. The story of the "Wise Hare," pages 712-716, is a Jātaka or Birth story.
[4] Translated by various hands under the editorship of E. B. Cowell, 6 vols., Cambridge, 1895-1907.

of Gotama. Next after all this prenatal biography comes the account of Buddha's birth into the existence which concerns us most nearly, the actual one of the sixth century before Christ, and this forms the subject of the second of Warren's translations, "The Birth of the Buddha." [5] That translation is from a later work. It is most instructive for the student of religious tradition to compare the meager statements of the oldest canonical account with such an account as this, in order to see how the loving imagination of devout disciples may embellish a simple and prosaic fact with a multitude of picturesque details. Thus the presages of Buddha's birth [6] are quite comparable, except for beauty of poetic diction, with those of the birth of Jesus in Milton's hymn "On the Morning of Christ's Nativity." [7] As an example of new accretions to the older story may be cited the later tradition that Buddha was born from his mother's right side, a trait that appears not only in the Lalita-vistara and in St. Jerome, but also in many of the sculptured representations of the scene.

THE TEACHINGS OF BUDDHA

The teachings of Buddha are indeed his life, his very self. In the house of a potter the venerable Vakkali lay nigh unto death. [8] The Exalted One (Buddha) came to his pillow and made kindest inquiries. "Long have I wished to go to the Exalted One to see him, but there was not enough strength in my body to go." "Peace, Vakkali! what should it profit thee to see this my corrupt body? Whoso, O Vakkali, seeth my teachings, he seeth me." Here the Teacher identifies himself with his teachings no less completely than does Jesus when he declares unto Thomas, "I am the way." And yet, despite Buddha's merging of his personality in his doctrine, it is of utmost importance to remember two things: First that Buddha most explicitly disclaims acceptance of his teachings on the score of authority; and secondly that it was, after all, their intrinsic excellence which (whether we take it as the fruit, of a

[5] *H. C.*, xlv, 617-626.   [6] *H. C.*, xlv, 622.   [7] *H. C.*, iv, 7.
[8] Samyutta-Nikāya, xxii, 87 (3.119).

transcendental illumination or as the outcome of his personality) has maintained them as a mighty world power for five and twenty centuries.

First then his position as to authority. The Exalted One, when making a tour through Kosala, once stopped at Kesaputta, a town of the Kālāmans. They asked him: "Master, so many teachers come to us with their doctrines. Who of them is right and who is wrong?" "Not because it is tradition," he answers, "not because it has been handed down from one to another, not because ye think 'Our teacher is one to whom great deference is due,' should ye accept a doctrine. When, O Kālāmans, when ye of yourselves recognize that such and such things are bad and conduce to evil and sorrow, then do ye reject them." [9] And again, "When a man's conviction of a truth is dependent on no one but himself, this, O Kaccāna, is what constitutes Right Belief." [10] It is hard for us of the twentieth century to estimate aright the significance of Buddha's attitude. He lived in a land and age when deference to authority was well-nigh universal. To break with it as he did, implies an intelligence far beyond the common and a lofty courage.

Secondly as to the intrinsic excellence of Buddha's teaching. That teaching is well characterized by a few brief phrases which occur as a commonplace in the canonical texts and are used as one of the forty subjects of meditation or "businesses" by devout Buddhists: "Well taught by the Exalted One is the doctrine. It avails even in the present life, is immediate in its blessed results, is inviting, is conducive to salvation, and may be mastered by any intelligent man for himself." [11] Frankly disclaiming knowledge of what happens after death, Buddha addressed himself to the problem of sorrow as we have it here and now, and sought to relieve it by leading men into the path of righteousness and good-will and freedom from lust. A would-be disciple once asked him to answer certain dogmatic questions about life after death. Buddha parried them all as irrelevances in the dialogue which Warren gives[12] and which is one of the finest presentations of

[9] Anguttara-Nikāya, iii, 65 (1.189).   [10] H. C., xlv, 677.
[11] H. C., xlv, 765.   [12] H. C., xlv, 662-667.

Religion versus Dogma to be found in antiquity. The holy
life, he says, does not depend upon the answers to any of
these questions.

If a physician of forty years ago had been asked to foretell the then presumable advances of medical science, his
guesses might well have included the discovery of new
specifics, such as quinine for malaria; for medicine was
then the healing art, its aim was to cure. True, we had
heard from our childhood that an ounce of prevention is
worth a pound of cure. But how was the ounce of prevention to be had? Doubtless by finding out the cause of
disease. And this is on the whole the most significant
achievement of modern medicine. Now it was precisely
this problem in the world of the spirit that Buddha claimed
to solve, the ætiology of man's misery. His solution he
publicly announced in his first sermon, the gist of which
was destined to become known to untold millions, the sermon of the Deerpark of Benares.

His most important point is the cause of human suffering,[13]
and that he finds in the craving for existence (no matter
how noble that existence) and for pleasure. If you can
only master these cravings, you are on the road to salvation, to *Nirvana*. This, so far as the present life is concerned, means the going out of the fires of lust and ill will
and delusion, and further a getting rid thereby of the round
of rebirth.

BUDDHISM AND OTHER RELIGIONS

Without attempting to discuss so many-sided a subject as
Nirvana, or rightly to evaluate Buddha's prescription of the
abandonment of all craving, it is clear that his ethical teachings, like his spotless life, have stood and will stand the
test of centuries. The Deerpark sermon urges the excellence of the golden mean between the life of self-castiga-
tion and the life of ease and luxury, and propounds the
Noble Eightfold Path, which is, after all, in brief, the life

[13] Buddha's Four Eminent Truths concern suffering, its cause, its sur-
cease, and the way thereto. They coincide with those of the Yoga system
and are indeed the four cardinal subjects of Hindu medical science applied
to spiritual healing—a fact which famous ancient Hindu writers have themselves not failed to observe.

of righteousness in thought and word and deed. Many
notable similarities between the teachings of Buddha and
those of Jesus have been pointed out.[14] These need not
surprise us. Nor is there any *à priori* reason for assuming
a borrowing in either direction. If I make an entirely
original demonstration of the fact that the inner angles of
a triangle amount to two right angles, my demonstration
will agree in essence with that of Pythagoras because
mathematical truth does not differ from land to land nor
from age to age. Nor yet does goodness. And accordingly
many of the teachings of the great teachers of righteousness must coincide.

On the other hand it is interesting to note that Buddha's
teachings lay great emphasis, and lay it often, upon things
about which in the Gospels comparatively little or nothing
is expressly said. Don't hurry, don't worry, the simple life;
don't accept a belief upon the authority of me or of anyone
else; don't let your outgo exceed your income; the relation
of master and servant; the duty not only of kindness but
even of courtesy to animals: these are some of the themes
upon which Buddha discourses, now with a touch of humor,
now with pathos, and always with gentleness and wisdom
and cogency.

To the readers of Warren's faithful translations a word
is due as to the extreme repetitiousness of much of the
Buddhist writings. The charming stories are free from it.
Not so the doctrinal discourses. Scientific opinion upon
this strange and tedious fault is rapidly clearing.[15] These
texts that claim to be the actual "Buddha-word" are in
reality the product of conscious scholastic literary activity,
and of a time considerably subsequent to that of Buddha.
This is quite certain. But no less so is it that they do in
fact contain the real sayings of Buddha. "Be ye heirs of
things spiritual, not heirs of things carnal."[16] This, we may
confidently assert, is in its simplicity and pregnant brevity,

[14] So by Albert J. Edmunds in his "Buddhist and Christian Gospels," 4th
ed., 2 vols., Philadelphia, 1908-9.
[15] See R. Otto Franke, Dīgha-Nikāya, Göttingen, 1913, p. x.
[16] The antithesis of this saying of Buddha, we may note in passing, is
familiar to readers of the New Testament.

an absolutely authentic utterance of Gotama Buddha. At the same time it is the substance, and indeed we may say the entire substance, of a discourse of about four hundred Pali words attributed to Buddha.[17] Of the lengths to which perverse scholasticism may go, the case is a luculent illustration.[18]

[17] Majjhima-Nikāya, vol. 1, p. 12-13.
[18] The method of the expansion one may easily guess after reading Warren's "Questions," H. C., xlv, 662-667. Its motive is probably pedagogical.

III. CONFUCIANISM

By Alfred Dwight Sheffield

CONFUCIANISM, although spoken of with Buddhism and Taoism as one of the "Three Teachings," or three major religions of China, can hardly be defined as a religion in the precise way in which we can define Mahayana Buddhism or Roman Catholic Christianity. It has neither creed nor priesthood, nor any worship beyond what Confucius found already established in his day. The commemorative service, performed by local officials throughout China in spring and autumn in the red-walled shrines known as "Confucian temples" is not worship of the sage, but a civil rite in his honor, quite compatible with the profession of another religion. Indeed, when a few centuries after his death veneration approached to worship, and women began offering prayers to Confucius for children, the practice was stopped (A. D. 472) by imperial edict, as something superstitious and unbecoming. Confucianism may be said to have a bible in the nine canonical books associated with the sage's name; but it claims for them no divine revelation, nor other inspiration than such as speaks for itself from their pages. What these books yield to one who would define Confucianism is a conception of enlightened living, a social ideal which entails some allegiance to an old national religion blending nature worship and ancestor worship. One might say that the essence of Confucianism is a type of "eligible" life, the regimen of which includes a worship only indirectly Confucian, much as Stoicism among the Romans included as a matter of principle some adherence to the established worship.

THE TEACHING OF CONFUCIUS

Confucius can be appreciated only in his historical setting. It has been made a reproach to the sage that his vision was retrospective and conservative; but he cannot be charged with a mere desire to bring back "the good old days." When, at the court of Chou, he first inspected the ancestral shrines and the arrangements for the great annual sacrifices to Heaven and Earth, he exclaimed: "As we use a glass to examine the forms of things, so must we study the past to understand the present." The past, moreover, really held models of statecraft from which his own times had fallen away. The great Chou dynasty, which through a succession of able princes had ruled the whole valley of the Hoang Ho, had in the sixth century B. C. dwindled to a shadow of its early power. The emperor (or rather king, for the title *Huang-ti* was then applied only to deceased monarchs) was reduced to a headship merely nominal, and the old imperial domain was broken up among turbulent vassals, each fighting for his own hand. The China of Confucius was pretty much in the condition of France before Louis XI broke the power of the feudal dukes and counts. With the tradition behind him of a nation united by wise leadership, Confucius is no more to be blamed for looking back than is Aristotle, whose Ethics and Politics show plainly that his sympathies were not with the advancing career of Macedon but with the old polity of Athens.

The first group of the Confucian books, the Five Classics, are fruits of this regard for the past, the sage being the reputed compiler of four of them, and author of the faith. These classics are the "Shu Ching" or "Book of History," made up of documents covering a period from the twenty-fourth to the eighth century B. C.; the "Shih Ching" or "Book of Odes," 305 lyrics dating from the eighteenth to the sixth century; the "Yi Ching" or "Book of Permutations," an ancient manual of divination; the "Li Chi," a compilation of ceremonial usages; and the "Ch'un Ch'iu," annals (722-484) of Confucius's native state of Lu. The second group in the canon, the Four Books, convey his actual teachings. They are the "Lun Yü" or "Sayings of Confucius"[1]; the "Ta Hsueh" or "Great Learning," a treatise by his disciple Tsang Sin on the ordering of the individual life, the family, and the state; the "Chung Yung"

[1] *Harvard Classics,* xliv, 5ff.

or "Doctrine of the Mean," a treatise on conduct by his grandson K'ung Chi; and the "Book of Mencius," his great apostle.

The distinctive features of Confucian doctrine may be summarized as follows:

(1) Filial piety is the cardinal social virtue. A dutiful son will prove dutiful in all the five relationships: those of father and son, ruler and subject, husband and wife, elder brother and younger, and that of friend. Such a tenet was naturally acceptable to a social system like the Chinese, with its patriarchalism and insistence on the family rather than the individual as the unit of society. Loyalty to family it raises to a religious duty in the rite of ancestor worship. Here Confucius did no more than emphasize with his approval a national custom—mentioned in the earliest odes—of offering food and wine to departed spirits. How far this family cult is to be construed as actual worship is disputable: some would compare it merely with the French custom of adorning graves on All Souls' Day. But it effectively strengthens the family bond, impressing as it does the sense of family unity and perpetuity through the passing generations.

(2) Between man and man the rule of practice is "reciprocity." "What you do not want done to yourself, do not do to others." Benevolence—an extension of the love of son and brother—is the worthy attitude toward one's fellows, but it should not be pressed to fatuous lengths. When asked his opinion of Lao-tse's teaching that one should requite injury with good, Confucius replied: "With what, then, will you requite kindness? Return good for good; for injury return justice."

(3) The chief moral force in society is the example of the "superior man." [2] By nature man is good, and the unrighteousness of society is due to faulty education and bad example. Virtue in superiors will call out virtue in common folk. The burden of Confucius's teaching is therefore "superior" character—character so disciplined to a moral tact and responsive propriety that in every situation it knows the right thing and does it, and so poised in its own

[2] In the version printed in *H. C.*, this term is translated "gentleman."

integrity as to practice virtue for virtue's sake. "What the small man seeks is in others; what the superior man seeks is in himself."

(4) Toward the world of spiritual beings the Confucian attitude is one of reverent agnosticism. The sage would have nothing to say of death and the future state. "We know little enough of ourselves as men; what, then, can we know of ourselves as spirits?" In his habit of referring to "T'ien" or "Heaven," Confucius may not have deliberately avoided the more personal term "Shang-ti" (Supreme Lord), and expressions of his are not lacking which suggest a personal faith: but speculation on the nature of being and the destiny of the world he treated simply as a waste of time. On a report that two bereaved friends were comforting themselves with the doctrine that life is but dream and death the awakening, he remarked: "These men travel beyond the rule of life; I travel within it."

In summary one might say that Confucius did not found any religious system, but transmitted one with a renewed stress on its ethical bearings. His interest was in man as made for society. Religious rites he performed to the letter, but more from a sense of their efficacy for "social-mindedness" than from any glow of piety. His faith was a faith in right thinking. The "four things he seldom spoke of—wonders, feats of strength, rebellious disorder, spirits"—were simply the things not tractable to reason.

THE GROWTH OF CONFUCIAN INFLUENCE

Confucianism has so long dominated the intellectual life of China that western scholars have fallen into the habit of speaking as if there were a sort of preestablished harmony between it and the national mind. As a matter of fact it has had to win its way against vigorous criticism and formidable rivals. The two centuries following Confucius's death were rife with conflicting theories of ethics. Yan Chu presented a cynical egoism: death ends all; so make the most of life, every man for himself. To this doctrine Mo Ti opposed a radical altruism, with universal love as the cure of misgovernment and social disorders.

Lao-tse impugned the Confucian idea of man's inborn goodness. Man's nature no more tends to goodness than water tends to run east, or willow wood to take shape in cups and bowls. Against all these contentions the teaching of Confucius was defended and elucidated by the greatest of his followers, Meng-tse (372-289), whose name has been Latinized as Mencius. But Confucianism had to meet systems of thought that carried a more positive religious appeal than it admitted of. Taoism was already in the field, preaching a wise passiveness toward the Way of Heaven, and enlisting in Chuang-tse one of the most brilliant writers that China has produced. His teaching was mystical: "The universe and I came into being together; and I, with all things therein, are One." The repulse of this doctrine by that of Confucius is perhaps correctly explained by the historian Ssu-ma Ch'ien: "Like a flood its mysteries spread at will: hence no one, from rulers downward, could apply them to any definite use." But the reticence of Confucius as to the state of departed spirits left an opening for Buddhism, which describes that state with the full detail craved by popular imagination. The pessimistic philosophy of Buddhism was indeed alien to the Chinese temperament, but its missionaries won a ready response to its doctrine of retribution and its offer of salvation. From the fifth century on it was increasingly in conflict with Confucianism, and succumbed only after sharp persecution. Even in its decline it has contributed many ideas and practices to the old animistic religion of the masses. The triumph of Confucianism in its fall, moreover, was not a mere reassertion of the teaching of Confucius and Mencius. Taoism and Buddhism had raised questions of cosmology which could no longer be ignored. The Neo-Confucianism, therefore, that began with Chou Tun-i (1017-1073) built upon the Yi Ching a cosmic philosophy, describing the world in terms of two principles: a primal matter and an immanent intelligence, which give rise on the one hand to the five elements and all sense data, and on the other to all wisdom and moral ideals. The greatest name in Neo-Confucianism is Chu Hsi (1130-1200), whose commentaries on the canonical books are now authoritative, and whose manuals of domestic rites and manners have brought the Confucian code into the homes of the people.

In 1906 Confucius was "deified" by imperial decree. With the rise of republicanism, however, there has appeared a disposition to reject not only such a canonization of the sage, but the whole conservative tradition for which he has stood. The movement has at the present writing called out a reaction, but the future of Confucianism amid the intellectual currents now flooding in from the West, can be only matter of conjecture. One may hope that the ethical code that has made so much of what is best in the national culture both of China and of Japan will keep its vitality under change of forms and formulas. Western critics sometimes talk as if Confucius had held his countrymen's regard by a sort of infatuation. If so, it has been given to no other man to captivate the imagination of his kind with sheer reasonableness.

IV. GREEK RELIGION

By Professor Clifford Herschel Moore

GREEK religion includes all the varied religious beliefs and practices of the peoples living in Greek lands from the beginning of history to the end of paganism. In contrast to Christianity it had no body of revealed teachings, no common dogma or fixed ritual binding at all shrines and on every worshiper, but each locality might have its own distinctive myths and practices, and the individual might believe what he pleased so long as he did not openly do violence to tradition. No priestly orders attempted to interpose their decrees upon society; local habit alone determined both ritual and belief.

The religion of the Greeks exhibited at every stage its composite character. As early as the second millennium B. C., so far as we can judge from the results of excavations in Greece proper and in Crete, the inhabitants of these lands had anthropomorphic ideas about some of their deities, that is, they thought of them and represented them in their art essentially as human beings; on the other hand, we find in the later centuries such primitive elements as the worship of sacred stones, trees, and symbols still existing. Yet it is a mistake to suppose that Greek religion had its origin in a worship of natural objects and forces; undoubtedly the worship of natural phenomena and of inanimate objects, of ancestors, and possibly of animals, all contributed to the religious sum total, but it is impossible to trace to-day all the factors which made up religion in historical times. We can only say that the Greeks worshiped a multitude of spiritual beings who filled all nature and were to be found in every field of activity. Man, therefore, was always in social relation to the gods. The ordinary Greek felt that the world was filled with divine beings of varying ranks whose favor he must seek or whose ill

nature he must propitiate by offerings and prayer. Only the most enlightened ever attained to anything like monotheism.

RELIGION IN HOMER AND HESIOD

The earliest Greek literature, the "Iliad" and "Odyssey," [1] shows a circle of gods bound together in a social organization similar to that of the Homeric state. At the head is Zeus, father of gods and of men, possessing a power on Olympus like that of Agamemnon among the Greeks before Troy. With Zeus, Apollo and Athena hold the first rank; Hera, although the wife of Zeus, is in the second rank with Poseidon; Ares and Aphrodite represent little more than the passions of rage for slaughter and love; the god of fire, Hephaestus, Artemis, the sister of Apollo, Hermes, the higher servant of the greater gods and the companion of men, and others are of still lower rank; while Demeter and Dionysus, although known, have no place on Olympus. All these divine beings are represented as larger, stronger, wiser than mortals, but they are no whit less subject to the passions of body and mind; their superiority over men lies chiefly in the possession of immortality. Now no such system of gods was ever worshiped anywhere in the Greek world. It was created by a process of selection and elimination from local cults, and adapted to please the Ionic courts at which the epics were intended to be recited. These epic gods did not drive out local divinities; but the Homeric poems acquired such universal influence in Greece that wherever possible the local divinity was assimilated to the Homeric type, so that Athena, for example, the patroness of Athens, was endowed with the characteristics given her in the epics. There was a constant tendency in literature and art to represent the greater gods in the Homeric way.

Hesiod (about 700 B. C.) also had a great influence on later times through his "Theogony," which was the first attempt to criticize myths and to bring the various accounts into a consistent and harmonious whole. Moreover, the Hesiodic poetry displays certain religious elements which

[1] See *Harvard Classics*, xxii, 9ff.

have little or no place in the Homeric epics. Of these the most significant is the worship of the dead and of heroes. On the side of ethics also we find higher concepts of justice and of the moral order; and in general there is much more reflection on man's relation to the gods and to society than we see in Homer.

In spite of the influence of Homer and Hesiod, no single god or system of gods ever became wholly universal, but each divinity was connected with some locality. The simple Greek conceived of his local god as individual, largely distinct from any other god of the same name, very much as the Greek peasant to-day thinks of his local saint. Yet with the growth of cities, when it became inconvenient to resort often to the ancient localities which might be remote, new shrines, offshoots of the old, were established in towns, so that there was, for example, at Athens, a certain concentration of cults. Furthermore, the chief divinity of a city acquired a position as patroness of a considerable area, as Athena of all Attica, but without completely overshadowing or expelling other gods. Likewise certain religious centers developed which served more than one state, such as the shrine of Apollo at Delos, which became a center for all Ionians, or that of Zeus at Olympia, where representatives of all the Greek world assembled every four years.

GROWTH OF PERSONAL RELIGION

It will thus be seen that Greek religion was largely social and local. The members of the family, the clan, the tribe, and the state were bound together by worship in which the individual shared by virtue of his membership in the social body. These conditions gave solidarity to society and made religion the common and permanent concern of all citizens; yet this common worship tended to check all tendencies to personal religion. But from the eighth century B. C. on, many influences operated to bring the individual to self-consciousness. Men began to be dissatisfied with the sacred tradition of the state and to seek to establish such personal relations with the gods as should give them as individuals religious satisfaction. This desire found outlet from the

sixth century B. C. in the Orphic Sect, whose members tried
to secure satisfaction for religious emotion and to gain the
warrant of a happy life hereafter through the mystic worship of Dionysus and a fixed method of life. At about the
same time the Mysteries began to be prominent. Of these
the most important were at Eleusis in Attica, where a
festival in honor of Demeter and certain associated gods
had existed from a remote period. This festival was
originally agricultural, intended to secure fertility and
prosperity for all admitted to it; but before 600 B. C. it
had been transformed into an eschatological mystery, by
initiation into which the individual was assured of a blessed
future life. The movements thus started in Greek religion
tended to break down men's real dependence on social worship, although the old cults continued to the end of paganism. Yet, in Athens especially, political events during the
fifth century checked the individualistic movements in religion temporarily. From the conflict with Persia (490-479
B. C.) Athens emerged as the chief state in Greece; during
the fifty years which followed she enjoyed an unprecedented
prosperity and an imperial position which bound all citizens
closely together, in spite of the strife of political parties.
Now in the preceding century Peisistratus had done much
to exalt and establish the Olympian type of religion at
Athens; and it was natural that in the time of the power
of Athens the ideal of the state religion should predominate.
All citizens united in dedicating to the gods their material
wealth and their noblest art.

RELIGION IN GREEK TRAGEDY

In this same time lived the great tragedians Æschylus,
Sophocles, and Euripides, who were also great religious
teachers. Æschylus endeavored to interpret the higher
truths of religion as he saw them, and to bring these truths
into relation with morals. He dwelt on the nature of sin,
the stain it brings to each succeeding generation, the punishment of wrongdoing which the divine justice must inflict,
and on the disciplinary value of suffering. These characteristics of his tragedies are well illustrated by the

"Prometheus"[2] and by the Trilogy.[3] Sophocles emphasized the divine source of the higher moral obligations which transcend all human laws. He further taught that pain may have its place even when the sufferer is innocent; and that purity of heart, faith in Zeus, and acquiescence in the divine will are fundamental principles of righteous life. These doctrines underlie the "Antigone"[2] and "Œdipus the King."[5] Euripides belongs in temper to the rational age which followed him. He had no consistent message to his time. On the whole he contributed to the rejection of the old Olympic religion, but at the same time he constantly stirred men to ask fundamental questions about life. In his "Hippolytus"[6] he shows his chaste hero brought to death because he will not yield to the goddess of love, and thus the poet belittles the sacred tradition; in the "Bacchæ"[7] he exalts enthusiasm and inspiration above reason, not, however, without a certain cynicism at the end.

From the close of the fifth century philosophy began to take the place of the traditional religion for thinking men; yet philosophy did not break with the religious sentiment of the time. Eventually the spirit of individualism and cosmopolitanism destroyed men's faith in the state religions, and although the ancient rituals continued to the end of antiquity, they never regained the position which they had in the sixth and fifth centuries B. C.

[2] *H. C.*, viii, 156ff.
[3] "Agamemnon," "The Libation-Bearers," and "The Furies," *H. C.*, viii, 5ff.
[4] *H. C.*, viii, 243ff.   [5] *H. C.*, viii, 107ff.   [6] *H. C.*, viii, 287ff.
[7] *H. C.*, viii, 349ff.

V. PASCAL

By Professor C. H. C. Wright

THE name of Blaise Pascal not only belongs to the list of great French seventeenth-century writers, he is also to be included among the greatest authors of modern literature. He affected radically the thought of countless religious men of his own and later times; he was, even though in part unconsciously, one of the masters of style in the chief age of French literature. Men of science, also, consider him one of the most important of their number as a mathematician and a physicist.

PASCAL AND JANSENISM

Pascal's name is inseparably connected with the history of Jansenism, and though varying phases of his intellectual development have caused him to receive all kinds of descriptive epithets ranging from skeptic to fideist, yet his temperament and his bodily condition reflect the austere and gloomy theories of the Jansenist Augustinians.

Born of a high-strung stock in a bleak part of the volcanic region of Auvergne, under the very shadow of the gloomy cathedral, built of Volvic lava, at Clermont-Ferrand, the child Pascal was from the beginning over-intellectualized. If we are to believe the accounts of a perhaps partial sister, this "terrifying genius" as Chateaubriand calls him, taught himself geometry and worked out problems in Euclid, while he still called lines and circles "bars" and "rounds." His intellect developed by leaps and bounds, and by the end of a life of recurring illnesses and of suffering, cut short at less than two score years, he had encompassed the field of knowledge, verified hypotheses of physics, descried unexplored realms of mathematics, and projected his thought into the vast chaos of conjecture concerning the relations of God and the world, of God and of created man.

Pascal's adherence to religion was not immediate, and he went through successive stages of hesitation and of partial retrogression. A man of the world, he consorted with brilliant talkers, entered into scientific discussions against the Jesuits, or argued on philosophy with other thinkers. But the real interest of his life for our purpose begins with his conversion to the doctrines of Jansenius.

Bishop Jansen of Ypres in Belgium had devoted his life to the study of Saint Augustine and to the elucidation of the doctrines of that great father of the church. Saint Augustine is the spiritual forefather of those who in religious thought are believers in determinism, in religious fatalism, with all the consequences which it involves, such as predestination and the doctrine of primitive sin which man is apparently endeavoring in vain to expiate. The theories of Jansen were propagated in France through the teachings of his friend the Abbé de Saint Cyran, a man of rigid and unbending principles, and the spiritual director of the convent of Port Royal. Port Royal was at the time dominated by members of the great Arnauld family, one of whom had in earlier days offended the strong and ambitious order of Jesuits. The Jesuits were by principle and temperament unfavorable to the theories of Jansen. A doctrine of self-concentration and of introspection, akin in almost every respect to Calvinism, which awoke in a human being a thousand cares and anxious doubts as to the why and wherefore of man's existence on earth—such a doctrine was diametrically opposed to the urbane teachings of the Jesuits, eager rather to acquire new converts by methods of amenity than to frighten them away by visions of dread. Therefore, with the Arnaulds and Jansenists all linked together at Port Royal, the convent became the storm center of religious discussion.

THE "PROVINCIAL LETTERS"

In the course of the controversy, Pascal was invited by one of the Arnaulds to help the cause of Jansenism. This he did by his "Provincial Letters," most of them purporting

to be a narrative of the condition of religious affairs at
Paris by a certain Louis de Montalte to a friend in the
provinces. In these letters, which are considered masterpieces of sarcastic polemic, Pascal did the Jesuits untold
harm. By methods which may seem sometimes technically
unfair, but which are after all employed by every controversial writer, he attacked the doctrines of certain Jesuit
writers upon religious dogma, such as questions of Grace,
and upon moral theories of casuistry, the science dealing
with the solution of dilemmas of conscience and the ex-
culpation of apparent offenses against righteousness. In
the long and violent contest which raged in the seventeenth
century, and of which the publication of the "Provincial
Letters" was an incident, the Jesuits succeeded in having
the Jansenists considered heretics, and they managed to
encompass the destruction of Port Royal. But, whether
rightly or wrongly (and here antagonists will remain un-
reconciled), Pascal dealt them severe blows from which, in
France at least, they have never fully recovered.

THE "THOUGHTS"

The "Lettres Provinciales" are, however, in some respects, ephemeral literature as compared with the "Pensées"
or "Thoughts." [1] In the "Thoughts" we have the sum and
substance of Pascal's religious views as well as one of the
masterpieces of French literary style. Pascal had long
planned a work on religion in which he intended to set
forth the defense of Christianity. This work never got
beyond the stage of disconnected and fragmentary notes and
"Thoughts," from which it is difficult, if not impossible, to
extract the definite plan of the whole work. But, none the
less, what we have deserves the deepest consideration.

Pascal was by temperament a pessimist, and therefore
he agreed the more easily with the gloomy Augustinian
determinism of the Jansenists and their ideas of the sinful-
ness of man and of the necessity of grace. He was no less
convinced of the impotence of man's reason to deal with the
problems of the unknowable and of the hereafter. Pascal

[1] *Harvard Classics,* vol. xlviii.

had fed on the jesting skepticism of Montaigne and realized how logically unanswerable it was in spite of its inconclusiveness. This realization made him feel that there was only one egress from the impasse, it was to reject all the help and conclusions of reason for or against, and to throw himself blindly into the arms of God, an act symbolized by his acceptance of faith and the influence of grace upon him. It is for these reasons that Pascal is sometimes given such varying designations as "skeptic," "mystic," or "fideist"; that, moreover, his religious feeling is called by some the expression of diseased hallucinations, by others visions of a seer into the other world.

The underlying idea of the fragmentary "Thoughts" is the despair of man, his weakness and powerlessness. But there remains something in man's own nature which protests against this despair. We have a certainty that all is not as bad as it seems. Let us accept the truths of the Christian religion and we then have the consolation that our suffering, is not without cause, that we are expiating the original and primitive sin of mankind. This will at least make us understand our condition. Thus we shall, in a way, be proving Christianity and even God himself, beginning with man.

The fragmentary state of the "Thoughts" makes it impossible, however, for the reader to work out the stages of this argument. He will find it more profitable to take them as they stand, and he will then be fully satisfied by words of imagination and of true poetry. The language is permeated with lyrical inspiration: the poet is a thinker who sees the abysses of immensity, spatial and temporal, the infinitely vast and the infinitely small. He brings back from the contemplation of them a feeling of terror and yet of self-confidence. For though man be a prey to brutal outer nature, though he may be but a frail reed beaten before the blast, yet he feels that one thing lifts him above it all, the consciousness that he is a *thinking* reed. The work is full of the vagueness of love for the divine; consequently, in spite of Pascal's mathematical brain, it is no geometrical proof for the persuasion of reason, but rather a way to take hold of the feeling. Pascal is the intuitionalist of French classicism, as Descartes,[2] his philosophical rival, is its great rationalist.

The influence of Pascal upon French thought has been tremendous. In his own day he helped to free French prose and its content from the stilted rhetoric of certain self-conscious Latinists like Guez de Balzac. He helped some of the men of letters of his age to acquire a new gentleness of feeling without the sacrifice of stoical self-control. He familiarized writers who were taken up by considerations of a petty nationalism with visions of the boundless immensity which enwraps this little earth. He helped to make the French prose of his day more clear and a mirror of the soul. And all this he accomplished by a work of which we have only disconnected fragments, and by a life tragic in its brevity, in its physical suffering, extraordinary by its mental torture and intellectual vigor, the life of an all-embracing genius such as the world produces scarcely once in many centuries.

[2] See pamphlet on Philosophy in this series, Lecture III.